3.95

Spain in the Fifteenth Century
1369–1516

Spain in the Fifteenth Century
1369–1516

Essays and Extracts by Historians of Spain

EDITED BY
Roger Highfield

TRANSLATED BY
Frances M. López-Morillas

Harper & Row, Publishers
New York, Evanston, San Francisco, London

A hardcover edition of this book was originally published in Great Britain by Macmillan.

SPAIN IN THE FIFTEENTH CENTURY 1369–1516

Editorial Matter and Selection

First HARPER & ROW edition published 1972.

STANDARD BOOK NUMBER: 06–138836–X

Contents

6 CONTENTS

List of Maps

The jacket-illustration shows detail from the tomb of the
Doncel Martín Vázquez de Arce in Sigüenza Cathedral.

Acknowledgments

JAIME VICENS VIVES, "The Economies of Catalonia and Castile" and "The Economy of Ferdinand and Isabella's Reign", from *An Economic History of Spain*, trans. F. M. López-Morillas (Princeton, N.J., 1969), chaps. 18, 20–22 and pp. 291–313. Reprinted by permission of Princeton University Press.

LUÍS SUÁREZ FERNÁNDEZ, "The Atlantic and the Mediterranean Among the Objectives of the House of Trastámara" ("El atlántico y el mediterráneo en los objetivos de la casa de Trastámara"), from *Revista Portuguesa de Historia*, V (1951), pp. 299ff. Reprinted by permission of Instituto de Estudos Históricos.

"The Kingdom of Castile in the Fifteenth Century" ("El reino de Castilla en el siglo XV"), from *Historia de España*, ed. R. Menéndez Pidal, Vol. XV (Madrid, 1964), chap. 1. Reprinted by permission of Espasa-Calpe, S.A.

JUAN TORRES FONTES, "The Regency of Don Ferdinand of Antequera" ("La regencia de don Fernando de Antequera"), from *Anuario de Estudios Medievales* (Barcelona, 1964), pp. 375–419. Reprinted by permission of the author.

JOSÉ MARÍA FONT Y RIUS, "The Institutions of the Crown of Aragon in the First Half of the Fifteenth Century" ("Las instituciones de la corona de Aragón en la primera mitad del siglo XV"), from *4 Congreso de la historia de la Corona de Aragón* (Palma de Mallorca, 1955) (iv), pp. 5–19. Reprinted by permission of the author.

JUAN AINAUD DE LASARTE, "Alfonso the Magnanimous and the Plastic Arts of His Time" ("Alfonso el Magnánimo y las artes plásticas de su tiempo"), from *4 Congreso de la historia de la*

Corona de Aragón (Palma de Mallorca, 1955) (ix), pp. 5–28. Reprinted by permission of the author.

V. BELTRÁN DE HEREDIA, O.P., "The Beginnings of Dominican Reform in Castile" ("Los comienzos de la Reforma Dominicana en Castilla"), from *Archivum Fratrum Praedicatorum*, XXVIII (1958), pp. 221–37. Reprinted by permission of Instituto Storico Domenicano.

JUAN BENEYTO PÉREZ, "The Science of Law in the Spain of the Catholic Kings" ("La ciencia del derecho de la España de los Reyes Católicos"), from *Revista General de Legislación y Jurisprudencia*, XXVI, pp. 563–81. Reprinted by permission of Instituto Editorial Reus, S.A.

FRANCISCO CANTERA BURGOS, "Fernando del Pulgar and the *Conversos*" ("Fernando del Pulgar y los Conversos"), from *Sefarad*, IV (1944), pp. 295–348. Reprinted by permission of Instituto Arias Montano de Estudios Hebráicos y Oriente Próximo.

JOSÉ GOÑI GAZTAMBIDE, "The Holy See and the Reconquest of the Kingdom of Granada (1479–1492)" ("La Santa Sede y la reconquista del reino de Granada"), from *Hispania Sacra*, IV (1951), pp. 43–80. Reprinted by permission of the author.

RAMÓN MENÉNDEZ PIDAL, "The Significance of the Reign of Isabella the Catholic, According to Her Contemporaries" ("La significación del reinado de Isabel la Católica según sus coetáneos"), and "The Catholic Kings According to Machiavelli and Castiglione" ("Los Reyes Católicos según Maquiavelo y Castiglione"), from *Los Reyes Católicos y otros estudios* (Buenos Aires, 1962). Reprinted by permission of Espasa-Calpe, S.A., Madrid.

MARCEL BATAILLON, "The Idea of the Discovery of America Among the Spaniards of the Sixteenth Century" ("L'Idée de la découverte de l'Amérique chez les espagnols du XVIe siècle"), from *Bulletin Hispanique*, LV (1953), pp. 23–55. Reprinted by permission of the author.

List of Abbreviations

And.	Al-Andalus
ANP	Archives Nationales (Paris)
AGS	Archivo General de Simancas
AHDE	Anuario de la Historia del Derecho Español
Arch.H.N.	Archivo Histórico Nacional
BAE, BAEE	Biblioteca de Autores Españoles
BAH	Boletín de la Real Academia de Historia
BEC	Bibliothèque de L'Ecole des Chartes
BH	Bulletin Hispanique
BHE	Bibliothèque des Hautes Études
CODOIN	Colección de documentos inéditos para la historia de España
EHM	Estudios de Historia Moderna
ER	Études Roussillonnaises
HAHR	Hispanic American Historical Review
MOPH	Monumenta Ordinis Praedicatorum Historica
RABM	Revista de Archivos, Bibliotecas y Museos
Rev.Est.	Revista de Extremadura

Textual Note

SPANISH CHRISTIAN NAMES

THE policy adopted for the translation of Vicens Vives' *Economic History of Spain* (J. Vicens Vives, *Historia Económica de España*, 3d ed. (Barcelona, 1964), translated by F. López-Morillas (Princeton University Press, 1969), has been followed here. The English equivalents of Spanish Christian names have been used for all the kings and princes of Castile, Aragon, Navarre, and Portugal. When this practice would cause ambiguity, if the name were left as it is, that of the relevant kingdom has been included. Isabella of Castile, Blanche of Navarre, and Joanna of Naples have also been left in their English forms since these are in common use.

NOTES

Each article or extract has been printed with its original notes; no attempt has been made to standardize the style of all the notes. Complete notes added by the editor have been indicated by placing them in square brackets. Subsequently all the notes have been renumbered right through each article in order to include the editor's notes in the sequence. Additional comments to existing notes have also been placed in square brackets.

CATALAN

In the essay by Sr. Font y Rius, *cortes* had been preferred to *corts*, as it is in common usage. But elsewhere Catalan forms have been used, as *diputació*, *generalitat*, etc.

LATIN

Latin in the text has been translated by the editor, where anything more than a phrase occurs. It has been left in the original in the notes.

OMISSIONS

One or two small omissions have been made in the text of phrases which would have been, if reprinted, inappropriate, and documentary appendixes have also been left out.

THE "CATHOLIC KINGS"

I have made no systematic attempt to alter the established use of this translation of *Los Reyes Católicos*, which strictly speaking ought to be translated the "Catholic Monarchs."

Introduction

THE history of Spain in the fifteenth century has not attracted the attention which it deserves. There are several reasons for this. The civil wars of Castile in the time of John II (1406–54) and Henry IV (1454–74) and the long-drawn-out social and political struggle between the Crown of Aragon and its opponents (1462–78) have made the great part of the century appear, at first sight, a meaningless night. Out of this darkness, it seems, rose the dawn of the reign of the Catholic Monarchs—to use the title which Pope Alexander VI gave to Ferdinand and Isabella. Again, until quite recently there did not exist enough basic investigations of the state of Spanish society to make it possible to do much more than repeat a detailed narrative of the political history. Even now there remain great areas of Spanish fifteenth-century history awaiting research in depth, and no effort will be made in what follows to conceal this fact. Yet much important work, especially by Spanish writers, has been published in the last twenty years. This book is an attempt to make the student who does not read Spanish aware of what has been going on. The essays and extracts themselves have been chosen to illustrate some of the more important historical themes of the Spanish fifteenth century. Sometimes it has been necessary to select a particular example to stand as a token for a much larger theme. Thus, for instance, the great and surprising story of the reform of the Spanish Church is represented by an essay of Father Beltrán de Heredia, O.P., on the small beginnings of reform in the Spanish province of the Dominican Order. The enthusiastic student will go on to read Heredia's larger work, *Historia de la reforma de la provincia de España (1450–1550)* (Rome, 1939). In instances in which no suitable essay was found, bibliographical suggestions have been made instead. No attempt has been made to provide an outline narrative of political events. This already exists in a number of forms (H. S. Merriman, *The Rise of the Spanish Empire*, I, The Middle Ages; II, The Catholic Kings (1918); J. H. Elliott, *Imperial Spain, 1469–1716* (London, 1963); and (in Spanish) in *Historia de España*, directed by R. Menéndez Pidal, XIV and XV (Madrid, 1964); these two volumes cover the years 1369–1474).

When the selection of essays was first made there existed no translation of the *Historia Económica de España* by Professor J. Vicens Vives of Barcelona University. It was, therefore, felt essential to begin with a series of extracts from that important outline of economic history. The whole of that book has subsequently been published by the Princeton University Press. Even so it has been decided to let the extracts from it retain their place in this book to maintain a balance of themes.

Above all it is hoped that the reader will be helped to understand the history of the Peninsula under the two branches of the Trastámara dynasty from its incoming in Castile in 1369 and in Aragon in 1412 to the death of Ferdinand II in 1516. The end of the fourteenth century and the early fifteenth century make a period in their own right—not just the background from which the Catholic Kings emerged. The first three Trastámara kings of Castile and figures like Ferdinand of Antequera tried more or less resolutely to deal with the major problem of stabilizing Iberian society.

The middle of the fourteenth century is a natural point at which to start for other reasons. The battle of Salado (1340), when Alfonso XI of Castile defeated the Moors in Andalusia, put a stop to the long forward movement of the Christian Reconquest. Economically the second half of the fourteenth century saw not only a halt but a setback which was at its worst in Catalonia. In that particular instance recovery was not to be reached until the very end of our period.

Demographically speaking, the situation in Catalonia can be judged from the figures of the hearth tax returns for 1359, 1376, and 1497. The post-Black Death figure of 85,222 hearths (say, 450,000 people) had recovered to 95,869 by 1376 (say, 500,000). But the subsequent epidemics and decline meant that in 1497 the population had still not returned to the 1359 position. A loss of more than 20 per cent occurred in this period. By 1516 the tide had turned (the 1515 returns give a population of more than 300,000) but only just, see Selection 8, p. 248. Not until well into the sixteenth century did substantial French immigration help to redress the situation. But in the other three kingdoms of the Crown of Aragon the story is by no means so discouraging. In Aragon itself (judging by the tax returns of 1404 and 1495) there seems to have been an increase from about 213,000 to about 270,000, though how far this was evenly spread over the period cannot be determined. For the island (though not the kingdom) of Majorca the figures are equally striking. A hearth tax of 1426 suggests a population of 45,000. In 1440 a comparable tax gives a total of 55,000. A general tendency toward increase in the first half of the century seems inescapable. It is a pity that comparable figures are not available for the kingdom of Valencia, since trade between Valencia, Italy, and France undoubtedly burgeoned during the course of the fifteenth century. Already in the first decade there was a considerable immigration of Italian merchants into Valencia. By 1510 the population of this kingdom stood at about 270,000.

Comparable figures for Castile are much more difficult to discover, see Selection 8, p. 248. The usual starting point is those produced by the tax return of 1482 made by Quintanilla. They give a total of 7,500,000. This seems much too high, judging by the next sets available, those of 1530 and 1541 (4,300,000 without Granada, allowance being made for Galicia and Murcia, and 6,272,000). Batista i Roca in the *Cambridge Modern History* thinks that the 1482 figure should be written down to about 4,500,000. There seems no means of estimating what it had been at the beginning of our period. Little is known about the population of the Pyrenean kingdom of Navarre, independent until its conquest by Ferdinand in 1512. But it was not large, perhaps 150,000. In 1336 its largest towns, Tudela and Pamplona, had about 5,000 and 4,500 inhabitants respectively.

Selection 1 (p. 31) begins with an extract which sets the economic scene against which the Trastámara dynasty was to establish itself in the kingdoms of the Crown of Aragon. The kingdoms lay across two important trade routes which sustained the commercial activity of its seaports, especially Barcelona, Valencia, and Palma de Mallorca. The first was the spice route to Alexandria, which was one of the outer channels by which the spices of the East reached Western Europe. The other route ran north and south to the Barbary states of North Africa. Along it traveled gold, slaves, and wool to help feed the Catalan textile industry. The gold was particularly important in an age when there was a European shortage of this commodity. In the first extract Vicens explains why the advancing capitalist economy of Catalonia was halted by a crisis which began in 1381, culminated in 1392, and dragged on to about 1420. Barcelona is famous for the establishment of its early deposit bank, the *Taula de Canvi* (1402). But this development is shown to have reflected a worsening, not an improvement, in the state of Catalan capitalism. This deterioration caused the breaking of the Gualbes bank only four years later.

In Barcelona itself the great quarrel between the merchant oligarchs (the *bigas*) and the popular party (the *buscas*) was directly stimulated by the economic difficulties of Catalonia. The landlords in the countryside who wished to preserve their social privileges over their backward serfs, known as *payeses de remensa*, tended to link hands with the merchant oligarchs and form a combination which several times sought to take matters into its own hands. The Crown often preferred to support the *buscaires* and to seek a lasting solution to the problem of the *remensas*. Its monetary policy was also directly related to *busca* and *biga* politics. When the *buscas* were in power the Crown was ready to follow the path of devaluation and also of protection. Eventually the problem of the *remensas* was solved by Ferdinand II at the Sentence of Guadalupe (1486), but only after years of effort and negotiation by all the Trastámara kings.

In the meantime the social problem was exacerbated by the Castilian/Catalan problem with which it became confused. Up

to the death of Martin I (1410) the reigning dynasty spoke Catalan
and much favored Catalonia among the possessions of the Crown
of Aragon. But Martin's line ran out with him, and the incoming
of Ferdinand I meant the triumph of a Castilian-speaking
dynasty; bringing in Castilian favorites and Castilian ways. The
disappointed Catalan nobleman the count of Urgel, Ferdinand's
main rival at the Compromise of Caspe (which had settled the
question of the disputed succession), refused to accept its decision.
His rebellion had to be fought to a standstill. He did not, however,
succeed in rousing enough Catalan support in his favor. But later
on, long after he had been defeated, the extended periods of
absence in Italy of Ferdinand's son Alfonso, the heavy taxation
to which his wars gave rise, the strong hand of his successor in
1458, John II, and the continuity of economic weakness all
combined to produce an attempt in the years after 1461 to over-
throw the Trastámara dynasty altogether. And this attempt was
based on Catalonia. The Catalan aim was to replace John II with
one of four princes, the Portuguese Pedro, John's son, Charles,
Prince of Viana, with a French prince; or even with King Henry
IV of Castile. More radically, some wanted to set up a republic.
Only when that threat had been defeated and the French under
Louis XI had taken the chance to lop off the trans-Pyrenean
provinces of Roussillon and Cerdagne could Catalonia go forward
again. Its lowest ebb economically seems to have been reached in
the years 1478–81, when the political situation had already started
to mend. Barcelona began to pick up notably after 1493. Castilian
military and naval power now backed a renewal of a forward
policy in Italy and the recapture of the spice route. The decadence
of Catalonia had in any case been something of a local phenomenon. To the south, Valencia, with a colonial economy, despite
the factional quarrels of the Centelles and the Vilaraguts, gained
at the expense of Barcelona—especially between 1455 and 1490.
Indeed Valencia entered a period of hegemony. Outside Spain, as
French and Austrian historians have shown, Toulouse, Marseilles,
and Genoa all profited and prospered in the middle years of the
fifteenth century. Genoa in particular was busy developing her

sailings of galleys through the Mediterranean and around the Spanish coast to England and Flanders. Systematically she exploited her alliance with Castile and the resources of the kingdom of Granada. At the same time she was engaged in the whole process by which she switched her colonization from the eastern to the western Mediterranean.

Three extracts from Vicens' work (Selection 1) paint the comparable background of the very different economy of Castile. A heavy reliance on stock-keeping of all kinds had already become the centerpiece of Castilian agriculture at the expense of arable farming. Castile was, it is true, one of the great corn-producing areas, like Sicily. Even so the kingdoms of the Crown of Aragon, which often needed to import corn, preferred to use the cheaper freightage by sea and to rely on Sicily and North Africa as their main suppliers. The frequent deficits in Majorca and Catalonia led the government of Ferdinand and Isabella to attempt more and more to control the import and export and the price of corn. By the end of the period there was an increasing anxiety about corn.

Castile, in contrast to Aragon, faced both ways, outward toward the Atlantic (north, northwest, and southwest) and inward toward the Mediterranean. The second half of the fourteenth century saw her emerge as a leading naval power. The intervention of the Castilian fleet in the Hundred Years' War was often a notable help to the French. Led by Genoese admirals, the Castilian fleet was dominant along her own coasts and beginning to strike out beyond them. The freeing of the Straits of Gibraltar led to a growth of commerce passing from the Mediterranean into the Atlantic and eventually to the annual galley fleet leaving Italy and sailing around the Spanish coast to Flanders. The Genoese aided and abetted Castilian naval and commercial development in many ways. As has been noted, they trained the Castilian fleet. They also settled in large numbers in Seville.

Certainly too they were on hand to exploit the sugar plantations and the colonization of the Atlantic islands of the Canaries, the Azores, and the Madeiras, when these came to be developed in the course of the century.

Professor Suárez in his essay on the Atlantic and Mediterranean aspects of Castilian policy (Selection 2) shows how the first Castilian Trastámaras felt their way forward from the strong naval positions that had been established on the Biscay coast in the north and in Andalusia in the south. Before an overall maritime policy could be constructed, two major threats had to be fought off: the Portuguese, dividing Andalusia from Galicia, and John of Gaunt. If Gaunt had succeeded in pressing the claims to the Castilian throne which he had acquired by marrying the heiress of Peter the Cruel, he would have overthrown the Trastámara dynasty itself. These two threats looked menacing indeed after the Portuguese land victory of Aljubarrota (1385). But Gaunt had no sustained backing once his expedition had failed. Wisely he came to terms. So eventually did Portugal, after the campaign of 1397–1402. Castile was free to build up her position and her trade on all her coasts, including her Mediterranean strip between the kingdom of Granada and Valencia. Here Cartagena began to be an important base. Portugal in the era of Henry the Navigator was preoccupied with her African destiny both at Ceuta and down the Guinea coast.

Internally and socially the great Castilian problem lay in the relations between the Crown and the nobility. In all the countries of Western Europe two different conceptions of the role of monarchy had emerged since the beginning of the thirteenth century—the monarchical and the aristocratic. But in Castile the aristocratic interpretation was supported by the unusually strong position of the nobility in military and territorial power. The Crown had to pay a very steep price for noble support throughout the Reconquest, both during the campaigns and in peacetime, in order to keep the southern frontier safe. Then in 1369 the new dynasty had had to add on the cost of rewarding its noble supporters with the series of grants known as the *mercedes enriqueñas*, or Henrician Mercies. More support was needed again in the 1380's to fight off the dangers from England and Portugal referred to above. It was not surprising that the Castilian nobility was strong. In his chapter from the *Historia de España* (Selection 3) Professor

Suárez sketches the Castilian fifteenth-century scene as it confronted the early Trastámaras. He shows clearly the differing conceptions of monarchy and emphasizes the decline of the Cortes and the weakness of the towns. A topographical assessment of the territorial power of the aristocracy brings out the immense strength of their position. His concluding assessment of the literature and ideas of the age in Castile reminds the reader of one of the most interesting features of Spain in the fifteenth century. It was a great and a formative period for Castilian literature. Latin was still used extensively, especially by the clergy. It remained the language of the Church and of diplomacy. It was to be the language of the humanist letter writers like Lucio Marineo Sículo and Peter Martyr. Catalan, however, was going into a decline from which it was going to take a long time to emerge. It survived most vigorously at Valencia, where Ausies March (1397–1459), a poet and royal official of Alfonso V, at the head of a small group of poets, upheld its honor in his love poetry. This was shot through with the same kind of preoccupation with death that appears in mural paintings and monumental sculpture in many countries of Western Europe in the fifteenth century.

Castilian flowered in a prolific manner. Both in poetry and in prose it produced a series of outstanding figures who rose above the political difficulties of their times: Juan de Mena, the marquis of Santillana, Fernán Pérez de Guzmán, Jorge Manrique, and Fernando de Rojas. The "Coplas" which Manrique wrote on the death of his father, the master of Santiago, and the *Comedia*, or *Tragicomedia de Calisto y Melibea*, otherwise known as *La Celestina*, of Fernando de Rojas are two of the notable achievements in the Castilian language of all time. Moreover, the writing of these men reflects the history of the Spanish fifteenth century remarkably. The problem of the nobility with which Professor Suárez deals in Selection 3 is reflected in the fact that no fewer than three of these outstanding figures were nobles of high rank and that the one of them who was not, Juan de Mena (the son of a corregidor), sets out in his great poem *El Laberinto* the poet's aspirations for a solution of the power struggle between the Crown and the nobility. His *Dezir* on the law links up with Sr. Beneyto Pérez's observations (cf. Selection 9).

The many ballads known as *Romances* included some which were either the equivalent of political pamphlets (like those in the Dom Pedro cycle which blackened the repute of the dynasty replaced by the Trastámaras) or idealized interpretations of the Moorish wars. Others were inspired by chivalry and the Carolingian or Arthurian legends. A few like the famous "Ballad of Conde Arnaldos" in its full version reached the level of Manrique's "Coplas" or *La Celestina*.

It was a great period also for the historical chronicle, from *El Victorial* of Don Pedro Niño by Gutierre Díez de Gámes, which strikes the right note for Professor Suárez's essay "The Atlantic and the Mediterranean" (Selection 2); to those of Diego de Valera, Alfonso de Palencia, and Fernando del Pulgar, to mention only three. All these writers stand close to the problems discussed in this book, none more so than the *converso* Pulgar (see p. 296 and Selection 10). The world of the *converso* equally, it seems, lay at the back of the brilliant if harsh impression made by the author of *La Celestina*—the so-called "first modern novel."

Until the last quarter of the century, moreover, external influences were chiefly those of Dante, Boccaccio, and above all Petrarch. Even Petrarch seems to have been more influential for his moral teaching than for his humanism. The introduction of printing into Spain (1473) and the publication of the first Spanish grammar (that of Antonio Nebrija, 1492) did not in themselves have much influence in bringing in Italian humanism. But with the arrival of Renaissance Italian influences at the court of the Catholic Kings, even if on a modest scale, it is not surprising that the period culminates in the high hopes which initiate the *Siglo de Oro* (ca.1540). Yet it will take the very finest products of the later sixteenth and seventeenth centuries to come close to the "Ballad of Conde Arnaldos," the "Coplas" of Manrique, or *La Celestina*.

In the fourth essay Professor Torres Fontes provides a careful and detailed picture of the solutions worked out by the co-regent

Ferdinand of Antequera to deal with the situation which faced him on the death of Henry III of Castile in 1406. In some ways they anticipated those reached by the Catholic Kings. Yet one must not leap at conclusions. The Moorish policy of the victor of Antequera certainly pointed the way to Granada. But in his attitude toward the masterships of the three military orders an important difference can be seen. Isabella, by working out a plan for consolidating the orders under her husband, was to make them a potential source of royal power. Ferdinand of Antequera, by securing Alcántara and Santiago for his two sons, and not for his royal nephew, John II of Castile, may have imagined that he was building up the power of the Crown. In fact he was guaranteeing intense difficulty for it once the regency was over. Ferdinand indeed at this point resembles John II or Charles V of France, or Edward III of England, when they set up *apanages* for their sons. Their attitudes were all intensely personal. Edward III stimulated the Wars of the Roses, the French kings prepared the Burgundian–Armagnac rivalry, and Ferdinand of Antequera precipitated the endless interferences of the Infantes of Aragon. The regency of 1406–16 also showed clearly with what difficulty the medieval polity faced a period when for some reason (weakness, madness, or minority) the king could not rule effectively. This problem, barely concealed during these years, remained in full view from the attainment of his majority by John II at the Cortes of Valladolid in 1419 to the death of Henry IV in 1474.

The kingdoms of the Crown of Aragon after the Compromise of Caspe were beset neither by minorities nor by weak kings. Both Alfonso V (1416–58) and John II (1458–79) were men of determination. They had difficult problems to contend with— the pursuit of expensive overseas ambitions abroad and the outbreak of a social struggle at home. Alfonso picked up the long-standing interest of the Aragonese in southern Italy, which went back to the marriage of the Hohenstaufen heiress Constance of Sicily and Peter III of Aragon. Alfonso himself was endowed by the childless Joanna II, queen of Naples, with the right to succeed her. Although she subsequently changed her mind and found a different protector in an Angevin husband, the king of Aragon did not let so valuable a claim pass by. Thus Aragonese Naples was eventually added to Aragonese Sicily (1442)—even if it soon passed (1458) into the hands of Alfonso's bastard son, Ferrante. The stage was set for the forward Italian policies of John II and Ferdinand II (1479–1516).

Thanks to the series of excellent articles produced by the Fourth Congress of the History of the Crown of Aragon we are able to study closely the institutions of those kingdoms in the first half of the fifteenth century. It was a crucial period for the development of the monarchy. Although Alfonso was frequently in Italy, the Crown was able to enhance its position as controller of feudal aristocracy and bourgeois oligarchy alike. It was moving steadily forward toward the clash which came when John II preferred to stay in Spain and face the issues of the power struggle. Alfonso's absence did mean that viceroys in Sardinia and Sicily, lieutenants general on the mainland of Spain, had to rule in his place. Sr. Font y Rius shows (Selection 5) how they prepared the way for the office of viceroy as it was to emerge in the sixteenth century.

The engagement of Alfonso in Italy in the fifteenth century posits the question of Italian influence in culture as well as politics. A careful study of the plastic arts in this period (Selection 6) shows that it is important not to anticipate events. Alfonso may have been a very influential patron of Renaissance artists and scholars in Italy—men of the caliber of Pisanello and Donatello—but this does not mean that his Spanish kingdoms were yet affected by Italian infiltration or example. For that, one must wait until the reign of the Catholic Kings. In the first half of the fifteenth century the Aragonese kingdoms (like the Castilian) still fell within the Late Gothic World.

In Castile while the monarchy seemed to languish (1416–74) under weak kings and a succession of favorites (Don Álvaro de Luna under John II, for instance, or Juan Pacheco, marquis of Villena, under Henry IV), in fact much leaven was working. This was nowhere clearer than in certain sections of the Spanish

Church. It is true that the Great Schism (1378–1417) had particularly affected Spain, since the Spanish kingdoms were the most resolute defenders of the Aragonese antipope Benedict XIII, whose cause eventually failed. But the movement in favor of reform was not to be stifled by the political disarray of either Church or State. This was nowhere more noticeable than in some of the monastic orders—especially the Dominicans, the Augustinians, and in some parts the Benedictines. Of the six great ecclesiastical figures of the century—St. Vincent Ferrer, Archbishop Talavera, Cardinal Mendoza, Torquemada the Inquisitor, and Cardinal Jiménez (or Cisneros)—four were members of the regular orders (Ferrer and Torquemada were Dominicans, Talavera a Jeronimite, and Jiménez a Franciscan). The Spanish orders had, in fact, won an unusually strong position as a result of the Reconquest. This they succeeded in maintaining spiritually as well as materially, partly as a result of individual movements of reform but also because of the continuation of the war against Granada from 1483 until its finale in 1492 and thereafter because of their importance in the mission field in America. Part of one of the Spanish reform movements is described by Father Beltrán de Heredia (Selection 7).

The remaining seven essays are devoted to the period of the Catholic Kings (1474–1516), with whose reign the century culminates. Naturally it is this heroic era which has attracted most attention from Spanish historians. Hence it has been very difficult to decide what to choose from a wide range of possibilities. The extracts from Vicens have been selected in order to emphasize the necessity of keeping one's feet on the ground in an epoch when there is a natural tendency toward extravagant utterance. The economic policy of Ferdinand and Isabella is shown to have been decidedly aristocratic. They also bear a considerable responsibility for the encouragement of stock-keeping at the expense of arable farming—a policy which produced an expansion of the wool trade and an increase in the revenue from taxation but which led to severe corn shortages soon after the turn of the century, if not before. Nor can these rulers be given very much credit for a protectionist policy which was full of inconsistencies.

However, there can be no doubt that the tendencies in favor of a strong absolutist monarchy, which had been fitfully glimpsed under Peter I, Henry III, and during the regime of Álvaro de Luna, were steadily made manifest in the last quarter of the century and in a wide variety of ways. The central administration was overhauled and reorganized (1476–83), even if there was still no capital and the court migrated in medieval style. To staff the bureaucracy, more and more use was made of the so-called *letrados*, graduates of the universities, often of middle-class origin, especially those who had taken the degrees of canon or civil law. The Spanish universities had all been essentially royal foundations, and it is not surprising that they were centers of enthusiasm for strong monarchical government. In the great law code known as the *Seven Parts* (*Siete Partidas*) Alfonso X had devoted a complete title to the universities. Castilian *letrados* came especially from Salamanca; Aragonese lawyers chiefly from Toulouse or Bologna, where the Spanish College founded by Cardinal Albornoz in the fourteenth century continued to draw "civilians" especially to the Italian university. In Castile the great problem to which the *letrados* began to apply themselves, as Sr. Beneyto Pérez shows in his essay (Selection 9), was the codification of the law. Men of the stamp of Alonso de Montalvo and Palacios Rubios showed the high standard which these *letrados* could reach.

The stronger monarchy found itself confronted with the long-standing problem of the two elements which were not yet integrated into the Christian body politic—the Jews and the Muslims. No other Western European country had to deal with such large non-Christian elements. Nor was the record of countries like England and France, which had been faced by very small numbers, much different from that of the Catholic Kings in 1492. For a long time Muslim and Jewish society and culture had found themselves side by side with Christianity in Spain, Some Christian rulers had been deeply influenced by this proximity. In the eleventh century Alfonso VI had married Zaida, the daughter of the

Muslim king of Toledo, and had called himself Emperor of the Two Religions. Alfonso X had patronized translations from the Arabic on a large scale, and if it is objected that this was already a long time ago, in the fifteenth century Alfonso V of Aragon always had with him in Italy his Moorish dancers and minstrels from Valencia, and Henry IV of Castile affected Moorish dress. Moreover, the sheer financial and demographic weakness of the Christian kingdoms prevented their rulers from pushing matters à outrance, as the papacy would have wished in the thirteenth century. By the middle of the fifteenth it was the monarchs who were being pushed along by the growing hostility of their subjects particularly toward the Jews and the converted Jews or conversos. Already by that time Toledo and Ciudad Real had excluded Jews and conversos from public office. The government of John II of Castile did not leap to their defense. Italian bankers, chiefly Genoese, later joined by the south Germans, seemed to offer an alternative source of capital and loans. The milder and never very effective methods of conversion advocated by Ramón Lull or Talavera were giving place to the strong-arm methods of a Torquemada or a Jiménez. Thanks to the so-called converso danger in Andalusia, and especially at Seville, the Inquisition was introduced in 1480. Twelve years later the Jews themselves were given the hard dilemma of conversion or expulsion. Of the two minorities they were by far the smaller (200,000 or so against about 1,000,000 Muslims). Even so the expulsion of three-quarters of the Jews made an exodus all too painful to those involved and one which did lasting damage to Spain itself. Those who chose conversion, or who had chosen it in the past, were by no means thereby saved. They included some of the ablest men in the country. The detailed essay by Sr. Cantera Burgos on Fernando del Pulgar, the chronicler of the Catholic Kings (Selection 10), highlights some of the difficulties of the intellectual converso in the early years of the Inquisition. (Cf. also Selection 8.)

The day of the expulsion of the Moriscos was not yet (it followed in 1610), mainly because there were too many of them. But the sack of the morería of Valencia in 1455 showed the kind of hostility which Muslims could arouse within a Christian kingdom. The Fall of Granada (in the same remarkable year in which the Jews were expelled and America discovered) meant that henceforth they were a conquered people. Then in 1502 (ten years after the Jewish expulsion) they too had to choose between baptism or expulsion.

The last stage of the conquest—from the end of the Succession War in 1477 for the next fifteen years—had absorbed almost the whole effort of the Catholic Kings. The siege of Baza in particular showed that the royal finances were inadequate. The essay by Sr. Goñi on Spanish-papal relations (Selection 11) reveals some of the stresses and strains experienced by the monarchy and papacy before the desired end was finally achieved. The popes on their side had the Turkish menance to consider—Otranto fell in 1480—and Innocent VIII proved especially reluctant to fall in line with Spanish policy until a hard bargain had been extracted.

Throughout these negotiations Spain was represented by her permanent ambassadors at the papal court, men like Bishop (later Cardinal) Joan Margarit, the count of Tendilla, and Francisco de Rojas, a fact which emphasizes the importance of the Spanish diplomatic machine. As Professor Garrett Mattingly has demonstrated, the recently united kingdoms of Castile and Aragon were the first of the Western European powers to follow Italian princes and republics in establishing permanent resident ambassadors abroad. Given the crucial importance of Spanish-papal diplomacy and the Aragonese (Spanish) stake in Naples, it was easily explicable. But from as early as 1475 a Spanish diplomatic offensive was launched by Ferdinand against France not only in Italy but in Germany and the Netherlands as well. After 1485 England was to be brought into the ring. By 1490 the king had created a grand alliance against France brought into being with the aid of the new diplomacy. It did not prevent the French invasion of Italy in 1494. But the invasion caused Ferdinand to redouble his diplomatic efforts. The result was the Holy League of 1495.

Lest the Spanish case for the greatness of Ferdinand and Isabella should seem to have been overlooked, two essays are included at this point (Selections 12 and 13). Their author is that notable Spanish historian—Ramón Menéndez Pidal. He shows the monarchs to us through the eyes of contemporary Spanish chroniclers and observers, men like Alfonso de Palencia, Fernando del Pulgar and the grammarian Antonio Nebrija, as well as through those of Italian humanists inside Spain like Lucio Marineo Sículo or outside it like Machiavelli and Castiglione.

The story of Spain in the fifteenth century has two sequels, one in Europe and the other in America. The last essay (Selection 14) has been chosen in order to give a good lead into the American sequel. So great is the weight of material which has been published on the Discovery that the student needs a guide with a good clear head to steer him away from the Sargasso Sea. Marcel Bataillon certainly has a clear head. He is also one of the most learned men in the field. And he wears his learning lightly. The last essay is a sheer delight.

FURTHER READING

M. Bataillon, *La Célestine selon Fernando de Rojas* (Paris, 1961).

J. M. Batista i Roca, "The Hispanic Kingdoms and the Catholic Kings," chap. XI in *New Cambridge Modern History*, ed. G. R. Potter, I, *The Renaissance 1493–1520*, 316–42.

A. D. Deyermond, *The Petrarchan Sources of La Celestina* (Oxford, 1961).

Gutierre Díaz de Games, *The Chronicle of Don Pero Niño, Count of Buelna*, transl. J. Evans (London, 1928).

W. J. Entwistle, *The Arthurian Legend in the Literature of the Spanish Peninsula* (London, 1925).

———, *European Ballads* (Oxford, 1939).

S. Gilman, *The Art of La Celestina* (Madison, Wisc., 1956).

A. Krause, *Jorge Manrique and the Cult of Death in the Cuatrocientos* (Berkeley, 1937).

P. Le Gentil, *La poésie lyrique espagnole et portugaise à la fin du Moyen Âge*, Vol. I (Rennes, 1949).

C. R. Post, *Medieval Spanish Allegory* (Cambridge, Mass., 1915).

Conde de Puymaigre, *La cour littéraire de Jean II*, 2 vols. (Paris, 1873).

Marqués de Santillana, *Prose and Verse*, ed. J. B. Trend (London, 1940), Introduction.

J. Vicens Vives, *An Economic History of Spain*, transl. F. M. López-Morillas (Princeton, 1969).

1 The Economies of Catalonia and Castile

JAIME VICENS VIVES

This book begins with an extract in which Professor Vicens underlines the strains put upon the Catalan economy at the end of the fourteenth century. The precocious establishment of the deposit bank, the *Taula de Canvi*, is shown to have been symptomatic not of expansion but of a crisis at Barcelona. By contrast, as is next seen, a stock-raising economy was characteristic of Castile, where the *Mesta* had already emerged and secured a position of great influence. The state of the famous Castilian fairs is then examined. A survey of coinage takes the reader back to the Moorish origin of the *maravedí* and *dobla* (the Aragonese, however, submitted early to French and Italian example). The incoming of Henry II as king of Castile spelled inflation, which, in its turn, stimulated devaluation. This proved an unsettling factor, depressing Castilian industry, which had never shown itself to be particularly vigorous.

PRICES, MONEY, BANKING, AND GENERAL ECONOMIC
CONDITIONS IN THE CROWN OF ARAGON

Catalonian banking: the crisis of 1391 and the founding of the "taula"
of exchange in Barcelona and Valencia

The most recent studies, among them those of the American scholar Usher,[1] assure us that in the thirteenth century the so-called *campsores* or *canviadors* already existed; they were those who engaged in money-changing. As coins were of different metals and fineness, and local and foreign money were used indiscriminately, the business of the money-changers was to weigh and appraise them. The profits they realized were considerable, and it was from the accumulation of these profits that the banking business, or the business of lending money, arose. The Jews had monopolized this type of operation up to the thirteenth century, for the Church completely opposed all forms of interest, which it considered usury. The bankers found a means to flout the canonical strictures by dealing in bills of exchange. Banking and commercial bills began their dazzlingly successful career at this time.

The importance of Catalonian banking began to grow within the thirteenth century itself. It appears for the first time in the legislation of 1284. Later, in the Cortes of 1300–1301, banking business became organized, and laws were passed concerning the rights, functions, responsibilities, and guarantors of the money-changer or banker.[2]

The second function of the *campsores* was to serve as depositaries for the assets of certain persons, especially merchants, who at times found it necessary to engage in credit operations and needed to draw money on a "taula" (in Catalonia the bank was named "taula," meaning "plank" or "table"). Very soon these exchangers had another function: that of lending money, sometimes to the monarchy, sometimes to the cities, as often for purposes of war as for problems of supplying the country in case of a grain shortage.

During the reign of Peter the Ceremonious,[3] constant warfare with Genoa and Castile caused an enormous development among the bankers in Barcelona, and in their train those of Valencia, Perpignan, Gerona, Lérida, and Tortosa. So much was this the case that in the last third of the fourteenth century Catalonian banking began to enter a phase of great prosperity. But just as it was about to achieve the stability necessary to assure normal functioning of the country's economy, the contraction of 1381 took place. This was characterized by a paralysis of business, reduction of the investment market, the ruin of *rentiers* owing to the breakdown in municipal finance, over-production, etc. In the face of this brutal shock, the slender stock of theoretical knowledge of the practising economists of the day failed them completely. Then two sets of parallel events occurred. The first was the massacre of Jews in 1391 . . . it was an explosion of popular anger against those who were being accused of the collective disaster. The second was the collapse of private banking. The bankers who had lent money to the king, unable to make good on the deposits which had been left with them, declared themselves bankrupt. Between 1381 and 1383 the chief bankers of Barcelona (Descaus, D'Olivella, Pasqual, and Esquerit), Gerona (Medir), and Perpignan (Garí) went into bankruptcy. This was a hard blow to the confidence placed in them by the public, as is shown by the edict published in Barcelona in 1397 reorganizing the system of money-changing.

As a result of the bankruptcies, the financial relationships which until that date had made up the normal network of public finance in the Crown of Aragon changed. The kings placed the credit of the Crown in the hands of foreign bankers, especially Genoese and Florentines, and in those of the families of converted Jews, particularly Aragonese, who had close ties with their friends and relatives, the *conversos* of Castile. As for the cities, the crisis resulted in the setting up of communal banking deposits known as "taules" of exchange.

When the historians of two or three generations ago spoke of the *Taula de Canvi* in Barcelona, they presented it as a product of our ancestors' creative genius, which had followed by only a few years its Genoese predecessor, the Bank of St. George. In fact, the origin of the famous *Taula* was the crisis of confidence which shook Barcelona after the events of 1381. So far from being an idea of genius, it was an event that demonstrated the financial insecurity of the bankers of Barcelona and their imitators in Valencia and Gerona. It was a short-sighted solution, for once they had lost confidence in the bankers and in national finance, the citizens and merchants decided to found the new institution (1401) by basing it on municipal credit and on the money which they were forced to deposit in the communal bank, whether its source was court orders, guardianships, estates, or attachments (edicts of 1412). In this way a great deal of capital was immobilized in the *Taula*, to the obvious detriment of the money market's flexibility in the crises subsequently to arise. It was, then, a blockade which froze money in Catalonia at the very moment when it should have been most fluid.

The *Taula de Canvi* of Barcelona, imitated in Valencia and Gerona, was under the control of the urban oligarchy. Its circle of operations included the *Bailía Real* (office of the king's bailiff), the *Clavariado* of the city (municipal treasurer's office), the small banks which had survived the catastrophe of 1380–1410, and foreign money (after 1446). Extremely careful regulations governed its workings in order to avoid any kind of fraud. Thus a period of financial conservatism was inaugurated which did not bode well for the future of Catalonia.

Development of the economic crisis in the first half of the fifteenth century: crisis of 1427 and devaluation of 1454

All efforts made after 1412, date of the definitive organization of the *Taula de Canvi*, to combat the economic crisis were fruitless. In 1427 there was a new collapse of the investment market and an even greater decline in economic activity. This was shown as much in the sharp drop in collection of taxes in the *Generalitat* of Catalonia and the city of Barcelona as in the *Bailía Real* of Valencia. The amount of the drop was extremely serious, ranging from 25 to 75 per cent. At the same time, mercantile activity and shipping declined. It is estimated that from 1432–1434 to 1454, shipping in the port of Barcelona declined by 75 to 80 per cent.

A currency reform was undertaken in order to offset these unfavorable conditions. It was an inevitable measure. The Valencians and Majorcans adopted it between 1426 and 1427, the Valencians by starting to mint the *timbre*, a 20-carat coin equivalent to 10 *sueldos*, supplanting the florin, which was worth 11. In Barcelona the monetary reform provoked a real battle between the two great urban parties, the aristocratic and the popular. The latter—the *Busca*—called for devaluation of the *croat* by dropping its ratio to the florin from 15 to 18 dineros. This measure, the *Busca* claimed, would prevent the flight of silver to France, increase the volume of trade, and stimulate industrial production. The other party, the *Biga*, opposed this on the grounds of the city's financial prestige, though in fact it was defending its own immediate interests: rural and urban revenues, bank deposits, debts, etc. It was necessary for some of the more adventurous aristocrats, like the Requesens de Soler family, to join the *Busca* before the Crown decreed devaluation of the florin in 1454. This measure was accepted by the bourgeoisie very much against their will, to the point that it was one of the causes which led the country into civil war in 1462. Then the value of money dropped to a point undreamed of by the conservative elements in the city.

The problem of economic decline in Catalonia

We have observed the development of the stages of very unfavorable conditions in the Catalonian economy. After the inflation of 1340 to 1380 and the crisis of 1381, we came to the collapse of 1427 and the total breakdown produced by the civil war of 1462–1472. This process ... was typical of Western Europe during the same period; but if in Catalonia it was serious enough to result in total stagnation of the economy, this was due to a number of specific circumstances which we would do well to examine. However, we must keep in mind that the heart of the problem was the inability of the oligarchy in Barcelona to see economic problems from a fresh point of view. This does not constitute a reproach to the oligarchy, for all such groups have failed when confronted with the same problem: namely, that of coping with depression conditions by truly adequate measures. Oligarchies have always taken refuge in the memory of the past, which brought them power and wealth.

There are a number of theories concerning the overall problem of Catalonia's economic decline, some working hypotheses, and a few proven facts. Let us sum up the main theses here:

Loss of control of the investment market. It went over into the hands of *conversos* and Italians. Consequently, the Catalonian bourgeoisie could not operate with its own assets; others handled them, and manipulated them for private ends. The country did not have money available to make productive investments during the whole long period of crisis in the fifteenth century.

Maritime terror and counterterror. The desire to make money rapidly caused the loss of the traditional markets for Catalonian trade in the Mediterranean. The slave trade, piracy, and privateering severely damaged Catalonia's commercial relations with other countries.

Closing of traditional markets in Barbary and Egypt. This was a direct consequence of the terrorism at sea that we have just mentioned.

Foreign competition. French on the one hand, English on the other. The French in the fields of textiles and spices, the English in shipping and the wool trade.

Lack of technological and social stimuli. People left Barcelona because trade was impoverished and because there was a climate of tension. In Barcelona, men fought in the name of theories which masked selfishness and personal antagonisms; but there was no view that looked toward the future. The protectionism of the popular party did not contain the seeds of positive reform in the industrial field. The fact was that the spirit of enterprise which had made Catalonian trade so powerful in the fourteenth century had been halted.

Lack of economic resistance in Catalonia's own commercial hinterland. This hypothesis of Robert S. Lopez[4] deserves serious consideration. Catalonia had neither the human resources nor a sufficiently powerful consumers' market to allow her to resist the onslaughts of the crisis. And the same was true in the south of France and the Crown of Aragon. On the other hand, Catalonia was faced with sharp competition from Valencia, a city which, by allying itself with Barcelona's enemies (Genoa and Marseilles), became the financial capital of the Crown of Aragon after 1462. . . .

STRUCTURE AND EXPANSION OF THE CASTILIAN HERDING AND AGRARIAN ECONOMY FROM THE THIRTEENTH TO FIFTEENTH CENTURIES

Organization of the Mesta

We shall have to study this organization in some detail, for it was perhaps the most important and most original feature of Castilian economy in the Late Middle Ages.

In the Early Middle Ages there existed local *mestas* for the flocks;

these were small common fields where sheep grazed. As the needs of these local mestas grew, cooperative groups of neighbors developed whose purpose was to look out for strayed sheep. In the course of time, mestas comprising more territory grew out of these local ones. These mestas must have coincided with the organic division of the Castilian flocks: the *Mesta of León*, which took in the whole mountain region in the north of that kingdom; the *Mesta of Soria*, including the highland zone of the Duero; the *Mesta of Segovia*, with the pastures of the Central System nearby; and the *Mesta of Cuenca*, on the slopes of the Iberian System. Soria especially contributed to the organization of the Mesta.

In 1273, Alfonso X the Wise consolidated the various Mestas and founded what later came to be called *El Honrado Concejo de la Mesta de los Pastores de Castilla*, or Honorable Assembly of the Mesta of the Shepherds of Castile. The motive was merely one of the king's financial embarrassments; he realized that it was much easier to assess taxes on livestock than on men, and formed the mestas into an organization that would provide considerable sums to the monarchy. In exchange for these taxes the herders wrested a series of privileges from Alfonso X, the most important of which was the extension of supervision over all migratory flocks, including stray animals, in the whole kingdom of Castile. This supervisory function was gradually extended, in time, even to "permanent" sheep pastured in local mestas and to the "riberiegas," animals which were pastured along the river banks within the district of a particular town.

The Mesta's principal function was to organize the *cañadas*, that is, the sheep highways which led the flocks from the mountains of the North to the *extremes* of the South, or from the summer pasturing grounds to the winter ones. The royal *cañadas* numbered three: the Leonese, the Segovian, and the Manchegan. These corresponded, generally speaking, to the three great areas of natural communication. The first brought together in León the flocks which were scattered in the northern mountains of the kingdom, and took them to Plasencia, Cáceres, Mérida, and Badajoz by way of Zamora, Salamanca, and Béjar. Béjar is important because it was a junction for one branch of the Segovian *cañada*. This one started in Logroño and went to Béjar through Burgos, Palencia, Segovia, and Avila, that is, along the northern slopes of the Guadarrama range. Another path branched out from this *cañada* to Talavera de la Reina, after which the flocks went on to Gaudalupe and then to the regions of Almadén and Andalusia. This same Segovian *cañada* included another eastern branch, which led from Cameros to Soria, Sigüenza, and El Escorial, and from there over the southern side of the mountains to join the western branch in Talavera de la Reina. Finally, the *Manchegan cañada* served the flocks raised in the mountains of Cuenca, which were then brought down to La Mancha and from there took one of two directions, toward Murcia or toward Andalusia.

The *cañadas* were protected by officials called "alcaldes entregadores de la Mesta," or judges of awards. Their maximum width was 90 Castilian *varas* (or about 250 feet). The officials seized every opportunity to remove the boundary stones from their places and widen the *cañadas* illegally. This produced long-drawn-out lawsuits with the farmers and teamsters.

According to rather late sources, for our knowledge of this matter dates from the reign of the Catholic Monarchs, the flocks were grouped together in *cabañas*, or droves. Each of these was in the charge of a chief herdsman. A drove was composed of at least a thousand head. The *hatos*, or flocks, were smaller. Each drove also included fifty *moruecos*, or stud rams, twenty-five *encencerrados*, the bellwethers which kept the sheep in line, and then one herder, four boys as assistants, five sheep dogs, and five pack animals carrying salt. Salt was an indispensable product for the good nutrition of the sheep.

The distances covered by these droves along the *cañadas* were: 830 km. for the Leonese and 270 to 370 for the Segovian and Manchegan routes. They traveled some 30 km. a day when going along the assigned path, and 10 in open country. The flocks left the South about the middle of April, and the sheep were sheared on the trip north, either while they were crossing the mountains or in the so-called *agostaderos*, or summer pastures.

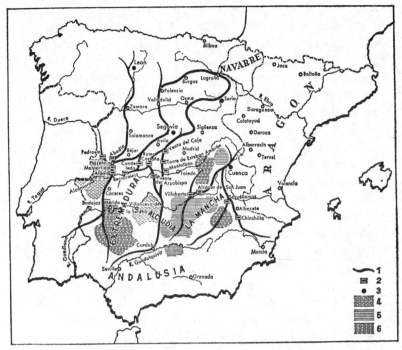

1. Migratory sheep routes in sixteenth-century Spain:
1, cañadas; 2, royal passes; 3, headquarters of cuadrillas of
the Mesta. Grazing grounds of the military orders: 4, Order
of Alcántara; 5, Calatrava; 6, Santiago

The Mesta's legal position is also interesting. The earliest code,
dating from 1379, has been lost, and we know only the text of the
statute of 1492 issued by Ferdinand and Isabella. But probably the
situation had not changed much. The essential basis of the organization was the "brothers of the Mesta," those who paid the tax or
servicio del ganado because they owned a migratory flock. Anyone
who paid this *servicio* was a "brother of the Mesta," and as such
had the right to attend the assemblies which were held twice a
year, one in the South and the other in the North. The southern
one occurred in January and February, most often in Villaneuva de
la Serena (where the Mesta's archives were kept), Don Benito,

Guadalupe, Talavera de la Reina, Montalbán, or Siruela. In the North they met in September and in autumn, especially in Ayllón, Berlanga, Riaza, Aranda de Duero, and Buitrago, and sometimes in Segovia and Medina del Campo. In order to be valid these assemblies had to have a quorum of forty brothers; generally 200 to 300 herders attended, representing a tenth of the total, so that by the end of the 15th century some 3,000 individuals were members of the Mesta. Voting was done by *cuadrillas*, or groups.

The decisions taken were of various kinds: internal organization, petitions to the king, protests, etc. The chief ones had to do with the duties and offices of the Mesta. On this point, Klein states that, following the ancient custom in Castile of choosing offices by lot, balloting by drawing members' names out of an urn was common in the Mesta. This is not true. In Castile this type of balloting was never used until the time of Ferdinand and Isabella, who brought the system from the Crown of Aragon. Therefore, before 1492 the common system must have been direct election to the various offices, except for that of president, who after the decrees of Alfonso the Wise was appointed by the Crown and generally had some connection with a person of high rank at court.

After the president, or *entregador principal*, the most important offices in the Mesta were the four *alcaldes de cuadrilla*, or *alcaldes de la Mesta*, who presided over the four *cabañas*, and then the judges, representatives, collectors, etc.

It is interesting to look at the social situation in the Mesta. Klein upholds a theory which might be termed a democratic one, saying that the flocks of the nobles represented only a very small proportion of the migratory flocks, and implies that the Mesta was an organization of small herdsmen. This theory, however, is in disagreement with the proven fact that the wool trade was controlled by the great Castilian lords. In support of his assertion Klein brings forward a lawsuit of 1561, in which there are declarations by a number of proprietors of flocks pastured on land owned by the Order of Calatrava. According to this document, of a total of 53,451 head, flocks of 50 head made up 32 per cent; those of 50 to 100 head, 35 per cent (that is to say, small flocks represented 67 per cent of the total); from 100 to 500 head, 23 per cent; from 500 to 1,000, 6 per cent; and more than 1,000, or whole droves, 11 per cent.

To Klein's opinion, which he bases on this lawsuit, we should have to object that these numbers are local, that they affect only one year, and that in consequence it is impossible to make generalizations from them. But on the other hand we must keep in mind that in 1561 the economic and social climate of the Mesta was at a peak, and that the concentration of great flocks had probably also reached its highest point; so that it is possible to believe that before the 16th century the percentage in favor of small proprietors compared to owners of large droves may have been greater.

Nonetheless, the existence of enormous flocks is evident well within the fifteenth century, For example, the monastery of El Escorial owned 40,000 head of sheep; that of Santa María del Paular, near Segovia, 30,000; the future Duke of Béjar, 25,000; the Duke of the Infantado, some 20,000. In view of the size of these flocks, it must be admitted that such numbers were very influential in the affairs of the Mesta. Therefore we may state without fear of contradiction that, in spite of the number of small proprietors who made up the Mesta, it was the great lords who ran it, who occupied the presidency and the offices of *alcalde de cuadrilla*, and those who, in short, had most to say in the autumn and winter assemblies. And finally, the person who controlled the money from the livestock *servicio* was neither the president of the Mesta nor the king but, after the time of Prince Henry, the Master of Santiago. Henry's father, Ferdinand of Antequera, had made him a donation of the taxes on sheep and cattle. Therefore, the structure of the organization may have been democratic, but the barons of Castile were those who really held the power. This was seen in 1462 with the failure of the Castilian cities' attempt to break the monopoly, which the herders were using to hinder development of the urban cloth industry. . . .

CASTILIAN INDUSTRY AND TRADE FROM THE THIRTEENTH
TO FIFTEENTH CENTURIES

Development of the great Castilian fairs

At the beginning of the thirteenth century, the local or regional markets which had become established during the early period of the Reconquest continued to develop in Castile. The fair—that is, the mercantile institution and activity distinguished from the market by the fact that it lasts a number of days, has more privileges, is more subject to regulation, and takes in a larger radius of economic action—appeared in the thirteenth century, not in the north, as it would be logical to suppose, but in the south. In fact, the first privileges granted to fairs were given in New Castile, Extremadura, and Andalusia during the reigns of Alfonso X and Sancho IV: in Seville in 1254; Badajoz in 1258; Alcaraz, 1268; Cádiz, 1284; Talavera, 1294; and Mérida, 1300. This phenomenon must be thought of as closely related to the commercial activity stimulated by the incipient wool trade.

As for the creation of fairs in the north, great confusion reigns, since the date of establishment of many of them is unknown. It is said that those of Valladolid and Sahagún date from the twelfth century, and that it is not known exactly when the fairs of Palencia, Segovia, Toledo, and San Sebastián were established. This leads us to think that these places probably had markets of more or less importance, and that at a given time which we can locate sometime during the fourteenth century they received the status of a fair. This is what happened at Compostela, which in 1351 received an authorization to celebrate a fair, extending its duration from two to fifteen days. The date for Burgos is 1339, and our first information about the very famous fair of Medina del Campo comes from the year 1321. This tends to confirm the theory that the southern fairs were the first to appear, owing to contact with the new commercial methods introduced by the Genoese and related to the Mesta.

This resistance to the development of fairs is linked to the position of the Castilian monarchy, which was never in favor of what was called a "free market." In the fifteenth century especially, when Castile's population was increasing rapidly, wool was selling well, and the textile industry was beginning to flourish, there was a tendency on the part of the nobles and clergy to concede one market to each town, the purpose being to stimulate trade and particularly to collect taxes from the merchants who attended the fairs. This practice cut down on the amount taken in by the royal treasury and threatened the privileged position of the old established fairs and markets. This is why "free" fairs and markets were banned by the Cortes of 1430, except for those which already possessed a royal dispensation.

After the middle of the fifteenth century the fair of Medina del Campo became more important than the others, for after its unsuccessful attempt to establish fairs all over Castile the monarchy was determined to concentrate the wool trade, and especially the money trade, in that fair. As the Castilian court was an ambulatory one and the flocks of the Mesta also traveled about, Mesta sales and payments to the monarchy were usually stipulated as payable in a certain place; and it was then that the famous phrase "to be paid in Medina del Campo" began to appear on bills of exchange. The concentration of the wool trade and the investment market made Medina del Campo, after 1450, the great financial center of the Crown of Castile. We must note, however, that after the end of the fourteenth century the great lords of the Mesta had excellent sources of income in Valladolid as well as Medina.

Merchants from Burgos, Seville, Lisbon, Valencia, and Barcelona, among those of the Hispanic Peninsula, traded in Medina del Campo. And among the foreigners were Irish, Flemings, Genoese, and Florentines. As for the types of goods exchanged, in Medina del Campo wool was sold and luxury articles were bought, for Castilian import trade was essentially in this kind of merchandise. There was no other luxury market in all Europe, not even in the courts of the Italian princes, that could compare with the one of Castile. This is understandable in view of the economic potential of the country's aristocratic class.

The financial role of the fairs was so important that, when the time of the monarchy's weakness arrived, the revenues brought in by Medina del Campo were usurped by the Archbishop of Toledo and the Count of Alba.

The taxes collected at the fairs were of two types, municipal and royal. As for the first type, the chief tax was the "fee of the ground of the fair"; that is, the one collected for putting up a stall there. In addition, there were taxes for guarding the merchandise ("constable's fee") and those paid on weights and measures. As for the royal taxes, the chief ones were the *alcabala* and the *sisa*, which appeared at the end of the thirteenth century. . . .

MONEY, USURY, AND PUBLIC FINANCE IN CASTILE

Castilian coinage and its fluctuations

[The] monetary circulation of the Astur-Leonese kingdom [was meager], based as it was not on coins of its own but on the introduction of Frankish, and especially Moslem, coins.[5] The advances of the Reconquest merely reinforced the entry of the kingdom, now Castilian-Leonese, into the dual monetary orbit of allies and invaders. *Dineros* and *dinars* from beyond its frontiers circulated more and more freely until the economic development of Castile brought about an emancipation. The first Castilian dineros were minted in Toledo shortly after its capture by Alfonso VI [1065–1109], and the first dinars (with Arabic inscriptions) much later, in 1172, after the Moslem king of Murcia, the habitual supplier of the Castilian-Leonese market, had stopped minting gold.

Let us survey the history of the two foreign coins transplanted to Castile.

Gold Coinage. The first Castilian version of the dinar, which we owe to Alfonso VIII [1158–1214], was called a *morabetí* or *maravedí*, taking its name from the Almorávides who at that time had restored the unity of Moslem Spain. Following the prescription of the Koran, this gold maravedí had a ratio of 1:10 in terms of silver; that is, it was worth 10 dirhems. A little later the monetary reform of the Almohades, the new invaders, also had repercussions on the Christian system. The *dobla* appeared, taking the place of the maravedí; this coin was equal to two dinarins (the name of the new Moslem dinar, of less value than the old) and was divided into half-doblas, or *mazmudinas*. As usual, the first doblas to circulate in Christian territory were foreign minted, until, when the power of the Almohades was crushed in 1212, Alfonso X [1252–1284] was obliged to mint them in his own kingdom. This Castilian version added to the existing coins a new fractional piece, the *cuarto*, or quarter-dobla. Also (though this did not influence specific coins, but did reflect the monetary evolution of Western Europe), it should be noted that Alfonso the Wise introduced the *mark* of Cologne as a unit of weight (233 grams of fine gold), as a substitute for the traditional Roman libra.

The dobla became firmly established (up to the time of Ferdinand and Isabella) as the Castilian gold unit. The only modification in it, a fairly unimportant one in the long course of its history, was its adaptation to the maravedí by Alfonso XI [1312–1350], who converted the latter into a simple money of account without any real value. Alfonso XI divided the dobla not into equal parts but into two fractions of 20 and 15 maravedís, the cause of this unequal division being the inequality of value between gold and silver. In fact, while the dobla was worth 35 maravedís in gold coin, it was worth 1 maravedí more, 36, in silver because of the difference in metal. This duality of value, depending on whether one counted in gold or silver, made the division into equal parts impossible, hence the separation into coins of 20 and 15. But what is really interesting with regard to the transplanted dobla in Castile is the fact that it survived until the end of the fifteenth century, outside the great European current which, beginning as early as the thirteenth century, caused the general adoption of Italian coins, with the florin at their head. Castile's fidelity to the Moslem system was to mark a profound divergence from the territories of the Crown of Aragon, which had joined the European movement, and would finally lead to the reform of Ferdinand and Isabella.

Silver Coinage. In contrast to what happened with gold, the silver coinage of the Western kingdoms developed within the orbit of European, that is to say French, mintings. Certainly the Moslem dirhem circulated in Castilian and Leonese territories, but at the time of the first Castilian mintings Alfonso VI introduced the *dinero*, a vellon coin (that is, a mixture of copper and silver containing 76 grams of fine silver). Although in France the dinero was worth one-twelfth of the *solidus* or *sueldo* (the ancient gold coin reduced after Charlemagne's time to mere money of account), in Castile the continuation of gold mintings permitted relating the dinero to the gold coin (the maravedí), using the same proportion. That is, the dinero was a twelfth, not of a fictitious sueldo, but of an actual coin, the maravedí.

Later, the amount of silver used in the dinero diminished so that the *pepiones*, the name given to these coins at the time of Ferdinand III, contained only 22 grams of silver. To correct this tendency and to revalue vellon, Alfonso the Wise instituted his reform. The basis of this was the introduction of the *maravedí blanca* or *maravedí burgalés* (note how, when it was replaced by the dobla, the old gold maravedí gave its name to a silver coin at the time of Alfonso the Wise), valued at one-sixth the original gold maravedí; that is, double the value of the dinero and pepión. But the "Burgos" coin did not last long, and the very king responsible for it was obliged to devalue its silver content by a third, bringing into existence the *alfonsíes* or *prietos* (that is, "dark in color"), or *coronados* and *cornados*, as they were called at the time of Sancho IV. The failure of Alfonso X's reform was underscored by Ferdinand IV when he minted the *novenes*, equal in value to the old pepiones.

At last Peter I achieved a true readjustment of silver coinage, so necessary after the confusion produced by repeated inflationary measures. In the middle of the fourteenth century this monarch established a new silver coin that was stronger than its predecessors. This was the *real*, the Castilian version of the Catalan *croat*, which in its turn had been inspired by the *gros* of St. Louis. The real, which contained 3.5 grams of silver and was worth 31 maravedís, was destined to attain great popularity, confirmed by Ferdinand and

Isabella's reform. However, between the two great reforms of Peter I and Ferdinand and Isabella, a long period of monetary convulsions and disorders intervened. Thus, in the time of Henry II, whose reign coincided with an extremely serious crisis in the Castilian monarchy, inflation knew no limits. The silver in vellon coins was reduced by half. Henry III minted a new coin, called the *blanca*, which was worth 5 dineros and contained 15 centigrams of silver. This new monetary unit was again debased by John II, whose blancas contained only 10 centigrams of silver. This plunged the country into a monetary chaos from which it did not emerge until the reign of Ferdinand and Isabella.

If we compare the course of the ordinary maravedí with the price of gold, we can establish two great inflationary periods in Castile, one between 1252 and 1258 (value falling from 4.22 to 2.87), and another at the moment of the European crisis of 1380 (1388, 0.90; 1390, 0.47). The Castilian monarchy's tendency towards inflation was enormously prejudicial to the industrial classes. The nobles had their real estate, and furthermore had infiltrated all the places where money was worth something, by means of the "vellum" of wool if not on the basis of "vellon." The constant devaluation of the currency was one of the essential reasons why Castilian industrial structure never solidified during the fifteenth century as it should have done.

Role of the Kingdom of Granada in the Castilian Monetary Economy

The majority of the Moslems who fled from Andalusia after the great rebellion of 1263 had become concentrated in Granada. A large number of farmers and many artisans from the cities emigrated to the little kingdom, defended by its high mountains, and with its rich flatlands and long coastline. Therefore Granada had a dense and industrious population, though it never reached the total of 1 million inhabitants which has so often been attributed to it. However, agriculture was prosperous, workshops were active, and a very remunerative trade was carried on with Africa through the ports of Almería and Málaga. Granada exported wheat, grapes, fruit, sugar, cochineal, and silk; manufactured goods, among which were velvets, damasks, and gold jewelry; and minerals such as gold, silver, and lead.

This wealth clearly benefited the Castilians. After 1430, the Nasrid dynasty of Granada undertook to pay a tribute of 20,000 gold doblas annually. It would be interesting to establish a graph of Granada's gold payments to the Castilian monarchy. And it would also be very significant to study the psychological process which accustomed the Castilian monarchy to count in its budget on a share of income which did not come from the labor of its vassals, drained off through taxes. Therefore, when it is stated that the treasures of America perverted the procedures of the exchequer and the royal officials, this important precedent is forgotten: that before the sixteenth century there was also a treasure which came to Castile from outside—the treasure of Granada.

The Gold Route

The flood of gold that inundated Castile from Granada brings up the subject of the gold route. The trade which Granada carried on with Morocco and the countries of the Barbary Coast (especially with Tlemçen) brought in gold from the Sudan. A very large amount of this metal constantly flowed into the ports of Almería and Málaga. At the beginning of the fifteenth century, however, the Castilians as well as the Portuguese, no doubt stimulated by the discoveries of the Majorcans who had reached Senegal, began a series of voyages of discovery along the coast of the Sahara in hopes of bartering for gold, slaves, and ivory. There was some romanticism in the voyages of Henry the Navigator of Portugal and the Andalusian sailors, but there was also a good deal of commercial activity. The grants given by Portugal to Henry the Navigator, and those which Castile offered to the Andalusian sailors on the Canaries route, were fundamentally grants for trading operations.

We do not know much about this struggle because each court, and each seaport, took great care not to announce its findings to its neighbors; a geographical discovery was a state secret. The

Castilians' main way station was undoubtedly the Canary Islands, from which they sailed to barter for gold, slaves, and ivory on the nearby African coast. In consequence, gold arrived on the Andalusian coasts not only along the route of Granada (through Tlemçen) but also from Senegal, through the Canaries and Cádiz. And from Cádiz it found its way into the pockets of the Genoese. This means that, long in advance of Columbus' discovery, we have an exact precedent for the gold route of the American treasure. Gold arrived in Castile only to be siphoned off by foreign powers, especially Genoa.

Genoese, Jews, and Conversos in the Castilian money trade

One of the studies which should be undertaken with the greatest urgency, if we are to understand something of the modern economic history of Spain, would have to do with the role played by the Genoese in the fifteenth century, not only in the Crown of Aragon but especially in Castile. There does exist a conviction that it was important; we know that the colonization of Spain by the Genoese after the thirteenth century marked a fundamental stage for the discovery of America, and that Valencia and Seville were their chief strongholds in the two Crowns of Aragon and Castile. But we know almost nothing about the precise manner in which they operated. Their role as great inter-mediaries between Andalusian Atlantic trade and that of the Mediterranean and Central Europe has not been properly clarified. And in particular, we do not know how they managed to get Sudanese gold into their country. Financiers rather than merchants, the Genoese of the fifteenth century must have financed the voyages of Atlantic exploration by Andalusians; they must have gained control of the Southern wool trade and lent money to the great Andalusian landowners. All these are mere working hypotheses. What is perfectly clear is that they established in Andalusia the mercantile and capitalist base which gave them such a leading role in the Castilian money trade of the sixteenth century.

A similar operation of cornering the money market, or rather, another concentration of capital, was in the hands of Jews and *conversos*. Since there was no long-term capital in the hands of bankers, and since the Jews, and later the *conversos*, were collectors for the military orders and the Church, it was logical that all the money which escaped from Genoese control wound up in their hands. From time to time there was a pogrom, and money went back into circulation; but it soon returned to its old owners. By the middle of the fifteenth century money was in the hands of the *conversos*, except for the small proportion under control of the Mesta (that is, of the great lords who engaged in the wool trade).

To sum up, the circulation of gold in Castile at about the middle of the fifteenth century can be reconstructed as follows: Granada and West Africa, as the great gold routes flowing into Seville; from there, disappearance of part of it to Genoa; the other, smaller part went north. In Medina del Campo it served to pay for luxury goods bought at the fair. Finally, when it reached Burgos it was swallowed up by the *conversos* in payment of their loans to the king, the nobles, and the magnates of the Mesta.

So the gold followed a straight line, without the country's profiting from it. And if we compare this circulation with that of the sixteenth century we will find the situation exactly the same. So the constant inflow of gold in the Late Middle Ages was the necessary precedent to the great machinery of the 1500's, which also swallowed up the treasure of America without the Castilian commoner's receiving any benefit from it.

Usury in Castile

Usury was calamitous in the early times of the Commercial Revolution. As neither capital nor credit institutions existed, money was very costly. The Jews in particular profited from this business, and it was then that they gained the reputation of usurers. But after the end of the fourteenth century their role declined all over Western Europe, with one notable exception—Castile—where their influence grew daily, to the point that, as we have said, they obtained control of most of the money in circulation.

Among the causes of this phenomenon was the incapacity of the Castilian bourgeoisie for creating banks and banking deposits.

But more important than this was the immoderate desire for luxury and ostentation which characterized their society and was, as Sánchez Albornoz points out,[6] one of its chief vices. The nobility, the clergy, and the bourgeoisie ruined themselves because of their desire to dazzle others with jewels, clothing, and ornaments. Chronically in need of cash, they found it in the tight purse of the Hebrew. Early in the thirteenth century, sumptuary statutes like those of Cuenca authorized the Jews to charge interest at the rate of one-eighth of a maravedí or one-twelfth of a solidus per week. This means a *monthly* interest of 50 and 33⅓ per cent respectively, a truly fabulous amount. Alfonso X limited this interest to 33⅓ per cent *annually* (1268), a tremendous reduction which was often flouted. Private documents prove this. The kings, urged on by the nobles, the clergy, and the municipal councils, repeated Alfonso's decrees. In vain. Money continued to be very costly in an ambitious society little given to work. Hence the violence of the upheavals of 1391, when Jews, accused of the high cost of living and the ruin of many important people, were persecuted everywhere in Castile. But really, as we know, the cause was a change in the general economic outlook. During the fifteenth century *conversos* took the place of Jews in loaning money to kings and aristocrats, churches and town councils. Burgos was the center of this business.

Usury came to a peak because the Jews had attained the rank of treasury agents of the Crown and the military orders. We have already mentioned this several times. The financial difficulties of the Castilian Crown gave wide scope to the activities of this group. After the twelfth century the monarchs had a Jewish *almojarife*, or taxgatherer, at their side. A century later these *almojarifes* had taken over the administration. The family of Zag de la Maleha played an important role in this respect at the time of Alfonso X, and that of Abraham de Barchilón (the Barcelonian) during Sancho IV's reign. From that time on, collection of taxes was the task of Jews and *conversos*. The Castilians hated them passionately. But their *raison d'être* is clear: they alone were the ones who understood the value of money in Castile.

Taxes and Levies by the State

Along general lines, the same principles for the collection of taxes and levies that had existed in the early period of the Asturian, Leonese, and Castilian monarchies were still in force; that is, the main weight of taxation fell, on the one hand, on those who owned land and, on the other, on those who worked or engaged in business. So it is no novelty to encounter again the fees, tithes, poll taxes, and war levies we spoke of before.

During the Late Middle Ages the most important new feature was the application of the country's growing economic resources to the royal treasury. This was achieved in two ways, by broadening the old taxes and by obtaining various grants and loans from the Cortes. The position of the aristocrats is also interesting. Since they were exempt from all taxes, they attempted—and partly succeeded in the effort—to wrest from the monarch the money which came in from taxes and levies. A large part of the social struggle in Castile in the fourteenth and fifteenth centuries was due to the nobles' eagerness to obtain control over the chief sources of collection of taxes on commerce.

Because of their nature, these can be divided into two large groups, taxes on *transit* and on *buying and selling*. In the first group we find the bridge tax, the turnpike tax, the ferry tax; the castle tax, paid by those who used a road under the jurisdiction of a castle; the road tax, which was paid for the safeguarding of highways; and the duty on the passage of animals. The *almojarifazgo*, or customs dues, can be related to these.

Taxes on buying and selling transactions were more important; these developed as commercial expansion took place, particularly expansion of the wool trade. In the thirteenth century two famous taxes appeared which were to persist in the history of the Castilian exchequer almost to the threshold of our time—the *alcabala* and the *sisa*. Both grew out of difficult moments for the monarchy, one in the time of Alfonso X and the other during Sancho IV's reign. The *alcabala* was a certain percentage on sales in the marketplace: first it was 5 per cent (in 1269), and later (in 1377) it was raised to 10 per cent. As for the *sisa*, or deduction made by the treasury from the sale price of a product, it was first applied during the time of Sancho IV at the rate of 1 per cent; shortly afterward, about the middle of the thirteenth century, it became fixed at 3 per cent.

To have an idea of what this constant succession of taxes, duties, and fees represented for the businessman, we must add to them the municipal and seigniorial levies.

We have left to the last any mention of the Crown's fattest source of income: the tax on sheep, or the fiscal organization which was set up over the great migratory flocks of the Mesta. From the earliest times of the wool revolution, the Crown had a very convenient area in which to collect taxes. When the general charter of the Mesta was granted by Alfonso X, one of its chief purposes was to establish the fiscal responsibility of livestock breeders. Four years earlier (in 1269, in fact), the so-called *servicio* had been established, voted by the Cortes, under the terms of which each flock of the Castilian drove was obliged to pay a certain amount. This service, voted for three or four years, kept on being renewed. In 1343 the *montazgo* was added to it. This was a purely municipal tax, but the Crown converted it into a general one, cancelling the local *montazgos*. "Servicio y montazgo," after that, became one of the chief resources of the Crown. Thus, it is logical and comprehensible that when Ferdinand of Antequera of the house of Trastámara, a very prudent man, exercised the regency of Castile for a few short years, he tried to insure the prosperity of his house by causing his third son, Prince Henry, to inherit, along with the mastership of Santiago, the right to collect the duties of *servicio* and *montazgo*. Hence the Castilian prince had an immense fortune in his hands: he controlled the uncultivated lands of the southern Meseta, many more in Andalusia, and furthermore had the right to collect taxes from the Mesta and turn them over to the Crown. Since Prince Henry turned out to be a good administrator, he formed quite a flawless tax organization; so when Don Álvaro de Luna took his job away from him, his system was adopted by the State. In 1457 a schedule of "servicio y montazgo" taxes was approved which remained in force until the end of the seventeenth century.

The Castilian Cortes and Fiscal Policy

In the Crown of Aragon, and more especially formulated in Catalonia, it had been a principle of political law that any economic relationship between the sovereign and the people had to be based on a pact which closely linked the sovereign with the Cortes to impose taxes, and the Cortes with the sovereign to vote them. In Castile this pactist theory, characteristic of a flourishing bourgeoisie, was formulated only by the Cortes of Henry IV, and then rather timidly. This is logical, for the Castilian monarchy never had to face a guild organization like the Catalan one, and at the same time it enjoyed much broader financial resources.

It is true, though, that in spite of the fact that the Castilian monarchs had large sums of money at their disposal, there were certain moments when they were not able to meet their responsibilities. This meant that they had to apply to the Cortes for grants and levies, and that the Cortes tried to take advantage of the situation to wrest from them certain special concessions on taxation.

During the reign of Alfonso XI (fourteenth century) the Cortes obtained from the king the promise that he would not assess any tax or levy without its authorization. This law appeared in all the fundamental codes of Castile, but in spite of it the monarchy never paid much attention to a concession which had been extracted from it at a tight moment. On the other hand, when the Cortes did vote a tax, it was the royal officials who collected it, thus giving an opportunity for the indefinite perpetuation of a tax granted for a special and transitory purpose.

Since no regulatory mechanism existed for the tax payments of the subjects to the monarch, the Castilian Crown quickly fell into the hands of moneylenders or issued certificates of indebtedness pledged on certain Crown incomes. These certificates were the so-called *juros*. There has been no careful study of the origins and development of these *juros*. We know that three types existed—those payable on demand, perpetual, and on one life—and that all of them were state issues of paper to legalize a debt or guarantee a loan. After the beginning of the fifteenth century the practice of issuing *juros* led the Castilian public treasury to the verge of inflationary anarchy.

Economic policy of the monarchy

If the Aragonese monarchy sometimes had political whims in the economic field and often sacrificed material realities to the pursuit of a fanciful objective, as in the case of Alfonso the Magnanimous, the Castilian monarchy scarcely had any idea of the country's real economic situation. Taken up with warlike enterprises, dominated by the feudal and seigniorial superstructure of the great landowners, it paid scarcely any attention to commercial relations, which were almost entirely the work of its more enterprising vassals. Fluctuating as it did between contradictory ambitions, its solution was always to seek the easiest path, and the easiest thing was to bow to the monopoly of the Mesta and the interests of the wool exporters: *conversos*, Genoese, and Flemings. The result of this was an internal contradiction between the needs of a country with a growing population and a burgeoning textile industry, and those of a monarchy accustomed only to solving its own selfish problems and the quarrels of those who grew rich from their connections with the throne.

Isolated figures opposed to this general trend, which was governed by the idea of consumption and freedom of external trade, were Alfonso X and Henry III. One author even speaks of a "controlled economy" when he refers to Alfonso the Wise. It was hardly that. It is true that this monarch reformed the currency standard and set up a severe tariff law (1268) which banned the export of precious metals, livestock, wool and silk, leather, wine, and wheat. It is also true that he favored the Castilian merchant marine and rescued it from foreign dependence. But this same Alfonso X was the monarch who created the Mesta, and was the adversary of the guild organizations. He was, therefore, not a very convinced protectionist. And in the end his efforts were a total failure.

His successors allowed themselves to be led by circumstances. They were incapable of dealing with economic factors. Only Henry III dictated an order in 1398 urging foreign merchants to embark their goods in Castilian ships. This was a measure taken in a period of crisis, no sooner published than flouted. Only during the reign of Henry IV—that king so little known to history—did an effective and intelligent protectionist policy begin to be practised, and it was to be continued by the Catholic Monarchs.

NOTES

[1. A. P. Usher, *The Early History of Deposit Banking in Mediterranean Europe*, I (Cambridge, Mass., 1943), 326.]

[2. *Cortes de los antiguos reinos de Aragón y de Valencia y principado de Cataluña* (Real Academia de Historia), I, *Cortes de Cataluña, 1064–1327* (Madrid, 1896), 167–80.]

[3. King, 1336–87.]

[4. R. S. Lopez in *Cambridge Economic History*, II (Cambridge, 1952), 347–48.]

[5. Cf. J. Vicens Vives, *Economic History of Spain*, trans. F. López-Morillas (3d ed.; Princeton, 1969), 134–5.]

[6. Cf. C. Sánchez-Albornoz, *España: Un enigma histórico*, II (Buenos Aires, 1956), 127–28.]

FURTHER READING

J. Brousolle, "Les impositions municipales de Barcelone de 1328–1462," *EHM*, V (1955), 1–164.

C. Carrère, "Le droit d'ancrage et le mouvement du port de Barcelone au milieu du XVe siècle," *EHM*, III (1953).

E. J. Hamilton, *Money, Prices and Wages in Valencia, Aragon and Navarre, 1351–1500* (Cambridge, Mass., 1936).

J. Heers, "Le commerce des Basques en Méditerranée au XVe siècle," *BH*, LVII (1955), 292–324.

——, *Gênes au XVe siècle* (Paris, 1961).

J. Klein, "Medieval Spanish Guilds," in *Facts and Factors in Economic History: Essays in Honor of E. F. Gay* (Cambridge, Mass., 1932).

——, *The Mesta: A Study in Spanish Economic History, 1273–1836* (Cambridge, Mass., 1920).

R. S. Lopez in *Cambridge Economic History*, II (Cambridge, 1952), 347–48; III (Cambridge, 1963), *passim*.

Ruth Pike, *Enterprise and Adventure: The Genoese in Seville and the Opening of the New World* (Ithaca, New York, 1966).

R. S. Smith, *The Spanish Guild Merchant: A History of the Consulado, 1250–1700* (Durham, N.C., 1940).

A. P. Usher, *The Early History of Deposit Banking in Mediterranean Europe* (Cambridge, Mass., 1943), Vol. I.

P. Vilar, "Le déclin Catalan du bas Moyen Âge, hypothèses sur sa chronologie," *EHM*, VI (1956–59), 3–68.

2 The Atlantic and the Mediterranean Among the Objectives of the House of Trastámara

LUIS SUÁREZ FERNÁNDEZ

In this survey of aspects of Castilian foreign policy, 1369–1420, the author, who is the rector of Valladolid University, gives special attention to the strength of the navy. In both the Atlantic and the Mediterranean, Castilian ships were increasingly important. It was no coincidence that the period saw the establishment of Castilian sovereignty over the Canary Islands in the face of keen Portuguese rivalry. Good use is made of documents in the archives of Murcia, Paris, Simancas, and the Vatican. Studies on the army also are at last coming into their own, thanks especially to recent work done by Sr. Ladero, whose *Milicia y Economía en la guerra de Granada* (Valladolid, 1964) and *Castilla y la Conquista del reino de Granada* (Valladolid, 1967) have given these subjects the revision which they badly needed.

HENRY II AND THE QUESTION OF THE ATLANTIC

Today there cannot be the slightest doubt that when Charles V of France encouraged and led the coup d'état which replaced the reign of Peter I in Castile by that of Henry II, he had as his almost exclusive objective the control of the Atlantic Ocean. And, looking ahead, we can see that this objective was fully achieved in the years which followed.[1] Castile had had a direct interest in exploiting this ocean—trade route for wool, iron, and wine from the Cantabrian ports to Flanders—for at least a hundred years. Though it seems that Peter I had allowed himself to be seduced by a Mediterranean policy, his father and predecessor, Alfonso XI, had pointed the way to gaining supremacy in the Atlantic. It is certain, however, that his methods were not feasible in 1369. That supremacy, destroyed at the battle of Winchelsea (August 29, 1350), has a curious parallelism with the success of France, or (which is the same thing) the weakness of England.[2] The Castilian defeat at Winchelsea had not interrupted either trade with Flanders or fishing activity in English waters.[3]

Mercantile[4] and security reasons were equally important in Castile; in France only reasons of security mattered.[5] In 1369 the Atlantic question was posed for Henry II—surrounded by enemies —in very harsh terms. The open warfare with Portugal had a marked maritime character; the fleet of Ferdinand I, who had assumed the title of king of Castile, launched two important points of attack: in the north, Nuño Martins de Goes, with eight galleys, captured La Coruña and swept the enemy from the Galician *rías*;[6] in the south, Lanzarote Peçanho, aided by Juan Focin, one of Peter's supporters, with more than sixty vessels, sealed off the mouth of the Guadalquivir.[7] In the face of these powerful naval forces Castile's sea power seemed ridiculous. Some of the galleys in the service of Portugal were Basque, faithful to the memory of Don Peter.[8]

SANLÚCAR AND LA ROCHELLE

The fact that the Cantabrian and Vizcayan sailors were able first to extricate themselves from the Portuguese pincers and then to defeat the English is an excellent proof of the vitality of these coastal cities and their men, who were accustomed to navigation in both peace and war. It is evident that in the battle of Sanlúcar de Barrameda, which freed the western approaches to the Straits, two important factors were the inexperience of the Portuguese admiral and the attrition caused by the length of the useless blockade.[9] Galicia, however, was reconquered by land. When the first peace was signed between Portugal and Castile, on March 31, 1371, Castile had taken her first step; she now had freedom of movement in the Atlantic.

The battle of the Atlantic was very far from being decided.

It was just at this point that the fiercest enemy the Trastámaras were to have during the next fifteen years appeared on the scene: John of Gaunt, duke of Lancaster, who married Peter I's daughter Constance in Roquefort (September, 1371) and assumed the title of king of Castile.[10] Immediately the Franco-Castilian alliance was strengthened. The following spring a fleet of twenty-three ships, commanded by Cabeza de Vaca and Ruiz Díaz de Rojas, sailed for France.[11] This time the objective was La Rochelle, a port which served as a link between the heavy ships of the Hanseatic League and the trade routes of the south.[12] The Franco-Castilian allies achieved a resounding victory before the city on June 23, 1372,[13] representing a terrible blow for the English trade in wine and salt. The city surrendered on August 15, and the efforts of Edward III, who was negotiating with Genoa behind the backs of the French, were shown to be useless; Castile now controlled the Bay of Biscay.

THE DUKE OF LANCASTER AND THE TRUCE OF BRUGES

This was the great principle which governed policies up to 1385. In 1373 England forced Ferdinand I of Portugal into a new war, solely so that Ambrosio Bocanegra could obtain another of his naval victories (March 7).[14] Within two weeks the inclusion of Portugal within the Franco-Castilian sphere of action was a fact.[15] With a free hand in the West, and completely ignoring the Mediterranean—a peace with Aragon was signed in 1374—Henry II and Charles V could devote future campaigns to an effort to dislodge their enemies from the Bay of Biscay and the English Channel. In 1374 an attack was carried out—an action by pirates as much as soldiers—on the Isle of Wight,[16] the doorstep of England. It was natural that Henry II, puffed up by his successes, should reject the English peace feelers made through Charles II of Navarre.

Only the duke of Lancaster, in England, understood that the great struggle was being unleashed in the Atlantic. Imbued with the same chivalrous spirit as his brother, he was also more practical, more of a realist, and more ambitious than Edward. Fate was to deny him the supreme ambition of ascending a throne, but his children, Henry, Philippa, and Catherine, were to be ancestors of kings. On June 12, 1373, he appeared in Bordeaux with the title of Captain General for Overseas, which implied broader powers than those ever attained by the Prince of Wales, now dead.[17] His objective was perfectly clear: to break the line of union between Castile and France. Four days after his appointment, on June 16, the duke, styling himself king of Castile, signed an alliance with England and Portugal.[18]

What a magnificent dream it was! Portugal, England, and Castile united, controlling the sea, exploiting the markets of Flanders, the routes to Africa, the wines of Bordeaux, the wool trade, the salt of Bourgneuf. But the facts did not respond to such high hopes. The great expedition launched in Calais on June 27, 1373, which was to lead the duke to Castile in triumph, ended in December of that year in Bordeaux, with only a handful of men remaining out of the splendid Lancastrian army. The victor of the hour was a gruff, silent, and choleric captain, Bertrand Du Guesclin.

The situation became stagnant. It was the Franco-Castilian allies who launched the attack on Bayonne, which, along with Bordeaux and Calais, was England's strong point on the Continent. On June 21, 1374,[19] Henry II besieged Bayonne, which "is on the sea, and he did great harm to all the coasts of Vizcaya and Guipúzcoa."[20] In spite of the use of a fleet and the large number of troops employed, Bayonne did not surrender.[21]

The military situation reached a stalemate. But England did not possess enough land to maintain a bridgehead in France, and resigned herself to admitting defeat. When the truces of Bruges were signed on June 27, 1375,[22] a page in history had been turned. The duke of Lancaster was relegated to a secondary role, and his ambitious plans seemed abandoned forever.

THE ATTACK ON ENGLAND

The truces were renewed, and they lasted two years; but they were powerless to prevent violent rivalries among merchant seamen. The English plundered fourteen Castilian ships; in retaliation, on August 10, 1375, the admiral of Castile struck another blow at English trade by burning thirty-six English ships in the bay of Bourgneuf.[23] This admiral was Fernán Sánchez de Tovar, one of the most famous seafaring personalities of the time and first in the ranks of Spanish sailors. The Genoese had taught him seamanship.[24] His second-in-command, representing France, was Jean de Vienne, a thirty-four-year-old Burgundian who had received his battle experience under the banners of Du Guesclin; he was an idealist dreaming of crusades, and brave to the point of recklessness.[25]

Victorious at sea, France and Castile were unable to resist the spell cast on the continental powers by the idea of an attack on England. In June, 1377, thirteen Portuguese and Castilian galleys[26] commanded by Tovar joined Jean de Vienne's fleet in Harfleur.[27] For a month the terrible allied attacks on the English coast continued relentlessly: Rye, Rottingdean, Lewes, Folkestone, Portsmouth, Dartmouth, and Plymouth felt the passage of the bold seamen. Edward III died, and a world died with him; the duke of Lancaster became regent for the young Richard II. The English forces seemed doomed to defeat: one squadron, formed with the help of Genoa and commanded by the earl of Buckingham, disbanded without result.[28] Relations between Castile and France were never so firm and solid as in those years.

But the power of the Franco-Castilians was a Colossus with feet of clay. On July 16, 1378, war with Navarre broke out, and in spite of the naval victory won by the Castilians over Sir Peter Courtenay[29] the English took Cherbourg,[30] thus adding this fine base in Normandy to those they already held in France.[31] It was a symptom. From Bordeaux the duke of Lancaster tried to lead his warrior bands to Castile—Thomas Trivet's ride through Soria during the winter of 1378–79—in search of friends. A few days before his death, in May, 1379, Henry II arranged peace terms with Navarre. Then the Portuguese seamen who were already in Santander to help Castile in the new theater of operations in Brittany returned home.[32] Circumstances were not decisively altered by the fact that Jean de Montfort, duke of Brittany, suffered a defeat on August 19, 1379,[33] nor that Spanish sailors captured the castle of La Roche-Guyon on the banks of the Loire,[34] nor even that in July, 1380, the joint fleet concentrated in Harfleur began the second of its terrible attacks on England, taking Winchelsea with blood and fire[35] and then sailing up the Thames to burn Gravesend, a district near London "where enemy galleys had never entered."[36] The death of Charles V (September 16, 1380) put a definitive end to a period of triumphs.

UNION WITH PORTUGAL

The Trastámara kings and their French allies based their strategy on an erroneous supposition. To conquer Ferdinand I was not to conquer Portugal. The monarch, that "unhappy creature," as Oliveira Martins calls him,[37] inspired very little confidence and respect in his subjects. But a profound transformation was taking place in Portugal during the second half of the fourteenth century, and from it a national conscience was to emerge in the long run; the sailors of Oporto and the merchants of Lisbon were to contribute to this more than any other group, for they were seeking outlets for their wool and wines, just as the Castilians were. The difference was that Castile had no single port, not even Seville, which could exercise an influence as considerable as Lisbon's in the political life of the kingdom.

On July 15, 1380, Portugal and England signed a new alliance;[38] the fact that their interests coincided was a strong motive for union in both countries. There were two consequences of this agreement: the disappearance of Castilian fleets in the English Channel, and renewal of the war between Portugal and Castile. Fernán Sánchez de Tovar won his last victory in the roadstead of Saltés on June 17, 1381.[39] It seemed to be the end; John I of Castile and Charles VI of France were caught up in the euphoria of victory and imposed humiliating peace terms on the Portuguese negotiators. Then Ferdinand—or rather, Leonor Téllez—made the great mistake and arranged a complex marriage treaty whose purpose was not to annex Portugal to Castile, as has been claimed, but to place the Castilian monarch on his throne, thus establishing, for the future, branches of the Trastámara dynasty on both sides of the frontier.[40]

REPERCUSSIONS OF THE CASTILIAN DEFEAT

The marriage of John I of Castile to the crown princess of Portugal, Beatriz, took place on May 17, 1383.[41] Immediately after the nuptial festivities, the chronicler Pero López de Ayala took the long road to Flanders in order to engage in some conversations on a general truce which were going on in Leulingham, between Calais and Boulogne.[42] The resulting Atlantic peace, essentially planned to be of long duration, was interpreted by Castile and France as the acknowledgment of their supremacy in that ocean. From the Straits to Bruges, the control of Castilian ships seemed indisputable.[43] The route between l'Écluse and Bilbao was at its peak of activity.[44]

It is not strange, then, that the anti-Castilian movement, on which the former master of Avis built his reputation, originated in Lisbon and was immediately supported by Oporto. Only the very energetic bourgeoisie of these cities could give impetus to a movement of a prenational character.[45] The maintenance of Castilian supremacy would have been fatal for them. Therefore we must consider as a foreshadowing of great future events the breaking of the blockade of Lisbon (June 17, 1384) by a fleet from Oporto commanded by Ruy Pereira; his opponent was Perafán de Ribera.[46] During the siege of Lisbon, Fernán Sánchez de Tovar died ashore as a result of plague. England collaborated actively in the task of building a Portuguese navy.[47]

In the spring of 1385 Castilian ships from Seville, Cádiz, and Sanlúcar dropped anchor for the last time in the mouth of the

Tagus.[48] It was too late. On August 15 of that year Nuño Alvares Pereira won his magnificent victory at Aljubarrota. It was there, on land, that Castilian control of the Atlantic was broken. It was also the beginning of the road that was to lead the Portuguese to Calicut. The treaty of Windsor (May 6, 1386),[49] between Portugal and England, was a direct reply to the treaty of Toledo in 1368.[50]

WAR WITH ENGLAND AGAIN

The duke of Lancaster's hour had struck. Castile was on the defensive, and a strong attack might pull the whole system to pieces. On July 25, 1386, in command of a powerful fleet of ninety ships,[51] he disembarked at La Coruña after having captured six unmanned galleys.[52] His expedition, undertaken with so many resources, was to end in failure, but the ease with which he had carried out the disembarkation and the capture of the ships was a sign of Castilian weakness. This weakness extended to the sea routes to Flanders: on March 24, 1387, the earl of Arundel surprised a combined French, Flemish, and Castilian fleet carrying great quantities of wine, and captured it.[53] There were new battles in La Rochelle,[54] which apparently played an important role in Castile's military relations with France.[55]

Since hostilities between England and France had been renewed, France continued to depend on naval help from Castile. A special agreement signed in Arnedo (February 13, 1388) provided for the naval armament necessary for a new attack on England.[56] Did Charles VI seriously consider an invasion of the British Isles?[57] It does not seem likely. The weariness of the combatants was general, and in Castile, now that the dynastic controversy had been settled, there was no interest in anything but the maintenance of her external mercantile policy. In Bayonne, on June 22, 1388, an agreement was made with the duke of Lancaster. The following year, in the previously mentioned town of Leulingham, general truces were arranged[58] in which Portugal joined[59] by the terms of the treaty of Monção (November 29, 1389). In these truces Castile saw the total freedom of her merchants recognized. When the truces were confirmed in 1393,[60] trade rights were to occupy an important place.

Thanks to the treaty of Bayonne and the consequent marriage of the future Henry III to Catherine of Lancaster, Castile moved almost imperceptibly toward a rapprochement with England. The Franco-Castilian alliance became less close, and for the same reason. For twenty years France and Castile had fought shoulder to shoulder against the common enemy; but this enemy had ceased to be dangerous for Henry, who also discovered that the truces, as they continued, gave him a freedom of trade with Flanders which was very necessary to his economic policy. Now there was no fighting to secure or conquer the sea routes; his policy, decidedly mercantilist—if it is permissible, as Pirenne proposes, to use this word—tried to win privileges rather than victories. There was the coincidental fact that France also regularly maintained her truces with England.[61] Between 1395 and 1399 it seemed that the Hundred Years' War was going to come to an end. Flanders, in the hands of a French duke, caught in an economic crisis in which its cloth industry was being transformed,[62] found friendship with Castile to its advantage.

There was still the question of honor in arms, lost in Portugal. The last war against Portugal, begun in May, 1396, was to give Castilian seamen the chance to mend it; in May, 1397, shortly after a Portuguese attack on Cádiz,[63] Admiral Diego Hurtado de Mendoza was able to intercept and destroy an auxiliary fleet coming from Genoa.[64] When on August 15, 1402, new truces were signed between the two Iberian monarchs,[65] primary attention was given to trade. From then on Portuguese and Castilians were to enjoy joint privileges of citizenship.

During these last years of the fourteenth century Castile slowly turned her attention to the Mediterranean. This was the result of

two converging forces: the attraction of Italy in the political interplay of the Great Schism and the geographical position of the
Iberian Peninsula. In the kingdom of Naples, as a consequence of
the schism in the Church, civil war broke out again between the
two branches of the Angevin dynasty. Joanna I was assassinated by
Charles of Durazzo in 1382. When Louis of Anjou took up the
war in the same year, in defense of Clement VII as well as his own
rights to the throne, he took a Castilian squadron into his service,[66]
under the command of Fernán Ruiz Cabeza de Vaca.[67] The
Angevin expedition was a failure, but it does not seem that the
Andalusian ships neglected to visit the coasts of Italy because of
this.[68]

During the second half of the fourteenth century, when the
prodigious advance of the Turks occurred in the Balkans and
there was a simultaneous intensification of the influence exercised
by Fez over Granada, the Castilian monarchs' concern for their
southern boundary increased. The inhabitants of Granada had
given dangerous signs of activity in the civil war. Thus there was
a return to the policy of the Straits, for motives of security as well
as for economic reasons.[69] We have little information about the
matter. One Chronicle tells us of the capture of Tetuán in 1400.[70]

We find one good example of Castilian activity in the Mediterranean, from a military point of view, in the raids of Pero Niño,
count of Buelna,[71] along the coasts of southern France, Sardinia,
Corsica, and Tunis in 1404.[72] It is important to establish that,
according to Gutierre Díez de Games' account, Cartagena appears
as a naval base even at this time. Perhaps even more instructive
than the count of Buelna's campaign is the reconstruction of the
logbook of a galley commanded by Juan Alfonso de Montemolín,
for it gives us the scope of Mediterranean navigation. It weighed
anchor in Seville on April 16, 1405, carrying an ambassador whom
the king of Castile was sending to Benedict XIII: Alfonso Egea,
archbishop of Seville.[73] It stopped in Cádiz for a few days, crossed
the Straits, put in at Cartagena, and with a constant light breeze
and by dint of rowing, arrived in Valencia on May 6. It weathered
a storm, reached Tarragona on the twelfth, and anchored in

Barcelona on the fourteenth of the month.[74] It reached Marseilles after a two-day voyage. On June 2 it dropped anchor in Genoa, where the pope's court was located. Here the ambassador disembarked.[75] We do not know how long it stayed in Genoa; it set sail from there in a southerly direction, put in at Sicily, and went as far as the Aegean to get news of the ambassadors whom the king, Henry III, had sent to Tamerlane. In Sicily it was joined by two Castilian galleys commanded by Juan Ruiz de Hoyos and Juan Castrillo. It was the month of September when these three attacked and captured two of Ladislas of Naples' galleys, which were trying to go to the aid of Pisa.[76] Later, Juan Alfonso de Montemolín appeared in Savona, the residence of the pope; his galley left there on October 13, and on the twenty-fifth of that month he passed through Barcelona on his way back to his base.[77]

Wool and hides were exported from Cartagena to the Italian cities.[78] Genoese and Venetian ships, which had made the voyage to Flanders ever since the beginning of the fourteenth century, put in there and at Seville; they brought gold and silk fabrics which were highly prized,[79] the so-called *paños bervíes*, precious metals, and all sorts of luxury goods.[80] After 1405 the presence of Italian ships in Castile became more frequent because of the advance of the Mongols and the occupation of the Levant by the Turks.[81]

Sometimes Cartagena became what Nature apparently intended it to be, a military port.[82] Operating out of Cartagena, a vessel commanded by Pedro Sánchez de Laredo captured a Moslem ship in 1411.[83] This happened at a time when the war with Granada was under way and the Straits were again a military problem. Alfonso Enríquez confirmed once again the control which the Christians exercised over them after the battle of Salado, when he defeated a Moslem squadron from Africa.[84]

Castile's attention turned in all directions; Henry III's ambassadors went off to the East to Tamerlane, and to the West went the first conquerors of the Canaries. These islands had been known for some time, but only in 1402 was an effort made by Béthencourt to capture them, with Castilian help. In the future Castile was to use him as its title to possession of the islands. Very soon Portuguese sailors were to take the place of the Castilians there, thus initiating one of the most glorious exploits of all time. In 1415 John I's sons took Ceuta; Galician and Vizcayan vessels participated in this operation, as in the later attacks on Arzila and Tangier.[85] In subsequent years, while Castile turned her attention to the north, where she encountered the powerful rivalry of the Hanseatic League, the Portuguese launched themselves into exploration of the western coasts of Africa. This was the great venture of Henry the Navigator, who set his face toward mystery, riches, and the future. From Sagres the arrow points went out which one after another discovered Madeira, Bojador, and Cabo Verde.[86] On the way lay the Canaries, and Don Fernando de Castro planted the flag of Portugal there in 1424.

The Portuguese sovereign asked the pope for a bull of concession. It was an embarrassing situation for Eugenius IV,[87] who was facing a rebellion in his council and was anxious to have any support the various monarchs might give him. In 1436 Alfonso de Santa María made a famous speech before the Council of Basel, in defense of the rights of his king, John II of Castile, to possession of the Canaries.[88] He used very similar arguments in 1438, when he protested the conquest of Africa.[89] In the end the question was solved very easily. The Portuguese monarch—and the pope's petition decreed the same—ordered his men not to put in at the Canaries. And at that time Castile needed a good alliance with Portugal.

POLICY OF PEACE IN THE ATLANTIC

Castilian policies were undergoing a great change in the Bay of Biscay. Henry III, keenly interested in the development of trade, had adopted the protectionist posture common to all princes; on January 27, 1398, he banned shipment of Castilian products in foreign ships,[90] and later backed up this order with one by which the freight rates on Castilian ships were to be fixed by two seamen and two merchants.[91] This mercantilism was to be jealously maintained in the future. The Castilian monarchs were concerned solely with keeping the routes to Flanders open, and this was accomplished with complete normality for more than ten years, beginning in 1393.[92] The Lancastrian revolution never changed the state of truce, nor could the truces do away with mutual acts of piracy.[93]

When the truce was concluded between England and France, the latter country requested naval help from Castile,[94] and in the spring of 1405 Henry III sent a fleet of forty ships commanded by Martín Ruiz de Avendaño, with specific instructions to patrol French waters.[95] Was not this action also of direct interest to Castilian merchants in Flanders? The fact that the notoriously untruthful Pero Niño was in the fleet, and that his chronicler was the no less untrustworthy Gutierre Díez de Games, may have led to error in the judgment of the campaign. The bloody raid of the count of Buelna and Charles de Savoisy was simply another act of piracy, among the many the Atlantic had witnessed.[96] Even "El Victorial" reproached Avendaño for his lack of aggressiveness.

The change in the Castilian attitude became apparent very soon. When the Franco-Castilian alliance was confirmed in 1408, any specific expression of naval support was eliminated,[97] and was replaced by a general permission to the Castilians, individually, to enlist under the banners of France.[98] Castile gained freedom of action when she was permitted to arrange truces for a year without consulting her ally. After that date the political norm to be followed was established: to maintain de facto peace with England by negotiating annual truces, and to form ever closer ties with Flanders.

Thus the immediate agreement, signed in Fuenterrabía on January 4, 1410,[99] was to have the effect of a total revision of Anglo-Castilian relations. A mixed tribunal of eight members was to undertake to resolve all questions of maritime law left pending since the death of John I of Castile.[100] It is easy to confirm the renewals of the truce in 1411, 1412, 1413, 1414, 1415, and 1416. When Henry V disembarked in France in 1415, shortly before the battle of Agincourt, a Vizcayan ship, the *Santa María*, was part of his fleet.[101] Castile calmly watched the defeat of her ally; at most a few ships, leased on the coasts of Spain, took part in isolated operations.[102] By early in 1417 Henry V felt himself powerful enough to break the alliance between France and Castile.[103]

CASTILE, THE HANSEATIC LEAGUE, AND THE ENGLISH WAR

The presence of the Castilians in Flanders, closely connected with the slow withdrawal of Flemish industry from English wool imports—for England now had her own cloth industry—became intensified during the first half of the fifteenth century. A trade agreement in 1428 guaranteed the safety of Castilian merchants in Flanders.[104] In the course of time, when Philip the Good banned wool imports from England, the new industry in his duchy would depend solely on shipments made from Spain. In 1456, when he was forced to choose, Philip cast his lot with Castile and incurred thereby the enmity of the powerful German League.[105]

It was natural that the protectionist measures adopted by the Spanish monarchs, and the harsh competition of Basque seamen in the Low Countries, should arouse the anger of the Hanseatic League. It became more closely allied with England. When Catherine of Lancaster died on June 3, 1418, Anglo-Castilian relations went sour again. Now it was not a question of defending the hypothetical rights of a dauphin, but of eliminating the interplay of commercial competition. Castile and the Armagnacs signed an agreement on June 28, 1419, and Castile prepared to make a great effort: 40 ships, 4,000 seamen, 200 men-at-arms, 30 captains, and 9 knights[106] were to be concentrated in Belle Île, off the southern coast of Brittany; the secret of the negotiations was revealed when a vessel from Bayonne captured a certain priest who was carrying a copy of the treaty.[107] Notwithstanding, on December 30, 1419, the English and the Hanseatic League suffered a total defeat near La Rochelle. The League lost contact with the Bay of Biscay.

As late as the summer of 1420 Juan Enríquez took a fleet out of Santander and sailed freely from Scotland to Poitou.[108] But it was the end. In that year Castile began the long series of coups d'état which were to make her fifteenth century a state of perpetual civil war. The struggle against the Hanseatic League, which was to last until 1443,[109] was left to the initiative of seamen and degenerated into a series of mutual acts of piracy. Once the Hanseatic League was eliminated, Castile had the markets of Flanders and Brittany for herself.[110] This situation was maintained until the end of the century. The alliances with France were confirmed with perfect regularity, and the truces with England renewed with the same regularity. Merchants were frequently issued safe-conducts so that they could enter and leave that country on business. The wool traders sailed to Flanders with their bulky ships stuffed to bursting, and sometimes returned bringing Flemish paintings of that new style which we call "Primitive" today. It was a wool trader from Carrión de los Condes, living in La Rochelle, who financed the journey of the admiral of France when he went to the royal interviews in Fuenterrabía in 1463.[111]

NOTES

1. "In the second epoch of the Hundred Years' War, the fleets of Charles V and Don Henry make common cause. England has lost the mastery of the seas: she cannot even hold the Channel." Sydney Armitage-Smith, *John of Gaunt, King of Castile and Leon, Duke of Aquitaine and Lancaster* (Westminster, 1904), p. 70.

2. See my *Intervención en Castilla en la guerra de los Cien Años* (Valladolid, 1950), pp. 38–40.

3. A peace agreement signed by England with the Brotherhood of the Castilian navy (August 1, 1351), which remained in force up to the civil war, provided for free circulation and fishing rights for Spanish ships in English waters. Published by Dumont, *Corps diplomatique universel du droit des gens*, Vol. I, Part II, p. 265.

4. On March 10, 1371, important privileges were granted to Spanish merchants in France. Published by Léopold Delisle, *Mandements et actes divers de Charles V* (1364–1380), Collection des documents inédits de la France, 35 (Paris, 1874), 449.

5. For France, the treaty of Toledo of 1368, establishing a close alliance with Castile, had only one aspect: the naval support she was to receive from her neighbor. To work out the details of this, she sent an embassy on July 19, 1369, among whose members was the "expert" Francés de Perellós, an

Aragonese in the service of France. Delachenal, *Histoire de Charles V*, III (Paris, 1926), 464–66.

6. Fernão Lopes, *Crónica de D. Fernando*, I (Barcellos, 1933), 82–83. [The *rías* of Galicia are long inlets.]

7. *Ibid.*, pp. 104–7.

8. C. Fernández Duro, in *La Marina de Castilla*, Madrid, 1891, p. 126, even says that the greater part of the fleet in the service of Portugal was from Guetaria and other towns in Guipúzcoa. We possess a document, published by T. Rymer, *Foedera, conventiones, etc.*, 2d ed., VII (London, 1728), 3–4, of February 20, 1373, which mentions one Pedro de Doyquina, master of the ship *Marye Sterlyng* of Villa Guetary, a vassal of the Duke of Lancaster, who was on his way from Portugal to Flanders with a cargo of wine. Guétary is the name of a small port south of Bayonne—at the time in English hands—but we see no reason to identify it with the Spanish Guetaria.

9. In 1370 there were only thirteen Portuguese galleys. Henry II managed to infiltrate through them seven of his own galleys, commanded by the Genoese Ambrosio Bocanegra; they recruited additional ships on the northern coasts and, skirting the coast of Portugal, attacked the Portuguese from behind. There was virtually no battle, for the Portuguese were exhausted by the blockade; they launched fire-arrows and were able to make their escape. Pero López de Ayala, *Crónica de Enrique II, BAE*, LXVIII, 6–7, and F. Lopes, *op. cit.*, I, 109–13, are in essential agreement about this occurrence.

10. Armitage-Smith, *op. cit.*, p. 93.

11. G. Daumet, *Étude sur l'alliance de la France et de la Castille au XIV et au XV siècles* (Paris, 1898), p. 35.

12. The economic importance of La Rochelle, chief port for the exportation of Bordeaux wines—they were called "wines of La Rochelle"—has been described by H. Pirenne, *Histoire économique de l'Occident médiéval* (Bruges, 1951), p. 298.

13. The sources—Ayala, *op. cit.*, p. 12, [T. Walsingham, . . . *Historia Anglicana*, ed. H. T. Riley (London, 1862), I, 314], Froissart, *Chroniques*, IX, ed. Kervyn de Lettenhove, 122–44—are in agreement on the fundamental points of the allied victory. A letter sent to Murcia by Henry II (Benavente, Sept. 27, 1372), published by Cascales in *Discursos históricos de la ciudad de Murcia*, fol. 132, tells us that the Castilian king's share of the booty was two-thirds.

14. Lopes, *op. cit.*, I, 194–95.

15. The agreements, drawn up March 19, 1373 (ANP K-1338, fol. 51), include, among other things, the alliance of Portugal to France and Castile against the English and that Castile would give help in the form of six galleys for three years, also promising not to receive the English in her territories or to give them aid.

16. Ayala, *op. cit.*, pp. 24–25.

17. After the Black Prince's death, Edward III had taken possession of the Duchy of Aquitaine (October 5, 1372), but he did not retain it (Jules

Balasque, *Études historiques sur la ville de Bayonne*, III (Bayonne, 1875, 359). The document of concession has been published by Rymer, *op. cit.*, VII, 13–14.

18. Rymer, *op. cit.*, VII, 15–19.
19. Balasque, *op. cit.*, III, 361–62.
20. Ayala, *op. cit.*, p. 23.
21. The siege—the only one undergone by the city in spite of Froissart's mistaken information—had been prepared for a long time. A document in the *Livre des Etablisements*, in the Municipal Archive of Bayonne, I, 310–311, tells how in 1373 military equipment was distributed to the inhabitants for the defense of the city. The episode has been brilliantly studied by René Cuzacq, in *Bayonne au Moyen Âge: Le Siège de 1374* (Mont-de-Marsan, 1952), pp. 6–10.
22. The text, published by Dumont, *op. cit.*, II, 1, 104, and Rymer, *op. cit.*, VIII, 68–78, was confirmed by two Castilians, Pedro Fernández de Velasco and Alfonso Barrasa. Daumet, *op. cit.*, pp. 38–40.
23. Ch. de la Roncière, *Histoire de la marine française*, II (Paris, 1914), 31.
24. F. Pérez Embid, *El almirantazgo de Castilla hasta las capitulaciones de Santa Fe* (Seville, 1944), pp. 134–35. J. Puyol, "El presunto cronista Fernán Sánchez de Valladolid," *BAH*, LXXVII (1920), 507 *et seq.*
25. Terrier de Loray, *Jean de Vienne, amiral de France (1341–1396)* (Paris, 1877), pp. 9–43.
26. A later agreement, on February 4, 1380, published by Terrier de Loray, *op. cit.*, Appendix LIII, gives us some idea of the crew of these galleys; each carried ten men-at-arms, thirty crossbowmen, a hundred and eighty seamen, three boatswains, and six "noguiers." [I.e., "mates" or perhaps "helmsmen," from the French *nocher*. Cf. E. Littré, *Dictionnaire de la Langue Française* (Paris, 1869), Vol. II, *s.v. nocher*. Mr. C. A. Robson kindly drew my attention to this entry.]
27. Delachenal, *op. cit.*, V, 24–25, has established the number of vessels and the presence of the Portuguese. See Charles V's order to pay 100 francs to John, a Scottish merchant, for the inspection of the Castilian fleet anchored in Harfleur (*Mandements . . . etc.*, *loc. cit.*, p. 722. [Cf. J. Campbell, "England, Scotland and the Hundred Years' War," in *Europe in the Late Middle Ages*, ed. Hale, Highfield, and Smalley (London, 1965), p. 208 and n. 3.]
28. Roncière, *op. cit.*, II, 57. A part of this squadron, commanded by Thomas Percy, captured twenty-two Castilian and Flemish boats laden with wine.
29. *Ibid.*, pp. 60–62.
30. This possession of Cherbourg, announced in principle for three years, was extended in 1381 (Rymer, *op. cit.*, VII, 315).
31. Delachenal, *op. cit.*, V, 231.
32. Ayala, *op. cit.*, pp. 65–66.
33. Roncière, *op. cit.*, II, 63–64.
34. Froissart, *op. cit.*, IX, 537.
35. Walsingham [*Historia Anglicana*, I, 438–39].
36. Ayala, *op. cit.*, p. 67.
37. J. P. Oliveira Martins, *História de Portugal*, I (Lisbon, 1942), 140.

38. Rymer, *op. cit.*, VII, 262–64.
39. As late as 1382 he commanded the Castilian fleet which cooperated in the battle of Roosebeke (Roncière, *op. cit.*, II, 73–75). For a description of the battle of Saltés, see Lopes, *op. cit.*, II, 90–94.
40. The virtual impossibility of a union between Portugal and Castile through the marriage of John I is what we have attempted to demonstrate in our article "Capitulaciones matrimoniales entre Portugal y Castilla," *Hispania*, no. XXXIII.
41. The notarial report of all the ceremonies is in the AGS, *Libros de copias de Patronato Real*, Book XXVI, fols. 183–204.
42. Castilian ratification, signed in Santarem on January 22, 1384, published by Rymer, *op. cit.*, VII, 439–41.
43. Shortly before this the Castilian ships had forced the surrender of a garrison on an island near La Rochelle. Daumet, *op. cit.*, p. 47.
44. Fernández Duro, *op. cit.*, pp. 443–44, has published two letters of contract, dated July 22, 1385, of two ships which made the run to l'Écluse, the great port of Bruges, the *San Bartolomé* out of Plencia and the *Santa María* out of Castro Urdiales. They carried wheat and hardtack.
45. "The revolution of 1383, when Don João, master of Avis, was on the Portuguese throne, gave rise to the establishment of greater political influence by the middle class; a number of merchants were appointed at that time to public offices of considerable importance, and the thorough reform of the royal council in 1385 introduced both jurists and burgesses into it, giving them a majority, with a noticeable reduction in the number of ecclesiastics and nobles." Damião Peres, *História dos descobrimentos portugueses* (Oporto, 1943), p. 30.
46. Fernández Duro, *op. cit.*, pp. 148–51; Ayala, *op. cit.*, p. 90.
47. An order by Richard II from Westminster, January 23, 1385, turns over to the Master of Avis all Portuguese ships which anchor in English ports. Rymer, *op. cit.*, VII, 455.
48. The importance of naval operations for the Castilian court is clearly shown in the letters of Don Pedro Tenorio, Archbishop of Toledo, dated March 21 and 22 and April 22. Biblioteca Nacional, Ms. 13103, fols. 97–99 and 100–102.
49. There is a copy of this agreement in Simancas, Patronato Real, Leg. 52, fol. 5. It has been published by Rymer, *op. cit.*, VII, 515–21.
50. In a protocol of May 9, 1386, Portugal promised to send ten galleys to England for a period of six months. Rymer, *op. cit.*, VII, 521–22.
51. See Richard II's order of May 15, 1386, published in Rymer's 3d edition, Vol. III, Part III, p. 195.
52. Duro, *op. cit.*, pp. 152–53.
53. Walsingham [*Historia Anglicana*, II, 154–55].
54. A Portuguese admiral, Juan Furtado, appeared in those waters in 1387. Roncière, *op. cit.*, II, 89. Jacques de Montmor was dispatched to give battle to him.
55. A report from Jacques de Montmor from La Rochelle on March 8, 1387, notes the presence of six auxiliary Castilian galleys (Fernández Duro,

"Una escuadra de galeras de Castilla en el siglo XIV," *BAH*, xii (1888), 243). In the same port, on June 10 of that year, the master of the ship *Santiago* of Bilbao, Juan de Sarria, was paid 730 *livres tournois* for the hire of his ship to carry troops and munitions. ANP, K-53, fol. 69.

56. The document showing French confirmation is in the AGS, K-1638, fol. 20.

57. Early in 1385 two French knights had visited John I in Seville to request naval aid for the invasion of England (Daumet, *op. cit.*, p. 47; Ayala, *op. cit.*, p. 93). They were given a negative reply. On September 2, 1388, Morelet de Montmor received authorization for new naval armaments (ANP (1603), fol. 67), which were cut down to the usual six galleys (Roncière, *op. cit.*, ii, 97–98). However, as late as March 29, 1388, the inhabitants of Montreal had been excused from payment of a tax for the expedition (ANP, K-53, fol. 57).

58. The inclusion of Castile in these truces bears the date of June 18, 1389. Rymer, *op. cit.*, vii, 622–30. John I confirmed them in Segovia on September 3, 1389. *Ibid.*, p. 644.

59. The agreement has been published by Alfredo Pimenta, *Idade-Média: Problemas & Soluçoens* (Lisbon, 1946), pp. 320–28.

60. Truces with Portugal, May 15, 1393, AGS, Patronato Real, Leg. 49, fol. 1.

61. Notice of the truces of March 13, 1395, in *Chronique du religieux de Saint-Denis*, ed. Bellaguet. Documents Inédits Français, ii (Paris, 1840), 367. We need not give excessive importance to the texts of the truces; they were regulative rules for trade which could not prevent acts of piracy. In this same year, 1395, Castilian freebooters attacked a ship from Hull, the *Christophe*. F. Michel, *Histoire de la navigation à Bordeaux, principalement sous l'administration anglaise* (Bordeaux, 1867–70).

62. H. Pirenne, "Une crise industrielle au XVI siècle: la draperie urbaine and la nouvelle draperie en Flandre," in *Histoire économique de l'Occident médiéval* (Bruges, 1951), pp. 621–43.

63. Duro, *op. cit.*, pp. 155–56.

64. Gil González Dávila, *Historia de la vida y hechos del rey don Henrique III de Castilla* (Madrid, 1638), pp. 129–30. About 400 crewmen were thrown into the sea by the victors (Ayala, *op. cit.*, p. 246); chivalry was not observed in the Atlantic. Genoa protested the attack (Martín Ruiz de Medrano's letter to Henry III, July 3, 1397. AGS, Estado, Castilla, Leg. 1-1⁰, fol. 154).

65. The original of the truces of August 15, 1402, is in AGS, Patronato Real, Leg. 49, fol. 1.

66. This squadron had been contracted for by the Pope, by means of an agreement which his legate, the Patriarch of Alexandria, had signed with John I of Castile, and confirmed by Clement VII on March 6, 1383. Vatican Archives, Inst. Misc. 3135.

67. We know this through the accounts of Don Pedro Tenorio, Archbishop of Toledo. (Burgos, May 20, 1386, Biblioteca Nacional, Ms. 13018, fols. 93–116.)

68. A brief of Benedict XIII to Fulco Pereira, collector of the *Cámara* in

Seville, ordering the payment of 600 gold francs for the lease of a ship as long as it stayed in Italy, shows us the presence of Castilian ships in the [Italian] Peninsula. Biblioteca Nacional, Ms. 13103, fol. 192.

69. From Avignon, on January 28, 1388, Clement VII granted authorization to John I to found a military order in Tarifa under the advocacy of St. Bartholomew, to fight against the Beni-Merins. Vatican Archives, Reg. Vat. 299, fol. 49 verso.

70. González Dávila, *op. cit.*, p. 148.

71. In addition to "El Victorial," of Gutierre Díez de Gámes, ed. J. M. Carriazo (Madrid, 1940), pp. 99 *et seq.*, see González Palencia, "Don Pero Niño y el condado de Buelna," *Homenaje a Artigas*, II, 105–46.

72. It is possible that Pero Niño's campaign was connected with the news sent from Murcia by Pedro Monsalve on June 14 of that year, in a letter to Henry III (AGS Estado, Castilla, Leg. 1-1°, fol. 59), that Agde had been attacked by Saracen pirates and that fifteen corsair vessels were infesting the Mediterranean.

73. Cádiz, April 26, 1405. Archbishop of Seville to Henry III. AGS, Estado, Castilla, Leg. 1-1°, fol. 55.

74. Barcelona, May 20, 1405. Archbishop of Seville to Henry III. AGS, Estado, Castilla, Leg. 1-1°, fol. 54.

75. Genoa, June 2, 1406. Archbishop of Seville to Henry III. AGS, Estado, Castilla, Leg. 1-1°, fol. 53.

76. Genoa, October 10, 1405. Pedro González de Medina to Henry III. AGS, Estado, Castilla, Leg. 1-1°, fol. 16.

77. Barcelona, November 5, 1405. Guillem de Fenollet to Henry III. AGS, Estado, Castilla, Leg. 1-1°, fol. 139.

78. Cartagena, May 21, 1406? Pedro de Monsalve to the king. AGS, Estado, Castilla, Leg. 1-1°, fol. 64. This letter gives information about the amounts of wool and hides sent to Genoa and Venice. In another letter from Monsalve to the king, dated June 1 (AGS, Estado, Castilla, Leg. 1-1°, fol. 60), Monsalve tells of the difficulties of a merchant captain, Luis López de Sevilla, in selling wool in Majorca owing to the threats of Moslem pirates.

79. Cartagena, March 1, 1406? Pedro de Monsalve to the king. AGS, Estado, Castilla, Leg. 1-1°, fol. 61.

80. Cartagena, June 8, 1406? Pedro de Monsalve to the king. AGS, Estado, Castilla, Leg. 1-1°, fol. 63. [*Paño berví* was an ancient cloth with warp and woof, but of uncombed wool.]

81. A substantial relationship between the merchants and the royal commissioners is shown in the letter from Bernal González Vieja to Henry III, written in Seville on June 26, 1406. AGS, Estado, Castilla, Leg. 1-1°, fol. 153.

82. Cartagena, July 9, 1406? Juan Ruiz de Hoyos to the king. AGS, Estado, Castilla, Leg. 1-1°, fol. 65. It undoubtedly refers to the war with Granada which began in that year. Six galleys from the kingdom of Granada had tried to join a fleet from Bougie.

83. June 3, 1411. Pedro Sánchez de Laredo to the king. AGS, Estado, Castilla,

Leg. 1–1°, fol. 163. The monarch, writing from Buitrago on November 15, ordered it to be sequestrated. (Archivo Municipal de Murcia. Registry of royal letters from 1411 to 1429, fol. 1 recto.)

84. Fernández Duro, *op. cit.*, pp. 179–80.

85. Richard Konetzke, *Das Spanische Weltreich* (Munich, 1943), p. 22.

[86. For Sagres, however, see now *Prince Henry the Navigator and Portuguese maritime enterprise* (Catalogue of an exhibition at the British Museum [Sept.–Oct., 1960]), p. 6; P. E. Russell, *Prince Henry the Navigator* [Canning House Lecture, May 4, 1960], Diamante XI [1960], p. 7.]

87. On December 28, 1434, he had ordered the payment of 2,000 gold florins from the *Cámara* of Castile for the evangelization of the Canaries. Vatican Archives. Reg. Vat., 367, fols. 10 recto–11 verso.

88. The text we possess is in the AGS, Estado, Francia, K-1711, 131 recto–146 verso. There is another copy in the Biblioteca Nacional, Ms. 11341.

89. Speech of May 9, 1438, in AGS, Estado, Francia, K-1711, fols. 416 recto–416 verso.

90. *Colección de documentos publicados por el Ministerio de Marina*, p. 171.

91. *Memorias de la Real Academia de la Historia*, v, 144.

92. An order from Henry IV of England to the Earl of Devon, July 6, 1403, ensured freedom of trade to the Castilians (Rymer, *op. cit.*, VIII, 312). The truces were extended until June 24, 1404, according to a letter from the same monarch, written January 28 (Rymer, *op. cit.*, VIII, 303). On February 27 of that year Henry agreed to be included in the truces with Portugal (Rymer, *op. cit.*, VIII, 351–52).

93. In 1404 the French and Castilians organized a fleet in Harfleur under a Scottish flag, to surprise the Earl of Somerset, who was returning from a privateering expedition. The attackers were defeated. (Roncière, *op. cit.*, II, 175.)

94. *Chronique du religieux de Saint-Denis*, *loc. cit.*, pp. 159–61.

95. Roncière, *op. cit.*, II, 185. An undated letter from Duke Louis de Bourbon to Henry III refers to this fleet. AGS, Estado, Francia, K-1482, fol. 22.

96. Roncière, *op. cit.*, II, 186; *Chronique du religieux de Saint-Denis*, *loc. cit.*, III (Paris, 1841), 317–23.

97. The original is in the ANP (1604), no. 76, and has been published by Rymer, *op. cit.*, VIII, 561–67; Dumont, *op. cit.*, II, 321; and Daumet, *op. cit.*, pp. 210–20.

98. It was at this point that a famous captain, Rodrigo de Villandrando, count of Ribadeo, went over into the service of France. Daumet, *op. cit.*, p. 60, n. 1.

99. The negotiations of Fuenterrabía took place during a period of total peace. There is a document dated Leicester, May 9, 1408, in which Henry IV gives permission to two Spanish merchants, Álvaro Carrillo and Alfonso Rodríguez, to sail in English waters. Rymer, *op. cit.*, VIII, 527–28. For the text of the truces, see *ibid.*, pp. 617–20.

100. There were frequent claims at this time. Rymer, *op. cit.*, VIII, 683, 722–23, 772–75.

101. Roncière, *op. cit.*, II, 212–13.

102. In 1416 Constable Armagnac made an unsuccessful attempt to recapture Harfleur with Castilian ships. The attackers retired on the arrival of the Duke of Bedford. Daumet, *op. cit.*, pp. 72–73.

103. This was the mission which brought John of St. John, mayor of Bordeaux, John Stokes, doctor of laws, and John Hull to Castile. Rymer, *op. cit.*, IX, 419–20. We do not know how it turned out, but it is to be supposed that the effort was useless. [Cf. A. B. Emden, *Biographical Register of the University of Oxford to A.D. 1500* (Oxford, 1959), III, 1781.]

104. Konetzke, *op. cit.*, p. 31.

105. Konetzke, *op. cit.*, p. 30.

106. Daumet, *op. cit.*, pp. 74–75.

107. Roncière, *op. cit.*, p. 185.

108. Fernández Duro, *op. cit.*, p. 185.

109. In this year a treaty of peace, with mutual concessions, was signed. Konetzke, *op. cit.*, p. 32.

110. Burgos, a concentration point for wool, played a very important role in relations with Flanders. These were interrupted because tariffs on merchants were raised, but in 1429 John II sent Sancho Ezquerra de Angulo to Burgundy, and peace was completely restored (Luciano Serrano, *Los conversos don Pablo de Santa María y don Alonso de Cartagena* (Madrid, 1942), p. 72). A nine-year agreement was signed with Brittany, in Nantes on May 15, 1430, creating a special judge in La Rochelle to settle questions among merchants (Fernández Duro, *op. cit.*, pp. 189–90). Confirmed in 1435 and 1452, this agreement was the basis for the Catholic Monarchs' alliances with the Dukes of Brittany.

111. St. Jean de Luz, May 3, 1463. Jean, lord of Montauban, to Jean Merichon. Private property of Don Jesús Casas.

FURTHER READING

G. Diaz de Games, *The Chronicle of Don Pero Niño, Count of Buelna*, trans. J. Evans (London, 1928).

G. Daumet, "Étude sur l'alliance de la France et de la Castille au XIVe et au XVe siècles," *BHE* (118) (Paris, 1898).

M. McKisack, *The Fourteenth Century, 1307–1399* (Oxford, 1959), chap. xiv.

Sir N. H. Nicolas, *A History of the Royal Navy*, Vol. II (London, n.d.), chaps. 2–4.

C. de la Roncière, *Histoire de la Marine Française*, Vol. II (1900), chaps. 1–8.

P. E. Russell, *The English Intervention in Spain and Portugal in the time of Edward III and Richard II* (Oxford, 1955).

3 The Kingdom of Castile in the Fifteenth Century

LUIS SUÁREZ FERNÁNDEZ

Professor Suárez Fernández has made a specialty of the relations between the Crown and the nobility. Here he outlines the main features of this crucial problem in the course of a general survey of the Castilian scene at the beginning of the fifteenth century.

POLITICAL REGIONS OF CASTILE

The Castilian-Leonese monarchy, resulting as it did from the successive incorporation of territories around a central nucleus through direct conquest, marriages, or political motives, displayed marked regional diversification at the beginning of the fifteenth century. The long title of its sovereigns at the head of state documents—king of Castile, Leon, Toledo, Galicia, Murcia, Jaén, Córdoba and Seville, lord of Vizcaya and Molina—carried with it a constant reminder of the kingdom's slow gestation, of the personal and dynastic character of the unions, and, in a period still dominated by the system of exception and personal privilege, of legislative complexity. The fusion of all these territories, with a common language though an abundance of dialectal variations, was already in a very advanced state of development. Regional variation included social and economic, but not political, aspects. The government and administration of all the regions combined under the name "kingdom of Castile" were substantially uniform.

The process of reconquest and resettlement of the country was reflected in the existence of four zones, each with a different economic structure. The northern coast, from Fuenterrabía to Bayona in Galicia, and the narrow strip which rises, through short valleys, to the high Cantabro-Asturian mountains, a region which

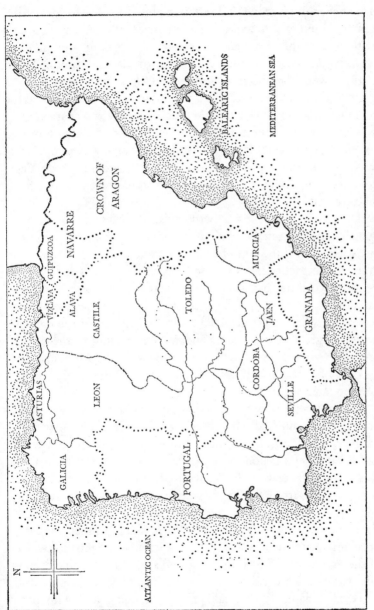

2. The kingdoms of the Crown of Castile in the fifteenth century

had never undergone colonization by Islam, had generally remained under a system of small or medium-sized landholding, with a type of exploitation combining farming and herding scarcely altered since the latter days of classical times. These regions were the ancestral home of *hidalgos*, who often sought their fortune in the center of the kingdom and founded powerful seigniorial families. This middle type of gentry is a characteristic and almost exclusive note; great seigniories could not occur, except in Galicia. As late as the sixteenth century everyone who was not an *hidalgo* was rejected in Vizcaya, and—Lope de Vega tells us—many sought an Asturian descent in order to prove their noble origin.

The second zone, the northern part of the Meseta, was a region which had been resettled under the *presura* system, and preserved its *behetrías* until the end of the fourteenth century.[1] It could not resist the impact of increasing seigniorial absorption, and we will see that two-thirds of the seigniories were formed there. This is the land of bread and wine—the symbol of wealth in the Late Middle Ages—essentially agricultural but crossed by the great *cañadas*[2] where migratory flocks came and went according to the season, from the pastures of Extremadura to those of the Montaña. The wool traffic sustained the great markets of Burgos, Medina del Campo, and Segovia.

The southern Meseta, including the southerly slopes of the central mountain chain, had been added to Castile from the end of the eleventh century to the beginning of the thirteenth, when the great phenomenon of European economic transformation was already under way. It had witnessed the birth, in the regions farthest away from the frontier with Islam, of the great cities: Segovia, Ávila, Plasencia, Toledo, Cáceres, Trujillo, Medellín, Talavera, etc., and, in the regions closest to the frontier, the three great military orders: Calatrava, Alcántara, and Santiago, which of themselves constituted the kingdom's most formidable economic strength. This was herding land which produced for export, not easily adaptable to small property-holding and with little population density. We shall see how in the course of the fifteenth century the cities lost their freedom, absorbed by very powerful seigniorial estates—in particular those of the Mendozas and Stúñigas—which took over their administrative functions without changing the style of life in the least.

The zone most recently incorporated into the kingdom was formed by the Guadalquivir and Júcar valleys. Herding also existed there, but it had given way in importance to olive oil, high-priced wines, hides, and irrigation crops. Strongly influenced by continuing Moslem influences because of its proximity to the frontier of Granada, its Morisco population was truly important. Here we find the principal mercantile city, certainly the most heavily populated one in the kingdom: Seville. The existence of *latifundia* was the logical consequence of the predominance of olive cultivation.

ECONOMIC STRUCTURE AND SOCIAL SYSTEM

Castile's chief economic characteristic in the Late Middle Ages was herding. Two-thirds of the country was given over to pasture land, and wool was certainly the chief product in export trade. Second place among exports was held by honey, obtained in large quantities from the Alcarria, Toledo, Talavera, and Ciudad Real. There was a certain productive relationship between honey and wool. The care of beehives and migratory pasturing of flocks had created in New Castile, some hundred years before, one of the most characteristic institutions in the kingdom: the *Hermandad Vieja* [Old Brotherhood].[3] Three great *cañadas* with many ramifications crossed Castile from north to south[4] to allow transfer of the flocks. Migratory pasturing was general, and stationary flocks very few before the sixteenth century.[5] Since 1273 Castilian herding had possessed a communal organization—whose purpose was, in substance, to guarantee the contracts between landowners and herders—called the Mesta. The Assembly of the Mesta had independent jurisdiction and became a great economic and political power controlled by the nobility. During the fifteenth century the direction of this body—with the title of *entregador* of the Mesta—was in the hands of members of a single family, that of Carrillo de Acuña. They were supporters of Don Álvaro de Luna, with whom they had a distant family relationship: first Gómez Carrillo, then Lope Vázquez de Acuña, and after 1454 Pedro de Acuña, count of Buendía and brother of the famous archbishop of Toledo, Alfonso Carrillo.[6] The three military orders were also great powers in herding, for their chief revenues came from wool. Especially the Order of Santiago, which, under the expert guidance of Don Ferdinand of Antequera and his son the Infante Don Henry, received a modern and efficient organization. By the middle of the fifteenth century the grand mastership of Santiago furnished its holders with exceptionally high revenues; hence the preponderant role played by its successive grand masters —the Infante Don Henry, Álvaro de Luna, Beltrán de la Cueva, the marquis of Villena—in Castilian politics, and the tremendous ambitions unleashed by possession of this office.

Castile was probably the only kingdom in fifteenth-century Europe which was still self-sufficient in foodstuffs.[7] This is a fact of great importance, and in part determines Castile's economic structure. Products derived from herding (wool and hides), from agriculture (olive oil and honey), or from the subsoil (iron) sustained a large foreign trade in raw materials and occasionally in manufactured products. The nobles were direct beneficiaries of this trade. They held the land and the overlordship of villages and towns, collected revenues, and owned flocks. On the other hand, herding imposed a peculiar character on Castilian society, permitting formation of a broad social class which did not cultivate the land but lived from it, and also permitting the formation of a type of latifundist property which always prevented the development of a class of well-to-do peasants. To hold a commandery in a military order, the right to impose taxes on pastures or the passage of flocks, hereditary ownership of grazing lands in Extremadura—as Cervantes could still say two hundred years later—meant being able to maintain high social rank and to receive revenues which permitted a relatively high level of existence.

It was undoubtedly because of this pervasive seigniorial economy that Castile did not succeed in creating industry. In the fifteenth century her economic evolution lagged behind that of the other European countries which, like England and France—not to speak of Flanders or Italy, which were exceptionally advanced— were then attempting, with relative success, the creation of power- ful national industries. The Castilian cloth industry, at that time just beginning, never succeeded in satisfying the needs of the internal market. Henry IV made really serious efforts to stimulate production of inexpensive cloth in Segovia.[8] In 1438 the Cortes of Madrigal asked for restrictive measures on wool imports[9] for the purpose of forcing greater internal use of the product; in 1462 Henry IV ordered one-third of the total production retained within the country.[10] Both attempts failed. The Catholic Kings returned to a free-export policy.

This inability to create an industry was reflected in the social order. There was no bourgeoisie conscious of itself as a class which might oppose the nobility, share political power with it, and serve as an effective support for the monarchy. Perhaps the special structure of the cities, organized from the top down and not from the bottom up, influenced this state of affairs. Merchants, very numerous in Burgos, Medina del Campo, and Seville, were extremely few or of very little importance in the rest of the country. And in the case of Seville the abundance of foreigners, mostly Genoese, deprived Spanish merchants of importance. All Henry IV's efforts to raise Segovia to the rank of a great mercantile city—for example, in 1459 he created two fairs lasting twenty days each[11]—failed. The social influence of the nobility had no counterweight, and thus Castile necessarily became a country of *hidalgos*. Their mental attitude, deeply rooted in a concept of aristocracy, had nothing in common with the utilitarianism which characterizes the nascent capitalism of the rest of Europe. Great fortunes were achieved by the accumulation of revenues.

FOREIGN TRADE

In the second half of the fourteenth century Castile had experienced a profound transformation which, with a number of fluctuations, had raised her to the rank of a great European power. Her economic and military resources were rated very high. All this was the result not only of the development of herding but also of a clear vocation for shipping which, in competition with the English, had given Cantabrian and Andalusian sailors control over the Atlantic within the relatively short period of twenty years. During the fifteenth century Castile's naval superiority was an undisputed fact, and the powerful German organization of the Hanseatic League had to bow to it. The Castilians realized the importance of this naval superiority: in 1436 the Cortes of Toledo laid down decrees for the construction of ocean-going ships and for the organization of large commercial fleets;[12] in the next Cortes, held at Madrigal in 1438, John II was able to announce that the kingdom's naval outfitting would be intensified and accelerated.[13]

Wool explains the rise of two cities, Burgos and Medina del Campo. Burgos was the favored concentration point for this product, which was then distributed through ports on the Basque coast. Almost fifty years before Bilbao, the great shipping city of the north, Burgos possessed a university of merchants, founded in 1443.[14] The existence of a numerous population of converted Jews was not unconnected with this exceptional prosperity. It would, however, be an error to suppose that this social phenomenon in Burgos was paralleled in other cities. In the course of the fifteenth century Medina del Campo became the most important fair in Castile. There were others in Villalón, in Medina de Ríoseco, in Valladolid, in Segovia, but none attained the international rank of Medina's, which lasted for a hundred days, divided into two periods, between the months of May and October. An unproved tradition attributes the origin of the fairs to Ferdinand of Antequera. In fact, Medina was the favored city of the regent, then of his widow and sons, and finally of Isabella the Catholic; its prosperity depended on freedom on contracting on credit,[15] whereas Burgos' depended on its geographical location.

From Burgos the bales of wool were carried by mule train to the frontier customs posts separating Vitoria from the towns of the Basque coast—Castro-Urdiales, Laredo, Bilbao, Bermeo, Lequeitio—among which they were distributed for shipment at regular intervals to Flanders. The customs duties and tolls levied on them in Vitoria as well as in the seigniory of Vizcaya were very burdensome. In 1453 Burgos attempted to detour this current of traffic toward Santander, which offered more favorable conditions.[16] The attempt failed because Santander could not compete with Vizcaya in shipping potential, and because in Bilbao or Bermeo wool shipments alternated with those of another important product in Castilian external trade: iron.

The direction taken by Castilian external trade was a decisive influence in the guiding principles of her international policy: a close approach to Flanders and the alliance with France.[17] During the course of the fifteenth century this first factor tended to become intensified, while the second was weakened. Protected by their war fleets and by diplomatic treaties, merchants and sailors established on the Atlantic coasts of Flanders and France a chain of trading posts whose origins go back to the first half of the fourteenth century. After 1430 these trading posts were consolidated and developed. The reconquest of France, to which Vizcayan sailors frequently contributed, directly favored Castilian trade. Castilian mariners, victors over the Hanseatic League in a long-drawn-out war of piracy (1419–43), succeeded in forcing a treaty on the Germans (August 6, 1443) which recognized their monopoly on trade in La Rochelle and on the shipment of Gascon wines.[18] Castilian naval supremacy in the Bay of Biscay was an incontrovertible fact up to the end of the century.

There were three chief Castilian mercantile colonies on the Atlantic. The oldest, and also the most important, was Bruges. It was made up of two communities, the Castilian and the Vizcayan—not always with cordial relations between them—which enjoyed privileges dating back to 1348.[19] After 1447

John II recognized the Spanish "nation" of merchants in Bruges as an autonomous body, authorizing free election of consuls and priors.[20] After its liberation in 1450 Rouen also had an important Spanish mercantile colony which supplied Normandy and the Seine basin with iron and hides, wine, figs, and raisins, in addition to wool, acquiring herrings and wheat in exchange. The organizers of this trading establishment appear to have been an influential merchant from Burgos, Iñigo de Arceo, and two brothers, Juan and Martín Pérez, who were natives of Durango. In 1458 the wharves of Rouen received a record cargo of 26,000 bales of wool from Castile.[21] The last of the great trading posts, in Nantes, was not set up until 1459, as the result of a solemn treaty of friendship with the dukes of Brittany.[22] In the second half of the fifteenth century, when an internal economic crisis occurred in Castile for political reasons, Brittany became the chief supplier of wheat to the Basque provinces.[23]

The development of her sea power also pushed Castile toward the Mediterranean. Ever since the end of the fourteenth century the Peninsula's southern ports had known an increase in the number of Italian merchants, for whom Ottoman expansion and the conquests of Tamerlane had made access to the coasts of Asia very difficult. Seville, and Cartagena too, experienced mercantile traffic such as they had never known before.[24] Wool and hides were exported from Castile to Italy. Moreover, Cantabrian mariners acted as intermediaries between Flanders and Italy.[25] When Marseilles slowly began to recover from the sack carried out by Alfonso V of Aragon in 1423, she called upon the services of Vizcayan and Guipuzcoan sailors, who had appeared on the western Mediterranean coast in large numbers after the middle of the century, for her communications with the outside world.[26] Wheat was also one of the chief objects of trade. A consul for the Spaniards in Marseilles, Vasco Gómez de Santiago, is mentioned beginning in 1439.[27]

Castile's wealth grew rapidly. It was, in fact, during Henry IV's reign that Seville reached her apogee,[28] and many cities—Valladolid, Burgos, Segovia, Toledo—attained the rank of chief cities of Europe. Fine cloth and paintings on wood were brought from Flanders. The nobles' homes became sumptuous, and their castles were a combination of rock-built fortresses and comfortable and luxurious palaces. However, this rudimentary economy, though prosperous, had a very narrow base, and in consequence very little stability. The distribution of wealth was most unequal; whole regions and broad sectors of the population were left out of this prosperity. Castile, an exporter of raw materials, was at the mercy of the ups and downs of a complex international market which she could not control; a drop in the price of wool or a wheat crisis, for example, could have the most dismal consequences for her. On the other hand, the two Castilian monarchs of the fifteenth century, who had received the legacy of an openly mercantilist policy from Henry III, did not know how to channel this commercial current to their own advantage. After the middle of the century John II placed in the hands of private persons the collections of export duties, which the Cortes considered to be the kingdom's principal revenues,[29] thus depriving the state of an unencumbered source of income. Issuance of debased coinage,[30] the flight of precious metals, restrictions and taxes on internal trade in wheat,[31] and fiscal disorder produced an almost continuous state of inflation. The victims of this situation were the peasants, among whom there was an observable tendency to emigrate to seigniorial lands where they could find the protection of the nobles. It does not appear, however, that this inflationary movement ever reached extreme proportions.

To sum up, the Castilian economy of the fifteenth century can be defined as both vulnerable and prosperous.

THE MONARCHY

The great political phenomenon which underlies fifteenth-century Castilian history, which explains the long series of violent actions, coups d'état, and civil wars, is the struggle between the nobility and the monarchy. Though neither of the two warring factions ever doubted for a moment the desirability of having the state ruled by a king, each brought to the field of battle its own interpretation of the political regime. Here we shall reserve—the historian can take this liberty in order to simplify concepts—the name "monarchial" for the party which sought to have the king's powers strengthened. The nobility was trying to give the state a structure which would link the monarchy in an almost contractual manner with the members of a powerful aristocracy whose resources were constantly increasing. It was a curious paradox that the struggle permitted the economic and social strengthening of the aristocracy in such a way that, at the end of it, the king succeeded in recovering his absolute power in the political, but not in the administrative, sphere.

The monarchy was not only a practical form of government; it was a theory which the jurists—Álvaro Pelayo, Alonso de Madrigal, Rodrigo Sánchez de Arévalo—insist on considering the most perfect foundation for a political regime.[32] There is no incompatibility between the fact of the monarchy and the principle that power resides in the community; on the contrary, the combination of these two principles gives rise to the idea of the royal power as a duty and not as a right, so characteristic of the Late Middle Ages. When in 1385, during one of the most severe dynastic crises, John I came before the Cortes of Valladolid after his defeat at Aljubarrota, he expounded in the royal speech before the representatives an interpretation of the monarchical power which was entirely in agreement with this concept, and compared it to the power exercised by a father over his children.[33]

The monarchy's prestige continued to grow throughout the century, in spite of its weakness and its failures; a broad segment of the population saw in the increase of the king's power the only remedy for the confused situation which the development of the seigniorial regime had caused in the economic and administrative spheres. Urgent appeals to John II's conscience were heard in the Cortes after 1440,[34] independently of whether the faction in power was being led by Don Álvaro de Luna or the Infantes of Aragon. Four days before the first battle of Olmedo, when he ratified Law xxv of the *Partidas*, John II promised the representatives of the cities that he would personally exercise his power in the future.[35] He did so again at the Cortes of Burgos on April 16, 1453, very soon after Don Álvaro de Luna was taken prisoner.[36] Empty gestures, but ones which show us, in the sense that they were intended for public consumption, what was then considered to be most acceptable to the country. And under Henry IV the representatives' petitions became very urgent: in the Cortes of Ocaña in 1469 the third estate, notwithstanding the fact that its influence had been reduced to almost nothing, reminded the sovereign that a king's first duty is to reign.[37]

Popularity of the monarchy as an institutional system: this is a principle which should not be forgotten when we are trying to understand fifteenth-century Castilian history. At a time when the state, in its modern sense, was taking its first steps, the king was the sole center of all political life. Theoretically his power was absolute and extended to all sectors of the country's public life—justice, treasury, army, and administration—but in practice this absolutism was subject to severe limitations on the part of the Church, the guardian of Christian ethics; the nobles, who formed a privileged estate; and the cities, which had a local administration of their own. Custom, stronger than law, enclosed the monarch in a ring of iron. There was, however, no contractual juridical instrument, no charter, between the king and his subjects; this made the limits of his authority very vague and diffuse. Omnipotent when he was face to face with an individual, the monarch was weak indeed when he dealt with communities of any kind. In the combined picture of the Western kingdoms Castile occupied an intermediate place between England and France.

THE ORGANS OF GOVERNMENT

French influence is very marked in the structure of public institutions, especially after the civil war of 1368, which produced the House of Trastámara's ascent to the throne. The bodies which aided the king in the exercise of his functions can be divided into four great groups: Court, Chamber, Audience, and Cortes. In the form in which they operate in the fifteenth century, it can be said that they are a direct creation of the dynasty, even though they have precedents whose origins go back more than a century. Before 1368, however, there had been no concept of the government as a structure of institutions clustered around a central power.

The Court, the former Curia, had to do with the public functions of the monarch, although there did not exist in Castile, as in England, for example, a clear distinction between such functions and private ones. The central organism of the Court was the Royal Council, which coordinated the action of the many officials. Court offices yielded emoluments known as *quitaciones*. By the terms of the Laws of the Cortes of Toledo in 1371, still in force at this time,[38] there were two types of offices at Court, one which did not have jurisdiction: *almirante, alférez*—after 1382, *condestable* —[39] and *monedero mayor*, and others which did have it: *entregador* of the Mesta, *alcalde mayor de sacas, adelantados*, and *merinos mayores*.[40] Numerous subordinate offices depended upon these.

The Royal Council, first organized by Henry II in 1371 and definitively by John I in 1385,[41] had been conceived in principle as a permanent representation of the Cortes, with twelve members chosen equally from among the three estates. In 1387 the representatives of the cities had been supplanted by legists,[42] and the Council had become an instrument of the monarchy, largely oriented to the exercise of justice.[43] The broad scope of its functions, which exceeded the councillors' capacity, caused this body to split up. John II was to create an independent Council of Justice, in more direct relationship with the Audience. The Royal Council, thus freed from burdensome tasks, became the center of government in Castile; with no concrete functions—and therefore no limitations on its power—and no fixed number of members, it was the governing instrument of the noble oligarchy. The Cortes opposed this evolution, though feebly, asking in 1419,[44] in 1425,[45] and in 1432[46] that representatives of the cities be admitted to it once again; but in every case their plea was answered with a disdainful negative. In the fifteenth century the Council's meetings were usually very well attended; there was no limitation on admission, and members of the upper nobility were almost automatically admitted to them when they were present at court. All provincial and local administration depended on the Royal Council; *corregidores*[47] were appointed there.

The Chamber was, strictly speaking, the fiscal organism of the king's household, while the Chancery was its diplomatic organism. Chamber and Chancery were closely linked together. The emoluments yielded by offices dependent on the Chamber were called *raciones*, a name which clearly alludes to their private origin. Ever since the Law of Lances of the Cortes of Guadalajara in 1390,[48] troops organized in permanent and direct service to the king also depended on the Chamber. These troops had fallen within the seigniorial ambit; the nobles—who received an annual revenue of 1,500 *maravedís* per lance—were in charge of the recruitment and preservation of their units. Thus the army was a source of income and power for the aristocracy. According to the Laws of Toro in 1371, the offices of the king's household were also divided into two classes: those without jurisdiction—majordomo, cupbearer, butler, porters-in-chief—which more clearly recalled their origin in private service; and those with jurisdiction—chancellor, notary, constables, and justices of the peace—who were, in practice, the executors of justice.

The Audience, the high court of appeal, regularly paid and holding regular sessions, was the supreme organ of civil justice, while the Council exercised the same function for criminal justice. Created in 1371 by Henry II, reorganized in 1387 by John I,[49] after that date its functions were restricted to civil suits. After 1419[50] it was composed of ten *oidores*,[51] five of whom sat alternately for terms of six months, and a presiding prelate. Installed in Segovia, except for a short period during which it was transferred to Valladolid, it functioned very imperfectly prior to 1474. There were frequent complaints from the Cortes,[52] but there was an excess of zeal in these: for the representatives, the Audience offered greater guarantees of independent and objective justice than the Council; in 1440 the Cortes even dared to request suspension of the latter's proceedings.[53]

The decline of the Cortes in the fifteenth century is very obvious. In any case, now that we have passed through the epidemic of laudatory literature aroused by these institutions through liberal influence, we are beginning to realize today how small their role always was in the Crown's governing process. Of the three branches which intervened in the Cortes, that of the representatives of the cities was the most important, for their function was to pay the subsidies agreed upon. When the cities succumbed to the impact of seigniorial expansion, the Cortes necessarily declined. And in any case the cities, governed by closed oligarchies, never defended anything more than a system of privilege. Let us use the example of Burgos, one of those which preserved its autonomy longest: the sixteen lifetime magistrates who constituted its City Council in practice succeeded each other by inheritance throughout the fifteenth century.[54] Two warring forces disputed future sway over the cities: the king, who aspired to their control through his *corregidores*, and the nobles, who were usurping municipal jurisdiction.

Unlike the Crown of Aragon, the kingdom of Castile had a single Cortes, a symbol in its turn of the country's advanced state of unity. One aspect of the decline of the institutions is shown in the fact that the great Laws which formerly had gone to swell the body of legislation were no longer published in the Cortes, as the fourteenth-century kings had done; John II and Henry IV merely received the list of petitions, to which they often replied after the subsidies had been voted and the representatives had returned to their homes. In the Cortes' deliberations—in most cases reduced to very unimportant matters—the nobility and clergy did not participate;[55] they had no right to vote or to pay subsidies.

We cannot compare the Castilian Cortes of the fifteenth century with any representative organism of a modern type. Only seventeen cities were usually called upon: Burgos, Toledo, León, Seville, Córdoba, Murcia, Jaén—capitals of kingdoms—Zamora, Toro, Salamanca, Segovia, Avila, Valladolid, Soria, Cuenca, Madrid, and Guadalajara, and not all of these always exercised their rights.[56] Whole regions of vital importance, such as Galicia, Asturias, Extremadura, and the Basque Country, were left outside the institution. Internal rivalries also afflicted Burgos, León, and Toledo, who disputed each others' primacy in voting, an empty honor. A whole enormous social sector, the one which might have found in the Cortes an opportunity to make its voice heard, was left outside it: for the Cortes of Palencia decreed in 1431 that neither peasants nor commoners could be appointed representatives.[57] Elections for representatives were never free; as the cities fell under the influence of the upper nobility, the nobility in turn imposed its own candidates, when the king did not directly appoint the representatives from each city. The insistence with which the Cortes called for free elections after 1430[58] is the best proof of how far it was from achieving them.

In conclusion: it may be stated that in the fifteenth century Castile lacked even the appearance of a representative government. The representatives of the cities were *hidalgos*, and often courtiers directly appointed by the king; the cities defended as an exclusive privilege the right to attend the Cortes, but it was the right to protest, not to deliberate; and these organisms included, socially and territorially, no more than a few restricted sectors of the country. Therefore their influence was necessarily very small. They could represent nobody. If we can consider that in a certain sense the government of Castile had a contractual and not an absolute basis, this was due to the existence of Catholic ethics, applicable to all, and to the existence of two forces which either helped each other or fought each other, according to the circumstances: the noble oligarchy—in which we must include the upper clergy—and the king. He could count on the adhesion of the people, for they saw in him—as the Cortes often insisted—the supreme expectation of justice; the oligarchy possessed wealth and power. Let us see, then, who the members of this noble oligarchy were.

THE NOBLE OLIGARCHY

Among the nobility of recent origin, a consequence of "Henry's favors,"[59] a few families emerge whose rapid accumulation of revenues and seigniories makes them arbiters of the Castilian political situation in the fifteenth century. In this respect the civil war of 1368 may be considered as a decisive event in Spanish history. The followers of Henry of Trastámara became beneficiaries of the new regime; some were natives of other regions of the Peninsula and had arrived in Castile as simple soldiers of fortune. The general tendency to found *mayorazgos*,[60] the continuity of their aspirations, and their keen sense of class permitted, in the course of years, a consolidation of families which, to judge from the wealth and prosperity we find them in during the fifteenth century, makes it hard for us to believe that their origin had been so humble and so recent. John I and Henry III, forced to do battle with their ambitious kinsmen, sought the support of this new and at the time modest nobility, bringing them to court to occupy key posts in the government. In general, the nobles responded by demonstrating their fidelity. At the beginning of the century the Mendozas, Stúñigas, and Velascos received the reward for this fidelity in the form of lands and titles.[61] Those of the new generation attempted to maintain themselves in power by inheritance, just as they maintained their possessions. Thus they came to constitute an oligarchy, with a sense of class and well-defined political ideals, whose influence on Spanish society has been enormously important. When we consider the political role of this oligarchy we must include in the number of its members the chief prelates of the realm, especially the archbishops of Toledo, Seville, and Santiago. But though these played an important political role, they did not take part in the task of intense social transformation fostered by the nobility.

Exactly fifteen noble houses, with an approximate total of two dozen seigniorial estates, were active on the fifteenth-century Castilian political scene. Their influence stemmed, in the first place, from their enormous wealth, from the large number of fortresses they possessed. A league made up of all these houses— something which never existed—would have been able, at least after 1430, to hold the king himself in check. Its members occupied the principal posts at court, as a result of the influence from which they derived their power. An important transformation which gives the period its character is that they did not achieve noble rank by occupying these posts, as had happened up to the fourteenth century, but occupied the posts because they were nobles. From time to time a new man appeared and immediately poured all his energies into founding a *mayorazgo*, into creating a noble house; it cannot be said, therefore, that the oligarchy was a closed one. The great lords served as a model for a large number of nobles of an intermediate type. There was perfect correspondence between their style of life, their concept of society, and the economic development of Castile. They were latifundists and felt a primary interest in herding—and the collection of taxes on the passage of flocks; they constituted the membership of the Mesta, and controlled and governed it. But the subsequent phase of economic evolution, industrialization, neither concerned nor interested them. They were highly conservative, and their conservatism was directed above all toward the economic structure which allowed them to develop their power. They can be called capitalists only in the sense that they had been able to accumulate enormous sums of money.

The Velascos were established on the borders between Old Castile and the Rioja region. "The good count of Haro," Pedro Fernández de Velasco, the descendant of a family from Álava or Vizcaya, owed his fortune to the services rendered by his father and grandfather to Henry III and John I, respectively. About the year 1446, after the first battle of Olmedo—the opportunity for a prodigious advance by most of these families—his domains included Haro, Arnedo, Herrera de Pisuerga, Frías, Medina de Pomar, Briviesca, Salas de los Infantes, Santo Domingo de Silos, Villalpando, Cuenca de Campos, and Tamarite, together with an indefinite number of towns and hamlets.[62] The county of Haro thus covered the greater part of the present-day provinces of Burgos and Logroño, and also spread into those of Palencia and Álava. The holders of the title had interests and influence in the city of Burgos, and in the latter years of Henry IV's reign aspired to reconstruct the ancient seigniory of the house of Lara; they reached the left bank of the Nervión and even, for a short time, attempted the conquest of Vizcaya.

On the southern borders of this seigniory we find the county of Medinaceli, founded in favor of Gastón de la Cerda; this was a family of half-French origin, descended from the famous *infantes* of that name. Medinaceli, which had an extensive fief, was its base; to it were added Somaén, Cogolludo, Almazul, Mazaretón, Miñana, and Alameda.[63] Constricted on one side by the Mendozas, with whom they soon intermarried, the counts of Medinaceli directed their attention to Soria.

The Manriques, a very numerous family and implacable enemies of Henry IV, boasted that they were descendants of Count Don Pedro de Lara. In fact the founder of this family's greatness, Diego Gómez Manrique, *adelantado mayor*[64] of Castile, owed much to his close relationship to influential men in the Church. In 1380 John I gave him Navarrete, the foundation of his *mayorazgo*.[65] After 1398 he apparently played a very important role in the government of Castile.[66] His son Pedro Manrique, *adelantado mayor* of Leon, was one of the strong supporters of the Aragonese faction. The combination of his sons—Diego, count of Treviño; Rodrigo, count of Paredes; Gómez, the poet and *adelantado mayor*—and their cousins, the sons of Juan Fernández Manrique—Juan, count of Castañeda, and Gabriel, count of Osorno—made up the most formidable family clan imaginable. They controlled the whole Campos region, from Palencia to the passes of Reinosa. Rivals of the Velascos in their expansion toward the north, under John II and Henry IV they constituted a permanent and belligerent opposition.[67]

The castle of Luna was located on the border between Leon and Asturias. Since 1369 its lords had been the Quiñones, a family from the Leonese highlands whose role in Asturian history was destined to be an eminent one. After the disappearance from the scene of the bastard Alfonso (1395) there was a vacuum to be filled, and to this they aspired. The three great figures in the family were, successively, Suárez de Quiñones, a supporter of John I and Henry III—from whom he received Cangas, Tineo, and Allande—Diego Fernández de Quiñones, who acquired Ribadesella in 1443, and Pedro Fernández de Quiñones, count of Luna, who by 1470 had added to these domains El Páramo, Astorga, Labiana, Gordón, Llanes, and Somiedo.[68] For eighty years the family battled untiringly to gain control over the entire principality. In 1471 it seemed to be on the point of attaining its objective: Isabella granted plenary powers to the count of Luna.[69]

Similarly, Fadrique Enríquez and Pedro Álvarez Osorio successively attempted to seize control in Galicia. In 1423 the former was count of Trastámara, duke of Arjona, and high mace-bearer of Santiago. The latter received the countship as a reward after the battle of Olmedo (1445). After 1453 Osorio was also count of Lemos.[70] But it was too late; Galicia was a much-divided land, where the archbishops of Santiago had strong influence. The venture ended tragically during the reign of the Catholic Kings.

In Benavente we find another great family: the Pimentels. The founder of this house, Juan Alfonso Pimentel, received the city, which had given its name to a duchy, from the hands of Henry III on May 14, 1398, after it had been wrested from the bastard Don Fadrique. Slowly and surely, the family gained wealth. Its initial alliance with Don Álvaro de Luna, its later opposition to this favorite, its constant participation in the intrigues and civil wars of Henry IV's reign, permitted the counts of Benavente to extend their possessions to Mayorga de Campos (1429), Villalón (1432)—seat of an important fair—Gordoncillo (1434), Puebla de Sanabria, Portillo (1465), and Castromocho (1468).[71] They aspired to the control of Valladolid, and even to extend their influence to Galicia. Located as it was on roads and sheep paths between Leon, Zamora, and Galicia, the county of Benavente could profit from the resources of a very intensive agricultural production, both in wheat and in wine.

In their aspirations to control of Valladolid and its surrounding district, the Pimentels found a formidable competitor in the Enríquez family. Two branches of it had existed since 1441, the major branch represented by the admiral Don Fadrique, the minor by his brother Enrique, count of Alba de Liste.[72] The only noble house—except that of the ruling family—left from the numerous bastards of Alfonso XI, the Enríquez were descendants, also illegitimately, of the grand master of Santiago assassinated by Peter I in Seville. They were firmly established in the Campos region, from Palencia to Valladolid. The seigniory of the major branch of the family, which never formed a county because its members preferred to be designated by the hereditarily transmitted office of Admirals of Castile, grew in increasing rhythm throughout the century. Listed chronologically, the places which became attached to it—to mention only the important towns— were Aguilar de Campoo (1389), Torrelobatón and Tamariz (1392), Villabrágima (1393), Moral de la Reina (1394), Berrueces (1395), Villalar (1410), Medina de Ríoseco (1421), which became the chief town of the *mayorazgo* and the seigniorial residence, and was granted fairs which competed with those of Villalón—for a rivalry of a commercial nature underlay the quarrel of the Enríquez and Pimentel families—Palenzuela (1429), Villapadierne, Villaverde del Arroyo, Cabanillas, and La Vega (1435), Rueda, Mansilla, and Castilberrón (1439), Vega de Ruiponce (1442), Valdenebro, Bustillo, and Melgar de Yuso (1465).[73] Ferdinand the Catholic was a grandson, through his mother, of the admiral Don Fadrique; this was to assure the family of a brilliant position in the future reign.

During a certain period of time, while John of Navarre's political control lasted, the Manriques, Velascos, and Enríquez had to endure the competition of Diego Gómez de Sandoval, count of Castro. But his family soon ceased to be dangerous. A partisan of Ferdinand of Antequera, who in 1412 gave him Lerma, an eagles' nest perched above the plain, Diego Gómez de Sandoval was wholly loyal to his protector's sons, especially John. They presented him with the county of Castro, which included Portillo, Osorno, and Saldaña with Castrojeriz, and helped him to acquire the estates of Cea, Villadiego, San Andrés, San Pedro, Renedo, Castrillo, Velilla, and Carvajal, together with Ampudia and Gumiel de Hazán (1419). At the time of the first great plunder by the Aragonese in 1430, this great seigniory fell into ruin. The family recovered very few of its former possessions.[74] Alfonso V, in compensation, made Sandoval count of Denia. This title was used by the most illustrious member of the family, a minister of Philip III: the duke of Lerma.

From the Cantabrian mountains to the Duero, the land was covered with seigniories. Only a few places were left—Valladolid, Burgos, Medina del Campo—like islands in a sea of nobility. The mountain passes of the Meseta from north to south, in both Extremaduras, passes traversed by two of the three principal *cañadas* and also obligatory for mule trains, were also in the hands of important family clans: the Stúñigas to the west and the Mendozas to the east. There was only one free strip in the middle, from Guadarrama to Arenas de San Pedro, where Madrid and Toledo were joined with Ávila and Segovia. Overlooking this territory, Don Álvaro de Luna was soon to build the formidable castle of Escalona on its southern slope.

The Stúñigas, poets and patrons of the arts, originated in Navarre and owed everything they had to the civil war. The founder of the family's greatness was Diego López de Stúñiga, chief justice of Henry III. He was able, knightly, and a great womanizer, and died in November of 1417. From Henry he received Béjar (April 5, 1396), which controlled one of the most lucrative inland ports of entry in the Peninsula.[75] His son Pedro de Stúñiga, count of Ledesma in 1429, a title which he changed for that of count of Plasencia, added Cáceres, Trujillo, and Curiel to these two cities. His grandson Álvaro, who served as jailer of the Constable [Don Álvaro de Luna], was already a great personage, an important figure during the reign of Henry IV. Eventually he acquired the title of duke of Arévalo.[76] Don Álvaro de Luna raised up a dangerous rival to the Stúñigas when in 1439 he named Fernán Álvarez de Toledo to the countship of Alba de Tormes; he was the grandson of a lord of Valdecorneja who had faithfully served John I, and a nephew of Gutierre Álvarez, bishop of Salamanca and Palencia, archbishop of Seville and Toledo, a great figure in the political life of the period.[77] The county of Alba, already in existence as a single seigniory at the time the civil war began

(June 8, 1369), included, in addition to Alba and its fief, Fuente-guinaldo, Salvatierra, Huéscar, San Felices de los Gallegos, Granadilla, Abadía, Castronuevo, Piedrahita, and El Barco de Ávila.[78] The Stúñiga and Álvarez de Toledo clans kept up a bitter warfare for control of Salamanca, a war which was later extended to Extremadura.

The Mendozas came originally from two humble villages in Álava, Mendoza and Orozco. The house of the Infantado arose from among them. The fortunes of this family were fabulous. They were to give the Spanish language one of its greatest poets, cover Castile with *mayorazgos*, fill the courts of Europe with their names, and even establish them on the American continent. The founder was Pedro González de Mendoza, who profited from the assassination of his kinsman Iñigo López de Orozco at the hands of Peter I, and from the great services he performed for Henry II and John I. Though his inheritance was in Álava, he[79] soon abandoned this region to settle in Hita, Buitrago, and Torija (1368). There he founded a seigniory, in a region of shepherds and beekeepers, and added to the original towns those of Robregordo, Somosierra, Palazuelos, Colmenar, Cardoso, El Vado, and Robredarcas.[80] He died at Aljubarrota. The family made capital of the legend that his last act had been to offer his horse to the king so that the latter could escape. By purchase, donation, or matri-mony, his son Diego Hurtado and his grandson Iñigo López de Mendoza acquired Casa de la Vega (Torrelavega and its fief), the Real de Manzanares (with Colmenar Viejo and Galapagar), Santillana, Carriedo, Piélagos, Villaescusa, Cayón, and Camargo.[81] In 1445, as a result of the battle of Olmedo, Iñigo López de Mendoza was created marquis of Santillana and count of the Real de Manzanares.[82] The second marquis of Santillana acquired the Infantado in 1470, which became the title of his duchy five years later. During Henry IV's reign the Mendozas became arbiters of the future destiny of Castile; for many, their intervention assured the victory of whatever faction to which they inclined.

To the south of the Tagus River were the domains of the military orders. No one succeeded in making the inheritance of a grand mastership permanent; fundamentally, the orders offered the possibility of obtaining wealth and power outside family tradition. This is why Isabella upheld from the very beginning the idea that the orders would have to go into the hands of the king if he wished to reimpose his authority. It was also impossible to create a seigniory. Not until much later do we see how two rival families, the Silvas and López de Ayalas, both of whom had settled in Toledo many years before, succeeded in founding small counties in Cifuentes and Fuensalida. Juan de Silva was a son of the *adelantado* of Cazorla, Alfonso Tenorio, who was nephew in his turn of one of the great ministers of John I and Henry III: the archbishop of Toledo, Don Pedro Tenorio. But López de Ayala was a grandson of a personage of the same name, a native of Álava, a diplomat and author of the most important series of medieval Castilian chronicles.

Between the frontier of Aragon, the kingdom of Murcia, and the central nucleus of the order of Santiago, a very important seigniory had been created: the marquisate of Villena. It was on the road from Alicante and Cartagena into the heart of Castile, and vineyards and market gardens alternated with herding. Muleteers were still very numerous there when Don Quixote's fancy passed through this region. The marquisate was composed of Villena, Belmonte, Alarcón, Chinchilla, Castrillo de Garcimuñoz, San Clemente, Iniesta, Alcalá, Gorguera, Beas, La Roda, Albacete, Hellín, Tobarra, Jumilla, Yecla, Sax, Almansa, Utiel, Villanueva de la Fuente, El Bonillo, Lezuza, Villarobledo, and Zafra.[83] Henry II had created it for one of his most important supporters: Alfonso of Aragon. Henry III reincorporated it to the Crown in 1398.[84] A vast and rich domain, it awakened greed: the Infante Don Henry, who was already grand master of Santiago, attempted to have it handed over to him as the dowry of his wife Catalina; finally it came into the hands of Don Juan Pacheco, the favorite of Henry IV.

On November 17, 1383, Alfonso Yáñez Fajardo was named *adelantado* of the kingdom of Murcia;[85] in 1387 Alhama was given to him as a seigniory.[86] From that time onward the office was kept in the family. Slowly and surely, the Fajardos extended their control over the whole kingdom, which in the end became their patrimony. The war between two cousins, Alfonso, called the Brave, and Pedro, the *adelantado mayor*, ending in the victory of the latter, was a mere episode, a family quarrel which did not affect the kingdom's future. After 1465 Pedro Fajardo was master of all Murcia, and acted there with absolute independence.

Two great Lower Andalusian houses, the Guzmáns and the Ponces de León, absorbed wealth and renown. No other families could compare with them, unless it were perhaps the Fernández de Córdobas, counts of Cabra, or the Aguilars. Both boasted, with justice, of their ancient lineage. The Guzmáns were descended from Alonso Pérez de Guzmán, the hero of Tarifa. They had been supporters of Henry II and had suffered losses in the civil war which that monarch repaid to them with interest. After 1371 Juan Alonso de Guzmán was advanced to the countship of Niebla —Huelva, Niebla, Alfarache, Almonte, San Juan del Puerto, Trigueros, and Valverde del Camino—to which were shortly added Vejer, Chiclana, Sanlúcar de Barrameda, Monteagudo, Ayamonte, Lepe, and Bollullos (1383).[87] Exporters of expensive wines, which commanded a high price in England after transit through Flanders or Portugal, they soon became wealthy. After 1470 they can be considered masters of Seville. On February 17, 1445, the county became the duchy of Medina-Sidonia.[88]

The Ponces de León, first the friends and later the bitter rivals of the Guzmáns, were lords of Marchena; their possession of this city goes back at least to 1309. Pedro Ponce de León was created count of Medellín (December 8, 1429)[89] out of the spoils of the Infante Don Henry. In 1440, when the Infante's possessions were restored, John II made Pedro Ponce count of Arcos and removed this city from the jurisdiction of Seville.[90] Mairena, Rota, Bailén, Pruna, Guadajoz, Paradas, and Cádiz were also added. The second count of Arcos, Rodrigo Ponce de León, was made marquis of Cádiz.

The central fact in fifteenth-century Castilian history is the struggle among these fifteen families—all ambitious to round out their domains—and the king. But once and for all, we must get rid of the oft-repeated idea that this was a struggle between the law and a flock of birds of prey. The nobles had their own political concept, a very respectable one indeed, whose results cannot be measured because they never achieved complete victory for their aspirations. Although it is certain that many [historians] see respect for law and order in the personal power of the king, it is no less certain that there were principles of lofty political stature in the programs of government advocated by the nobles. As in all conflicts of far-reaching importance, it is very difficult to say which side was in the right in this one. What matters to the historian is to demonstrate that in fifteenth-century Castile a phenomenon of *aristocratization* occurred; the economy, society, culture, and life itself were organized in the service of this ruling class, whose influence reached down to the lowest levels of the population. It was at this time that, as a style of life was imposed, the concept of *hidalguismo* became basic; and this concept was to be the chief characteristic of Spanish society under the Hapsburgs.

THE STYLE OF LIFE

The noble oligarchy's predominance was not restricted to a merely political ambit. It created standards of life, an ideal, which was absorbed by the whole society of the period, the era of "flamboyant Gothic." This was all the more true because the counterweight of a strong bourgeoisie did not exist. There is always a natural tendency in men to form part of the dominant and privileged social class. Thus, while the nobles took advantage of the vicissitudes offered by political changes and civil wars to elevate their titles and to round off and increase their seigniories, a very broad social stratum—all the city dwellers or peasants who enjoyed a comfortable economic situation—tried to reach the ranks of the lower nobility and attain knightly status, not only to escape payment of taxes but also to become included in the social ambit of the privileged classes. On certain occasions this movement was alarmingly rapid. It was the economic aspect of this tendency toward knighthood that was being attacked in John II's decrees of December 20, 1442, the agreements made by the Cortes of Palencia in 1431[91] and the more explicit ones issued by the Cortes of Ocaña in 1469.[92] But the effort was vain: the monarchs knew that a promise of conferring knighthood was the most effective stimulus of all, and often resorted to it when they needed aid.

The knightly ideals of this last period in the Middle Ages have been summed up by Huizinga in a shrewd phrase: "nostalgia for a more beautiful life." The artifice of the heroic takes the place of the truly heroic; forays into Moslem territory, the hard-fought ancient task of the reconquerors and colonists. This artifice, which bears a close relationship to the convolutions and redundant foliage which cover spires and vaults in the late Gothic period, is certainly the most characteristic sign of the times.[93] Tournaments and excursions take the place of war: chivalrous love—as in the amorous manual which Gutierre Díez de Gámes includes [in his *Victorial*]—supplants erotic passion. The kings extend their protection to knights-errant. In[94] 1428 the whole city of Valladolid was transformed into a stage for splendid tournaments in which the Infantes of Aragon and Don Álvaro de Luna carried their rivalry to the point of prodigality.[95] Wooden castles, fantastic dress, pagan allegories, were all combined in the competition. The Infante Don John, who made a gift of golden spurs to his servants, then loaded them with sacks of gold so that they could graphically exhibit his wealth in the streets of the city.

When chivalrous ideals were translated into the political sphere, we find the case of Granada. From the time of Ferdinand of Antequera—referred to throughout the century in a self-seeking court literature as the model of the perfect knight—the war against Islam in Granada became the great propaganda base for politicians: Don Álvaro de Luna, the victor of 1430, threw himself into a war with Granada; the marquis of Santillana, many years later, gloried in that exploit of his when "he entered into Huelma to loot." Henry IV began his reign with a series of campaigns which were no less brilliant for being useless. But in all these anti-Islamic ventures—sometimes elevated by the popes to the level of Crusades

—the form was more important than the content. And yet the frontier, that breeding-place of warriors, exerted considerable influence on the Castilian spirit. It was where danger ceased to be fiction and became reality, where battles were bloody and deaths were real. In the heat of daily hazard, artifice resolved itself into that magnificent series of frontier ballads which preserve the typical Spanish realism.

The type of life imposed by the aristocracy was a fertile field for the development of literature. We are in the period which it is fashionable to call the pre-Renaissance. Courtly poets, whose works are collected in *Cancioneros*—the most famous of these songbooks is that of Baena, compiled for John II in the very year of the battle of Olmedo—and palace chroniclers who write to praise the deeds of their lords are the typical product of this period. Not in spite of political circumstances, as has been said again and again since the days of Menéndez y Pelayo,[96] but precisely because of them. The great poets of the century, Gómez and Jorge Manrique, the marquis of Santillana, Juan de Mena, Lope de Stúñiga, either belong to the most important families or live at their expense. Careful reading of the *Cancionero* is highly recommended for an understanding of the period's mental attitudes.

The themes of this literature give the historian a clear picture of the ideals which inspired that society.... Eloy Benito has pointed out the artificial nature of love, the superfluity of the theme of woman once it had become a literary topic.[97] The heroic theme is forgotten, and literature passes from reality to the allegory, Italian in origin and influence. Taken all together, Castilian society in the fifteenth century, as in most European countries, appears to our eyes as a revival of paganism, dominated by the pathos of death. Death and life, in dolorous contrast, are filled with nostalgia even when they are made to serve, with bitter sarcasm, the oft-repeated theme of the Dance of Death.[98]

This revival of paganism affects customs but not beliefs. The Church is in crisis—a process of monastic reform is under way which it is not our purpose to examine here, but which makes

Castile an enormously interesting source of new ideas. There is a renewed zeal for enjoying life which takes the form of extreme immorality, but which does not show signs of any grave heretical influence such as that which troubled most of the Western European kingdoms after the middle of the fourteenth century. The heretics of Durango, led by Fray Alonso de Mella, or Canon Pedro Martínez de Osma—Nebrija's teacher in Salamanca—who wrote against indulgences, are isolated exceptions, museum pieces.[99] Though a religious problem did exist, it was due to the existence of a large population, growing in numbers after the beginning of the century, of converted Jews. The *conversos'* wealth and influence aroused the hatred of the lower levels of society. Riots, plunder, and massacres took place from time to time.

The fifteenth century has an epitaph in the verses of Jorge Manrique, dedicated to his father, Rodrigo, count of Paredes, grand master of Santiago, who is one of the best examples of noble activity both for good and for ill. The author was unaware that, in expressing his nostalgia, he expressed a whole era with it:

> Tourney and joust, that charmed the eye,
> And scarf, and gorgeous panoply,
>   And nodding plume.
> What were they but a pageant scene?
> What but the garlands, gay and green,
>   That deck the tomb?[100]

NOTES

[1. From Low Latin *benefactoria* = commendation—a village or town in Asturias, Leon, or Castile, occupied by men of *behetría*, peasant proprietors who had been free to choose their overlord in exchange for the incurring of obligations. Their rights in 600 or so such villages were recorded in the *Libro de Becerro*, or Book of *Behetrías* (1353).]

[2. Sheepwalks; see above, p. 37.]

3. L. Suárez, "Evolución histórica de las Hermandades castellanas," *Cuadernos de Historia de España*, XVI (Buenos Aires, 1951), 29.

4. J. Klein, *The Mesta: A Study in Spanish Economic History, 1273–1836* (Cambridge, Mass., 1920) [p. 19. The original references were to the Spanish edition (1936)].

5. *Ibid.* [p. 25].
6. *Ibid.* [pp. 81–83].
7. L. Serrano, *Los Reyes Católicos y la ciudad de Burgos* (Madrid, 1943), pp. 18–19.
8. We possess a curious undated report which Henry IV had drawn up by a certain Pedro de Buitrago, expert clothmaker, concerning the qualities of cloth it would be suitable to manufacture in Segovia. AGS, Estado, Castilla, Leg. 1–2, fol. 100.
9. *Cortes,* III, 340. All notes in this form refer to the *Colección de cuadernos de Cortes,* published by the Academia de la Historia.
10. J. Klein [p. 36 and n. 4].
11. The first of these began a week before the Monday of Carnival, the second on the feast day of San Bernabe (June 11). J. Torres Fontes, "Las ferias de Segovia," *Hispania,* LIX (1955), 168–72.
12. *Cortes,* III, 264.
13. *Ibid.,* 325.
14. Robert Sidney Smith, *The Spanish Guild Merchant: A History of the Consulado, 1250–1700* (Durham, N.C., 1940), p. 41.
15. Ramón Carande has shown how the limitation of bills of exchange produced the collapse of the fair after 1551.
16. E. García de Quevedo, *Ordenanzas del consulado de Burgos de 1538* (Burgos, 1905), pp. 39–41.
17. C. Viñas Mey, "De la Edad Media a la Moderna: El Cantábrico y el estrecho de Gibraltar en la Historia política española," *Hispania,* II (1941), 72–73; IV, 65–66.
18. E. García de Quevedo, *Ordenanzas,* pp. 32–33. R. Konetzke, *El Imperio Español* (Spanish trans., Madrid, 1946), p. 39.
19. J. Finot, *Étude historique sur les relations commerciales entre la France et l'Espagne au Moyen-Âge* (Paris, 1899), pp. 55–59, 97–105.
20. *Cartulaire de l'ancien consulat d'Espagne à Bruges,* ed. L. Gilliodts van Severen, second part (Bruges, 1901), p. 31.
21. M. Mollat, *Le commerce maritime normand à la fin du Moyen-Âge* (Paris, 1952), pp. 113–14.
22. C. Fernández Duro, *La marina de Castilla* (Madrid, 1891), p. 196.
23. We possess an interesting report from the *Junta* of Usarraga to Henry IV, undated as to year, in which details of this trade are explained. AGS, Estado, Castilla, Leg. 1–2, fol. 89.
24. L. Suárez, "El Atlántico y el Mediterráneo en los objetivos políticos de la casa de Trastámara," *Revista portuguesa de Historia,* V (1951), 299 *et seq.* [and see above, p. 68].
25. H. Laurent, *Un grand commerce d'exportation au Moyen-Âge: La draperie des Pays-Bas en France et dans les pays méditerranéens (XIIe–XIVe siècles)* (Paris, 1935), pp. 181–83.
26. E. Baratier and F. Reynaud, *Histoire du commerce de Marseille,* II (Paris, 1951), 319–27.
27. *Ibid.,* 546.
28. C. Viñas Mey, "De la Edad Media," *Hispania,* V, 75.

29. Cortes of Burgos in 1453. *Cortes*, III, 659–60.
30. Complaints in the Cortes of Madrid in 1435 and the Cortes of Córdoba in 1455. *Cortes*, III, 232, 691–92.
31. See *cuadernos* of the Cortes of Valladolid, 1442, and Toledo, 1462. *Cortes*, III, 411, 469.
32. J. Beneyto Pérez, *Textos políticos de la Baja Edad Media* (Madrid, 1945), p. 145, has brought together three texts of the authors mentioned which give us a precise idea of the monarchical doctrine. Álvaro Pelayo: "Optimus autem regnum multitudinis est ut regatur per unum, quod patet ex finis regiminis quae est pax." Alonso de Madrigal: "Non est discordia in uno principante sicut in multis." Sánchez de Arévalo: "Toda comunidad es mejor e más perfectamente regida por un príncipe que por muchos."
33. *Cortes*, II, 330.
34. *Ibid.*, III, 369–73.
35. *Ibid.*, 456–94.
36. *Ibid.*, 669–70.
37. *Ibid.*, 767 *et seq.*
38. *Ibid.*, II, 165.
39. The document creating the office of constable, July 6, 1382. Biblioteca Nacional, Ms. 6932, fols. 314–19. [Alférez = (royal) standard-bearer.]
[40. *Monedero mayor* = chief moneyer, head of the mint. *Entregador* of the Mesta or *alcalde entregador de la Mesta* = principal judicial protector of the Mesta. It was his job to keep the *cañadas* open and supervise any quarrels which might arise from disputes over pasture rights. *Alcalde mayor de las sacas* = the officer in charge of the officials who were posted at the Castilian frontiers to scrutinize those leaving the country in order to prevent the export of forbidden goods. *Adelantados* and *merinos mayores* = provincial governors with military and political powers. By the end of the Middle Ages there were twenty *merindades* in the north and center of the country, i.e., one each in Galicia, Leon, and Asturias and seventeen in Old and New Castile. The *adelantados mayores* had originally been placed in charge of the provinces on the frontier with Granada. Thus Murcia and Andalusia had *adelantados mayores*. The *adelantado mayor* of Andalusia was *adelantado mayor de la Frontera*.]
41. During the Cortes of Valladolid. *Cortes*, II, 314–35.
42. Cortes of Briviesca. *Cortes*, II, 363–78.
43. The definitive by-laws of the Royal Council are laid down in the royal ordinances of July 1, 1389, and August 24, 1390. Biblioteca Santa Cruz, Valladolid, Ms. 25, fols. 251–85.
44. *Cortes*, III, 20–21.
45. *Ibid.*, 56.
46. *Ibid.*, 120–21.
[47. Lit. "correctors"; the *corregidor* was a special kind of royal magistrate usually appointed to a town. His term of office ran for a year but could be extended. Cf. R. S. Chamberlain, "The 'Corregidor' in Castile in the Sixteenth Century and the 'Residencia' as applied to the 'Corregidor,'" *HAHR*, XXIII (1943), 222–57.)

48. *Cortes*, II, 460–70.
49. L. Suárez, *Juan I rey de Castilla (1379–1390)* (Madrid, 1955), pp. 127–28.
50. *Cortes*, III, 10 *et seq.*
[51. Lit., "auditors," from Latin *auditores*, but here judicial, not financial, officers, the equivalent of *letrados*, in particular trained legal members of an *Audiencia*, or court of appeal.]
52. In almost all the *cuadernos* of the fifteenth century we find petitions for reform: 1425 (*Cortes*, III, 51–52), 1430 (*ibid.*, 85), 1433 (*ibid.*, 162–63), 1436 (*ibid.*, 299–303), 1438 (*ibid.*, 312), 1447 (*ibid.*, 521), 1462 (*ibid.*, 702), and 1469 (*ibid.*, 767–70).
53. *Cortes*, III, 383–84.
54. L. Serrano, *Los Reyes Católicos y la ciudad de Burgos*, pp. 12 *et seq.*
55. W. Piskorski, *Las Cortes de Castilla en el período de tránsito de la Edad Media a la Moderna, 1188–1520* (Spanish trans., Barcelona, 1930), pp. 45–46.
56. *Ibid.*, p. 38.
57. *Cortes*, III, 101.
58. *Ibid.*, 85.
[59. The *mercedes enriqueñas*, or "Henrician Mercies"; cf. p. 21.]
[60. From the Latin *mayoratus*, originally the law by which the eldest son of a nobleman inherited an entailed estate; by the fifteenth century it had come to mean such an estate which could be inherited by anyone named in the royal document setting it up. Thus a noble could establish a whole series of *mayorazgos*. By the sixteenth century the *mayorazgo* had been taken up by the bourgeoisie.]
61. A subject which I have already discussed in my *Estudios sobre el regimen monárquico de Enrique III de Castilla* (Madrid, 1952).
62. M. Lasso de la Vega, Marqués de Saltillo, *Historia nobilaria de España* (contribución a su estudio), I (Madrid, 1956), 137–38. [For a map showing some of the possessions of the Velascos in 1458 see M. T. de la Peña Marazuela and Pilar León Tello, *Inventario del archivo de los Duques de Frías*, Vol. I (Casa de Velasco), plate ix. Almost all the places named as possessions of other members of the nobility can be identified on the map in R. Menéndez Pidal, *Historia de España*, Vol. xv, ed. L. Suárez Fernández, A. Canellas López, and J. Vicens Vives (Madrid, 1964), p. 272 opposite.]
63. *Ibid.*, I, 183–84.
[64. See above, n. [40].]
65. L. Salazar y Castro, *Historia genealógica de la casa de Lara*, II (Madrid, 1697), 5.
66. L. Suárez, *Estudios*, p. 122.
67. J. B. Sitges, *Enrique IV y la excelente señora llamada vulgarmente doña Juana la Beltraneja (1425–1530)* (Madrid, 1912), pp. 115 *et seq.*
68. Saltillo, *Historia nobiliaria*, I, 173–75.
69. Jovellanos, *Colección de Asturias*, II (Madrid, 1948), 47–48.
70. A. López Ferreiro, *Historia de la Santa A. M. Iglesia de Santiago*, VIII (Santiago, 1905), 225.
71. Saltillo, *Historia nobiliaria*, I, 101–4.
72. *Ibid.*, p. 61.

73. *Ibid.*, pp. 177–80.
74. *Ibid.*, pp. 169–71.
75. L. Suárez, *Estudios*, p. 87.
76. Saltillo, *Historia nobiliaria*, I, 91–93.
77. Diego Ortiz de Zúñiga, *Anales eclésiasticos y seculares de la ciudad de Sevilla* (Madrid, 1677), p. 325.
78. Saltillo, *Historia nobiliaria*, I, 59–60.
79. From Henry II he received Foncea (A. Andrés, "Don Pedro González de Mendoza, el de Aljubarrota, 1340–1385," *BAH*, LXXVIII [1921], 162), Arciniega, and Llodio in 1371 (Academia de la Historia, Colección Salazar, D_{10}).
80. F. Layna Serrano, *Historia de Guadalajara y sus Mendozas en los siglos XV y XVI*, I (Madrid, 1942), 54.
81. Saltillo, *Historia nobiliaria*, I, 162–66.
82. F. Layna Serrano, *Historia de Guadalajara*, I, 218.
83. Saltillo, *Historia nobiliaria*, II, 268.
84. L. Suárez, *Estudios*, p. 122.
85. F. Cascales, *Discursos históricos de la ciudad de Murcia* (Murcia, 1621), fols. 148 verso–149 recto.
86. Academia de la Historia, Colección Salazar, O_{20}.
87. Biblioteca Nacional, Ms. 13102, fols. 31–32.
88. Ortiz de Zúñiga, *Anales eclésiasticos*, p. 329.
89. *Ibid.*, p. 308.
90. Saltillo, *Historia nobiliaria*, I, 82.
91. *Cortes*, III, 113–15.
92. *Ibid.*, 782–84.
93. E. Benito Ruano, *Los infantes de Aragón* (Madrid, 1952), pp. 42–43.
94. As an example, which could easily be duplicated, see the letter given by Alfonso V of Aragon on March 2, 1417, on behalf of three German knights-errant, published by A. Jiménez Soler, *Itinerario del rey don Alfonso V de Aragón* (Saragossa, 1909), p. 7.
95. *Crónica del Halconero de Juan II, Pedro Carrillo de Huete*, ed. Carriazo (Madrid, 1950), pp. 20–26.
96. In fact, this distinguished writer on so many subjects saw clearly that the confusion of the fifteenth-century civil wars was a sign of what he called "sanguineous exuberance" and not of decadence. M. Menéndez y Pelayo, *Poetas de la Corte de Juan II* (Madrid, 1943), p. 17.
97. E. Benito Ruano, *Los infantes*, pp. 67 et seq.
98. A. Valbuena Prat, *Historia de la literatura española*, I (Barcelona, 1937), 206 et seq., has successfully caught this contrast of ideals by including in a single theme death, magic, and knightly adventure.
99. M. Menéndez y Pelayo, *Historia de los heterodoxos españoles*, II (Madrid, 1947), 365–67.
[100. *Outremer*, II, trans. H. W. Longfellow (Harpers, 1835), 87–88, stanza XVI.]

FURTHER READING

Apart from the works of Merriman, Klein, Puymaigre, and Trend already mentioned:

Ars Hispaniae, Vol. VII, ed. L. Torres Balbás, *Arquitectura Gótica* (Madrid, 1952); Vol. VIII, ed. A. Durán Sanpere and J. Ainaud de Lasarte, *Escultura Gótica* (Madrid, 1956).

B. Beavan, *The History of Spanish Architecture* (London, 1938), chaps. 9–15.

J. Huizinga, *The Waning of the Middle Ages* (London, 1924, and later editions).

C. R. Post, *History of Spanish Painting*, vols. 4 and 5 (Hispano-Flemish), 6 (Valencian School in the Late Middle Ages and Early Renaissance), 9 (Beginning of the Renaissance in Castile and Leon), 10 (Early Renaissance in Andalusia), 11 (Valencian School in the Early Renaissance), 12 (Catalan School in the Early Renaissance), 13 (Schools of Aragon and Navarre in the Early Renaissance), and 14 (Later Renaissance in Castile) (Cambridge, Mass., 1934–66).

4 The Regency of Don Ferdinand of Antequera

JUAN TORRES FONTES

Professor Torres Fontes of the University of Murcia describes the government of Castile between 1407 and 1416—an interlude of comparative stability following the death of Henry III, when Ferdinand of Antequera, as one of the two regents for the minority of John II, was able not only to renew the Reconquest and capture Antequera but also to help in solving the overwhelming European problem of the Great Schism. At the same time the difficulties of a medieval minority, which were to be clearly exemplified after his death, and again in the reign of Henry IV, were equally clearly foreshadowed in the period of the co-regency of Ferdinand and Queen Catalina.

THE SUCCESSION OF HENRY III[1]

On December 25, 1406, a date which, according to the computation of Christmas then in use in Castile, marked the beginning of the year 1407, Henry III lay dying. The Cortes was being held in Toledo, hastily convoked to request the concession of an extraordinary loan for the war with Granada; and since the monarch was ill, it was presided over by his brother Don Ferdinand. The Infante, exercising skill and prudence and always mindful of his sovereign's instructions, succeeded in getting approval for the requested subsidy, and also received a vote of confidence enabling him to collect a larger amount if the exigencies of war should demand it.

Henry III's premature death left Castile under the threat of a long regency, for the dead king's only male child, Prince Don John, was only a little more than a year and a half old. Not many years had passed since the disturbed and disordered period of

Henry III's minority, so that the prospects ahead were very disquieting, and there were well-founded fears of a return to anarchy within the state and further development of the nobles' ambitions.

In view of this possible lack of government, some of Henry III's counselors proposed to the Infante Don Ferdinand "that he take the government of those realms in his charge and reign in them." This was a bold stroke, but one which represented the opinion of many other members of the court. Zurita, who finds this reference in Lorenzo Valla and in instructions given years later by John of Navarre as regent of Aragon to his ambassadors in Castile, names the constable Ruy López Dávalos as the leader of this group of grandees and representatives who offered their recognition to Don Ferdinand.[2]

As a precedent for this political attitude, Zurita himself cites the fact that even before Henry III's death, because of the monarch's physical ailments which made it impossible for him to carry on properly the governing of Castile, more or less public suggestions had been made to Don Ferdinand to take over the government, and that the Infante had always refused to listen to those self-seeking counsels in spite of the possible complaints he might have had of his brother's character.

Henry III's jealous hold on his authority and his high esteem for the royal office were limitless, even with persons so closely attached to him and of such proved fidelity as his brother. There is an anecdote which tells us of his sometimes irascible character. González Dávila says that once when Henry III was in Valladolid, as he passed from one room to another in his palace he saw his brother sitting in the chair that he customarily used for his audiences; he rushed into the room, and though the Infante got up and doffed his hat as soon as he saw the king come in, Don Henry said to him, after ordering the chair thrown out the window, "And be grateful that I do not order you to be thrown out with it."[3]

It had not been so many years before that the founder of the Trastámara dynasty had occupied the throne of Castile by a *coup de force*. A similar opportunity, though absolutely no violence was involved, was being offered to his grandson. Historians represent this offering of the crown to Don Ferdinand as if it had occurred immediately following Henry III's death, and that it was then, when the news was made public, that Don Ruy López Dávalos, in the name of the grandees, prelates, and representatives present at the session of the Cortes, went to the Infante to ask him for whom they should declare themselves as king of Castile, and that in this question was implied the certainty that they would unhesitatingly accept his decision; but that Don Ferdinand, giving proof of his loyalty to the monarchy and to his brother, immediately proclaimed his nephew Don John as king of Castile.

This event, to judge both from these sources and from what we know of the personalities of both protagonists, may seem doubtful if it is presented to us as having taken place in Toledo on the very day of Henry III's death. It was, in fact, the most propitious moment, for Don Ferdinand had all the power in his hands, the Cortes was prepared to confirm the action, and the young king and his mother were in Segovia and entirely remote from what was happening in Toledo. It all seems possible, but one doubt remains: Did it really happen that day? We believe not. For the narrator, the scene is centered on the opportune moment: Henry III's death. But the truth is that this offer, if it existed, could only have taken place in the days previous to the king's demise; that is, when it became completely certain that he would not recover. The rest of the story was distorted later and placed on the most appropriate date, December 25.

It is precisely this precedent mentioned by Zurita, the counsel given to Don Ferdinand to take over the governing of Castile during his brother's illness, which is the only real fact that can be admitted or accepted, and for the following reasons: John II had not been sworn as king in advance of his father's death, as was customary in the kingdom, though he had been recognized as prince of Asturias by the Cortes; there were also the factors of his extreme youth and distance from Toledo, the declared hostility of Granada, "which was a bad neighbor," and the lack of certainty about a stable peace with Portugal. Other, positive reasons can be ranged on the other side: the personality of the Infante, known and esteemed for his considerable gifts; his intervention in the administration of the Cortes of Toledo, and the certainty of a stable and energetic government which would avoid the intervention of various persons as guardians for John II, whose extreme youth meant a long minority and possibly a period even more anarchic than the one Castile had undergone under Henry III himself.

These arguments are supported by documentary proofs that the offer was previous to Henry III's death. One of them is a letter from the Infante Don Ferdinand himself, dated in Toledo on December 25 and addressed to Fernán García de Herrera, marshal of Castile and *frontero mayor*[4] in Lorca. In the letter he wrote that Don Henry, the king, was dangerously ill; he also ordered him to disregard completely any news which might reach his ears, and to prevent any movement or attempt at desertion by the troops concentrated in Lorca, and that he should be prepared to begin the offensive against Granada as soon as he received the order to do so. After these instructions, the Infante's words take on a more solemn tone as he writes, "Be of firm heart, and do all that is required for the service of our lord the king and for the good and safekeeping of all those lands, for in case that God requires any other thing of my lord and brother the king, thanks be to God we have a lord and king in his son the prince, my lord and my nephew, whom I intend to obey and guard and serve and have for my king and my lord. And since I am here in Toledo together with the prelates and grandees and knights of the realm and the representatives of the cities and towns, orders will very soon be given for the ordering of the things necessary and fit for the conduct of the war. . . ." But this letter, signed by the Infante, does not end here, for there is a postscript which adds the following: "Moreover, know that after this letter was written, our lord the king made his will very fittingly, so that with the help of God the realm might remain in peace and order. I the Constable. Diego López. Juan de Velasco."[5]

This long paragraph shows us many things. On the one hand, the existence of the offer of the Castilian crown to Don Ferdinand, for there can be no other explanation of the Infante's insistence on declaring that if his brother died, they had a king in his son, whom he was prepared to obey, guard, serve, and have for his king. If there had not been such a conspiracy there would have been no need for this excess of assurance regarding Ferdinand's loyalty to the king and his son, precisely during Henry III's last hours. On the other hand, it is clear that this offer was made previous to his death, a fact also demonstrated by the insistence of Don Ferdinand's words. And to all this we must add Ferdinand's attitude of following faithfully the procedure established by Castilian law. The postscript and its signers give us further proof, for they indicate that the king made his will "very fittingly," which presupposes their knowledge and approval. And to make proof even more positive, we can see that the first signer, knowing the terms of Henry III's will and the Infante's intentions as stated in this letter, was none other than the constable Ruy López Dávalos, one of the executors named by Don Henry in his will and the person to whom the offer made to Don Ferdinand of the crown of Castile is attributed; the other two signers are precisely the persons to whom the monarch had entrusted the guardianship and possession of his son. If the plan had been the opposite one, this letter would never have been written, nor would the three nobles have added the final lines of this extremely valuable document.

And if these arguments were not sufficient, there are other documents which fully confirm it. A letter from Don Ferdinand, whose purpose was to assure the lives and property of the Jews of Murcia against any attempt at violence or robbery, was also dated in Toledo on December 25, but after Henry's death, which "was today, Saturday, on Christmas Day, and I with the prelates and counts and *ricos omes* and knights and squires and representatives of the cities and towns who are here in this city of Toledo swore the oath and raised as king the Prince Don John, my lord and my nephew."[6] A third letter, also written in Toledo on

December 26, was the means by which the Infante announced that he had been appointed as guardian and regent for John II, jointly with the queen Doña Catalina, and ordered all the cities and towns of Castile to take the necessary measures to prevent any disturbance of public order or any change in the government of the cities.[7]

These three documents, so closely linked in both chronology and intent, make perfectly clear that the counsel to Don Ferdinand mentioned in the chronicles really did exist. But the offer was made previous to Henry III's death, for John II's succession was already assured before his father's demise through a personal decision of his uncle the Infante Don Ferdinand; a decision which corresponds to a character, a mode of being, firmly maintained both before and after this event, and throughout his life.

To all this we may add the Infante's personal declaration, made two years later, when he offered the Castilian kingdoms his justification for the differences between him and his co-regent in the guardianship of John II: "As soon as the said king died, I, with all the aforesaid prelates and counts and *ricos omes* and knights who were there, swore the oath with all due solemnity for my lord and my nephew the king Don John, as was only right, placing his standards on his *alcázar* in the said city of Toledo."[8]

An eyewitness, Álvar García de Santa María, tells us: "A great throng entered the church of Santa María, making great moan for the king Don Henry, who it seems had just died, and then the said Infante mounted on a mule and took the royal standard in his hand and passed through the city of Toledo, and he and those who went with him calling out in a great voice: Castile, Castile, for the king Don John. And he saying: My lords, if until now you have been faithful, be faithful from this day forward and loyal to my lord and nephew the king Don John. And after he had passed through the city with the standard, he ordered it to be placed on the said *alcázar*."[9]

Pérez de Guzmán, in the short biography he gives of Don Ferdinand in his *Generaciones y Semblanzas*,[10] also repeats this account and, with full knowledge of the event, places all these happenings as having occurred before Henry III's death, "and as he was tempted and induced by some grandees of the realm, that since the king his brother being gravely ill could not fitly reign or govern, that he should take charge of the government; but he never consented to it, leaving to the will and disposition of Our Lord the governing of the kingdom as well as all that which pertained to his person, preferring to await the solution God would give to both matters, rather than any disposition he himself might make, for it would have been done with scandal and by force." We consider, therefore, that this question is solved and that there can be no doubt whatever about it.

THE INFANTE

The second son of John I and his wife, Doña Leonor de Aragón, Don Ferdinand was born in Medina del Campo in November, 1380. López de Ayala's *Crónica*[11] gives the date as the twenty-seventh, feast day of San Facundo, but according to a letter from the Infante himself it was really November 28.[12]

From 1390, the year of his father's death, to November 14, 1401, birth date of the Infanta Doña María, the first child of Henry III and Doña Catalina of Lancaster, he was the heir to the throne of Castile. After that date he continued to be an effective helper to the monarch, aiding him in the affairs of government, to the point that when Henry III's health prevented him from personally carrying on the affairs of state, it was Don Ferdinand, a fervent defender of the monarchical idea, who took over and directed Castilian policies. Particularly in the year 1406, there was a period during which the Infante's intervention was continuous, and although there were no innovations in the plans marked out by his brother, there can be no doubt of the effectiveness of his efforts. An example is what happened in the Cortes of Toledo, where he succeeded in getting an authorization from the representatives to freely augment the subsidy granted for the war in Granada, if there should be need for it, without having to recall the Cortes specifically for the purpose.

The political circumstances through which Castile had passed offered him an advantageous marriage. During the turbulent years of Henry III's minority, one of the nobles who produced the greatest unrest in the unstable regency was Don Fadrique de Trastámara, duke of Benavente, a restless and ambitious man. His political position as John I's brother, his economic strength, with vast properties everywhere in Castile, the protection of his sister Leonor, queen of Navarre, and of other nobles, carried a great deal of weight during the first years of Don Henry's minority. Using the argument that, having been betrothed to the Infanta Doña Beatriz of Portugal, the second wife of John I, he had lost a kingdom when the marriage had not taken place, he considered, and almost demanded, a marriage to Doña Leonor de Alburquerque, daughter of Count Don Sancho, one of Henry II's brothers, whose extensive domains had earned her the sobriquet of *la rica hembra*. Hence Don Fadrique lusted to add his cousin's colossal fortune to his own domains of Benavente, which would have meant a considerable increase in his position and his decisive influence in the government of Castile.

It was Don Pedro Tenorio, archbishop of Toledo, who, by agreement with the council of regency and in order to prevent the execution of this plan of the duke of Benavente, but without having to give an official denial to Don Fadrique's plan, arranged Doña Leonor's marriage to the Infante Don Ferdinand, thus preventing a vast increase in the duke of Benavente's power to the detriment of the monarchy and Henry III's council of regency.[13] This marriage was not to take place at the time; it was decided to wait until Don Henry attained the age of fourteen, and with it his coming of age and the beginning of his reign in Castile; for by the terms of the treaty of Bayonne, to assure the position of Catalina of Lancaster it had been agreed that if Henry died before being crowned, Don Ferdinand would marry her.[14]

Doña Leonor Urraca "was then the lady of best inheritance to be found in Spain," for besides being countess of Alburquerque she held the seigniory of Haro, Briones, Cerezo, Belorado, Ledesma, Codosera, Alzagala, Alconchel, Medellín, Alconétar,

Villalón, Urueña, and other lesser towns. Don Ferdinand was to add his own possessions to these. At the Cortes of Guadalajara in 1390, John I made public his plans to leave a legacy to his son Ferdinand, and that "it was his wish to grant him, and he gave him, the seigniory of Lara, which the King Don John had as an inheritance from the side of his mother the Queen Doña Juana, who was grandaughter to Doña Juana de Lara, mother of Don Juan Núñez de Lara, and that the said Don Juan Núñez de Lara had not left a legitimate heir. And that on that day he gave him arms for a scutcheon, on the right-hand half a castle and a lion, for his legitimate son, and on the other side the arms of the king of Aragon from the queen Doña Leonor, his mother, who was daughter to the king of Aragon; and on the orle of the scutcheon cauldrons for the seigniory of Lara. And further, he said that he gave him the town and castle of Peñafiel, since it had come from his grandfather Don John, son of the Infante Don Manuel, and that he should inherit it through the queen Doña Juana his mother, who was daughter to the said Don Juan Manuel; and he said that he made the said Infante Don Ferdinand duke of Peñafiel; and to show that this was so, he took a chaplet of pearls and set it on his head. He further said that he gave him the town of Mayorga, and made him count of that place; and that he gave him the town of Cuéllar, and the town and castle of San Esteban de Gormaz, and that he gave him the town and castle of Castrojeriz; and that he ordered that he should have from him 400,000 *maravedís*[15] every year for his estate. . . . And the king also said that as he was giving Castrojeriz and San Esteban de Gormaz to the Infante Don Ferdinand, that he wished him to have also, when the duchess of Lancaster came to die, the towns of Medina and Olmedo, which she had of him for life, and that they should be for the Infante Don Ferdinand, and that the Infante should then give up Castro-jeriz and San Esteban de Gormaz."[16]

Years later Henry III was to confirm his brother's possession of these properties, beginning with the seigniory of Lara and continuing with the duchy of Peñafiel, the county of Mayorga and the towns of Paredes de Nava, Olmedo, Medina del Campo and its surrounding lands, Cuéllar, and other lesser towns: a donation which permitted the formation of a vast seigniory, the greatest in Spain, and rich revenues which Don Ferdinand was always to hold ready to assist the Crown.[17] It is known that during the two campaigns he waged against Granada during his regency, he spent large sums out of his own funds either to maintain his own forces or to pay the wage-lists of the royal army.

Álvar García de Santa María and Fernán Pérez de Guzmán coincide in many of the accurate strokes with which they sketch Don Ferdinand's physical portrait; or rather, they repeat each other's most telling adjectives. Both point out that he was "very handsome, with a calm and benign expression;" both also repeat the impression of his great religious feeling, chastity, and uprightness. They describe him as rather tall and well formed, slender, with a pink-and-white complexion; well-rounded legs, cheeks slightly full, and "very beautiful eyes, a little bloodshot, his hair neither fair nor dark, but rather lighter than chestnut color."

Apart from his physical appearance, he is described as "speaking slowly and softly, and although in all his acts he was slow and unhurried, he was so patient and forbearing that it seemed there was no perturbation of passion or wrath in him; but he was a prince of great discretion, who did all his deeds with good and ripe deliberation."

All his acts of government at the head of Castilian affairs as regent of John II, both before and after he was king of Aragon, are praised without exception by contemporary historians. Prudent, just, upright, conscientious, frank, humble, gentle, forbearing, patient, loyal, active, faithful, obedient, and humane are the adjectives applied to him by Pérez de Guzmán and Álvar García de Santa María.

But he was also accused of greed, especially for his active maneuvers to obtain the grand masterships of Alcántara and Santiago for his sons Sancho and Henry. Pérez de Guzmán rejects this accusation, considering that it was a common thing for those who attained power to appropriate as many honors, offices, and vassals as they could. Álvar García, however, maintains the accusation in spite of the friendly feeling and affection he had for Don Ferdinand's person, although perhaps he was influenced by later events, when the pernicious results of the intervention and ambitions of the Infantes of Aragon came to light. The chronicler tells us that he was "very covetous of realms and honours and lands for himself and his sons," though he does recognize that "he labored much and did great deeds, but no riches could suffice to carry them out, and he was always in debt; the lands he held in Castile, as well as the fees which his guardianship brought him in Castile, came to more than clxxx [180] thousand florins, and he gave in lands and subsidies more than cc [200] thousand florins, so that he was always in need and his personal jewels in pawn."[18]

THE INFANTES OF ARAGON

There is no doubt that Don Ferdinand procured a preponderant role in Castilian political life for his sons, with the idea that at his death they would succeed him and would occupy the same position of proximity to the monarch that he held, as protector of the royal power and one step above the higher nobility, protectors of the monarchy and in fact carrying on the government of the Castilian kingdoms; that is, an intermediate step between the king and the nobles, based on a broad economic foundation and with strong forces and fortresses scattered all over Castile, from which his sons could not be dislodged if they continued to be closely united.

This idea was the basis of the Infante's plan to give two of his sons—not, however, the eldest two—the grand masterships of Alcántara and Santiago. But, anticipating immediate criticism, Don Ferdinand tried to justify himself in advance against any possible accusation. When Don Fernando Rodríguez de Villalobos, grand master of Alcántara, died in 1408, the Infante decided that his son Don Sancho should succeed him. He called Don Sancho de Rojas, bishop of Palencia, and told him that in former times the kings had granted seigniories and privileges to the sons of Infantes, giving them inheritances on a scale worthy of their state and social position. Henry III's premature death and the fact that his nephew was not yet of age, together with the oath he and Doña Catalina had sworn not to dispose of anything belonging to the Crown, made it impossible for him to assure his sons' future. On the other hand, all the towns and villages with which the royal power customarily rewarded and benefited its subjects and relatives were at that time given over to *ricos hombres* and knights, and nothing was left except the concession of some royal revenues, which would represent a serious loss to the Crown and which he consequently could not assign.

This line of reasoning was the one Don Ferdinand used to explain his intention to the bishop of Palencia; his intention was to take advantage of the opportunity offered by the vacancy in the grand mastership of Alcántara, which he believed would satisfy a legitimate aspiration without prejudicing the royal revenues. Hence his declaration that "I intend to give them an inheritance with as little sin as may be." To soften possible criticism, he added that if his son were named grand master of Alcántara he would spend all the revenues of the mastership on the war with Granada during his son's minority. Don Sancho de Rojas' acumen, of which he was later to give abundant proof, would suffice to assure the candidacy of Don Ferdinand's son without great difficulties. Don Ferdinand's good relations with Benedict XIII would also help to obtain papal dispensation for the fact that Don Sancho was not yet of age.

Greater difficulties appeared in the matter of obtaining the grand mastership of Santiago. Though there were some resentments and veiled objections to Don Sancho's appointment, the mastership of Santiago represented an office which was not only representative but to which extraordinary economic power was attached. The importance of herding, fundamental basis of the Castilian economy, and the fact that the order was one of the great livestock powers, gave its grand master a decisive role, even though so far none of them had intervened actively in Castilian politics; to it were added its numerous commanderies, revenues, and military forces distributed all over Castile, which supported the considerable power and influence attainable by its grand masters.

When Don Lorenzo Suárez de Figueroa, grand master of Santiago, died in 1409, Don Ferdinand wrote to all the commanders of the order recommending the appointment of his son Henry. Since Don García Fernández de Villagarcía, commander-in-chief of Castile, also aspired to the grand mastership, the Infante had to use all the power and influence he wielded as regent, as well as the good offices of the commander-in-chief of Leon, of the constable Ruy López Dávalos, and of his high chancellor in order to attain his ends. At the same time he requested from Benedict XIII both the direct appointment and the waiver of the age clause. Once the Infante Don Henry was elected, he received the habit in Becerril in the presence of his father, who very shortly thereafter was obliged to choke off the open rebellion and indignant protest of the commander-in-chief of Castile. The good offices of Doña Beatriz, widow of John I, the use of large sums of money, and promises of future favors quieted down the commander Fernández de Villamayor and the other commanders who had also expressed their dissatisfaction with the manner in which the Infante Don Henry's appointment had been carried out.

Since both Infantes were minors, the administration and governance of both orders remained in Don Ferdinand's hands. Thus he was able not only to assure his sons' economic and political future but also to assure his sons' economic and political ideal, owing to the fact that the former grand master of Santiago had not always been sympathetic to his plans. A complement to this policy was concession to the grand master of Santiago of the right to collect the Mesta's taxes and the *servicio y montazgo*[19] taxes, to be turned over to the Crown. As Vicens Vives points out, this put an enormous fortune into the Infante's hands.

Don Ferdinand had other aspirations for his eldest son, even before fate set him on the throne of Aragon and assured the succession of his son Alfonso. It had been Henry III himself who, grateful for the aid and loyalty given him by his brother, and also having in mind the need for his son to have a protector within the family, had arranged in his will for the marriage of his brother's eldest son to his daughter María, marchioness of Villena. And Don Alfonso, as lord of Lara and heir to his father's fortune, was acting as early as 1408 both in the Royal Council and in the Cortes of Castile as a representative of the nobility. Later, after he had been declared prince of Gerona, he was to take part with his father in the government of Aragon, as real executor and capable lieutenant of Ferdinand I's orders and policies in Aragon. But this did not prevent Don Ferdinand from carrying out the terms of his brother's will, and the wedding of Alfonso and María was celebrated in Valencia on June 10, 1415. The Aragonese succession prevented the Infanta from bringing the marquisate of Villena as her dowry, and its place was taken by the delivery of 200,000 gold *doblas mayores*, and possession of the strongholds of Madrigal, Roa, Sepúlveda, Arévalo, and Dueñas held as security until the sum was paid.[20]

This family policy of Don Ferdinand of Antequera also had its public side, in relation to his son John. Though in principle he was destined to inherit his mother's vast possessions, the turn of events made Don Ferdinand change his mind. In a meeting at Mallén, in 1414, he arranged the marriage of his son John to Blanche of Navarre, heiress of Charles III the Noble and future queen of Navarre; and since his brother Alfonso had been proclaimed prince of Gerona, the family patrimony passed into Don John's hands, while his mother's properties were turned over to his brother Henry. Thus Don John became heir to Navarre, lord of Lara, duke of Peñafiel and Montblanc, count of Mayorga, and held the seigniories of Medina del Campo, Cuéllar, Castrojeriz, Olmedo, Villalón, Haro, Belorado, Briones, Cerezo, etc. Don Henry was grand master of Santiago, count of Alburquerque, and had the seigniories of Ledesma, Salvatierra, Miranda, Montemayor, Codosera, Alzagala, Alconchel, Medellín, Alconétar, Urueña, Alba de Liste, etc. The marquisate of Villena was added to this list somewhat later, though not in a very lasting form, by his marriage to Doña Catalina, sister of John II.

Don Ferdinand did not intervene in the marriages of his son Henry to the Infanta Doña Catalina, of John II to his daughter María in 1418, or of his daughter Leonor, queen of Portugal after 1430 as a result of her marriage to Don Duarte. But these marriages must have been the result of his political ideals. The Infante Don Peter did not receive an inheritance in Castile—he died at the siege of Naples in 1438 after having taken part in the Castilian civil war—but undoubtedly one of Don Ferdinand's plans was that his brothers, from their positions in Aragon, Navarre, and Castile, would provide him with a position suitable to his rank.[21]

This family policy of Don Ferdinand's, ably carried forward throughout his regency, both before and during the time he was king of Aragon, was, Suárez Fernández believes, the result of a tenacious and prolonged effort; and if it did not bear fruit it was because of Don Ferdinand's sons' lack of unity. Suárez Fernández thinks that "the first ten years of John II's reign represented a step backward, for a government made up of the king's relatives had been established. Ferdinand's hope was that while his sons kept on being united, no one could govern without them. The possession of foreign, though Peninsular, kingdoms gave Henry, Sancho, and Peter—who were entirely Castilian—a guarantee of effective aid. The installation of scions of their dynasty on every throne in the Peninsula—a course leading to Spanish unity—meant that very strong control was exercised on the country as a whole. The Infantes of Aragon were to represent a real epoch in Spanish history, and not only in the poet's nostalgic expression. In the interplay of institutions they were destined to change the Royal Council into the supreme organ of government, quite outside the king's will in the matter."[22]

But this plan and these policies of Don Ferdinand's were all projected toward an immediate future, for after his death. While he lived no one could trouble him, nor was there the slightest possibility of danger, though there might have been some attempts to weaken his political position. Thus he was able to maintain the regency of Castile after being declared king of Aragon, and death surprised him on the way to Castile, where he was going to stamp out some attempts at resistance which had begun to crystallize around the queen, Doña Catalina.

THE REGENCY: 1407–AUGUST, 1408

An unpublished document of extraordinary interest helps us to understand fully the disagreement produced between the regents of John II in regard to the form in which the governing of Castile was to be handled. This document, which verifies and completes the information given us in the chronicles, is a written report from Don Ferdinand of Antequera to the city of Murcia, in which he explains in detail the differences which had arisen between him and his co-regent, and the reasons why it had not been possible to adopt a common criterion or come to a mutual understanding. These causes justified the energetic measures he had adopted to keep this antagonism from continuing and to avoid Castile's remaining without an effective government or a lasting set of policies.

The Infante tells how he had proclaimed his nephew king of Castile as soon as Henry III died, and his decision to move from Toledo to Segovia, where the king and his mother were, in order to carry out his official recognition as king of Castile. He immediately goes on to describe the differences he had had with Doña Catalina, which hindered the close cooperation he had wished for.

In accordance with the terms of Henry III's will, the custody and upbringing of the young king were to be held jointly by Diego López de Stúñiga, chief justice of Castile, and Juan de Velasco, the high chamberlain, and in addition Don Pablo de Santa María, bishop of Cartagena, who was to be in charge of his education. And in this respect the will made special mention of John II's guardians, designated as regents during his minority, saying that, "in the possession and custody of the said prince . . . I order and command them not to interfere. . . ."

This arrangement was precisely the first to be objected to by Doña Catalina. As soon as she learned of her husband's death, she wrote an emotional letter to her brother-in-law in answer to the one the Infante had sent her, in which she expressed her sorrow and told him of her intention to consider him as her guide and elder brother, hoping in her turn that he would protect and defend her honor and estate, and declaring herself ready to follow his counsels. But when Doña Catalina learned of the clauses in her husband's will, her attitude was to change.

On January 1, 1407, Don Ferdinand left Toledo accompanied by all the grandees, prelates, and representatives, carrying with him Don Henry's will, and proceeded to Segovia to make the official recognition of John II. García Fernández de Córdoba and Fray Martín, the queen mother's confessor, came out to meet him, and in her name expressed the sorrow that she felt and her plea not to be deprived of the possession and upbringing of her son, for there was no one with more reason and right to have custody of the king than his own mother. A short time later, when Don Ferdinand was resting from his journey in Torreferreros, Don John, bishop of Segovia, appeared before him with a second letter of persuasion from Doña Catalina. His embassy had the same purpose, that of imploring the Infante to let her continue to have possession of her son, offering in exchange to renounce the regency. Don Ferdinand could not give a definite reply at the moment, but could only beg her to have patience and tell her that as soon as he arrived in Segovia they could jointly adopt measures which would be most appropriate for all.

The retinue arrived in Segovia on January 7, and as Diego López de Stúñiga and Juan de Velasco were among its members, the queen, fearing that the clause in the will calling for delivery of her son would be carried out, ordered the guard at the gates reinforced and refused to allow any of them to enter the city. This rebuff, the first of innumerable such acts that Don Ferdinand had to suffer from the queen, was received with dignity by the Infante. He ordered his people lodged in the outskirts of the city, while he went to stay in the monastery of San Francisco, and from there began dealings with the queen so that she would permit entrance to the city to the representatives of the Cortes, trying to convince her of the damage she was doing her son with this attitude, since he still had not been recognized as king of Castile. The chronicler tells us that he had great difficulty in making the queen change her mind and recognize the desirability of doing as her brother-in-law advised. The gates of the city were opened, and the Cortes and representatives of the cities carried out the recognition of John II as king of Castile.[23]

There were two reasons why Don Ferdinand wanted to end these disagreements as soon as possible. He feared that delay might give rise to the formation of factions and to a division of Castile, which would usher in a period of anarchy with grave consequences, for these were decisive moments for the future government of Castile; and on the other hand he was concerned about the war with Granada, which had been declared officially, and because the approach of spring permitted no delay in the necessary preparations, both to wage the proposed campaign and to place the frontier under suitable conditions of defense. And he must also have realized that to carry on the war in Granada would mean that he could order the nobles to go to Andalusia, thus giving him sufficient time to make his regency secure.

When John II's recognition had been accomplished, and while the official documents were being prepared for the Cortes to proclaim him king of Castile and designate Doña Catalina and Don Ferdinand as regents, the Infante used all his talent and powers of persuasion to convince Juan de Velasco and Diego López de Stúñiga not to exercise their right to physical custody of the king. The *Crónica* itself says that it took him several days to accomplish this agreement, that the two nobles argued bitterly against renouncing their right, and that only in the last instance, after many negotiations and an advance indemnity of 12,000 gold florins contributed by the queen, did they finally give their consent. Thus, though Doña Catalina succeeded in her purpose and had reason to be grateful to her brother-in-law, the nobles lost a valuable hostage with whom they could have put major obstacles in the way of either of the two regents.

After the regency was set up, Doña Catalina and Don Ferdinand began to rule jointly with the Royal Council. From the very beginning of their activities, the affairs of state were not carried on in the way which the circumstances warranted. The unstable and wavering temperament of the queen influenced the Royal Council; and she, taking the advice of some persons who were attempting to hinder a normal understanding between the regents, maintained an attitude of resistance to her brother-in-law. The *Crónica* tells us that "some bad servants, the queen's as well as the Infante's, who were displeased by the harmony between the queen and the Infante, tried to further their own interests, and sowed so many suspicions between them that they did not trust one another." As the persons most likely to benefit from the regents' drawing apart, the document to which we refer—reflecting the Infante Don Ferdinand's opinions—singles out Juan de Velasco, Diego López de Stúñiga, Doña Leonor López de Córdoba, the bishops of Cuenca, Sigüenza, and Mondoñedo, and Doctor Pedro Sánchez.

Since Don Ferdinand's attention was on the Granada campaign, he made no move for the time being, though "no matter how much the Infante tried to discover who were doing this, he was never able to find out for certain." Nor did Don Ferdinand wish to remind his sister-in-law of her promise to give up the regency in case she was permitted to continue having custody of her son, an offer which she personally repeated to him in Segovia on several occasions. For the moment he was also unwilling to exacerbate the disagreement between them, fearing a rupture which might become permanent and of which the nobles would take advantage, for according to Henry III's instructions, "There shall be two guardians of the said prince my son, to rule over the said realms and seigniories; and because they are two and no more, some divisions and disagreements may arise between them on some matters, so that one of them may have one opinion and the other another, and both of them may not be in agreement; therefore, I order and command that when one of said divisions and disagreements arises between them, that the members of my Council be summoned, and the opinion of the one of them with whom the greater number of the Council shall agree, that shall be done and fulfilled, just as if both of the said guardians had commanded it."

Differences continued between the two regents, and there were few agreements which could be adopted. They did manage to agree about the assignments of the companies of soldiers corresponding to each—three hundred lances to the queen for John II's bodyguard, and two hundred for the Infante—and in holding a public audience on Fridays in the bishop of Segovia's residence, each taking thirty men-at-arms. But there was no decision on what was to be done about the war with Granada, for the chronicler tells us, "And the Infante, being thus greatly irritated by the attitude that was being shown to him, and that the proper measures were not being taken, in the governing of the realms as well as in the war that had been begun against the Moors, was much disturbed and did not know how to remedy the matter."

This state of things produced first discontentment and finally a protest from the knights who were serving as *fronteros mayores*, for three months' pay was owing to their troops; the admiral Alonso Enríquez wrote about the poor condition of his fleet and the need for making repairs, which he could not do for lack of money. These protests decided the Infante to demand of Doña Catalina that she give or advance money to him from the royal treasury, and the queen was forced to agree in view of the Infante's attitude and the seriousness of the situation. An estimate was made of what the payment of these expenses would necessitate, and she turned over twenty million *maravedís*, on condition they be returned once the royal revenues and the subsidy granted by the Cortes were collected.

Another result of this disconcerting attitude of Doña Catalina's, influenced by her private councillors and her antagonism to the Infante, was that the centralizing measures adopted by Henry III were reversed. One of these was to return to their posts all the *oidores* of the *Audiencia Real* whom he had stripped of their positions, with the sole exception of Doctor Juan González de Acevedo, because of the abuses they had committed in their posts. Much the same thing happened in matters affecting the government of the cities, at least in regard to Córdoba, Seville, and Murcia.

The substitution of *corregidores* nominated by the king for the former *alcaldes* had not only reestablished order in the cities by causing the disappearance of factional agitation and of control by certain groups of nobles and *hidalgos*, but also established the monarchy's direct control there. Through a decision of Doña Catalina, who once more allowed herself to be swayed by the self-seeking counsels she was given and by her desire to maintain an attitude different from that of her brother-in-law, the *corregidores* were relieved of their duties and the cities regained the autonomy they had lost.

A new difficulty arose when the time came for Don Ferdinand, as commander-in-chief of the army, to march to the Granada frontier. This caused a repetition of Doña Catalina's contradictory behavior, accepting a solution one day only to oppose it the next. She feared that if one of the conditions of Henry III's will were carried out, ordering the division of Castile into two provinces if the regents should have to be separated, her brother-in-law's position would be too greatly strengthened. Therefore she decided to go to some place near the frontier, thus avoiding the necessity of dividing the government. The Infante accepted this decision in the hope that Doña Catalina would at last adopt a reasonable point of view beneficial to her son's monarchy. But the Royal Council was opposed to the queen's departure, in view of John II's tender age and the danger involved in his being close to the frontier.

This decision involved an obligatory division of Castilian territory into two provinces, as well as the division of the Royal Council, Chancery, accounting department, etc. This gave rise to a new series of contradictory actions by the queen regent, and to intrigues by some councillors eager to have a hand in the administration of the Infante's province. But none could make up his mind to intervene, perhaps because Don Ferdinand was suspicious of several of them. Only two, obliged to do so by their social rank, took part in the campaign against Granada under Don Ferdinand's orders; they were Juan de Velasco and Diego López de Stúñiga.

Thus a period of apparent tranquillity was achieved in relations between the two regents. This was the period between April 13, 1407, and early January, 1408, when Don Ferdinand returned to Guadalajara. But it was only apparent, for all kinds of plots and intrigues against Don Ferdinand were brewing around Doña Catalina during this time, to the point that the queen mother, from the contradictory and vacillating policy she had maintained up until then, passed to direct accusation against her brother-in-law.

On his return from the Granada frontier, when he was still in Córdoba, Don Ferdinand received information that the calumnies against him had increased during his absence, and that Doña Catalina's complaints of him had been made public, with the clear intention of creating an atmosphere hostile to his administration. This information was repeated while he was on the road, and its truth could be observed as soon as he reached Guadalajara. What he learned was that certain of the queen's partisans were advising her privately, without consulting the Infante at all; that she was granting privileges and money payments to certain knights, and receiving oaths from them that they would continue in her service and faithfully carry out her orders; and that when Doña Catalina left Segovia she had demanded an oath from its city councillors that they would not allow anyone to enter the city without her express order, no matter what her brother-in-law might decide upon. As a culmination of all this, and as confirmation of Doña Catalina's attitude, the Infante was unable to meet her and deal with the affairs of the kingdom in the first few days after his return to Guadalajara.

On her side, Doña Catalina made known her complaints regarding some of the decisions the Infante had adopted in the province administered by him. We know what these accusations were: that when Don Ferdinand was in Seville he had ordered Pedro de Monsalve to mint money of less value than that struck by Henry III, without her consent and approval, and that he had handed over certain amounts of money and granted various favors to many persons, under the pretext of paying wages, by attributing to them more men than they actually had.

Don Ferdinand defended himself against these accusations. He stated that because of the scarcity of coinage, and by previous agreement with the royal councillors who were with him in Andalusia, he had ordered Pedro de Monsalve to strike currency in order to pay the wages of the army fighting on the frontier. The order had been to mint coins of the same metal content as those issued during Henry III's lifetime, and he had informed Doña Catalina of this by letter; but when he did not receive an answer and found it necessary to pay the soldiers' wages, he had then ordered Pedro de Monsalve to mint coins in accordance with the Council's decision; he later received a reply from the queen stating her dissatisfaction, and though he could have continued to do so without her approval, because of both the Royal Council's agreement and the fact that the mint was in Seville and thus within his administrative province, he had ordered Pedro de Monsalve to stop minting in order to avoid further unpleasantness.

He was also accused of minting coins of lesser value than those made by Henry III, and to this accusation Don Ferdinand replied that he wished justice to be done. If Pedro de Monsalve had adulterated the minting he should be punished, but if he had not, the queen, on her side, should turn over the authors of the libel to the law. So that this imputation could be cleared up, the Infante ordered the coinage tested, and it was found to be of equal metal content with that minted during Henry III's lifetime. With this proof in hand, he asked the queen to punish the authors of the libel, but she refused to give their names or allow them to be tried.

Don Ferdinand denied the accusation that he had given unjustified sums to certain knights, replying that it was an insult to think any such thing about his person. He explained that he had made two distributions of wages, overseen by officers of the king and made when some companies had already deserted for lack of food and because their wages had not been paid. These distributions had been protested by many commanders, who grumbled that such a thing had never been done in Castile. In fact, one of those who had advised him not to make the second distribution was

Juan de Velasco, and that the more he had insisted on the contrary course, the more determined the Infante had been to carry it out. He had not been able to gather all the troops together, but most of them were present, and he had had to pay the wages in accordance with the oaths made by the respective captains, since it had not been possible to hold a complete muster.

To these concrete replies Don Ferdinand added the statement that if he had committed some error—though he firmly believed that this was not the case—that no charge be made against him; for in addition to the absence of intent was the circumstance that in the agreement of Segovia, before his departure for the frontier, it had been stipulated that neither of the regents should pay any attention to what might be said about the other, and that when they met again they would clarify and explain the differences which might have arisen. As the queen did not accept the Infante's explanations, and insisted that judges be named to give a verdict on the truth of those accusations, Don Ferdinand, in order to avoid a total break and even though it might be injurious to his person, was forced to accept the procedure that two judges, one from each side, should examine the facts. The bishops of Palencia and Cuenca[24] were named, and their verdict could only be favorable to him.

But the matter did not end there, for the regent's renewed attempts to reach a personal agreement with the queen always encountered Doña Catalina's refusal to grant an interview; her advisers feared that an understanding between the two might arise, and that in consequence Don Ferdinand's sensible view would prevail. The Infante tried very hard not to let these disagreements spread to the whole court, especially since the Cortes was being held in Guadalajara and the nobles, prelates, and representatives of the cities were all present; if these were to take the side of one or the other regent, disunity would be produced in all the Castilian kingdoms. The result was that when the representatives received a petition for extraordinary subsidies, they made public the heavy taxes burdening the people and asked that part of the royal revenues and the monarch's own treasure be spent on the war. Don Ferdinand beat down this feeble attempt, succeeding in obtaining a grant for the sixty million *maravedís* he had requested to continue the campaign against Granada.

Political events and the attitude of the king of Granada combined to favor Don Ferdinand's position. At about that time the Moslems of Granada laid siege to Alcaudete, taking advantage of the small number of Christian troops deployed along the frontier. Because the siege of this stronghold lasted for five days, and the divided forces of the king of Granada were defeated only by the intrepidity and resolution of the small frontier forces, the news which reached Castile was alarming. The knights and representatives of the Andalusian cities in the Cortes, indignant over what they felt to be an abandonment, made a written request to John II's regents, stressing the great shame represented by the circumstance that Alcaudete had been besieged for so many days without receiving aid, and that there were not adequate forces on the frontier for its proper defense, demanding that soldiers be sent to Andalusia and making the regents responsible for the possible consequences of that abandonment.

The queen and her councillors quickly changed their policy and, in agreement with Don Ferdinand's petitions, gave orders that the grand masters of the military orders, the constable, Don Pedro Ponce, the *adelantado* Perafán de Ribera, and Pedro López de Ayala were to set out with 1,500 lances to reinforce the armies on the Granada frontier.

This decision did not suffice for the regents to arrive at an agreement and the maintenance of a common policy, and since according to Henry III's will disputes were to be solved by a majority of votes in the Council, and the queen had a larger number of councillors on her side than the Infante, the Council merely voted what the queen mother wanted despite Don Ferdinand's arguments and petitions. One of the chief agreements adopted, over the Infante's protests, was that of not continuing the war with Granada, and this was followed by the granting of truces for eight months. These events are also noted by the chronicler, and "whenever the Infante had something to say in the administration of the realms, he was immediately contradicted, and what was agreed upon one day was changed the next. And the Infante was amazed by this, and could not find out for certain who was giving such bad counsels to the queen, though he suspected whence this discord had arisen; and so he dissembled, and kept on a straight path, always striving for the service of the king and the queen and the good of these realms."

The granting of the truce had a clear enough motivation. There was no intention of maintaining the advantage involved in continuing hostilities against Granada, but simply of preventing a new division of Castile into two provinces and keeping Don Ferdinand from achieving greater power as commander-in-chief of the army and in sole charge of its administration; for, according to Doña Catalina's advisers, "the Infante was becoming very powerful with the war, and had all the knights at his command, and in the proportion that the power of the Infante waxed, her power waned; and that it was not just that she should suffer this, for she was mother to the king; and with these things they beclouded the resolution of the queen, and things were not done as they should have been done."

This state of affairs lasted until Don Fadrique, count of Trastá-mara, returned to court after having secured the frontier. Since he knew everything that was going on in Andalusia, and could appreciate from that point of view the queen's disconcerting behavior and Don Ferdinand's excessive patience, the count of Trastámara could not resist advising him to seize power, assuring him of support from the armed companies he had in the district. Hence his words, "My lord, I am much amazed that you are willing to suffer the things I am told you suffer and endure, dissembling before some whom you know do not love you; but if you would punish them, my lord, you would do a service to God and to the king my lord and to the queen, and things would go differently from the way they are going now; and if you, my lord, could be certain of who the persons are that are concerned in this, you have only to command, my lord, no matter who they be, and I will seize them."

Don Fadrique did not stop with offering this aid and counsel to Don Ferdinand privately, but made it public. As soon as they learned of the count of Trastámara's decision, two councillors, Juan de Velasco and Diego López de Stúñiga, must have had an uneasy conscience; for after sunset the next day, on the pretext of going out to talk in the country, they left Guadalajara and took refuge in the castle of Hita. That same night they sent the *adelantado* of Galicia, García Sánchez de Arce, and Juan Hurtado de Fondecha to the Infante to explain why they had left, so that he would not be angry with them for going away without taking leave of him. Their explanation was that they had been told that the Infante suspected them of being the cause of his differences with the queen, and as this information was untrue, they had decided to go away so that no one might think they were a barrier to good relations between the regents.

The count of Trastámara's attitude was helpful to all concerned, and especially to Don Ferdinand. Don Fadrique represented a large group of knights, especially those who lived in places near the Granada frontier, who understood the need for an energetic policy which could be implemented only by expelling from the court those persons who were intentionally maintaining disagreement between the regents. This action of Don Fadrique's became the point of departure for a decisive change in John II's regency, for it obliged Don Ferdinand to abandon his excessive caution and to break off energetically the interference of a number of councillors who were seeking their own advantage. The immediate result of the count of Trastámara's attitude was that two of the most important persons on the Council, the high chamberlain and the chief justice of Castile, had voluntarily left the court in advance of possible consequences.

The effects of this, though not immediate, began to be felt very soon. When Doña Catalina learned that Juan de Velasco and Diego López de Stúñiga had gone away, her hostility toward Don Ferdinand grew even more extreme, but since she had been deprived of the counsel of the two absent nobles and her popularity was diminishing, she was also unable to count on the help of her private councillors, who were fearful that the Infante would take steps against them.

At this point there occurred an event of minor importance, but one which at bottom reflected the beginning of the formation of two parties or factions. A quarrel between two youths, Rodrigo de Perea and Diego Pérez Sarmiento, led to an armed clash between two groups in which members of the young men's respective families took part, such as the admiral Alonso Enríquez, the count of Trastámara, and the grand master of Santiago, and in which eight men died.[25] The queen refused to let Don Ferdinand intervene, and gave to the bishop of Palencia the task of making peace and reestablishing order. Don Ferdinand appeared later and in a few well-chosen words seconded Don Sancho de Rojas' action, giving explanations to Don Lorenzo Suárez de Figueroa and expressing regret for his nephew's death, succeeding in making him understand what had happened, so that he would not try to avenge the death.

These events, and the consequences they might have had, decided Don Ferdinand to write to his sister-in-law and explain to her that "these things happened because of the disagreement and lack of understanding between them, and that other and much greater evils might be expected for this reason, and that he implored and begged her as a favor that in the service of God and the king she might be pleased to see him, for he wished to speak to Her Ladyship at length, and show her what bad counsel she was heeding." Private interviews were then to take place between the two regents, and if the desired result were not quickly obtained, it would also be a reason to put an end to that duality of authority which was in no way beneficial to the Crown.

Doña Catalina must have come to these interviews full of suspicion and fear, which her councillors attempted to instill in her so that she would not accede to her brother-in-law's wishes. There were proposals on both sides, although the queen's demands did not concur with the Infante's arguments; but he accepted her conditions for the sake of reaching an agreement. On Don Ferdinand's side it was proposed that he would not spend any sum from the royal treasury under the queen's custody in the *alcázar* of Segovia except in case of extreme necessity, and that both would make efforts that this necessity should not arise; in case there were differences between them, the Royal Council would decide according to the terms of Henry III's will. The Infante was pursuing two purposes with this proposal, which was not accepted by Doña Catalina. One was that if the war with Granada or any other contingency demanded larger than normal expenditures there would always be a reserve to satisfy them temporarily, and the other was that if the royal treasury were placed under fiscal control the queen could not use it freely, and none of her private councillors would be able to obtain any benefit from differences which might arise between the two regents.

Another article proposed by Don Ferdinand was that neither of the two regents could hold private council; that whenever both were in the same city their councils should be joint, and that in case there were private councils each would be obliged to give an account of them and of the names of the councillors who proposed any sort of innovation, appointments, or a decision of any kind; for if their names and the responsibility they assumed were made public, the councillors would try to be prudent in their proposals and advice.

The third article proposed by the Infante had to do with the need for adequate preparation of the army and the fleet during the short space of time represented by the truce; he would take charge of this in order to prevent a repetition of what had occurred, for lack of time, in the previous campaign. The preparations had been made too late and without sufficient resources, and had not obtained all the desired success. Another reason for this petition was the fact that the king of Granada had died, and according to custom this meant that the life and validity of the pacts expired when one of the signers died, so that the frontier was exposed to surprise attack.

Reference was also made to the oaths and promises made by some knights to the queen, to faithfully follow her personal orders; this was contrary to Henry III's will and to the good feeling which ought to exist between the two regents. Don Ferdinand believed that these oaths should disappear, so that the councillors and knights could vote and express their opinions freely, aiding the regents with their knowledge and experience the better to govern the realm.

The agreement was given its finishing touches during the private meeting held between the two regents in the *alcázar* of Guadalajara on June 23. The assurances offered by the Infante momentarily convinced the queen, although he found it necessary to dispel two suspicions still harbored by his sister-in-law. Doña Catalina feared a coup on her return to Segovia, for she had been informed that there were armed forces in the district and that they would attempt to seize her person; she had also been told that the Infante intended to deprive her of the possession and upbringing of the king and to make himself sole regent of Castile.

Don Ferdinand had to use persuasive words to allay her fears, explaining to her that the armed companies in that province were those which had returned from the frontier and were waiting to collect their pay, and that they were there only because their return journey happened to cross that district; though he made no mention of the fact that the commander of those companies was the count of Trastámara, whose attitude a few days previously, ready to act in favor of the Infante, was not easy to forget.

The queen's demands did not stop there, however, for she asked her brother-in-law to grant a letter of surety, signed and sealed with his seal, so that Diego López de Stúñiga and Juan Velasco could return to court without fear of reprisals for having left without his knowledge. Since the flight of these nobles had been caused by the count of Trastámara's threats to seize anyone who advised the queen against the Infante, this request for surety was not made simply because of their departure, but to cover any risk they might run because of their interventions in the queen's private council. Thus the Infante's reply was that both could return to court, that he felt no more than the natural annoyance because they had left without telling him, and that therefore it would not be necessary for him to sign any letter, for he would limit himself merely to reprimanding them in the queen's presence.

For once both regents were in agreement on the most essential points in their difficulties, and the accord was made public on that same day, June 23, in the presence of the royal councillors, bishops, representatives, and notables who were present at court; and at the same time letters were sent to all the cities and towns of Castile to spread the good news.

But after a few days had passed, when Don Ferdinand sent a request to the queen to confirm the ordinances decreed for the governing of Castile, the reply was negative; for Doña Catalina demanded in exchange the letter of surety for Juan de Velasco and Diego López de Stúñiga. This event is reflected in the words of Álvar García: "Those who were trying to produce discord between the queen and the Infante told the queen not to sign those articles unless the Infante were first to give his letter of surety . . . and this was done to keep the discord alive." This time Don Ferdinand's refusal was conclusive. He could not grant such a surety to persons who had no need to ask for it, nor could he permit them such lack of trust in his person; and he added that, were he to grant this surety when there was no cause for it, everyone would believe that the said nobles had good cause to ask for it, and that it would also be a bad example; for in the future any person, no matter how small the cause, would feel justified in asking for such a letter and would then be outside his jurisdiction and prevent him from administering true justice.

If the Infante's patience had a limit, he did not lack the prudence necessary to do things in good order. He convoked the Royal Council to set forth all the acts of the regency since Henry III's death and the reasons why there had not been a common and continuous point of view between them, blaming the queen's private councillors for keeping these differences alive and for perniciously influencing her decisions. The Council's reply was also conclusive: "My lord, if you do not send away these bad counsels that the queen has, no good thing will ever be done." Then the councillors went to talk to the queen to tell her of their agreement and of Don Ferdinand's reasonable attitude, exhorting her to sign the accord made on St. John's Eve which had been made public in their presence. The queen once more refused to sign, and with this reply the councillors returned to Don Ferdinand.

This time the regent's decision was final. Since he could count on the help of the Royal Council, the Cortes, and the larger part of the nobles, he proceeded to the expulsion and exile from the court of the persons "who were and are close to the said lady the queen, who until today have continually tried to foment dissension and discord." These were the bishops of Cuenca, Sigüenza, and Mondoñedo[26] and Dr. Pedro Sánchez. They were ordered to leave the court and not to stay "near the said lady our queen, fomenting and creating discord between her and me, and damaging and hindering the affairs of the realm." Four councillors, together with the two who had already left, Juan de Velasco and Diego López de Stúñiga, who had formed the group most closely allied with Doña Catalina.

Don Ferdinand did not want to carry this coup d'état to an extreme by forcing the departure from court of Doña Leonor López de Córdoba, the friend and closest confidante of Doña Catalina, for he did not wish to make these decrees seem like an action against the queen in his own favor. But although he refused to proceed against her directly, and tried in vain to get the queen to dismiss her, he did make public her greed for wealth, her lamentable interference in all the affairs of government having to do with Doña Catalina, and her capture of posts for her relatives. His declaration to all the kingdoms of Castile in this regard is emphatic: "The said Leonor López has suborned and continues to suborn all those in this realm who have some favor to ask of the said lady our queen ... they are suborned by the said Leonor López, who accepts from them large sums of money and jewels."

The "account ... of what has taken place in the kingdom," sent by Don Ferdinand to all the Castilian cities, and the support given him by the Royal Council and the Cortes, spelled Doña Leonor's eclipse, the end of her intimate status, and her prompt departure from the court. But though an attempt was made to soften the accusation against the queen of lack of capacity to continue heading the regency, the contents of the "account" are also conclusive and imply the queen's removal from the tasks of government.[27]

After Juan de Velasco and Diego López de Stúñiga had left the court voluntarily, the bishops of Cuenca, Sigüenza, and Mondoñedo and Dr. Pedro Sánchez had been exiled, and Doña Leonor intimidated, Don Ferdinand's authority increased, and from that time onward his personality asserted itself without contradiction. Doña Catalina, deprived of her chief advisers, was incapable of competing with her brother-in-law on her own and was relieved of the tasks of government. Though she is mentioned officially, she no longer intervenes in public affairs, and her figure is clouded over for a few years. It is more than probable that the threat of depriving her of the king's custody and upbringing was held over her.

And so this troubled period in John II's regency, short in time but long in activity, came to an end, spelling Don Ferdinand's victory over a group of courtiers who aspired to the intervention of the nobles in the regency. The victory also meant that John II's minority was a peaceful one, and that the royal power prevailed in it; for Don Ferdinand loved the royal estate for its own sake, even though he believed, to his own advantage, that the monarchy's best defense was government by relatives of the king.

THE REGENCY: 1408–1412

This short period of time has decisive importance in John II's regency for various reasons, among which the conquest of Antequera, Don Ferdinand's election as king of Aragon, and the achievement of personal government by the Infante are important factors; he made clear, through some decrees known to us, his desire to carry out an improvement in the government, strict control to counterbalance the excessive power that had been attained by the Royal Council, and various reforms in the administration of the cities. His intention was to improve city life and correct the abuses which lack of government had produced in all the important towns and cities in the kingdom.

The measures adopted by Don Ferdinand in decreeing exile from the court for those councillors whom he considered to be hostile elements and prejudicial to the good governing of Castile were as effective as timely. Deprived of these persons' cunning counsels, Doña Catalina did not dare to confront either the Royal Council or her brother-in-law, and was unable to adopt any decision to oppose the triumph of her victorious rival.

The queen could count on the effective help of Doña Leonor López, who, because she was the daughter of the grand master Don Martín Pedro López de Córdoba, killed at Carmona because of his total fidelity to Peter I, had managed to gain an extraordinary ascendancy over the granddaughter of that Castilian monarch. Her position and influence in the queen regent's inner circle permitted her not only to bend her desires to her own profit, but to take advantage of her circumstances to accumulate a large fortune by accepting bribes from everyone who wished to obtain a favor from Doña Catalina, and raising her relatives to the most remunerative positions in Castile. The favor she enjoyed from the queen regent, who was pleased to call herself in the letters she wrote her "the Queen, your loyal daughter,"[28] made Doña Leonor the real arbiter of Castile's internal policies for some time.

The public accusation made against her by Don Ferdinand in his "account" ended her position of prominence in the court. We do not know the date, but it must have been soon after Don Ferdinand's coup d'état, for the Crónica tells us that Doña Leonor "was in Córdoba, for she had been ordered by the whole Council to leave the court, since her presence there was of little benefit to the king and the queen." In spite of this she did not lose the friendship of the queen regent, with whom she maintained an active correspondence in the hope that circumstances would change and she would be able to return to court.

We do not have news of her again until 1410. She was in Córdoba, where she probably founded the monastery of San Pedro in which she was eventually buried, when Don Ferdinand, who was engaged in the conquest of Antequera, requested her aid. The length of the siege and the heavy expenses it entailed forced the Infante to ask her for help, begging her to convince Doña Catalina, whose best friend she still was, to turn over to him some sums from the royal treasury to enable him to maintain the siege of Antequera. Doña Leonor did not hesitate to lend assistance to Don Ferdinand, and her letter to the queen advising her to grant the economic aid requested by her brother-in-law was successful. Although many chroniclers have accused Doña Catalina of being miserly, she decided to advance six million *maravedís*, probably as much to grant her friend's request as because she realized that she would be blamed if the siege were lifted for lack of money. These funds were used to pay overdue wages and to continue the siege of the Granadine fortress.

Some time later, when Don Ferdinand was in Cuenca, busy with the defense of his pretensions to the Aragonese throne, he received a letter from Doña Leonor asking his pardon and consent to return to court in Doña Catalina's service. "The Infante was troubled in his mind about this, for she had many times given occasion for the discord that had occurred between the queen and the Infante; and he resolved to write to Doña Leonor López telling her to come to the city of Cuenca where he was." It must have been an effort for Don Ferdinand to make this decision, but he could not overlook the favorable response she had given him when he had asked for economic aid from Doña Catalina.

While Doña Leonor was on her way to Cuenca the queen learned of her journey and of her plan to return to the queen's side; but Doña Catalina had been misinformed, for "they made her believe that her former friend was trying to enter the palace to be an agent of Don Ferdinand close to her person, and that she was entirely in his power."[29] Doña Catalina wrote to her brother-in-law, begging him to make Doña Leonor return to Córdoba, "swearing to him that if Doña Leonor should go to her, she would have her burned." When she arrived in Cuenca and learned from the Infante what the queen regent's decision had been, Doña Leonor, to quote the words of Castro, "was so perturbed that she thought she would die." It was Don Ferdinand himself who advised her to return to Córdoba and to resign herself to her fate so as not to arouse further anger in the queen, who formerly had done her so many favors.

The *Crónica* states that the author of the false imputation against Doña Leonor was a lady named Inés de Torres, the queen's new adviser, a person who actually owed her entrée at court to her friendship with Doña Leonor López de Córdoba. Since she was occupying her position, when she heard of Doña Leonor's attempt to return to Doña Catalina's side she was fearful of losing her intimate status and lost no time in arousing the queen's ire. The latter, not satisfied with forbidding her to return, expelled Doña Leonor's brother and son-in-law from the court, as well as other relatives and protégés who occupied important posts in the king's and queen's households.

It was at this time, after the departure of the instigators who had kept him estranged from the queen, that Don Ferdinand's position achieved maximum strength. From then on he had all of the Royal Council on his side, his decisions were not contested, and there was no voice or authority other than his. This solid position made it possible for him to accept Doña Catalina's petition to grant a letter of surety to Juan de Velasco and Diego López de Stúñiga, so that they could return to court without fear of reprisals. And although he had firmly forbidden this in June, 1408, and it had been the decisive cause of the break between the two regents, he had no objection to granting it in March, 1409, almost exactly eight months later, for during this short space of time everything had changed. And both nobles, Velasco and Stúñiga, returned to court, asked the Infante's pardon, and became members of the Royal Council again; but they took great care not to arouse Don Ferdinand's enmity this time, though their ambitious plans had not changed; for not many days had elapsed after the death of the king of Aragon before they were already intriguing actively at court, and managed to recover the possession and guardianship of John II, together with Don Sancho de Rojas, and for a short time to control Castilian policy with the approval of Doña Catalina.

Don Ferdinand did not wish to maintain the decision taken in June of 1408, to avoid the unpopularity which would be aroused by his "tyranny" and the enmity of all the nobles. Sure of his position, he now reestablished the Royal Council in its entirety, permitting the return of the exiles, who unhesitatingly voted for all the proposals the Infante presented to the Council. Doña Leonor López was the only one still away from court, in her golden exile in Córdoba. All this meant a return to normality and legality, with the only controlling voice the Infante's, though the ambitions of many nobles and courtiers were still latent.

Considerations of security as well as his conviction that he was necessary to the government of Castile caused him, when it became necessary for him to go to Aragon (thus defeating the hopes of Doña Catalina and many nobles), to decide to keep his regency. Therefore, in accordance with the terms of his brother's will, he reestablished the division of Castile into two provinces and named for his province a council of regency composed of very prominent persons. Following the thread of previous events and the political line maintained by the Infante, we are not surprised to find the names of Don Juan, bishop of Sigüenza, and Dr. Pedro Sánchez in this council of regency. They were two of the four councillors who had been partisans of Doña Catalina, exiled from court by his personal decision in June, 1408. He was also to use the services of the bishop of Cuenca in the matter of the Great Schism. The only person whom we do not find mentioned again is the bishop of Mondoñedo.

There is nothing strange in this. Don Ferdinand had realized that his excessive caution was seriously endangering the monarchy, and once he had the power in his hands he was not going to offer any opportunity to have his will or his decisions questioned. We are, however, surprised by the abrupt change which took place in the person of Doña Catalina, for she passed from a position of great strength to almost complete compliance with her brother-in-law's wishes. We can find an explanation for this in her limited intelligence, ignorance of politics, and the Castilian character, and especially in the lack of councillors willing to oppose the Infante's authority. This was Don Ferdinand's view, and the words he uses about her in his "account" are not empty ones intended to gloss over Doña Catalina's mistakes. "You may be certain without any manner of doubt, that once the aforesaid bishops and doctor and the said Leonor López are removed from the said queen, that the said lady our queen is of such good understanding and such good will that she will accept all the things that are done in the service of the said lord our king, and for the good of these realms; and between her and me, with the help of God, there will be no dissension or discord as there has been up until now." And in fact there was not, though certain symptoms of disagreement remained.

We could say the same of many other events. Suffice it to cite two of the most important. When Doña Catalina decided that the candidacies of John II and Don Ferdinand to the throne of Aragon were to be defended jointly, the Infante disagreed and obliged the Royal Council to decide which of them had the better right. Naturally, the councillors had to do so, and they recognized the priority of Don Ferdinand. Almost the same thing happened in the concession of the forty-five million *maravedís* granted by the Cortes for the war with Granada. It was Doña Catalina, a very different person from the regent of five years before, who requested from the pope and the Castilian cities the authorization necessary to employ this money in the defense of Don Ferdinand's candidacy to the throne of Aragon—though we have ample reason to suspect that the sole object of this solicitous intervention by the queen was to achieve the possibility of her brother-in-law's removal from and renunciation of the regency.[30]

The fact that, when the new division of Castile into two provinces was carried out because Don Ferdinand had to go to the siege of Antequera, Doña Catalina made no effort to recover the lost ground probably has the same meaning. On the other hand, the victory of Antequera gave Don Ferdinand even more prestige, which the popular ballads increased to an incredible degree, thereby consolidating his position still more; and on his return Doña Catalina gave public proof of her respect for her brother-in-law's decisions. When he decided to move from Valladolid to Ayllón, to be closer to the frontier of Aragon, and asked the queen to come there with the king, Doña Catalina obeyed; and "though the queen was very sorrowful to leave Valladolid, she left there and went to Riaza[31] to please the Infante, whom she loved much for his great virtues ... and the queen, to content the Infante, was pleased to go to Ayllón, and brought the king with her."

During this period of John II's regency there was also another problem, which displayed the differing points of view held by the king of Castile's two guardians. In Valladolid on November 9, 1408, both regents signed a law concerning the *Mudéjares*[32] who lived in Castile. Its only importance was "to implement the plans of Henry III, which John II's guardians, who at that time had differing views on many matters of government, put into effect because of their desire to maintain as political objectives of their regency the precedents which had existed in the previous reign; this was always the basis of their governing program, and a similarity of views on those precedents always existed between them." These edicts coincided with the anti-Semitic movements which were taking place all over the Peninsula, and which "in a way served as a brake to the unreasonable pretensions of some sectors of the public, whose anti-Jewish feeling, exacerbated for several years and especially since the preachings of the archdean of Écija,[33] could also be turned against the Moslems." But when John II's guardians contented themselves with merely requiring the obligation to wear distinctive marks on their clothing indicating their race and when "they did not insist on the maintenance of some previous edicts, they seemed to show a benevolent attitude, whose only purpose was to carry out Henry III's plans."[34] The date of promulgation of this edict, as well as its mildness, shows the inspiration and caution of Don Ferdinand.

But when a new division of the government of Castile took place between the regents, necessary because Don Ferdinand had to be located near the Aragonese frontier, Doña Catalina again allowed herself to be influenced by the prejudiced counsels of the converted Jews in her province and the zeal of St. Vincent Ferrer; and, acting on her own initiative, she dictated a new edict against Jews and Moslems extending to all the Castilian kingdoms. And it is abundantly clear that she did not consult Don Ferdinand, whose opinions on this matter were entirely different. The Edict of Valladolid was extremely harsh, for it not only revived older edicts but added new prohibitive laws and put Jews and Moslems on the same footing. The Infante was forced to oppose its legality in the Castilian province under his jurisdiction, and even to order all that had been done under its terms canceled. Nor did Don Ferdinand introduce any change in future years, and thus the laws laid down by Doña Catalina gradually lost currency until they were eventually ignored or, as in the case of Seville, there was a wait until the queen's temporal power over that city had expired, in order to request and obtain from Don Ferdinand the suppression of all the measures adopted against the Jews.[35]

Another facet of the Infante's personality, of which we have several documentary proofs, was his concern for the betterment of living conditions and government in the Castilian cities.[36] Though we consider ill-advised the decree laid down by both regents in 1407, restoring to their posts the city councils of Seville, Córdoba, and Murcia, among others, and wiping out the intervention of the *corregidores* and the rules which had been established for the governing of the cities during Henry III's lifetime, we must also note that it was the policies of Doña Catalina and her advisers which dominated the Council at that time. This explains why, when Don Ferdinand's will was imposed in the Royal Council later, although he did not try to return to the absolutism of Henry III, he did try to lay down decrees leading to "the well-being of the subjects of the territories under his control. In his visits to a number of cities he therefore took a personal interest in their condition, hearing the complaints that were made to him, finding out as much as he could about everything, and then correcting abuses of every sort with appropriate decrees which reflected his thoughtful and judicious spirit."[37] An example of this is his edicts to the cities of Toledo and Seville on March 9 and December 29, 1411, reforming the administrative system, cutting down on political liberties, and restricting the citizens' participation in the system of representation, elected by vote and renewable every two years. Thus he initiated a thorough reform of local constitutions, which was not destined to succeed because of the Infante's short stay in Castile, his accession to the throne of Aragon, and his premature death.

We do not intend to judge or comment here on Don Ferdinand's activities in war, his pretensions to the throne of Aragon, or other facets of his external policy, which have already been studied elsewhere, but only to point out that both chroniclers and historians praise this historical period as an oasis of peace in the turbulent history of medieval Castile, and that they apply all sorts of favorable adjectives to his efforts. We find only one isolated protest, a complaint of a purely local character, perhaps motivated by the collection of royal taxes or the repeated and interminable payments of the extraordinary subsidy for the war with Granada. This took place in San Antolín, a remote suburb of the city of Murcia near the Moorish quarter of that city. In the council session of September 27, 1410, some council members revealed to their companions that certain women of San Antolín were saying "many foul words against the Infante Don Ferdinand, saying of him that he would be beheaded in Antequera, and saying, let him take Antequera, and saying many foul things and words of him." The councillors of Murcia judged such insults to be an act of contumely against the Infante's person, and ordered the *alcalde* to make an investigation and to administer corporal punishment to the women immediately. There is no further mention of the incident in the council's records.

THE REGENCY: 1412–1416

The proclamation of the Infante Don Ferdinand of Antequera as king of Aragon did not have official repercussions on his position as regent of Castile, for he retained the government of his province and the administrative division of Castile by means of successive postponements, granted every six months until his death.

In the official sphere everything stayed the same. Don Ferdinand named a council of regency to act for him in Castile, and it was charged with solving judicial and purely bureaucratic matters. Don Ferdinand kept his most essential prerogatives as regent, in the concession of posts, offices, privileges, and favors as well as in everything affecting the internal and external politics of his Castilian province. When one evaluates his conduct as regent of Castile during these four years in a more concrete sense, it is noted that activities diminished considerably compared to the previous period, and the balance of advantage and disadvantage acquired an unstable equilibrium, with small oscillations in one direction or the other.

Benefits for internal peace were: the disappearance of strong forces outside and antagonistic to the monarchy; renewal of external trade with Aragon, Navarre, and countries outside the Peninsula; safety along the frontiers of Portugal and Granada; good relations with North Africa, England, and France; outstanding intervention in the solution of the Great Schism; solution of frontier problems with Aragon, especially those which arose on the borders of the jurisdiction of Orihuela[38] and the *adelantamiento* of Murcia; reestablishment of royal absolutism and renewal of town government with the appointment of *corregidores*; closing of the Cortes, since the previous annual meeting was replaced by letters of authorization approving the petitions or decisions of the Infante, without giving the cities a chance to adopt joint agreements or express their petitions and complaints in a public form, etc.

To counterbalance these factors there were unfavorable ones of greatly varying kinds, economic in particular, which Álvar García de Santa María sums up under the following thirteen headings:

1. When the war with Granada was not renewed the Moslems lost their fear, and tributes, taxes, and delivery of captives, agreed upon when the truces were signed, fell off considerably.

2. Proper government of his own province also declined, for since Don Ferdinand kept the solution of the most important matters in his own hands, it was necessary to go to Aragon to deal with them, and this obviously meant delays and lack of direct information.

3. When the opening of the passes between Castile and Aragon was authorized, articles which previously had been prohibited began to be taken out of Castilian territory, such as gold and silver coins, wheat, horses, droves of sheep, arms, and pack animals.

4. Serious damage to the Castilian treasury also, for all the rich revenues held by Don Ferdinand in Castile, as well as the tithe he received for his guardianship and the forty-five million *maravedís* granted for the war with Granada and later turned over to Don Ferdinand in support of his claim to the throne of Don Martín the Humane, were spent and continued to be spent in Aragon.

5. The inconvenience for the Castilian subjects in his province, representatives of the cities as well as private persons, involved in having to journey to Aragon to make their petitions, request vacant posts, or simply obtain commissions; this meant great expense and delay in resolving these matters, with the further nuisance of having to carry silver and gold for their living expenses, which were spent in Aragon, where prices had risen sharply.

6. Because Benedict XIII was living in Aragonese territory and only Aragon and Castile were under his jurisdiction, all the revenues from vacant bishoprics went to Aragon; this produced a constant economic drain for Castile for which she received no compensation. To this were added the expenses incurred by anyone who went to the pope to request a canonry, benefice, or prebend, and who inevitably had to take gold and silver coins for his maintenance and journey.

7. The wages paid to the 2,000 mounted Castilians who spent

more than a year in Aragon on Don Ferdinand's service, and spent their pay in Aragon.

8. When Don Ferdinand was besieging the count of Urgel in Balaguer,[39] 1,500 men-at-arms and other foot soldiers came to help him, also paid in Castilian money.

9. A great deal of money was also spent in Saragossa on the nobles and the large number of Castilians who went there for the coronation of Don Ferdinand as king of Aragon.

10. More or less the same thing happened when the Infanta Doña María married the prince of Gerona in Valencia in 1415; the wedding was attended by a brilliant Castilian delegation headed by Don Sancho de Rojas.

11. The meeting at Perpignan also cost a large sum of money, for a great number of bishops, doctors, knights, and representatives came from Castile, interested in ending the Schism.

12. Because the knights who accompanied Don Ferdinand to Aragon were given an inadequate maintenance allowance, they had to supplement it with the revenues from their Castilian possessions, which, naturally, stayed in Aragon.

13. The opening of the frontier passes led to large-scale export of droves of sheep, mares, mule colts, asses, and mules of both sexes. Álvar García estimates that more than 3,000 mules and mule colts alone came into Aragon in the space of a year, besides many other things whose lack was felt in Castile.

To these thirteen points specified by the chronicler as economic losses, we could add the large sums spent by Don Ferdinand in Aragon to attract important Aragonese knights to his side, as well as the concession to these of privileges, landed property, and posts in Castile. Nor does he mention another fact which had profound economic consequences. This was the action of Diego Fernández de Vadillo in Valencia. A document of the Valencian Council tells us that he remitted payment of more than 300 florins in fees for sealing documents, owed by the merchants of Valencia "for the matter of the said prisoners and ransomed captives, on account of victuals as well as safe-conducts for the merchants."

This liberality had repercussions on the royal revenues of Castile.

Don Ferdinand of Antequera's election as king of Aragon represented, therefore, according to Álvar García de Santa María, a very heavy loss in gold and silver spent in Aragon, to the consequent impoverishment of Castile in these precious metals and the rise in price of many articles. And to all this the same chronicler adds two other serious consequences: famine and a rise in the death rate.

In 1412 there was a good wheat harvest in the irrigated lands of Castile, and there were also good supplies in Andalusia and the lands owned by the order of Santiago. The harvest was poor in Portugal, and prices went up to two gold *doblas* per *fanega*,⁴⁰ so that the Portuguese were authorized to buy wheat from those districts. Simultaneously, as Don Ferdinand was about to take possession of the kingdom of Aragon in 1412, he discovered that wheat was also scarce there, and because he wished to gain the gratitude of his new subjects he sent Pedro García de Medina, his personal scribe, to buy wheat in Andalusia and send it to Valencia and Barcelona by sea.

This scribe bought more than 50,000 *fanegas* in Seville and Jérez, and other large amounts in Córdoba. But, tempted by the possibility of earning greater profits, he sent only a part and sold most of it at high prices in the same places where he had acquired it. The result was a scarcity of wheat in Andalusia before there was one in Castile, and a long period of famine ensued.

Added to this was lack of rainfall, which not only reduced the harvest of 1413, but the drought combined with lack of food produced an epidemic of plague which in Andalusia lasted more than a year and caused a great many deaths.

This calamitous year of 1413 also had the result that the Andalusians did not have enough money to harvest their wheat, wine, and olive oil. The scarcity of horses, for they were being exported to Aragon in large numbers, also made itself felt, and the drought killed off many of them; this too had unfavorable consequences in Andalusia.

The black colors with which Álvar García seems to enjoy

painting this somber picture, blaming it all on Don Ferdinand's election as king of Aragon, display few mitigating touches, and in summing up he says, "Castile was greatly weakened in everything; empty of inhabitants because of the many deaths; drained of gold and silver and beasts; poor in the government of her province, and the inhabitants of the same suffering great hardships."

However, the *Refundición del Halconero*, which seems to use the same terms as Álvar García de Santa María, changes the sense of his words when it says that the election of Don Ferdinand "did great harm to the kingdom of Castile, as much because this noble Infante left the conquest of the Moors, which he was so anxious to pursue, as because he absented himself from the government of the kingdom that he had ruled with much peace and justice. This was soon evident after he left Castile, in the great evil and harm that befell the kingdom for lack of good government."[41]

In general terms we must accept Álvar García de Santa María's words as true, for Don Ferdinand's election did indeed have unfavourable repercussions on some aspects of the Castilian economy. The kingdom of Aragon benefited circumstantially from the events which took place at that time, and from Don Ferdinand's policy of ingratiating himself with his subjects. There is no doubt that the precious metals, wheat, animals, and other articles which went to Aragon caused obvious losses to the Castilians. But if we are to judge these events impartially we cannot make a list of the damages without a balancing list of benefits, and this the chronicler does not do.

We must also understand that in the political sphere Don Ferdinand's absence from Castile had a number of unfavorable aspects for his Castilian subjects. What Álvar García says about Castilian-Granadine relations is equally true, for the power of Granada increased, and this caused a diminution of the tributes and delivery of captives which were renegotiated when the truce was renewed. But he has nothing to say about the security of the frontier, stronger than ever now that Castile and Aragon were united under Don Ferdinand, which made superfluous the very large expenditure involved in maintaining troops along the border.

The same could be said of matters of internal policy. Since the division of Castile into two provinces continued, not many innovations were put in practice, and things slowly reverted to the time previous to the regency, to the constructive policy of Henry III which favored the monarchy. There were only three disadvantages affecting the two provinces into which Castile was divided. On the one hand, Don Ferdinand's non intervention in the territory governed by his sister-in-law, which permitted the nobility to wield influence over Doña Catalina, to their private advantage and to the detriment of the nation. On the other hand, in the province administered by the king of Aragon, since the persons designated to form the council of regency, though they did not fail to carry out their duties faithfully, had only limited authority, they could not resolve matters of a certain importance on which the Infante himself reserved decision. Therefore the lords and representatives of the cities had to go to Aragon to deal with them. This involved long stays in Aragon, greater expense, and delay in solving these matters. The exhausting task which fell to Ferdinand I when he took possession of his kingdom, involving not only Aragonese and Mediterranean affairs, with whose laws and customs he had to familiarize himself, but also in the convocation of Cortes, the journey to Perpignan for an interview with the emperor Sigismund, and all the other problems arising from the count of Urgel's rebellion and his own coronation, did not prevent him from spending all the time he could spare on Castilian affairs, though there was obviously a delay in resolving them.

He never intended to give up the regency of John II, as his sister-in-law hoped and many nobles desired. True to his political idea of family protection, which he had consolidated by his enthronement in Aragon, he continued to hold fast to the idea of maintaining his sons in the privileged position he considered necessary for his family and for the monarchy; and in addition, he felt himself morally obliged to continue to help his nephew.

Proof of this is found in the fact that during the last months of his life, when he was painfully traveling from Valencia to Perpignan to cooperate with his presence and personality in the healing of the Great Schism, he should have been concerned to have Castile worthily represented in that transcendental act. And his hasty return to Catalonia, on his way to Castile, also proves it; he intended to reconcile his differences with Doña Catalina so that Castile could retract its obedience to Benedict XIII. His last thought, his last effort, was to return to Castile, though he did not arrive there, for his journey ended in Igualada.

Before this, despite his physical ailments and the important business which kept him in Perpignan, Don Ferdinand did not neglect even the most minor Castilian affairs. He gave an immediate reply to a petition from the city of Murcia brought personally by one of the Murcian councillors, protesting the supposed appointment of the constable López Dávalos as *corregidor* of the city: "We answer you that We have dealt with the matter . . . ," a letter which he ends by saying, "because of our infirmities, signed by our firstborn son Don Alfonso."[42] On the same day he made the decision that "so that the concerns and affairs which We, as guardian of the king of Castile, must dispatch, shall not be delayed because We are unable to sign our name,"[43] since he was "lying abed ill" in his castle at Perpignan, in the future letters sealed with his secret seal and released by the private scribe of the king of Castile should be valid. These letters were to be given equal credence, validity, and authority as if they bore a signature written in his own hand, for he was now not strong enough to be able to sign.

Everything was to change after his death. According to the terms of Henry III's will, Doña Catalina was left as sole regent of Castile. But instead of remaining independent and holding herself above the groups of courtiers eager to meddle in the affairs of government, guided only by the Royal Council and following the political lines laid down by her brother-in-law, Doña Catalina took a step backwards. In 1407, at the time she took over her son's regency jointly with Don Ferdinand, she requested, and made as much trouble about it as she possibly could, that it would be she who would assume the guardianship and upbringing of her son, and was even ready to give up the regency to do so. She succeeded, thanks to the energetic intervention of the Infante, who convinced Juan de Velasco and Diego López de Stúñiga to renounce the responsibility Henry III had laid upon them, in exchange for a heavy compensation in money and their subsequent enmity.

It was precisely these two persons who very shortly afterward became extremely friendly with Doña Catalina and tried to keep her out of sympathy with her brother-in-law. The nobility, then, did maintain a certain attitude toward the regent's policies, which came to light when these two nobles fled at the time Don Ferdinand decided to end their pernicious meddling in the queen's affairs. His influence and the pressure he brought to bear were also shown in 1408 when, just as the agreement between the two regents was about to be signed, the queen demanded as a prerequisite a letter of surety from Don Ferdinand for both men. The Infante's refusal and his sister-in-law's intransigence led to the coup d'état of September, 1408.

Later, when his power over the Royal Council was assured and he was trying to return to a state of normality, Don Ferdinand forgave the two nobles' rebellious attitude and permitted them to return to court and to be readmitted to the Royal Council. Years later, when Castilian territory was definitively divided between the regents, Velasco and Stúñiga became members of the part of the Royal Council that stayed with the queen; and it was then, with full freedom for their intrigues, that both nobles were offered an opportunity to achieve the fulfillment of their ambitions, though they were very discreet about it up to the time of Don Ferdinand's death for fear of new reprisals.

The *Crónica* states that Diego López and Juan de Velasco, seeking a means of gaining the queen's confidence and thus attaining a position of preponderance in the government of Castile, persuaded Don Sancho de Rojas, archbishop of Toledo, to recover custody of John II jointly with them. Doña Catalina accepted this proposal under the pretext that she would be carrying out the terms of Henry III's will, although she received a previous oath that they would return possession of the king to her and that their intervention in the matter would be purely symbolic. Once they had made this agreement, each of the three councillors assigned his own guard to the king's retinue and signed a firm alliance against the other councillors. Thus they tried to make public, in an official form, that only an act of force by Don Ferdinand had prevented the terms of Henry III's will from being carried out, and in particular gained the queen's favor against the group of councillors who had been loyal to Don Ferdinand; and they tried to increase Doña Catalina's natural resentment against this group.

When the queen informed the Castilian cities of these events, she began by explaining the care and trouble she had taken in the upbringing and education of her son, to whom she had tried to teach everything necessary for his high destiny. She also referred in her letter to the agreement with her three councillors, saying that she had made it in the belief that she would be preventing the formation of "any sort of partisanship," and as a measure beneficial to the Crown. However, to assuage any possible displeasure on the part of the other councillors, she announced money payments and privileges to all the nobles and knights who were at court.

The whole letter, and especially the last part of it, has but one intention, one concrete purpose, that "you may see my good and manifest intention, so that in case other things are said, you will not believe them."[44] Indeed, some things were doubtless being said in Castile, owing to the wide repercussions of Doña Catalina's act, and its immediate consequence was the division of the Royal Council, the formation of two political factions, and the beginning of an unstable period which made everyone wish to have Don Ferdinand's government back again. The *Crónica de Don Pedro Niño* says in so many words that when Doña Catalina became sole regent "respect died and justice sickened in the greater part of Spain."

In Doña Catalina's letter this resurgence of the nobles is shown unequivocally, in phrases which offer no doubt of her intention, as when she refers to "the great houses whence they come," or in the announcement of concession of honors and favors to the nobility "according to what is required by their estates." Indirectly, too, we find a condemnation of the policies maintained by her brother-in-law, with the consequent return to an alliance and formal agreement between the monarchy and the nobility.

This piece of stupidity on the queen regent's part, with its clumsy partisanship, created a confusion which afflicted the rest of John II's reign, while at the same time, by contrast, it emphasized the years of peaceful existence Castile had known during Don Ferdinand of Antequera's regency.

Eleven years after the king of Aragon's death, when John II referred to the period of his minority and sketched the political development of those years of his guardianship as an antecedent to the years he had been governing Castile, since he could not betray his mother's memory and also knew a good deal about the personality of his uncle Don Ferdinand, whose sons Henry and John were at his side and taking part in the governing of his kingdom, he attempted to put the work of the two regents on the same plane, making the causes of the existing anarchy rest on both of them. According to the Castilian monarch, the differences and disagreements kept up by Doña Catalina and Don Ferdinand had led to the formation of factions and therefore to the political division of Castile, and hence to civil war. But he could not help recognizing the fact that after the death of his guardians, when he was already of age, anarchy, factionalism, and scandals had continued and increased.

This is a sad summary made in the name of a man who felt himself incapable of personally carrying on the government of Castile, unjustly criticizing a task which is worthy of praise on many counts. For even though there were disagreements and even enmities in high places in the state, in general these did not have direct repercussions on the Castilian nation. This is why Don Ferdinand's administration was remembered with nostalgia as the only period of peace and tranquillity to be found in the restless course of the kings of the Trastámara dynasty during nearly a century and a half of battles, alarms, anarchy, and civil war.

In the letter of pardon granted by John II to all who had become liable to punishment because of participation in leagues, confederations, or factions, he said, referring to his minority, "For at the time when the king my father and my lord, of illustrious memory (may his soul be with God), took leave of this life, I became king at a very tender age; therefore there were great debates and quarrels over my guardianship as well as possession of my person. And after the said guardianship and possession were agreed upon, there were differences of opinion between the queen, my lady and mother, and the king Don Ferdinand of Aragon my uncle, then the Infante (may they be in Paradise), my guardians and the rulers that were of my kingdoms; and the grandees of my kingdoms, prelates as well as knights, were forced to divide, for some adhered to the opinion of the said lady the queen my mother, and others to the opinion of the said king of Aragon my uncle. And there followed from this many difficulties and divisions and scandals and unrest in my kingdoms; and after the said guardians died these continued, and in order to carry out their plans the nobles formed leagues and confederations, swearing great oaths and vows and pledges and homages and bonds, which continued even after I took the rule and governance of my realms and seigniories into my own hands, and they continue to the present day. . . ."[45]

A period of peace in the Castilian province governed by the king of Aragon, and a more unstable one, to judge from the little we know, in the territories governed by Doña Catalina. A brilliant record in international politics, under Don Ferdinand's exclusive direction, and in which we should point out as the most outstanding events the good relations maintained with Granada, Portugal, France, England, Germany, and Navarre. A period of consolidation of Don Ferdinand's policies, in which the most outstanding event was his intervention in the solution of the Schism, although Doña Catalina delayed her withdrawal of obedience to Benedict XIII at the instigation of Don Sancho de Rojas, archbishop of Toledo, who out of motives of gratitude attempted to maintain his support of the Luna pope up to the last moment; in another sphere, the heir of Aragon's marriage to the Infanta Doña María, and that of Don John to the heiress of Navarre, both of which reaffirmed Don Ferdinand's intentions concerning Castile's political future, as well as his skill in calming the anti-Semitic furor of the early years of his regency, and bringing things back to their normal course.

Don Ferdinand's regency offers us a combination of positive events, and though we cannot find accomplishments of genius or transcendental acts, it can be summed up as a period of shrewd government beneficial to the monarchy. The initial failure before the walls of Setenil had ample compensation in the resounding conquest of Antequera and Castile's continued superiority in war, resulting in the prolongation of the truces in exchange for higher tribute and delivery of captives. His international policy is also a positive aspect, for it resulted in Castile's more cordial and intimate relations with other Peninsular states, and her implicit control and predominance over them. He also kept down for ten years an unmannerly and ambitious noble group, though this was offset by the preference given to the Infantes. Although this amounted in Don Ferdinand's eyes to government by the king's closest relatives, as an intermediate step between the monarchy and the nobility, there is no doubt that an energetic king would have been able to take advantage of both these factors to the benefit of the Crown. Marriage connections with Aragon, Navarre, and Portugal, which meant progress toward Peninsular unity; the final disappearance of the third estate as a power opposed to the monarchy, with carefully controlled sessions of the Cortes and intervention of the Crown in city government; a prosperous economy, extension and strengthening of external trade, and tolerant solutions to the religious and racial problems which presented such a somber prospect at the outset of the regency. These and other facts of less importance permit us to assess Don Ferdinand's achievement at the head of the Castilian government, generally speaking, as prudent and shrewd to a considerable degree.

NOTES

1. This article is part of a complete study on the regency of Don Ferdinand of Antequera, written with the help of a grant from the Fundación Juan March, 1958.

[2. Cf. G. Zurita, *Anales de Aragón*, Book x, chap. 84, ii (Saragossa, 1610), 446, col. B.]

3. González Dávila, *Historia de Enrique III*, pp. 9–10.

[4. The chief military officer at Lorca, a town in the modern province of Murcia, then close to the Castilian frontier between Murcia and the kingdom of Granada.]

5. The letter is included in *La regencia de don Fernando de Antequera: Las relaciones castellano-granadinas, 1406–1416*, Doc. 1, soon to be published.

6. Published in Torres Fontes, "Moros, judíos y conversos en la regencia de don Fernando de Antequera," *Cuadernos de Historia de España* (Buenos Aires, 1960), pp. 92–93. [*Ricos omes* = *ricos hombres*, the highest nobility of Castile, possessing extensive estates, often also offices at court.]

7. Published in Torres Fontes, "Las Cortes castellanas en la menor edad de Juan II," *Anales de la Universidad de Murcia*, xx (1961–62), 1–2, f–68.

[8. Printed in the original appendix, Doc. 1.]

9. Ms. in Paris, quoted by I. Macdonald, *Don Fernando de Antequera*, p. 20.

[10. Cf. Fernán Pérez de Guzmán, *Generaciones y Semblanzas*, ed. R. B. Tate (London, 1965), pp. 9–13.]

11. Pedro López de Ayala, *Crónica de Juan I*, BAEE, p. 70.

12. Enrique Flórez, *Reinas de España*, ii, 121. He publishes the letter, taking it from the *Historia de Santo Domingo*, Book i, chap. 84.

13. Don Ferdinand, then ten years of age, accepted the betrothal in the presence of Henry III; Doña Leonor did likewise, being able to give her personal consent since she was sixteen. Public contracts were signed obliging the countess of Alburquerque to put up all her possessions as a guarantee that she would fulfill her promise. This ceremony took place in 1390 (*Crónica de Enrique III*, p. 162). The marriage went into effect in 1393, when Henry III attained his majority (*Crónica*, p. 217).

14. *Crónica de Enrique III*, p. 217.

[15. The *maravedí*, originally a gold coin minted by the Castilian kings in imitation of the Moorish *morabetín*, was replaced in the reign of Alfonso X by the gold *dobla*. The silver *maravedí* (60 new silver to 1 old gold *maravedí*) in turn gave place to the silver *real de plata*, and under Peter I three silver *maravedís* = 1 *real de plata*; 12 *reales* = 1 gold *dobla*. Henry III had vainly tried to maintain this ratio (in 1388 there had been 50 *maravedís* to the gold *dobla*; in 1406 there were 95). But by the early fifteenth century the *maravedí* was rapidly becoming depreciated. It was to continue its existence either as a *vellón* or as a copper coin or simply as money of account. At the time of the coinage reform of the Catholic Kings in 1497 there were 34 *maravedís* to the *real de plata*, 375 to the ducat, 265 to the Aragonese florin. For all this see N. Seternach, "El maravedí—su grandeza y decadencia," *RABM*, xii (1905), 195–220; "La dobla, el excellente o ducado y el escudo," *ibid.*, xiii (1905), 180–99.]

16. *Crónica de Juan I*, p. 130.

17. Grants of John II exist, bearing the royal seal and the signature of witnesses, all dated Alcalá de Henares on July 11, 1408, confirming others of Henry III, in which the Infante Don Ferdinand is given Peñafiel with the title of a dukedom; Mayorga with the title of count; the town of Paredes de Nava; Cuéllar and its lands, etc. (AGS, Patronato Real, nos. 5016, 5015, 5011, 5012, 5013, and 5014). Also a transfer, requested by the monastery of Santa María de Dueñas of Medina del Campo, of a privilege of Henry III granting 11,000 gold *doblas* to Don Ferdinand, duke of Peñafiel, given November 20, 1406 (AGS, Patronato Real, Doc. 5010).

18. Álvar Garcia de Santa María, *Crónica de Juan II*, fols. 250–51 (cited by I. Macdonald, *op. cit.*, 233).

[19. *Servicio y montazgo* = A Castilian royal toll levied on sheepowners for revenue purposes, to be distinguished from *montazgo*, which was a local penalty for trespass; cf. Klein, *Mesta*, p. 149.]

20. In a contract drawn up in Valencia on June 10, 1415, Don Ferdinand and Don Alfonso promised to restore to the Infanta Doña María, or to her brother, King John of Castile, in case of the dissolution of this marriage owing to the death of either spouse or in case of their separation, the sum of 200,000 Castilian gold *doblas* which Doña María was to receive as a dowry; John II, as a guarantee of payment, mortgaged and turned over to his sister and the aforesaid Don Ferdinand and Don Alfonso his towns of Madrigal, Roa, Sepúlveda, Arévalo, and Dueñas (AGS, Patronato Real, Leg. 12, fol. 13; ed. by Emilio Sáez, *Colección Diplomática de Sepúlveda*, i (Segovia, 1956), 364–72). On the date of the wedding, see Emilio Sáez, "Semblanzas de Alfonso el Magnánimo," *Estudios sobre Alfonso el Magnánimo* (Barcelona, 1960), p. 28, n. 7.

21. The wedding of John II and María de Aragón was celebrated with great solemnity in October, 1418, but after the death of the queen Doña Catalina, who had opposed the match. On the other hand, the Infante Don Sancho, grand master of Alcántara, died in 1416, shortly before his father; but Don Ferdinand made no move to maintain his mastership within the family, and therefore Don Juan de Sotomayor was elected without opposition. On the sons of Don Ferdinand, see the excellent monograph of Eloy Benito Ruano, *Los infantes de Aragón* (Madrid, 1952), 112 pp.

22. Luis Suárez Fernández, *Nobleza y Monarquía* (Valladolid, 1959), pp. 81–82.

23. The city of Murcia's recognition, on February 21, can be seen in *Las Cortes castellanas en la menor edad de Juan II*, f. 69–71.

[24. Sancho de Rojas I, bishop of Palencia, 1403–June 10, 1415; Juan, bishop of Cuenca, *ca.* 1407–1408, but not after March 16, 1408.]

25. This dispute, undoubtedly representing the rivalry of the two factions, since apparently all the courtiers, knights, and prelates were inclined toward the side of one or other regent, took place on June 19 (*Crónica de*

Juan II, pp. 309–10). Its most immediate result was the agreement signed four days later between the regents.

[26. For the bishop of Cuenca see note [24]; the bishop of Sigüenza was Juan de Illescas, 1406–November 15, 1415; the bishop of Mondoñedo, Álvaro de Isorna, 1400–1415.]

27. If the coup d'état of September 28, 1408, involved the forcible setting aside of the queen, when Don Ferdinand gave a public explanation of what had happened he had to censure his sister-in-law's part in it; however, he speaks kindly of her, and of his conviction that once her evil councillors have departed, her excellent qualities would come to light, as well as "her good understanding and good will so that she will do all things necessary for the service of the said lord our king and the good of these realms."

28. Adolfo de Castro, "Memorias de una dama del siglo XIV y XV (de 1353 a 1412): Doña Leonor López de Córdoba," *España Moderna*, CLXIII, pp. 120–46, and CLXIV, pp. 116–33. The *Memorias* break off in the year 1400, but Castro continues them by using references from the *Crónicas* of Pérez de Guzmán and Álvar García de Santa María. The letter he publishes, undated as to year, is dated in Valladolid on December 9.

29. *Ibid.*, p. 124.

30. See Torres Fontes, *Las Cortes castellanas en la menor edad de Juan II, op. cit.*, fol. 65.

[31. Riaza and Ayllón are in the modern province of Segovia, northeast of the Somosierra pass in the Guadarramas.]

[32. *Mudéjares*, "Moslims living under Christian rule"; from Arabic, *Mudaggan* —"one permitted to remain."]

[33. Ferrán Martínez, archdean of Écija, was a famous preacher who led the attack on the ghettoes of Écija and Alcalá de Guadaira in November and December, 1390, in the wave of pogroms which followed the death of John I; cf. R. Menéndez Pidal, *Historia de España*, XIV (ed. L. Suárez Fernández and Juan Reglá Campistol), p. 310.]

34. Torres Fontes, "Moros, judíos y conversos en la regencia de don Fernando de Antequera," *op. cit.*, pp. 63–69.

35. *Ibid.*, pp. 77–78.

36. Emilio Sáez Sánchez, "Ordenamiento dado a Toledo por el infante don Fernando de Antequera, tutor de Juan II, en 1411," *AHDE*, XV (1944), 499–556; and by the same writer, the edicts issued in Seville in "El libro del juramento del Ayuntamiento de Toledo," *AHDE*, XVI (1945), a reprint of 99 pages.

37. Sáez Sánchez, "Ordenamiento . . .," pp. 499–500. In his preliminary study of the transcription of Don Ferdinand's Edict to Toledo, he makes a brief summary of the chaotic state of Toledo at the time and the need to reestablish order and morality, end abuses, and make rulings on the attributions of public functionaries; this was Don Ferdinand's purpose in issuing his edict, a "model of municipal law."

[38. In the modern province of Alicante on the Segura River.]

[39. The famous siege of Balaguer lasted three months in the summer and

autumn of 1413 and marked the end of the resistance of Jaume, count of
Urgel, to the decision of the Compromise of Caspe by which the
Aragonese throne was awarded to Ferdinand of Antequera.]

[40. *Fanega* was a dry measure for corn. It varied from one part of the country
   to another but was usually something over 1½ bushels.]

41. *Refundición de la Crónico del Halconero*, ed. Carriazo (Madrid, 1946), p. 20.

42. In Perpignan, January 21, 1416. Archivo Municipal de Murcia, Cartulario
   Real 1411–29, fol. 38 recto.

43. *Ibid.*, fol. 38 recto–verso.

44. In the original appendix, Doc. 2. In Valladolid, June 3, undated as to year;
   I believe it to be 1416 because Juan de Velasco and Diego López died in
   1417. Suárez Fernández, *Nobleza y Monarquía* (Valladolid, 1959), p. 83.

45. In Segovia 28-xi-1427. A. M. Murcia, Cartas originales, Vol. II, fol. 2.

FURTHER READING

I. Macdonald, *Don Fernando de Antequera* (Oxford, 1948).

5 The Institutions of the Crown of Aragon in the First Half of the Fifteenth Century

JOSÉ MARÍA FONT Y RIUS

J. M. Font y Rius assesses the state of the institutions of the Crown of Aragon in the first half of the fifteenth century. He shows how the equilibrium established in the course of the fourteenth century between monarch and institutions was breaking up in Aragon, even if until 1462 the country did not flare into civil war as Castile had done much earlier. Though the Compromise of Caspe (1412) emphasized the elective nature of the monarchy, and though the powers of the Cortes of Catalonia, Aragon, and Valencia were stronger than those of the Cortes of Castile, the tendency of the Aragonese monarchy to enhance its position was marked—especially in Catalonia. The municipalities meanwhile tended to become pinched between aristocratic factions. The establishment of the *Diputació del General* in Catalonia and Valencia and the introduction of the policy of picking the Officers of the towns by lot were not enough in themselves to slow down the movement toward a head-on collision.

NO aspect of history, much less that which refers to the progress of political, economic, and social institutions, can be rigidly confined within a predetermined chronological scheme, even though this may coincide with the temporal limits of the reigns of certain sovereigns. Thus we shall have to call attention in advance to the difficulty of offering an accurate treatment of these matters, without exceeding the limits imposed by the fundamental objective of this Congress [4 Congreso de la Historia de la Corona de Aragón (1955)], especially if we keep in mind that, in the institutional sphere, the period to which its themes are confined[1] does not offer special peculiarities or witness appreciable changes. It is a period of evolution and transition between the ordering of the state which had become consolidated in the thirteenth and fourteenth centuries, and the profound and transcendental transformation of the end of the fifteenth. Thus its significance and most characteristic features should be sought, perhaps, in the prefiguration and foreshadowing, in a number of areas, of the new world of concepts and structures which, less than a century later, would come to replace the previous organization.

STATE AND MONARCHY

The first half of the fifteenth century, the period to which the historical consideration of the two reigns we are studying is for all practical purposes confined, represents from the point of view of the political institutions of the Crown of Aragon the beginning of a fundamental transformation which, vaguely foreshadowed in previous decades, was to attain full development during the second half of the century. The political equilibrium and constitutional harmony, achieved as the regulatory system of an enduring co-existence, was breaking up in favor of the growing power of the sovereign, which was to assert itself eventually in the form of a monarchy which, though not absolutist, was certainly authoritarian.

In recent years a number of writers have touched upon this interesting and important evolution, and have offered us shrewd suggestions and viewpoints which, though they display different shadings of opinion, show a clear and unanimous view of the historical reality of the period. Professor J. Vicens Vives, who had tackled this subject in his previous studies on the politics of Ferdinand the Catholic, has returned to it in his *Consideraciones sobre la historia de Cataluña en el siglo XV* (Zurita, *Cuadernos de Historia*, Vol. I), later incorporated into his magnificent work *Juan II de Aragón: Monarquía y Revolución en la España del siglo XV*.[2] This work is the fruit of new meditations, as is the admirable contribution of Professor S. Sobrequés in his substantial analysis of the Cortes of Barcelona of 1454–58 (*Estudios de Historia Moderna*, II), both of which are so significant for this area. From another angle, Professor Elías de Tejada, in the vivid pages which he dedicates to the study of *Las doctrinas políticas en la Cataluña medieval* (Barcelona, 1950), also offers us a shrewd and profound interpretation of the constitutional evolution of the principality—nerve center of the Crown—both in its political reality and in the doctrines of its authors.

Analysis of legal texts, of juridical works, and of the realities of government permits us to establish some apparently definitive data, at least along general lines. The Catalan-Aragonese State was, at the beginning of the fifteenth century, a true Mediterranean imperial community, based on the most absolute respect for the autonomy of its individual kingdoms. In the internal sphere, as we have just mentioned, a system of true constitutional equilibrium had been reached between the royal power and the different estates, which Professor Vicens does not hesitate to assess as "one of the great contributions of fifteenth-century political practice to the needs of Western society." This formula was based on "conditioning the exercise of power through the exercise of freedom, giving to the first element the effectiveness necessary to maintain law and order, and protecting the second behind the indispensable guarantees which would assure the healthy development of institutions and individualities." A deeply rooted doctrinal tradition (Lull,[3] Eximenis[4]) undoubtedly served as preparation for the flowering of this system, fed by the contingent historical circumstances of the period (struggle against feudalism, development of the bourgeoisie in the cities). And at its moment of splendor—the beginning of the fifteenth century—it received the support of a brilliant constellation of jurists who worked out, in the name of a synthesis which superseded the old feudal mentality and the new Romanist current, a true theory of the constitutional state. This rested on the concept of a monarchy limited by a system of freedoms, on a legal order established to give equal rights to all; in a certain sense—in the opinion of Mieres[5] and Marquilles[6] in particular—what has come to be called in modern times a state founded on law.

This concept, a reflection of the thinking of the fifteenth-century Catalonian bourgeoisie at the moment of their greatest ascendancy, but equally alive in Aragon and Valencia, has been described by Vicens with the word *pactism*. In this writer's opinion, the pactist idea achieved a new development with the installation of the Castilian dynasty, because of the incontrovertible fact (which seems to be established as early as the chronicler Turell[7]) that the Castilian monarchs had an elected authority, conditioned to a certain degree by the people who had had a part in choosing them. A resounding affirmation of pactism was the recognition, in the Cortes of 1413, of the political powers of the *Generalitat* of Catalonia—defense of the country's political liberties, protest over breaking of the laws. On the popular side, certain actions in the Cortes, such as the impugnation of the powers of the syndics of Barcelona in the Cortes of 1454 under the pretext that, since city offices had been assigned that year by royal decree, such syndics should be considered in their turn as royal officials and therefore disqualified from acting in the Cortes, since it was impossible for the monarch to pact with himself.

However, we cannot ignore the fact that after the Castilian dynasty's ascent to the throne royal authoritarianism continued to progress, and aspired toward taking advantage of the break in that equilibrium, which, as Elías de Tejada has so accurately pointed out,[8] became even more unstable. The tendency toward absolutism was not, to be sure, characteristic of the House of Trastámara, but it was in the air; it was the fruit of the Romanist renaissance, and had already been evident in some traits of the policies of previous Catalonian monarchs (Peter the Ceremonious, for example). But with the House of Trastámara, more imbued with these ideas because of its Castilian origin, the evolution speeded up. During the periods when Alfonso the Magnanimous' powers were delegated to a lieutenant, relations between the monarch and the Cortes became very strained, sometimes to breaking point. In the struggle between the royal authority and the bourgeoisie to seize the heritage of the feudal nobility's declining power, royal authority was unequivocally established, not as an absolute and arbitrary power (as historical writing of a few decades ago attempted to show), but as the only force capable of overcoming the tyrannies of an anachronistic feudalism and the ambitions of the bourgeois oligarchies in the large cities. John II's war represented the culmination of this process.

THE CORTES AND THE *Diputació*

We have just noted some reflections of the pactist concept in the Cortes held under the first two Trastámara kings. The organic structure of these bodies, representative of the different estates of the respective kingdoms, underwent virtually no change during this first half of the century. Their significance was strengthened in some respects, as is shown by the growing power of the popular arm of the Catalan Cortes, which in 1449 and 1454, through the initiative of Alfonso the Magnanimous, came to be composed of forty cities instead of fifteen as before. Professor Sobrequés, in the study to which we referred above, shows with the aid of very eloquent figures the degree to which the Cortes, however, constituted an effective representation of the country. In the area of its functional activity and its effective role in the country's political processes, we still have no good studies on the institution in the different kingdoms, perhaps because the proceedings of the Cortes in Aragon and Valencia during this period have not yet been published. For the Catalonian Cortes, apart from Coroleu-Pella's old book,[9] we have only the very useful pages in which Sobrequés discusses the Cortes of Barcelona of 1454–58, and which we should like to see extended to the other Cortes of the realm. An overall view of the development of the legislatures of these two kingdoms soon reveals the symptoms of an initial crisis in this institution. It is not only the attitude of greater tension between the Crown and the different arms of the Cortes, almost always caused by royal petitions for subsidies and granted only very conditionally by the estates, which contrasts so sharply with the cordial and benevolent accord of former times. It is also the repeated disagreement among the estates themselves, and even within the bosom of the same branch, where group and factions were formed which fought among themselves on various questions. If in the Cortes of 1419–20 and 1421–23 the military arm was split between the faction of the count of Pallars and that of Cardona, in the Cortes of 1436 a dissident splinter group from the ecclesiastical arm, under the leadership of the Castellan of Amposta, took a position of its own in a question of peace and truce which was under discussion. And in the famous Cortes of 1454–58, we already know of the dissension between the syndics of Barcelona and a number of like-minded municipalities, and those of other cities, who impugned the validity of the powers of the Barcelona syndics. Problems of substance were often complicated by demands of form on the part of the estates (extemporaneous convocations or those held outside the usual place, lack of qualifications of members, presentation of grievances, etc.), making the position of the sovereign or his lieutenant annoying and difficult.

On the other hand, the *Diputació del General* acquired full maturity during this period, and after its initial activity at the end of the fourteenth century, when its predominant character was that of a permanent delegation of the Cortes, it became progressively transformed into a representative and permanent institution of the respective countries, which to its original financial functions soon added others of a different kind, both political and social. Especially in Catalonia, the *Generalitat* reflected the polarization of a political concept, in that equilibrium of powers between the royal authority and the country's various estates, assuming the representation of these last, or rather of the whole principality, after the manner of a "mystical body." The reigns of Ferdinand I and Alfonso V witnessed, in Catalonia as well as in Valencia, the organic structuralization of their respective deputations and the first steps in a meaningful evolution. Perhaps the actions of some of these bodies during the interregnum which followed the death of King Martin definitively consolidated their position, as Professor Vicens believes. This would explain the fact that in the first Cortes convoked by the new monarch, in 1413, the definitive structure of the Catalonian *Diputació* was established, with three *Diputats* and three *Oidors*, renewed triennially by the system of cooptation, a method of selection which was undoubtedly taken as an example by the sister organization of the Valencian *Generalitat* a few years later, in 1418. It seems that by means of this system these bodies were trying to prevent any royal intervention in the appointment of their leaders, but they also incurred the opposite risk of winding up in the stranglehold of a closed oligarchy, more mindful of its personal or group interests than of the common good. The rectification can be observed in Valencia in the following year, 1419, when the previous system of designation was changed into a new one which combined cooptation with balloting by drawing lots, while in Catalonia this change was not made until 1455, in a similar form, although in previous years different methods had been adopted tending toward the elimination of all private favoritism in the appointments. All these aspects, sketched out in regard to Catalonia in the works by Professor Vicens to which we referred before, are scarcely treated more fully in the book ·by Rubio Cambronero (*La Diputació del General de Catalunya*, Barcelona, 1950) and outlined in regard to Valencia in Martínez Aloy's book (*La Diputación de la Generalidad del Reino de Valencia*, Valencia, 1930). There is, however, no comparable contribution in respect to the Aragonese Deputation, owing perhaps to the vicissitudes undergone by the archives there. Nor do we know much about the internal procedure, function, methods, etc., of these Deputations. We await with interest the result of Professor Camarena's researches on taxes under the Valencian *Generalitat*.

THE COURT AND THE CENTRAL ADMINISTRATION

Undoubtedly the changes undergone in the early part of the fifteenth century by the central bodies of administration in the Crown of Aragon were of less importance. The king, the court, and its officials, together with the array of civil servants and

bureaucratic services, had received a regulated and stable organization a century earlier with the *Ordenanzas* of Peter the Ceremonious, which encompassed earlier attempts at organization; this
body of rules was fundamentally adhered to until the reign of the
Catholic King. We need only mention here the introduction by
Alfonso V, in 1419, of a new *Maestre Racional*, or chief accountant,
exclusively for the kingdom of Valencia, independent of the office
which had previously existed for all his kingdoms, as has been
described by Srta. Ángeles Masiá ("El Maestre Racional en la
Corona de Aragón: Una pragmática de Juan II," *Hispania*,
no. XXXVIII); an indication, perhaps, of the importance of the
royal patrimony in that kingdom, or of the Crown's increasing
concern for the improvement of its accounting services, revealed
in John II's pragmatic restating of the functions of this office.
Mateu y Llopis' studies[10] have assessed the interest offered by the
documentary material on the *Maestre Racional* in the Archive of
the Kingdom of Valencia, for knowledge of this post as well as
the majority of the magistracies of the kingdom.

In a manner similar to that of the Court, the structure and
functions of the Royal Council had been organized ever since the
days of Peter IV, and this was also the case in the judicial sphere,
in the so-called *Audiencia*. But in regard to this latter high
institution—which Ferdinand the Catholic was to reorganize
separately in both its aspects, in consideration of new times and
new circumstances—we possess extremely scanty and vague
references, and we know nothing about its life and development
in the fifteenth century, for it is scarcely mentioned by authors
and writers of monographs, and then only in a most general and
contradictory fashion. The documents in the section pertaining
to the *Audiencia* in the respective regional archives await the
diligent treatment of researchers who can wrest their secrets from
them. It would be interesting to discover just what the composition of this Royal Council was, and its integration into the heart
of the Chancery, as well as its function as a supreme tribunal and
its conjoint or separate functioning in the different spheres of
government. This would permit us to assess the evolution and

crystallization into new molds of the traditional king's justice, the elements of its counseling function, the respective roles of nobles, ecclesiastics, and learned men, etc. We know a little more—but not in much depth—about the Aragonese magistracy of the *Justicia Mayor* in the fifteenth century, thanks to the somewhat outdated pages of Giménez Soler.[11] This learned professor clearly pointed out the profound crisis through which that institution, like the other offices and organs of justice, passed in the middle decades of the fifteenth century, owing to the flagrant abuse in its positions made for the benefit of illicit interests. The royal dismissals of the justices Cerdán and Díez de Aux, in spite of the juridical victories obtained for these posts at this time, making them lifelong and inviolable and responsible only to the Cortes, clearly prove to what an extent the original significance and meaning of this prestigious magistracy had been perverted; it was a prelude to the events involving the ill-fated Juan de Lanuza[12] a century later.

GOVERNMENT OF THE KINGDOMS AND GREAT TERRITORIES

The decades upon which our study is concentrated are of particular significance in the development of certain high magistracies in territorial administration: lieutenants and governors. Until recently our only information about this institution came from a few marginal references by Professor Giménez Soler (*El poder judicial en la Corona de Aragón, Don Jaime, Conde de Urgel*, etc.) which, though they inquired closely into the origins and earliest significance of the office of governor, were marred by confusion between this office and that of the lieutenancy. Some years ago, in an attempt to investigate the possible Peninsular precedents for the viceroyalties of the Indies, the question arose, though indirectly, of describing in detail and distinguishing between these high positions, delegated by the Crown, and of characterizing their true attributes and functional content. With this aim, Professors Vicens and García Gallo[13] wrote some brief but extremeley informative pages about the development and

evolution of these offices in the fifteenth century, thinking, however, more of their role as possible precedents of the magistracies
of the Indies. These contributions have cast considerable light
on the problem, and we await its final solution from the thorough
research promised by Professor Vicens on a certain occasion.
Provisionally, it seems that we can conclude with little possibility
of doubt that these offices can in no way be confused with each
other; on the contrary, they seem to be perfectly differentiated,
if not in the beginning at least later on, except for occasional
confusions or coincidences having to do with the identification
of persons. The post of governor general is older, and was linked
after the middle of the fourteenth century with the heir to the
throne; it was characterized from the outset as a permanent post
with ordinary jurisdiction, which for its effective exercise in the
various kingdoms or territories was provided with its respective
delegates or *gerenti vices* in each of them. Independently of this
office, and owing to the necessities imposed by the government
of the Mediterranean dominions, there appeared after the end of
the fourteenth century the royal appointment of some uncon-
ditional officials with delegated jurisdiction, for one or several
territories and as an exceptional procedure (absence or illness of
the monarch): the *Lugartenientes*, or lieutenants. Apparently (and
this is Professor Vicens' opinion) in the course of the fifteenth
century, while the office of governor became progressively more
honorary, that of lieutenant general of a territory gained special
importance, possibly through the influence of the two viceroyalties
across the Mediterranean, Sicily and Sardinia, which were
organized just at that time, in the first half of the century. García
Gallo believes that this mutation of roles was brought about
especially by the circumstances existing in the kingdoms about
the middle of the fifteenth century. The office of governor was
vacant most of the time because Alfonso V had no children, and
because of John II's disagreements with the prince of Viana, and
the post lost its effectiveness; at the same time, the lengthy exercise
of the lieutenancy during the prolonged absence of Alfonso the
Magnanimous, by either his wife María or his brother, the future

John II, strengthened its nature. Therefore, since the title of governor came to be more of an honor than a governing post, the general lieutenancy stood out as the most important office of all, for it presupposed a full delegation of the monarch's functions, and thus also came to be called the office of viceroy, using the Mediterranean term. This impression is corroborated by the fact pointed out by Vicens, that some functions which at first were peculiar to a governor passed over (or at least there was an attempt to pass them over) to the lieutenancy—such as the right to convoke Cortes—and, on the whole, as this office took over more and more functions the governorship lost them.

Our period constitutes a sort of transition between these two extremes, and thus it is to be hoped that as research advances along the trail blazed by these two illustrious scholars, we shall soon come to know more precisely the development and characteristics of these high ministerial posts in the Crown of Aragon.

A good deal of progress has been made on the lower levels of territorial administration, in our knowledge of the lesser offices and the way in which they functioned—*vegueres, justicias*, etc.— although within the period of time to which our study is confined these bodies doubtless underwent no special transformations.

THE LOCAL SYSTEM

In the sphere of municipal life, the reigns of the early Trastámaras are of extraordinary importance. The crisis of the great cities, and their development toward new forms in their structure, which were to culminate during the reign of Ferdinand, can already be observed in the decades we are studying, with their symptoms and peculiar characteristics clearly in evidence. On this point also, we can count on the valuable insights of Professor Vicens—one of the most knowledgeable students of our fifteenth century—who since his earliest works has indicated directions in the study of these problems different from those traditionally followed by the previous literature. A good number of his pupils

and followers have worked together, in the form of local contributions, toward establishing along general lines and filling in the
details of the municipal policies of the fifteenth-century Aragonese
monarchs, destined to result in the great reforms of Ferdinand the
Catholic. It is becoming more and more evident that the beginnings of this policy originated during the reign of Alfonso the
Magnanimous. Balloting by lot for offices and municipal posts,
replacing the old systems of voting or cooptation—under cover of
which a powerful oligarchy composed of the upper bourgeoisie
had flourished everywhere—was begun by this monarch or his
lieutenants, tried out in a timid and occasional manner in the cities
of his different kingdoms, generally in places of secondary importance. So far there has not been an overall study on the development of this process; and the local monographs which have
appeared in the past few years do not permit us to obtain more than
a fragmentary view of it, without being able to capture its essential
pattern. It is possible that such balloting reforms were first tried
out in Majorca, as A. Santamaría tells us in a thesis as yet unpublished. But we know that in 1446, in some ordinances dictated by
the Infante Don John as lieutenant of the kingdom, this system was
established in the city of Castellón de la Plana in the kingdom of
Valencia, with the object of ending the disorders and immorality
afflicting municipal life there, once the obstinate resistance of its
Council had been overcome (Roca, *Ordinaciones municipales de
Castellón de la Plana durante la Baja Edad Media*, Valencia, 1952).
Less than four years passed before balloting by casting lots was
solemnly established in the Catalonian municipality of Vich
(Privilege of Alfonso V in 1450), in this case precisely as an
integral aspect of a new and broader organization of the city's
municipal system, requested and prepared by none other than the
representatives of the city themselves, when it was incorporated
into the Crown. A few years later balloting by lot reached the
kingdom of Aragon and was established in Barbastro by means
of some royal ordinances issued in 1454. And, toward the end of
the reign, the lieutenant Don John extended it to Gerona, a city
which also suffered from the irregularities and abuses of its

reigning oligarchy. This plan to reform local government through balloting—similar to the plan used for the *Generalitat*—did not imply meddling by royal authoritarianism in the internal functioning of the government, for the Crown did not claim any intervention in the compiling of lists or in the bags into which the names of candidates were put. It was aimed solely at freeing the cities from the perpetuation of the oligarchies which dominated them, entrusting the renewal of offices to chance, and with it the introduction of new elements into the Councils. It was later that, upon this foundation, the monarchs—Ferdinand the Catholic, Charles I[14]—in addition to extending the system to the chief cities of their kingdoms, placed it at the service of their attempts to centralize the Councils, reserving for themselves in one way or another the designation of the candidates. In this sense too, the period we are studying was one of transition. And this impression is buttressed by the eloquent fact that, when Alfonso the Magnanimous was forced to take action in the reform of the city government of Barcelona—where, aside from the evils of the oligarchy, the struggles between the *Busca* and the *Biga* demanded an immediate decision—the modification which he established in its internal organization (reforms of 1455) did not depend in the least on the system of balloting by casting lots, in spite of the fact that at the time this system was in its period of fullest application in the smaller cities, and that in the same year it was applied to the *Generalitat*. As we know, the privilege of 1455 fundamentally attempted to fix a numerical equality in the components of the municipal Council according to its respective estates, giving effective representation to the lower classes of artisans and workers, who had been passed over until then. The failure of this reform in the sense which had been intended was to be the basis of Ferdinand's later intervention.

But these famous and spectacular reforms in municipal organization should not conceal other interesting aspects in the functional development of communal corporations. Monographs on towns and municipalities usually emphasize the attainment of a certain degree of administrative and social development in them, undoubtedly corresponding to the urban development and economic prosperity of cities and towns and the subsequent proliferation of services. If we search the pages of some recent studies we will find, for example, the rise in many places of the urban office of *mostaçaf*, so representative in local economic life. If it is true that this office owes its chief establishment to Peter the Ceremonious, it is also true that in this first half of the fifteenth century the *mostaçaf* attained considerable importance in the exercise of his office, as is proved by the numerous versions of the Ordinances or Books of the Mostaçaf in various localities (Vich, Castellón, etc.). An indication of the same phenomenon—the broadening of the circle of municipal concerns—was the creation by Valencian jurists of the office of *afermamossos*, in 1439, with promulgation of its respective Ordinances, for the prosecution of idlers and false paupers, either giving them work to do or expelling them from the city. In another sphere, the prestige and importance of the great cities is clearly demonstrated, during the years we are studying, by the numerous concessions of *carreratge*, by means of which the cities broadened their juridical radius of action and their supremacy in the political interplay of the period. Between 1423 and 1445 a number of important Catalonian municipalities (Granollers, Mataró, Vilanova and Geltrú, Caldas de Montbuy) placed themselves under the protection of Barcelona in exchange for various royal privileges.

ECONOMIC AND MERCANTILE INSTITUTIONS

In the fifteenth century the flowering of economic institutions, corporative bodies, guild organizations, and the like reflects the degree of development achieved by the arts and industries, and by mercantile traffic, as well as the rise of the new world of capitalism in the kingdoms of the Crown of Aragon in the period preceding the wars of John II. I shall leave for another occasion the treatment of these economic phenomena as such, and will merely point out here the valuable contributions to our knowledge of institutions and bodies of this type which were either created or developed in the course of the decades we are studying, especially the guilds, maritime consulates, and *Taules de Canvi*, or exchange banks.

As for the guilds, we know that the bibliography is both large and growing, in studies of some length as well as in special and local contributions, to which the nature of the subject lends itself. But we lack an overall study of the Catalan-Aragonese guild organization of the middle of the fifteenth century, a crucial moment because it was at this time that the transition began from the old beneficent-social confraternity to the true, closed professional guild. The city of Valencia, with its deep-rooted guild tradition, can offer us much information in this regard, as was foreshadowed in Tramoyeres' classic book, and which will be confirmed with the work of Gual Camarena now in preparation,[15] based on the documentary resources and bibliography of the Valencian guild structure.

There can be no doubt that the performance and importance of the *Consolats de Mar* in the Spanish Levant during the fifteenth century are an index of the volume and scope of mercantile relations between Spanish ports and those of the coasts of the entire Mediterranean. A worthy but insufficient contribution to the study of the Consulates is Robert Sydney Smith's little book *The Spanish Guild Merchant* (Durham, 1940), which for all its sketchiness would be worth translating into our Peninsular languages. Smith has made use of many documentary sources which are either unknown or generally forgotten, and the book is useful as an overall view. But what interests us more is the possibility that historians will arise who are also jurists, who can undertake the study of the vast amounts of unpublished documentary material concerning the Consulates and use it to write thorough monographs on different aspects of them, as economic corporations and as tribunals, on their juridical system and judicial activities, on the application of the customs and standards of maritime law contained within the *Llibre del Consolat de Mar*[16] or outside it. Good scientific constructions should be built on the solid foundations provided by Capmany in the treatment of these institutions, for they are subjects of general interest.

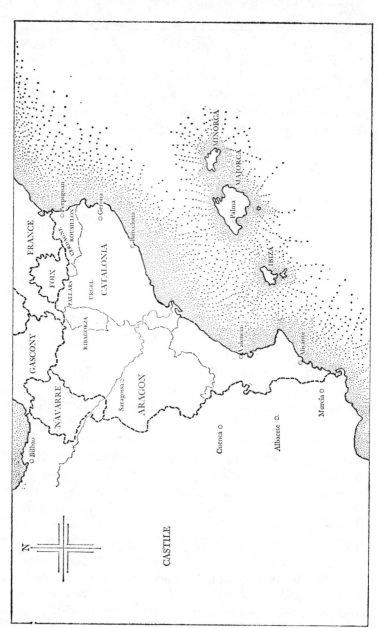

3. The Crown of Aragon c. 1400

In relation to the period which occupies us at the moment, it should be remembered that the great Consulates of Valencia, [Palma de] Mallorca, Barcelona, and Perpignan, created at the end of the thirteenth and throughout the fourteenth centuries, achieved very broad development; and others were established in places of secondary importance but with an old mercantile-maritime tradition: Tortosa in 1401, San Feliú de Guixols in 1443 (this last as a result of its struggles with the city of Gerona), which along general lines followed the pattern established by the earlier Consulates. The full development of the life of the larger Consulates can be observed in the privileges and ordinances which made up their organization during this period, and which regulated their judicial activity. Separate privileges of 1418 and 1420 set forth the form of appointment of the consuls of Valencia, while some extremely detailed procedural ordinances, apparently drawn up between 1410 and 1423, organized the functioning of the Consulate of Barcelona with certain features peculiar to it. The Valencian type was based on the election of consuls by important persons in the maritime community themselves; the Consulate in Barcelona, however, gave this function to the municipal council, and the Consulates of Mallorca and Tortosa, Perpignan, and San Feliu de Guixols functioned along the same lines, almost always distributing the two positions of consul, and the appellate judge-ship when there was one, among the different classes of persons with commercial interests (citizens and merchants or merchants and ship owners, etc.). In the area of the objective competence of these tribunals as well, a number of decisions made by the Crown are important—1443 and 1444—giving the *Consolat de Mar* in Barcelona the exclusive examination of cases and institution of proceedings in maritime litigation, except for the admiral or vice-admiral of the sea, and also authority to carry out the "commands and seizures" ordered by that official. As for trial procedure, Professor Fairen has stressed the interest taken by the Consulate in this area,[17] as the first manifestations of a type of rapid plenary justice which has had great influence on modern regulations in this field.

At the same time we must express our regret that the documents on Catalonian consulates in the Mediterranean, whose publication was promised some time ago by Durán y Sanpere and Camós Cabruja, have not seen the light; the latter scholar is unfortunately no longer in our midst.

In the financial sphere the *Taula de Canvi* of Barcelona, undoubtedly the prototype of those established in other Levantine capitals and even in cities of secondary importance in the interior, has had a splendid presentation by Professor A. Payson Usher, in his book *The Early History of Deposit Banking in Mediterranean Europe* (Cambridge, [Mass.] 1943), the second part of which is dedicated entirely to banking in Catalonia. The *Taula* of Barcelona, created in 1401 (with Ordinances dating from 1412), certainly inspired the creation of the *Taula* of Valencia, requested by the municipality and obtained from Martin the Humane by a privilege of 1407, also as a semi-official deposit bank (Carreras Zacares, *La primitiva Taula de Cambis de Valencia*, Valencia, 1950). But both seem to display a certain lack of solidity in their beginnings, or perhaps the times were not yet ripe for such undertakings. The same phenomenon seems to affect the *Taula de Canvi* of Gerona, created in 1443 by a privilege of Queen María in answer to a petition by the city authorities (L. Marqués Carbó, *La Tabla de Cambio y comunes depósitos de la ciudad de Gerona*, Madrid, 1952). The *Taula* of Valencia ceased to function in 1414–18, Carreras believes, as a result of the circumstances the kingdom was going through, and was not reestablished until a hundred years later. The one in Gerona, in spite of its foundation as described above, did not achieve effective operation until a century later, in Marqués' opinion because of the semi-anarchic state of disorder in which the city of Gerona must have lived, first owing to the war of the *remença* serfs and then to the struggles among parties and factions. The *Taula* of Barcelona was somewhat more fortunate, but it also showed the effects of the critical situation of the years of the revolts, and suspended payments in 1468, after which it was reorganized. Usher's book offers us a valuable body of information about the internal life and fluctuations of this *Taula* (floating and funded debt, budgetary regulations, relations with private bankers, etc.). We should like to see this book translated into Spanish, and it could serve as a basis for the creation of new and more profound studies of the economic and financial life of Catalonia during the 1400's.

THE LAW AND ITS EXPANSION

It seems fitting to close this contribution with an allusion to the development of the law and its sources in the different countries of the Crown of Aragon, and its expansion through the Mediterranean. The first half of the fifteenth century does not represent any significant moment in transformations of a juridical nature. Territorial laws, largely the result of the great Romano-canonical revival, had been developing increasingly and progressively ever since the thirteenth century and displacing local laws. In this sense, the period we are studying accentuated the official force of this *common law*—both canonical and Roman—and it gained authority in the tribunals as a law in its own right, though supplemental to the systems of the respective countries. In Catalonia, where jurists had been asserting and applying it in both forensic life and notarial practice, it received the official sanction of possessing this supplemental nature in the Cortes of 1409, at the end of King Martin's reign, and since that time it has retained this characteristic up to our own day. But, in addition, the law of the principality itself was compiled at this time, and this gave an organic and coherent structure to the mass of *usatges*, constitutions and privileges which had been promulgated over the course of nearly five centuries. The first Cortes convened under Ferdinand I—in 1413—turned over this task to a commission of famous jurists. We do not think that F. Soldevila's interpretation is correct[18] when he considers this to be a defensive attitude on the part of the Cortes in the face of possible royal highhandedness in the observance of those laws. The movement toward compilation was widespread during the period, and was also carried out in Castile, Aragon, and Valencia toward the end of the century, simultaneously with the definitive promulgation of the Catalonian compilation, though this was not done through official initiative in every kingdom. The penetration of Romanism, however, assumed different characteristics in other territories. Thus, in Aragon, it has been established that it was the work of jurists, especially the justices of Aragon, through the collections of *Observancias*, by means of which they interpreted and completed the traditional Aragonese laws along with the common law. This task was begun with the *Observancias* of Jacobo del Hospital—as yet unpublished; it gained greater importance with those of Díez de Aux, finished by order of Alfonso V in 1437, and they acquired a certain official character. The denaturalization undergone by many Aragonese institutions as a result of this doctrinal task had important consequences in some spheres; this was analogous to what happened in Catalonia, such as, for example, the aggravation of seigniorial rights over the peasants, with absolute recognition of the *ius maletractandi* as a result of applying to the peasants the juridical status of the serfs in Roman law.

Besides territorial law, local laws also underwent formulation and compilation during this period, in spite of the decline of their role in legislative life. Between 1430 and 1439 the *Costumbres de Gerona* were drawn up by the jurist Tomás Mieres, utilizing earlier elements. In Majorca the *Ordinaciones* of Pelayo Unís and Berenguer Unís were promulgated. The municipalities themselves carried out a careful work of promulgation of *Ordenanzas*, sometimes in the civil and criminal fields—such as those of Barcelona in 1425 and 1442, and Huesca in 1445—and sometimes in the economic and mercantile area. Among these latter we must not forget the Ordinances of the city of Barcelona on navigation and maritime trade (1435–36) and those on marine insurance (1435, 1436, 1458), these last, in Goldschmidt's words,[19] a truly complete codification of the law of insurance, which essentially fixed mercantile practice and caused it to advance in a positive manner.

If to these remarks we add a reference to the brilliant group of Catalan and Valencian jurisconsults who wrote their books—doctrinal works, or glosses on the principal texts—during those years (Callís, Vallseca, Marquilles, Mieres, Belluga . . .), we shall have a general but very lively impression of the maturity achieved by juridical life in the Mediterranean countries of the Peninsula.

It would be a suitable ending for this study to mention the expansion of Catalan law and institutions into the trans-Mediterranean territories: Sicily and Sardinia. A number of years have passed since Genuardi,[20] Era,[21] Anguera de Sojo,[22] etc., first dealt with this subject, making notable first-hand contributions. We need only point out here the special significance of the decades we have been studying, in regard to this phenomenon. During those years autonomous parliaments were organized in both Sicily and Sardinia, obviously inspired by the Catalan Cortes, as was the Deputation of Sicily, though in lesser degree. Through royal privileges in 1440 and 1441, the *jui de prohoms* was extended to Sardinia. And its Royal Council, *Audiencia*, *Vegueres*, etc., can likewise be traced back to Catalan models. The question of the origin and structure of lieutenancies and viceroyalties, in relation to the governor general of the territories of the Crown, is more problematical, and we have alluded to the problem elsewhere in this study. We can anticipate the successful prosecution of this sort of research from the eminent Sicilian and Sardinian historians, who will be able to illuminate and complete our knowledge of these important problems, to the benefit of the common history of the countries bathed by the western Mediterranean Sea.

NOTES

[1. 1412–1458.]
[2. Barcelona, 1953.]
[3. Ramón Lull, outstanding Majorcan philosopher, *ca.* 1235–1315. He developed a complete philosophical system of his own.]
[4. (Francesc) Eximenis, or Eximeniç, *ca.* 1340–1409. His chief work was an encyclopedia of Christian moral philosophy.]
[5. Tomás Mieres, fifteenth-century jurist, author of *Costumbres de Gerona*, written 1430–39; see below, p. 288.]
[6. Marquilles, Catalan jurist, author of *Usatges* (1448); cf. p. 290.]
[7. Gabriel Turell, author of *Recort*, a fifteenth-century chronicle on the history of France, Spain, and especially Catalonia.]
[8. Cf. Elías de Tejada, *Las doctrinas políticas en la Cataluña medieval* (Barcelona, 1950).]

[9. J. Coroleu e Inglada and J. Pella y Forgas, *Los fueros de Cataluña* (Barcelona, 1878).]

[10. F. Mateu y Llopis, "Notas sobre los del Maestre Racional, Real Audiencia y Justicias," *RABM*, LVIII (1952), 23–52; cont. in *ibid.*, LIX, 7–37.]

[11. A. Giménez Soler, "¿El poder judicial de Aragón es de origen musulmán?" *RABM*, V (1901), 201–6, 454–65, 625–32.]

[12. Justicia, 1564–1591, beheaded during the revolt of Aragon against Philip II.]

[13. Cf. J. Vicens Vives, "Precedentes mediterráneos del virreinato Colombino," *Anuario de Estudios Americanos*, V (1940), 571–614; A. García Gallo, "Los orígenes de la administración territorial de las Indias," *AHDE*, XV (1944), 16–100. Cf. also now *5 Congreso de Historia de la Corona de Aragón. Estudios*, II, 139–56. Professor Vicens died in June 1960 with the researches referred to incomplete.]

[14. I.e., Charles V.]

[15. L. Tramoyeres Blasco, *Instituciones gremiales, su origen y organización en Valencia* (Valencia, 1889). The general work of Sr. Gual Camarena on the guilds of Valencia does not yet seem to have appeared. Cf., however, his "Concordia entre los gremios de zapateros y chapiñeros de Valencia," *Saitabi*, IX (Valencia), (1952–1953 [1956]), 134–44.]

[16. A collection of maritime laws and customs written in the early thirteenth century.]

[17. Fairen. I have not been able to trace this reference.]

[18. Cf. F. Soldevila, *Historia de Catalunya*, II (Barcelona, 1935), 27.]

[19. L. Goldschmidt, *Universalgeschichte des Handelsrechts: Handbuch des Handelsrechts* (3d ed.; Stuttgart, 1891), I (i), 209.]

[20. L. Genuardi, "La influencia del derecho español en las instituciones públicas y privadas de Sicilia," *AHDE*, III (1927), 158–224.]

[21. A. Era, *La raccolta di carte specialmente di re aragonesi e spagnoli, 1260–1715, esistenti nell Archivio del Comune di Alghero* (Sassari, 1927).]

[22. Anguera de Sojo. Reference untraced.]

6 Alfonso the Magnanimous and the Plastic Arts of His Time

JUAN AINAUD DE LASARTE

Sr. Ainaud de Lasarte, in describing the development of the plastic arts in the first half of the fifteenth century under Alfonso V of Aragon, concentrates on the two centers of Barcelona and Valencia, although he allows his eye to travel over the other parts of the "empire" of the Crown of Aragon. Despite the renewed interest in Italy itself, occasioned especially by the conquest of Naples, the plastic arts in eastern Spain did not yet show any notable Renaissance influence. Late Gothic was the predominant architectural style, and if the Catalan economy had suffered a downturn (as has been stated elsewhere), there was still no lack of royal, seignorial, or municipal patronage in Catalonia as well as in the more prosperous Valencia and Majorca. The art patronage of the king at Naples raises special problems of its own, not the least of which concerns the famous triumphal arch of the Castel Nuovo. In Catalonia and Valencia, however, Flemish influences were still more important than Italian.

THE study of the plastic arts at the time of Alfonso the Magnanimous is of an exceptional, though understandable, complexity, owing to the geographical extent of his domains as well as to the beginning and end dates of his reign (1416–1458). It includes centers and artistic trends of such diverse origin as the Hispano-Arabic decorative arts or Flemish painting, and successive periods which, in the field of painting alone, extend from the Gothic International Style to the Italian Renaissance.

I shall have to limit myself, therefore, to sketching a general outline of these varied styles and arts, noting at most a few very representative names and works, and perhaps suggesting some points of departure or conjunction of results and antecedents.

Within these limitations I shall try to take as a center the figure of the king and of his court, sometimes as a guiding element and always as a reflection, at every moment and in a superlative degree, of the highest artistic values attainable.

I shall begin, therefore, with architecture and sculpture and then take up painting, which forms a particularly complex picture because of its abundance and the diversity of styles and artists, and also the facility of movement of paintings and painters. I shall end with the decorative arts, with special reference to Moorish art, in the appreciation of which Valencia played a very important role during Alfonso's lifetime, as well as in other aspects of the artistic life of the period.

Without forgetting other more or less peripheral areas such as Roussillon, Sardinia, Sicily, or Aragon (especially during the time of Archbishop Dalmau de Mur[1]), the two artistic centers with the greatest tradition and continuity were Barcelona and Valencia. Naples achieved exceptional interest only when the Court resided there, and had an extraordinary, though factitious and heterogeneous, atmosphere.

In Majorca there is one name of the first rank, that of Guillem Sagrera, who stands out above the other artists.

In the world of the plastic arts, the Renaissance affected the monarch only very slightly during the last years of his reign, after the conquest of Naples; and except in the isolated case of a few imported works, it found no immediate reflection in his kingdoms outside the court of Naples.

ARCHITECTURE

At the moment when the princes of the House of Trastámara began their reign in Aragon, Gothic architecture of the Catalan style had reached full maturity. The principal cathedrals and palaces of the principality were already planned in their essentials and had attained a perfection and refinement which can be summed up in the name and personality of Arnau Bargués, author of the Gothic façade of the City Hall of Barcelona, the palace of

King Martin in Poblet and the castle-palace of the Cabrera family in Blanes.

The flowering of this same architecture in Valencia or the Balearic Islands, and its expansion through Sardinia and Sicily, is a subject of particular interest. It began especially during the reign of King Martin, and has been the subject of important studies in recent years; we may note as a typical example the case of Guillem Abiell, architect of the General Hospital and so many other buildings in Barcelona, a participant in the famous Congress of Gerona in 1416,[2] who died in Palermo in 1420.

The Majorcan Guillem Sagrera was, during the reign of Alfonso the Magnanimous, the loftiest exponent of this tradition—which he renewed with very personal contributions—in which architecture and sculpture were united.

His formation belongs to the previous period. The oldest reference to him goes back to 1397, when he was working on the cathedral of Palma de Mallorca with his father and a brother, stonecutters by profession.

There followed a long period of activity as an architect in Perpignan, where he married, and for whose cathedral he served as master builder; and, as Ponsich has demonstrated,[3] he transformed the design and gave the cathedral its present appearance. As master for that church he participated in the Congress of Gerona referred to above, and precisely during those years he was in contact in Roussillon with the architect Rollin Valtier, of the diocese of Verdun, who a few years later was to be the master builder of the cathedral of Gerona.

The quality of his production after his return to Majorca is well known. Appointed master builder of the cathedral in 1420, for whose Mirador portal he carved the figure of St. Peter two years later, he was the architect of the admirable *Lonja* [merchants' exchange] contracted for in 1426 and finished by his collaborators —Guillem Villasolar, among others—when he left for Naples about 1447, summoned by the king. Among other minor works left in Majorca by the master or his assistants I shall mention here only the side chapel of the palace of the Almudayna, in which the devices or personal emblems of Alfonso can still be seen.

In Naples his chief work was, of course, the rebuilding of the Castel Nuovo, and especially the Great Hall, designed by him and finished by his relatives and assistants in 1457, three years after his death. Its style is pure Gothic, and it is a definitive and improved version of the star vaulting used by Arnau Bargués when he designed the old chapter room in the cathedral of Barcelona. The Neapolitan writer Summonte, at the beginning of the sixteenth century, could still write of the hall that "è cosa catalana."

The style of his sculptures is very personal and also purely Gothic, and it shows very clearly in a much-photographed window in the Great Hall, as well as in the *Lonja* of Majorca.

Among the many examples of the expansion of Sagrera's architecture into the kingdom of Naples, we should mention the palace of Marino Marzano in Carínola, which can probably be dated between 1449 (or 1453) and 1458.

Among the most outstanding architects of the second quarter of the fifteenth century in Catalonia, we may mention several members of the Safont family: Marc, Joan, and Jordi, responsible among other works for a large part of the palace of the *Generalitat* in Barcelona, the wing added to the *Lonja* of that city, and, perhaps, the house or small palace of the *Generalitat* in Perpignan, built between 1447 and 1458. They are all buildings along very stylized lines, in which the tradition of Catalan Gothic is fully followed. The decoration was the work of independent sculptors, to some of whom I shall refer later.

Another personality, not often studied but apparently very interesting, is Andreu Pi, appointed master builder of the cathedral of Lérida in January, 1457, as successor to Jordi Safont (about 1425–1456). Andreu Pi had been since 1454, the year when the first stone was laid, the master builder of the Hospital de Santa María in that city, on whose façade the angel figures below a large niche are identical in style—a very personal style indeed—to that of another very beautiful work of this period, the Chapel of San Jorge, built in Poblet between 1442 and 1458 by order of Alfonso

the Magnanimous. Old historians of the monastery speak of the
sculptured reredos in the chapel, no longer in existence, and
assume that it was done in Naples; however that may be, other
details still extant, and in particular the interior brackets, make us
think of an artist who might have known Sagrera's work; this
does not detract from the tradition that Pi may have worked
previously with the architect and sculptor Guillem Solivella, for
the mobility of medieval artists has been fully demonstrated on
many other occasions, and Solivella himself was no exception to
this rule.

Outstanding among the constructions of this period in Valencia
are the Torres de Quart, towers which flank the gate of the same
name in that city. They were built by Pere Bonfill between 1441
and 1460, and are not inferior to those of the Castel Nuovo in
Naples.

Aragon, more bound to the Mudéjar tradition of construction
in brick, has nevertheless preserved notable examples of Gothic
architecture. We may mention here the castle-palace of Valder-
roures, begun in the fourteenth century but finished during the
time of Archbishop Dalmau de Mur.

SCULPTURE

In spite of the simplicity of ornamentation which characterizes
Catalan Gothic, the study of sculpture cannot be separated from
that of architecture. In the case of Sagrera or Pi, for example,
both activities are even combined in a single person; but the
existence of sculptors who rarely—or never—designed architectural monuments was also frequent.

In Catalonia early in the fifteenth century we find a solid local
tradition which showed itself in a number of forms. In the first
place, the old workshops which had done work for Peter the
Ceremonious; in this line of descent, but with a completely new
artistic feeling, was Pere Johan, son of Jordi de Déu, a Greek from
Messina who had been a slave of Jaume Cascalls, a native of Berga
and certainly the best Catalonian sculptor of the third quarter of

the fourteenth century. Pere Johan's artistic personality is very well known. We need only mention his decoration of the lateral façade of the *Generalitat* in Barcelona, sculptured in 1418 when he was only twenty years of age; the main altarpiece in Tarragona (1426), with reliefs of admirable quality; the predella[4] of the great altarpiece of Saragossa (1434–49), commissioned, like the one in Tarragona, by Dalmau de Mur. Finally, but only through documents published by Filangieri di Candida and by Madurell,[5] we know that in 1449 King Alfonso summoned him to go to Naples with two or three helpers, his tools, and a supply of alabaster. In March of 1450 we find him on his way through Barcelona, and during the course of the same year he arrived in Naples. Unfortunately, I believe that works so far attributed to him in Naples are not well documented, and even though I run the risk of committing a similar error, I feel that I must in my turn propose a new attribution, of a work which I unfortunately know only through photographs: that of the magnificent seated figure of King Alfonso belonging to the famous Italian historian Tammaro de Marinis.[6] I do not believe that its attribution to Laurana is based on any other argument than that of the Dalmatian sculptor's intervention in the triumphal arch of the Castel Nuovo during the king's lifetime, to which I shall refer later. I seem to see in this sculpture a strong Gothic flavor, more intense than in the majority of Italian works of the same period, and easier to explain if it is attributed to a Catalan artist.

Returning to the early years of the fifteenth century, we find other parallel lines in the Catalan tradition of sculpture. The chief of these is made up of the artists formed at the end of the previous century around Pere Sanglada, in the excellent collective work of the carving of the choir stalls in the cathedral of Barcelona. One of the artists employed there, first as apprentices and then as journeymen, was Pere Oller, well known for the great alabaster altarpiece in the cathedral of Vich and a number of tombs and images carved chiefly in the second quarter of the fifteenth century. The only royal commission of which we are aware—a very early one however—was for the reliefs with hooded figures on the tomb of

Ferdinand of Antequera, carved by order of Alfonso the Mag-nanimous beginning in 1417; some have been returned to the monastery of Poblet, but others are found in places as distant as the Untermeyer collection in New York; a relief with a figure of a mounted man may have belonged to one of the lateral surfaces of the tomb, inspired perhaps by Pere Johan's St. George.

We should also mention a number of other less known or less important Catalonian sculptors, among them Joan Aimeric, apparently the son and heir of a sculptor of the same name, a native of Ager, who died in Perpignan in 1410, whose executor had been Guillem Sagrera. Joan Aimeric II was the author, among other works, of the decoration of the tympanum of the church of Sant Martí de Provençals in Barcelona (1432), and of the Virgin which decorated one of the doors of the parish church of Sabadell (1421), according to documents discovered by Madurell.

In the second quarter of the century Antoni Claperós and his son Joan, son-in-law of Berenguer de Cervià, master builder of the cathedral of Gerona, were working in Barcelona. Apart from some terra-cotta figures, the most important work of these artists is the decoration of the canopy over the fountain in the cloister of the cathedral of Barcelona (about 1449), culminating in a keystone with the figure of St. George, more stylized and more in the decorative manner than that of Pere Johan.

The discussion of sculpture in Catalonia at the time of Alfonso the Magnanimous can be closed with a work of exceptional quality which shows a new, German-influenced style, parallel to that of Flemish painting. This is the tomb of Bishop Bernat de Pau (died 1457)[7] in the cathedral of Gerona; in the same temple there is a direct echo of it—lower in quality, however—in the tomb of his vicar general, Canon Dalmau de Raset (died 1452).

Besides the sculptors properly speaking, we must make at least a brief allusion to the numerous carvers in wood, with the names of Macià Bonafè and Francí Gomar at their head, who carved an enormous number of choir stalls and pulpits in Catalonia, Aragon, the Balearic Islands, and even in Sicily (for example, the choir of the cathedral of Palermo).

In Aragon the patronage of Archbishop Mur was generally given to non-Aragonese artists, such as Pere Johan or Gomar. About 1453 an artist, perhaps French or Burgundian, carved in alabaster the predella of the altarpiece in the archiepiscopal palace of Saragossa (Metropolitan Museum, New York), the equivalent for Aragon of the tombs in Gerona which we mentioned. Nor should we forget that in the second quarter of the century a sculptor from Daroca named De la Huerta worked independently in Dijon.

The Valencian sculptors of this period seem to have been of less importance, especially in comparison with the painters or silversmiths of the same time. We shall name the various artists who worked on carving the sumptuous ceilings in the city hall: Joan del Poyo, Bartolomeu Santalínea (of Morella), Mateu Llop, and Joan Llobet (who died soon afterward, in Sigüenza in 1435). Joan de Castellnou is better known as a silversmith than for his sculptures.

In Majorca, except for the works of Sagrera and his relatives or immediate collaborators, the only works which may belong to the reign of Alfonso the Magnanimous—though we cannot be absolutely certain—are the stone altarpiece of San Salvador de Felanitx, and a Calvary, probably by the same artist, which has been preserved in Palma de Mallorca.

Works by Italians in Barcelona and Valencia are something entirely apart from the production of local artists.

One extremely fine group is still in existence in Valencia: the twelve carved-marble reliefs made for the retrochoir of the cathedral. In spite of the fact that Jaume Esteve, a sculptor from Játiva, contracted to make them in June, 1415, their true author seems to have been "Julià lo florentí," to whom we find documentary references in Valencia between the years 1418 and 1424. The reliefs show the influence of the best Pisan and Florentine tradition, and thus Schmarsow[8] proposed the identification of their author with Giuliano di Giovanni da Poggibonsi, an artist who appears in 1407 in connection with Ghiberti and who is then mentioned in Florence in 1410, 1422, and 1423. The theory does not seem very well founded, especially in view of the presumptive incompatibility of dates between his last years in Tuscany and the references to his presence in Valencia.

Still another hypothesis may be suggested, which though it does not involve a contradiction of dates does not have, at the moment, a full confirmation in regard to style. This is the possible identification of the artist active in Valencia with the Florentine Giuliano di Nofri, who worked on the cathedral of Barcelona in 1422, 1434, and 1435, and between 1443 and 1448 collaborated with Bartolo di Antonio in the Brunelleschi screen for Santa María Novella.

The Italian sculptors and architects active in Naples seem to have formed in still greater measure a world completely independent of their colleagues who had come there from Majorca or Barcelona.

Pisanello, one of the best artists of his time, worked at the court of King Alfonso between 1448 and 1449. We know of two admirable medals carved and signed by him which bear likenesses of the monarch. The king appears on them with the epithets "Triumphator et pacificus" (planned in 1448, dated in 1449; on the reverse, an eagle with the motto "Liberalitas augusta") and "Venator intrepidus." A third, unsigned medal of Alfonso is also generally attributed to Pisanello, the reverse containing a Latin prayer: "Fortitudo mea et laus mea Dominus, et factus est michi in salutem."[9]

Pisanello's drawings in the Codex Vallardi (Louvre) contain sketches and studies for these medals and for another, apparently never made, with an equestrian portrait of the king. A number of authorities, especially Degenhart,[10] have tried to connect with these the series of plans made by Pisanello for other Neapolitan works, from the coverings or tapestries with the motto "GUARDEN LES FORCES" to models for artillery pieces. A large group of studies of heads (some with surprising resemblances to those of Bernat Martorell) have been linked by Degenhart with the first sketches for the triumphal arch of Alfonso the Magnanimous in Naples.

This supposition does not seem to me to be well founded, but the presence of Pisanello during the genesis of this work cannot be completely discounted, for there exists a drawing attributed to his immediate circle which refers precisely to the arch in question.

This is the sketch or plan which was acquired from the Lagoy Collection by the Boymans Museum in Rotterdam. Many of the architectonic elements are still Gothic (except for architraves and medallions), but its style is purely Italian, with no relationship to Catalan Gothic. The sketch shows the complete arch, including the two orders existing in the finished work, and an equestrian statue of the king in a niche in the upper part, placed in a frontal position. This in itself gives the lie (in addition to innumerable complementary arguments) to a fanciful suggestion made a few years ago according to which, in the face of all documentary proofs, the authors of the plan and its execution were Catalans instead of Italians. The fact that Sagrera was the master builder (*protomagister*) of the Castel Nuovo is no bar to the Italians' independence of creation, especially in view of the fact—as seems certain—that the idea had been developing since 1443, years before the great Majorcan artist arrived in Naples.

The sketch in Rotterdam bears only one name, "Bonomi de Ravena," which has been linked with that of Francesco Bonomo, who was in charge of the construction of the Castel Nuovo between 1444 and 1448. There is one more doubtful point in relation to these same dates, that of the intervention of Daniel Florentino, who was in Naples in June of 1446, whom Alfonso calls the *maior fabrice magister* of John II of Castile and wishes "to retain here with us and employ in any special work in this our new Castle of Naples and other castles and works that we are causing to be built in this our realm"; ideas which, as Dr. Rubió has pointed out,[11] do not seem to fit in with his presumed identification with Dello Delli, and still less with the Nicolás Florentino who, a year earlier, had painted the altarpiece for the high altar of the old cathedral of Salamanca.

But whoever the author of the Gothic design was (either related or unrelated to the marble arch whose foundations had originally been begun in a different spot), we know, thanks to other studies, in particular those of Filangieri di Candida,[12] a good many details about the men who carried out its Renaissance adaptation in successive stages.

To begin with, in 1451 the idea of constructing the arch was already in the king's mind, for when Luciano di Martino Laurana (one of Sagrera's collaborators) raised the two great towers "before the gate of the castle," it was specified that he prepare the space between them "except for the marbles and pavements."

This marble decoration was the part reserved for other artists. Certainly the monarch's idea, or that of his councillors, was to turn over the architectural construction to Pietro di Martino da Milano (died 1473) and the sculptures to Donatello, for Alfonso wrote simultaneous letters to the republic of Ragusa asking it to authorize Pietro's journey, and to the Doge of Venice (according to documents published by Dr. Rubió), requesting him to facilitate Donatello's journey and settle accounts with Gattamelata for his monument, since "we have heard of the skill and cunning of the mind of Master Donatello in making bronze and marble statues, it has been our great desire to have him with us and in our service for a while."[13]

According to the anonymous writer of the Gaddi, who seems to represent the least altered tradition, Donatello did only one horse's head in bronze—which was still preserved years later in Naples—as a sample for an equestrian statue of Alfonso which was never made.[14] I think it very possible that this incident may be perfectly true, and that the equestrian statue must have been intended for the niche, now empty, in the upper part of the arch, just as was anticipated by the sketch in Rotterdam.

The king's petition in 1452, as well as later documents, leave no room for doubt concerning the decisive role played by Pietro da Milano in the construction of the arch, proved after July, 1453. At that date he was already working with Francesco Laurana, de Zara, and Paolo Taccone di Mariano da Sezze (Paolo Romano), as head of a team of more than thirty workers. The inscription on the tomb made for him in 1470, three years before his death, commemorated several notable events in the life of Pietro da Milano, among them the fact that he was knighted by Alfonso "on account of the triumphal arch of the new Arch recently constructed."[15] Pietro must have been the author of the *Roman* adaptation of the decoration of the arch, in both its stages (since he worked on it between 1453 and 1458, and then again beginning in 1465); the Roman arch of Pola (in Istria) has often been mentioned as an obvious model for this adaptation. The degree of Laurana's collaboration, documented between 1453 and 1458, continues to be imprecise, and the importance of his role is at present supported only by a late text of Summonte.

We can refer only incidentally here to the importance of his work in Sicily during the years after Alfonso the Magnanimous' death, together with Domenico Gagini (Domenico Lombardo), who worked on the arch between 1457 and 1458. It is precisely to this Sicilian period of the work of these two artists that two beautiful images of the Virgin belong, preserved in the Hospital de la Sang in Palma de Mallorca, one of which follows with considerable fidelity the composition of the Virgin sculpted by Laurana in 1471 for the façade of the chapel of the Castel Nuovo.

Another important artist who worked on the arch was Isaia di Pisa. He had previously done, in Rome, the tombs of the cardinal of Portugal and of Eugenius IV. The humanist Porcellio Pandone, in his poem "Ad immortalitatem Isaiae Pisani marmorum celatoris,"[16] cites various examples of his art:

> Testis et Eugenii mirabilis urna sepulchri
> Testis et Alphonsi regius arcus erit.[17]

This artist had begun his work in June, 1455, and continued with it until the king's death.

And lastly, we can name two disciples and direct collaborators of Donatello, who worked on the same project and represent the Florentine contribution in the absence of their famous master. They are Antonio di Chelino, of Pisan origin, and Andrea dell' Aquila. This last is listed as having been paid in January, 1456, "for the work he has done on the marble stones of the Triumphal

[Arch] for the entrance of Castell Nou," and he died a short time
before Alfonso the Magnanimous. The fact that after 1457 he
continued to work on the Castel Nuovo but not on the arch has
resulted in an attempt to attribute other works to him, among
them the decoration of the tympanum of the palace chapel.

Aside from the famous and controversial arch, the monarch's
sculptural iconography can be followed through other works.
In the first place, the medallion in relief from Poblet (National
Archaeological Museum, Madrid) with a bust of the king in
profile, which can clearly be related with Pisanello's medal
"Triumphator et pacificus," the first word of which is repeated
on it, but not the helmet, which is replaced by a sheaf of millet.
It may be a work brought from Naples in the seventeenth century,
when Alfonso's remains were transferred to Spain.

Another very notable piece, by an unknown author, is said to
have been found in Ibiza. On one side it has a representation of the
Virgin and Child, in a Byzantine style, and on the other, in char-
ming and extremely low relief, a bust of the prince in old age with
the lofty words, "Alfonsus in eternum referens memoriam sui."[18]
This figure, very human and intimate in spite of the motto, is in
strong contrast with that of another medal known to be by Cristo-
fano da Geremia, in a strongly Neo-Pagan style, on the reverse of
which Mars and Bellona are shown crowning the king, in Roman
dress, while on the other side there is a bust of the sovereign.

PAINTING

When Alfonso arrived in Catalonia and Valencia, he found the
pictorial style known as "International" already established in its
first phase. By about 1400 it had spread throughout Europe, in
spite of the fact that in Castile the Italianist style of the artists
patronized by Don Sancho de Rojas, archbishop of Toledo,[19] was
still maintained.

During the first quarter of the century the most outstanding
artist in Catalonia was the painter Lluís Borrassá of Gerona,
established in Barcelona before 1385 and in the service of John I

in 1388. There were artists from Roussillon and Valencia in his workshop. On December 19 [1388] the Majorcan carpenter Gabriel Vila sold him an eighteen-year-old Tatar slave named Lluc. We have only one document of Alfonso's—a simple legal transaction, it appears—in which the name of the painter is mentioned: it is an order from the king, still a prince (November 20, 1413), stating that the Licentiate in Laws Joan Llobet is to handle the suit between Lluis Borrassà and the barber Pere Jaca of Barcelona.

During Alfonso's reign Borrassà painted, with the aid of various collaborators—among them his slave Lluc—five works which have been documented and preserved: the altarpiece of San Miguel de Cruïlles (1416), those of Santa María de Seva and San Andrés de Gurb (simultaneously, in 1417-18), and that of San Esteban de Palautordera (1424), shortly before his death (which occurred in 1425 or 1426).

His slave Lluc returned to Majorca, where he became established with a number of members of his family, and died there (in Sóller, before March, 1434). Indeed, in the church of Roser Vell (Pollensa) there is still a panel of a Pietà which can be attributed to Lluc because of the similarity of its style to Borrassà's.

Two contemporaries of Borrassà were Jaume Cabrera, whom documents show to have worked between 1394 and 1430, in an archaic style, and for whom no dated works exist during the Trastámara period, and Joan Mates of Vilafranca del Penedés, who in 1391 collaborated with Pere Serra, and was active in Barcelona until his death forty years later. Two of his works are dated during the reign of Alfonso the Magnanimous: the altarpiece of Santa María de Vilarrodona (1422) and certainly one other, dedicated to St. Sebastian (1421-25).

The Valencian masters Jaume Mateu (1402-1449), Anton Pereç (1404-1423), and Gonçal Pereç (1411-1423) are successors of Pere Nicolau and Andreu Marçal de Sax, and belong to the same phase of the International Style. Only one work has been proclaimed as attributable to the last-named of these: the Saint James of Algemesí, now in the Museum of Catalan Art.

During the second quarter of the century painting acquired greater refinement, even though it continued to remain within the International Style.

Lluis Borrassà was improved upon in many respects by his successor Bernat Martorell, a native of Sant Celoni, of whose activity in Barcelona we have proof from 1427 until his death in that city in 1452. Consequently, his complete work coincides with the central period of Alfonso's reign.

We know of no direct relationship between this painter and the king or even Queen María, in spite of the fact that he personally received payment for a miniature (perhaps the work of a close collaborator) in a manuscript of the Commentaries on the *Usatges*, executed by order of the Council of the city of Barcelona, which contains a magnificent portrait of the queen (1448). Also commissioned by the councillors, in 1434 he had painted a number of works for the funeral obsequies of another queen, Violante of Bar, the widow of John I.

The altarpieces of St. Martin (Museum of Valencia), St. John the Baptist (Ródenas), and St. Barbara (Museum of Catalan Art, Barcelona) are among the works of the best Valencian painter of the second quarter of the fifteenth century: the so-called Maestro de Martí de Torres, who can be placed in the same category as Martorell in Catalonia, for both the value and the quality of his work. According to Saraleguí, this artist may perhaps be identified with the Gonçal Pereç we mentioned above.[20]

One very enigmatic case is the relationship (or identification) of the Valencian artist whom Post calls "Gil Master"[21] with the Italian named "Maestro del Bambino Vispo." Whether or not these are the same person, perhaps related to the Valencian Miquel Alcanyis, established in Majorca after 1434, the work of this group or groups demonstrates the link between Valencia and the Florentine painters of the International Style. We could also name many other local masters, among them Bernat Serra, active in the Maestrazgo region.

Dello Delli must also have received his artistic formation in Florence, and within the same style. Thanks to a Florentine document of 1433 we have information about his relationship to Bernat Martorell. As we suggested when we were describing the triumphal arch in the Castel Nuovo of Naples, the discussion is still open as to his presumed identification with the "Nicolás Florentino" who decorated the apse of the old cathedral of Salamanca about 1445, and who died in Valencia in 1470.

In Perpignan the International Style had its best exponent in the artist Post calls "the Master of Roussillon." His quality is excellent; he comes midway between Borrassà and Martorell, and Durliat, in his recent magnificent survey of the painting of Roussillon, offers the hypothesis of his identification with Jaubert Gaucelm (1380–1434).[22]

The spread of the painting of Barcelona into Sardinia during this period may be traced through a few documentary references and in some secondary works.

In Sicily painting generally maintained a more individual character, though the artists there were not unaware of Catalan painting. In the group of paintings of the first half of the fifteenth century we may point out the polyptych of the Virgin Mary, and the master who painted the altarpiece of St. Laurence (in the Museum of Syracuse), or, to use the nomenclature proposed by Bottari, the "Maestro di San Martino."[23] Nor should we forget that during this same period there is documentary evidence of the presence of a Syracusan painter, Pietro Scaparra, in Puigcerdá and later (1465–1472) in Perpignan.

The International Style must have been current in Naples before its definitive conquest by Alfonso the Magnanimous, but the known examples of its oldest manifestations are related to the field of the miniature, with which we shall deal later.

Pisanello's stay in the court of the Aragonese monarch between 1448 and 1449 must have marked the apogee of his style in its most perfect and refined phase, even though the examples which have been preserved are limited to drawings, as we said when speaking of the medals of this artist. When Pisanello left—or perhaps died—the king had to content himself with replacing him by a Milanese painter, Leonardo da Besozzo, whose rhetorical appointment (published by Dr. Rubió) was signed by Alfonso in the Torre d'Ottavio on September 10, 1449. In the document it is established that the king wishes him to do mural painting, panels, standards, and miniatures. In reality, except for one manuscript and part of the murals of San Giovanni in Carbonara, very little is left to us of the production of this Lombard painter who, at least in the field of painting on wood, must have been displaced by Jacomart and still more by the original Flemish paintings that Alfonso possessed, for within a short time the naturalism of the court of Burgundy found as strong an echo in Alfonso's court as in that of his competitor René d'Anjou.

In 1444 the king was sent from Valencia "an oak panel four handbreadths high and three wide, on which is painted and drawn by the hand of Master Johannes (Jan van Eyck), the great painter of the illustrious duke of Burgundy, the figure of St. George on horseback and other works, very finely done." It appears that in addition the king possessed an Annunciation, also by van Eyck, and a great tapestry of the Passion acquired in Flanders for 5,000 ducats, which according to Summonte was by "Maestro Roger" (certainly van der Weyden).

Valencia appears to have played an important, though naturally not exclusive, role in this transmission of Flemish art to Naples. This was partly due to the sending of the St. George panel already mentioned, or to the presence of unmistakably imported works such as the triptych of the convent of the Incarnation (now in the Prado Museum, no. 2538,) with coats of arms of the Roïç de Corella family, and also because of the significance of two painters active in Valencia, Lluís Dalmau and Jaume Baço (Jacomart).

Dalmau's trip to Castile (1428) is well known, at the same time as van Eyck arrived in Portugal, and later the Valencian painter's journey to Flanders (1431). On his return to Valencia (documents of 1436 and 1438, concerning works for the Court) or later in Barcelona (after 1443, at least), he must have contributed decisively toward the diffusion of van Eyck's painting. In 1439 Louis Alimbrot of Bruges was already living in Valencia, where he obtained citizenship in 1448. He made a will in 1460, and three years later we have evidence that he had died. As for his artistic production, we know only that he painted a curtain, but the suggestion of the name of Bruges makes us think of the possibility of attributing to him some other Flemish works, such as the triptych in the convent of the Incarnation; however, there are no proofs to confirm this, and the triptych is so small (78 centimeters high) that it is easy to believe that it is an imported work.

Jacomart, in the best works which can be attributed to him— the altarpiece of Játiva, panels in the cathedral of Valencia, and a St. Francis receiving the stigmata (Balanzó collection, Barcelona) —shows a delicate personality and a rather personal adaptation of Flemish formulas, according to the style which was to appear in a more popular and varied form in the panels of his follower Joan Reixach. It is impossible to learn of his activities in Italy at the Court of Alfonso the Magnanimous (at least between 1443 and 1450) by means of authenticated works, and the same occurs with the celebrated Neapolitan painter (later, in part) who through vague literary references in the sixteenth century has sometimes been identified with a supposed Colantonio, for whom we have no contemporary documents as yet. The importance of this master is even greater because he displays to a certain degree the local point of departure of the Neapolitan formation of Antonello da Messina, whose earliest date of proved activity at the present time is a commission for Reggio (Calabria) in 1457, possibly before his journey to Venice, which was to have such a decisive influence on his splendid art. He belongs, at least during the period in which we know his work, to a time later than the death of Alfonso the Magnanimous.

On the other hand, the study of Sicilian painting of the immediately preceding period does not give us any clear ante-cedent, in spite of the fact that there exists on the island a work of such high quality as the fresco of the Triumph of Death, which passed from the Palazzo Sclafani into the collection of the National Gallery in Palermo. It is a work of capital importance, and I agree with Müntz and other authors that it is much more closely linked to the circle of Pisanello, and in general to the painting of northern Italy, than to the Catalonian school.

In Catalonia the purest Flemish style obviously came in with the works of Dalmau, though there was no lack of imported works. As an example of the introduction of the new style into the homes of the bourgeoisie, we might mention the inventory of a citizen of Barcelona, Antoni Cases (1448), which I owe to a kind letter from Sr. Madurell. Besides tapestries and bench covers from Arras and Tournai and a "candelabra, very large, of Flemish brass, with six branches, and the image of Our Lady with Jesus in her arms," there is also a painting which is described as follows: "an oak panel from Flanders, on which is painted Our Lady of Sursum Corda and Jesus in her arms, to whom she is giving suck, done by a very fine hand."

The figure of the Virgin on the central pinnacle of the altarpiece of the Holy Doctors in the cathedral of Barcelona, painted between 1452 and 1454 by the Valencian Miquel Nadal (died 1457, can be related to the Maestro de Altura), is also inspired by a Flemish composition of the Virgin giving suck, of the circle of van der Weyden.

But the painter who best succeeded in adapting Flemish naturalism to the spirit of the country was Jaume Huguet, born in Valls and established in Barcelona after 1448 (where he died in 1492). Still more than Jacomart and Reixach in Valencia, he displays for the principality and Aragon a style of his own, in which the spirit of the country and Flemish contributions converge, adopted with more independence and sense of proportion than in Dalmau and tempered with a sense of monumentality which is closer to that of Italian painting.

Jaume Huguet, unlike his Valencian contemporaries, does not appear to have worked for the Court, though he had other official commissions. Among them is a painting for a tapestry cartoon (1453) with the legend of St. George, made for the deputies, at the same time as Miquel Nadal was painting two others at a lower price, all of them to be sent to Flanders as models. Within the period of Alfonso the Magnanimous' reign (December, 1456, and March, 1457), the councillors of Barcelona came to him and the cardinals with the request that they intercede with the pope to permit the collection of special offerings—with granting of indulgences—to finish paying for the magnificent altarpiece of St. Anthony Abbot, one of Jaume Huguet's best and most delicate works, contracted for in 1454 and unfortunately destroyed in 1909. Huguet's art was to serve as a model for Catalan painting from the last years of Alfonso's reign to the tardy introduction of the Renaissance into the principality about the year 1500.

In the Maestrazgo, the painter who introduced this same style was the Tarragonian artist Valentí Montoliu, established in Sant Mateu about 1447.

In 1455 two Catalan painters appeared in Sardinia, Rafael Thomás of Barcelona and Joan Figuera of Cervera, who worked together to paint the altarpiece of San Bernardino, now in the Museum of Cagliari. Figuera may have stayed in the island for several years, but Thomás later went to Perpignan, where his activity is documented between 1463 and 1470.

His best-known predecessor in Roussillon during the second third of the century was Arnau Gassies, son of a painter from Gandía who had become established in Perpignan. Arnau must have been sent by his father to Valencia to perfect his artistic skill there. In 1432 he was working on the cathedral of Valencia, but two years later he married in Perpignan, and was never to leave it again until his death, which occurred in 1456. About 1454 he painted the altarpiece of St. Michael and St. Hippolytus in Palau del Vidre, a work that has been carefully studied by Durliat, in which the lessons he learned in Valencia and Barcelona are combined, these last received either through a stay in that city or thanks to his work (1437) in the studio of Pere Tortós, a painter from Barcelona established in Perpignan.

In Aragon the introducers of the new style were possibly, as in the case of sculpture, the artists brought in by Archbishop Mur. We have, in fact, a text of 1443 which is very indicative: the contract of Pascual Ortoneda and Pere Joan, apparently written by the latter, for the sculpture and polychrome work of an altarpiece intended for the House of the Commons of Saragossa. The contract states that the work will be "painted very much in the new style, and all in colors of linseed oil, and in very fine colors," and it is stipulated that on the outside surface there are to be figures in monochrome: "four prophets in black and white, wrought in the new style, in relief on stone."

It would be hard to find a more complete definition of the characteristics of the new style, which, in general terms, must soon have undergone adaptation to make it more suitable to the country's tastes, through the style of Jaume Huguet, Pere García the so-called Maestro del Arzobispo Mur (possibly Tomás Giner), Bernat d'Aras, etc.

As for the full impact of the Renaissance in painting, it does not seem to have affected the court of Alfonso the Magnanimous except occasionally. I can only mention here the altarpiece in three sections painted for the king by Fra Filippo Lippi between 1457 and 1458, as a gift from the Medicis, and which was already in Alfonso's possession on May 27, 1458, a few weeks before the king's death.

The two side panels, with St. Anthony Abbot and St. Michael, were acquired by the Cook collection (Richmond Hill, Surrey) early in this century, and their quality makes the loss of the central panel even more lamentable; it is known only through a drawing by the artist in which the frame can also be seen. Instead of architectonic features, it was surmounted by vases of fleurs-de-lis, Alfonso's emblem.

In the case of two other Renaissance Italian pictures which have preserved portraits of the monarch, there are no proofs of a direct link with Naples.

One of them is the handsome bust, in profile, with the inscription "RE DIRAGONA," preserved in the Musée Jacquemart André (Paris). It belongs to the circle of Piero della Francesca and is a work of high quality.

The other is a *cassone* [dower chest] attributed to the Master of Anghiari, an anonymous Florentine of the middle of the fifteenth century. It belongs to the John and Mabel Ringling Museum of

Art in Sarasota, Florida, and represents the assault and capture of a city by Alfonso's troops; he appears on horseback at the left of the picture, and the inscription "R. ALFONSO" on the horse's bridle confirms the identity of the figure, already suggested by the banners, coats of arms, and other elements. Two other panels which form a series with the preceding one and are preserved in the same American museum show a detailed scene of combat between Gauls and Romans and a representation of the triumph of Scipio.

MINIATURES

At the beginning of the reign of Alfonso—whose interest in books is well known—the illumination of manuscripts was still being carried on in the area of the International Style, following more or less the local tradition of Barcelona, Valencia, and Naples.

As for the court, even more than in the case of painting, Alfonso's years of residence in Valencia and his continuing relations with the city, principally through the chief bailiff Joan Mercader, must have had a decisive influence in this area. This continuity was favored by the continued existence of the workshop of Domingo Crespí, who had done work for the court and the *Jurados* of Valencia during the reigns of King Peter and King Martin, and who probably lived until 1438. Of his son Lleonard Crespí, who was already working for himself in 1424, we have information as late as the year 1459.

In addition to the "Consolat de Mar" in the Municipal Archive of Valencia, the "Liber Instrumentorum" in the cathedral of that city, and part of the breviary made for King Martin, illuminated in Valencia about 1403—very early works, therefore—we can attribute to Domingo Crespí the magnificent folio with the scene of St. George and the dragon added during Alfonso's time (about 1430, perhaps) to the breviary mentioned above. In the capital we see the figure of Alfonso, very young, with two Cistercian monks and the devices of the *siti perillós* [or *siège périlleux*], the millet, and the book. The presence of the *siti* is no obstacle to this, for it is documented at least as early as 1427. Lleonard Crespí is the

painter of the miniatures of the "Liber Successionum," a work by
Pau Rossell, done during 1437 and 1438 by Crespí and the scribe
Daniel Baró. The manuscript (Biblioteca Universitaria, Valencia,
no. 2086), contains an allegorical portrait of the king entering a
doorway, symbol of his accession to the rights of the crown of
Naples. This work was written at the request of Joan Mercader
and was intended for his son Berenguer, the friend of Roïç de
Corella.

However, the Crespís' supreme work is the Book of Hours of
Alfonso the Magnanimous (London, British Museum, Ms. Add.
28962). A receipt dated October 19, 1437, proves that the manuscript had been started (but not finished) by Domingo Crespí,
commissioned by Joan, bishop of Elne and the king's confessor.
Three additional receipts (1439–42) show us that Lleonard Crespí,
through the intervention of this same dignitary, was commissioned
to finish the book, and, in fact, in the miniature on folio 263 verso,
the date 1442 can still be read; this must have been the date of the
completion of the decoration, since we know from other sources
that the book was bound the following year.

As for Catalan miniature work during this period, the traditional
style is represented by works like Manuscript 49 of the Biblioteca
Catalana in Barcelona, copied in 1432 by Joan Font, the parish
priest of Riudoms, for Dalmau de Mur; but the work with the
highest quality and most developed style is linked to the name of
Bernat Martorell, with a Book of Hours made prior to 1444
(Historical Archive of the City, Barcelona), and the manuscript
of the Commentary to the *Usatges* already mentioned (1448).
A Rule of St. Benedict written in Ripoll in 1457 (Biblioteca
Universitaria, Barcelona), after Martorell's death, shows the
continued existence of this art in Catalonia.

At the court of Naples the best representative of this same style
was the painter Leonardo da Besozzo, to whom we alluded earlier.
We should also include in this tendency two pages illuminated by
different artists in the *Libro de la Cofradía de Santa Marta* (in the
National Library, Naples), which correspond to the inscription
in the confraternity of King Alfonso himself (1422) and of Joan

de Cardona (1423). In the same book there is a simpler group of pages in the local tradition, to which belongs, among others, the folio corresponding to the prince of Viana (about 1457).

There were other Italian manuscripts of the same style in Alfonso's library, donated by their authors and illuminated in different cities; for example, the codex containing the satires of Francesco Filelfo (Biblioteca Universitaria, Valencia, no. 1791), apparently illuminated in Milan, in which there is a scene showing the author offering it to the king.

I can present only two examples (magnificent ones, however) showing the reflection of Flemish art on Neapolitan miniature work of the period: the pages in the book of the confraternity of Santa Marta which correspond to Arnau Sanç, who entered the confraternity in 1439, and to Pere Roïç de Corella, archdeacon of Játiva. They were published by Filangieri in 1950 with the first of the two pages reproduced in color.[24] Their style is clearly derived from van Eyck, and there is no direct relationship with Jean Fouquet, as there has been an attempt to show. If they were painted about 1440, during King René's period of ascendancy—when he had recently arrived at the court of Burgundy—there would be no room for doubt as to their chronology, but the persons shown in them were, it appears, linked exclusively with Alfonso; the style of the miniatures, on the other hand, even though it has a parallel in some manuscripts of King René, has closer links with van Eyck, either through the painter of the triptych of the Valencian convent of the Incarnation—which bears, as a matter of fact, the coat of arms of the Roïç de Corella family—or through artists like Jacomart or Lluís Dalmau, who was working in Valencia between 1436 and 1438—on his return from Flanders—for the king's household.

The first phase of Renaissance humanism became established in Naples during the last years of Alfonso's life, but did not attain the perfection or interest of the second half of the century. Some quite luxurious, though monotonous, manuscripts which had been presented to the king must have been used as models; for example, George of Trebizond's translation of Cyril of Alexandria (Biblioteca del Catedral, Barcelona, Ms. 119) or the translation of St. John Chrysostom by Theodore of Thessalonica (Biblioteca Universitaria, Valencia, Ms. 1223). In a few cases we know the name of the scribe, for example that of the Bolognese Gandulfo Fantuccio in a codex of St. Ambrose which is preserved in Madrid (Biblioteca Nacional, Ms. 9482).

The manuscripts produced in the king's own court, masterfully studied by Tammaro de Marinis, were the work of calligraphers from various places. Among them were a number of Neapolitans —naturally—and some from the Spanish countries. The style of this latter group does not appear to be personal, but imitated from the humanistic manuscripts which were available to them. We do not know of any documented work of Alfonso de Córdoba, certainly one of the best of the calligraphers, but we do possess some works by Gabriel Altadell, a native of Barcelona, who was librarian for Alfonso and for the prince of Viana while the latter was in Naples. We can find Aristotle's *Ethics* in the British Museum in London (Ms. Add. 21.120), and in Valencia two manuscripts of the year 1450 (Biblioteca Universitaria, Mss. 943 and 1072) with grammatical works by Bartolomeo Fazio and Guarino di Verona; another example of a text of the latter calligrapher is mentioned in a group of eleven manuscripts executed by Gabriel Altadell, which the royal chronicler Pere Miquel Carbonell acquired in Barcelona in 1470.

As for Queen María, although we can assume the interest she must have had in manuscripts from the inventory of her books, I know of only one volume attributed—without very firm proof —to her personal use. This is a Book of Hours written in silver and gold on a black background, and it is at present in the library of the Hispanic Society of America (Ms. B 251).

DECORATIVE ARTS

I have given especially full treatment to miniatures in order to call attention to Alfonso's propensities as a bibliophile; however, the desire to avoid excessive length prevents me from doing the same with the decorative arts. On the other hand, in this area there is an excessive disproportion between the abundance of documentary references and the small number of works which have been preserved, chiefly those belonging to the Court.

In regard to tapestry, I have only a few scattered references and the information offered by the tapestries shown in the miniatures of the king's Book of Hours. These are of a completely French-Flemish character, as is the magnificent tapestry of the Passion which belonged to Archbishop Dalmau de Mur, at present preserved in the cathedral of Saragossa.

In these miniatures we can see carpets of various styles. We know that in 1456 Alfonso had a "master carpetmaker" in Naples named Francesc de Perea, possibly of Valencian origin. I know of no example of the models shown in the manuscript. However, up to the nineteenth century there was in the convent of Santa Isabel in Toledo a magnificent group of carpets, probably of Murcian manufacture, with the coat of arms of María de Castilla, the wife of Alfonso the Magnanimous. They have been studied recently by Miss May and Dr. Kühnel. One of them now belongs to the Hispanic Society (New York), another to the Detroit Institute of Arts, and a third to the Textile Museum of the District of Columbia (Washington). They are exceptional pieces (the one in New York is more than five meters long) and are considered among the best and oldest examples in existence.

These works put us into contact with the world of Moorish decorative arts, which we will also find in Queen María's or Alfonso's courts. His inventory, made before he ascended the throne, lists various objects of the same kind, the majority coming from his father Ferdinand of Antequera, perhaps as trophies of his campaigns against the Saracens. Among them are short swords adorned with gilded silver, enamels and carved ivory. Also, in the same inventory, begun in Barcelona in 1413, foreign arms from a number of sources are described: German and Rumanian (Byzantine) crossbows, Turkish, Damascus, or English bows, coats of mail from Paris, Italian lances, etc.

The prince's wardrobe also included many garments in the

Moorish style: three shirts, three jubbahs, and three *alferemes* (turbans). In some cases they are indisputably of Moslem manufacture, such as a jubbah described as "Moorish, of Moorish silk cloth, made with long stripes, and white Moorish letters, and other ornaments of divers colors."

One magnificent group, a gift from the king of Granada, is described in a letter from the *alcaide* Yamin (1418). In it he describes the saddle, the gold sword, a shield, and a complete outfit of clothing including a burnoose, and the *alcaide* himself observes to the king, "And, my lord, these precious things are for jousting."

The custom of using Moorish dress for jousts persisted in Valencia up to the end of the sixteenth century, and thus we should not be surprised to find that whole costumes in the Moorish style were often made there. This was also true in regard to the trappings or harness of the horses and to the swords themselves, and the Valencian silversmiths of Jewish origin specialized in the manufacture of these. Sanchís Sivera has published valuable documentary references of this type,[25] and I shall mention a few of the most significant. The *converso* Daniel Martínez of Gandía, a resident of Valencia, made between 1426 and 1427 a "Moorish blade" for the king with a matching harness, and in 1434 "two short swords" for the monarch's use (and certainly for the use of his companions in the joust). In 1428 a silversmith from Játiva, Diego Rodríguez, made other Moorish gold trappings for the royal service. Among the proofs of the survival of this same style years later, we find the detailed description of the sumptuous outfit made between 1467 and 1468 by Vidal Astori, a Jew from Sagunto, for the prince and future king Ferdinand the Catholic. It consisted of a gold sword adorned with letters, and trappings for a horse with all kinds of decorations in gold filigree.

We also know of other Valencian gifts in the Moorish style received by the king, as is shown in the case of "a piece of Moorish silk cloth with Moorish letters and other ornaments of different colors, which was presented to him by the Moorish community of the city of Valencia."

Along the lines of these tastes—though it has nothing to do with the decorative arts—we should mention the king's interest in always having in Naples Moorish minstrels and dancers of both sexes, sent from Valencia.

Also, gilded ceramic pieces and the tiles of Manises, both in the Moorish and Gothic style, manufactured chiefly in the establishment of the Murcí family, were frequently sent to Italy, and not only to Naples but to Rome, Florence, or Venice. Osma,[26] Van de Put,[27] González Martí,[28] and Mrs. Frothingham[29] have made special studies of these products and of all the documentation referring to them. Some tiles are still in existence today out of the thousands ordered by the king and queen for their palaces in Valencia and Naples, with the devices of the millet, the book, the *siti perillós*, and various mottoes or legends. The Museum of Sèvres possesses two examples of about the year 1430, with the coats of arms of María of Castile and her sister-in-law Blanche of Navarre, part of a set of tableware in the Moorish style which belonged to the kings of Navarre and was found in the sixteenth century in the castle of Pau. María of Castile also ordered other pieces made in Manises for her personal use in the year 1454. A magnificent platter 51 centimetres in diameter, now in the Victoria and Albert Museum, may have belonged to this second group.

To close the discussion of the decorative arts, we should say a a few words about jewelry—words which are almost elegaic since it is only through documents that we know something of the royal table service or the gold oratory in the chapel, embellished with diamonds, pearls, and sapphires.

The inventory begun in 1413 contains many references to the pieces of table service which Alfonso received from the cities and towns of his domains; there are also frequent later references, in large part from municipal documentation (such as the *Llibre de Solemnitats* of Barcelona).

In Barcelona, silversmiths' work of the first half of the fifteenth century gives us four illustrious names: Marc Canyes (died 1436), the teacher of other artists; Bernat Llompart, a native of Valencia, the richness and originality of whose work are exceptional;

Berenguer Palau, and Francesc Ortall or Artau of Gerona, who often worked in Barcelona.

It has been demonstrated that the silversmiths Artau, Palau, and Llompart worked for King Alfonso. In 1451, when the councillors of Barcelona decided to present a gift of jewelry to the king, they displayed their intentions in a way that deserves to be quoted:

> ... it is reasonable and very necessary ... that the said gift or service be made to the said lord, but that it be beautiful and striking in appearance; for this city is very famous there in Italy, and through the impression made by the said gift or jewel, the fame of the said city shall resound in those parts. ...
>
> And by some of the said Council it was argued that it would be well if the said service or jewel be an image of St. Eulalia, patroness of this city, that it be made all of gold and placed in the chapel of the said king.
>
> And moreover, a large and beautiful shell of gilded silver, to be placed on the sideboard of the said king. And that in each of the said jewels shall be placed the arms of the said king and the said city; and when the said king sees the said jewels, he will call to mind the said city.

Both were made by Francesc Artau, one of whose documented works has been preserved: the monstrance of the cathedral of Gerona. The magnificent coffer of San Martinián, in Banyoles, dated in 1453, can also be attributed to him, at least in part; a complete study of it was made by the historian M. Constans,[30] unfortunately no longer alive.

As for Valencia—apart from the Santalínea family, studied by M. Betí[31]—Sanchís Sivera has published an almost inexhaustible number of references which are difficult to summarize in a brief survey. Among them are references to tableware, church images, jewels or prizes for poetry competitions, and objects for the king's personal use, such as a gold ring with a seated figure of the monarch made by a jeweler named Llorens of Constance, perhaps a German, in 1424.

This leads us to speak, even though briefly, of the art of seal-making, for the makers of royal seals were always silversmiths, and in the case of Alfonso and his wife always Valencians.

The oldest was Bartolomeu Coscolla, who in 1373 was already working with the famous royal silversmith Pere Bernés, and who made seals and jewels for Sibila of Fortià and kings John I, Martin the Humane, and Ferdinand of Antequera. Through a document of the year 1417 we know that he made the first *flaó*, or royal seal, for Alfonso as king, as well as the gold or lead molds for bulls. And, in fact, his design does not differ substantially from that used by previous monarchs. Sagarra lists at least fifteen molds used in the different kinds of royal seals up to 1458.[32] Only a gold bull of 1445 is different from the traditional ones; it may possibly have been made in Naples.

In regard to Queen María, we know the name of the last silversmith who prepared the mold for her ordinary seal. He was García Gomis Sorio, who lived in Valencia, also the maker of the queen's testamentary seal and the first seal used by John II of Aragon.

We might also note here, in connection with the decorative arts, a person who in the course of his restless life went into the service of Alfonso the Magnanimous almost by accident—and then only as a soldier. This was a young man born in Ulm in 1406 who, after having learned the art of staining glass in his native city, went to Rome, and between 1431 and 1435 (at the time of the battle of Ponza) enlisted in Alfonso's army. He then went into the service of a citizen of Capua, and about the year 1440 entered the Dominican monastery of Bologna as a novice. He died there in 1491, and is known as the Blessed Giacomo of Ulm. After taking his vows as a monk he developed his artistic abilities very notably as a stainer of glass and was responsible for the formation of good disciples within his own Order. Although it is possible that he had no opportunity to give proofs of his art because of the special circumstances of the king's campaigns, I believe that this is a not unworthy example of how subject to chance the life of some medieval artists was, and of the infinite and unfathomable complexity of the crossing of personal relationships or artistic currents which often took place.

CONCLUSION

And so we come to the end of this review, incomplete of course but also perhaps excessively prolix in some of its sections. In any case, I think it has been useful to help us, as far as is possible, to form an idea of the artistic ambiance during the reign and at the court of Alfonso the Magnanimous.

It is more difficult to establish the degree of intensity and sincerity of the prince's tastes. But this would involve as a previous question the much-discussed value of the statements contained in the official correspondence of our medieval monarchs.

Be that as it may, even though these may not always reflect a sincere and personal opinion, they do have the interest of being the highest expression of the world in which those monarchs lived.

An autograph letter from Alfonso to the cardinal of Aquilea is often cited as an important piece of evidence, in which the king emphasizes his decision to "satisfy the spirit before satisfying the body," as a result of his having arrived one evening after the chase and having stopped before eating to contemplate a piece of sculpture and some paintings which he had just received.

In a comparable sphere of ideas we can also cite his praises of Donatello or Leonardo da Besozzo, in expressions which attempt to reflect the king's tastes and ideas. He wrote to Duke Francesco Foscari in these words:

"Indeed, you are not unaware that We take great delight in these statues and works of art, in bronze as well as in marble."

When Arnau Fenolleda, the same secretary who wrote the letter to the duke, drew up in Latin the appointment of Leonardo da Besozzo, he set forth a real theory of the relations between the prince and artists. He emphasized the usefulness of royal patronage and placed artists on the same plane with chroniclers and poets in a phrase from Horace: "Poesis nichil aliud est quam pictura loquens."[33] And he stresses the fact that, thanks to both poetry and art, posterity can learn of a king's greatest and most illustrious deeds.

The king entered fully—and in a very personal and sincere way—into the clearly pagan concept of many of his Italian contemporaries. This was the unmistakable making divine of the individual and his heroic deeds, and is expressed in the title DIVUS ALPHONSUS on Pisanello's medals. However, in spite of the headiness of his triumphs and the Neapolitan atmosphere in general, from the marbles of the arch of the Castel Nuovo to his treatment of Queen María, cruelly passed over in the monarch's will, the king's ardent desire to spread his fame sometimes took on a more generous character. This is shown through both official and sumptuary commissions, such as the provision in his will for the creation of two silver altarpieces for El Puig and Montserrat, or the enigmatic relief described before, on one of whose sides there is also a figure of the Virgin and on the other the bust of the king, with the inscription which shows his constant desire, a desire that we, in a sense, are helping to satisfy today:

Alfonsus in eternum referens memoriam sui

NOTES

[1. Archbishop of Saragossa, 1431–1456.]
[2. The Congress of Gerona met to decide whether Gerona cathedral should have a nave and two aisles, or simply one great nave—the solution finally reached. (Cf. L. Torres Balbás, "Arquitectura Gótica," *Ars Hispaniae*, VII (Madrid, 1952), 175; the proceedings of the *Junta* printed in E. S. Street. *Gothic Architecture in Spain* (London, 1869), 501–13).]
[3. P. Ponsich, "La cathédrale S. Jean de Perpignan," *ER* (1953), 137–214.]
[4. The painting on the altar step.]
[5. R. Filangieri di Cadida Gonzaga, "Archittetura e scultura Catalana in Campania nel secolo XV," *Boletín de la Sociedad Castellonense de Cultura*, II (May–June, 1930), 121–36. I have been unable to trace the reference to the work of Sr. Madurell Marimón.]
[6. Editor of the standard work on Alfonso's library, *La biblioteca napoletana dei re d'Aragona* (Milan, 1950).]
[7. Bishop of Gerona, 1436–1457.]
[8. A. Schmarsow, "Juliano Florentino ein Mitarbeiter Ghibertis in Valencia," *Abhandlungen der K. sächs. Gesellschaft der Wissenschaft philolog.-hist. Klasse*, XXIX, 3 (Leipzig, 1911), 6 ff.]

[9. "The Lord is my strength and song, and he is become my salvation."]

[10. B. Degenhart, *A. Pisanello* (Turin, 1945).]

[11. J. Rubió i Balaguer, "Alfons 'el magnanim' rei de Napols, 'Daniel' Florentino, Leonardo da Bisuccio i Donatello," *Miscellània Puig i Cadafalch* (Barcelona, 1947–51), pp. 25–35.]

[12. R. Filangieri di Candida Gonzaga, "L'Arco di Triunfo di Alfonso d'Aragona," *Dedalo*, XII (1932), 439–66, 594–626; "Rassegna crítica delle fonti per la storia di Castel Nuovo," *Archivio Storico Napoletano*, II, III (Naples, 1938–39).]

[13. "Cum audiverimus ingeni sol[l]ertiam atque subtilitatem magistri Donatelli in statuis tam eneis quam marmoreis fabricandis, magna nobis voluntas recessit eundem penes nos et in nostris serviciis per aliquod tempus habere."]

[14. Cf. Cornel v. Fabriczy, *Il códice dell'Anónimo Gaddiano* (Florence, 1893), quoted M. Cruttwell, *Donatello* (London, 1911), p. 118 and n. 1.]

[15. "Ob triumphalem Arcis novae arcum solerter structum."]

[16. "To the Immortality of Isaiah of Pisa, Carver of Marble."]

[17. "His witness is the urn of the wonderful tomb of Eugenius, and witness too will be Alfonso's royal arch."]

[18. "Alfonso reproducing for eternity the memory of himself."]

[19. Archbishop of Toledo, 1415–1422.]

[20. L. Saraleguí, "Gonzalo Pérez," *Archivo de Arte Valenciano*, XXVIII (1957), 3–24, and cf. C. R. Post, *History of Spanish Painting*, XII, pt. 2, 593–97.]

[21. C. R. Post, *History of Spanish Painting*, XI, 424.]

[22. M. Durliat, *Arts anciens du Roussillon* (Perpignan, 1954), pp. 86–90.]

[23. S. Bottari, *La Pittura del Quattrocento in Sicilia* (Messina, Florence, 1954).]

[24. R. Filangieri di Candida Gonzaga, *Il códice miniato della confraternità di Santa Marta di Nápoli* (Florence, 1950).]

[25. J. Sanchís Sivera, "Arquitectos y escultores de la catedral de Valencia," *Archivo de Arte Valenciano*, XVIII (1932).]

[26. G. J. de Osma, *Apuntes sobre cerámica morisca . . . textos y documentos Valencianos* (3 vols.; Madrid, 1907–1909; rev. 1923).]

[27. A. Van de Put, *The Valencian Styles of Hispano-Moresque Pottery 1404–1454* (New York, 1938).]

[28. M. González Martí, *Cerámica del Levante Español* (3 vols.; Barcelona, 1944–52).]

[29. Alice Wilson Frothingham, *Lustreware of Spain* (New York, 1951).]

[30. M. D. Luis G. Constans, "Los claustros del monasterio de Bañolas," *Centro de estudios comarcales de Bañolas* (1952).]

[31. M. Betí Bofarull, *Los Santalínea, orfebres de Morella* (Castellón de la Plana, 1928).]

[32. Cf. F. de Sagarra y de Siscar, *Inventari, descripcio i estudi dels segells de Catalunya* (Barcelona, 1932). I have not been able to consult this work myself.]

[33. "Poetry is no more than a painting which speaks." Cf. Horace, *Ars Poetica*, 11, 361–62, "Ut pictura poesis: erit quae, si proprius stes te capiat magis, et quaedam, si longius abstes."]

7 The Beginnings of Dominican Reform in Castile

V. BELTRÁN DE HEREDIA, O.P.

Father Beltrán de Heredia, the outstanding historian of spirituality in Spain, in describing the beginnings of the reform of the Dominican Order in the province of Salamanca opens up a particular aspect of a very large topic—the reform of the Church in Spain, usually, and rightly, associated with Cardinal Jiménez. This essay shows that already in the second quarter of the century the Dominicans were starting on the lengthy task whose achievement was to make the Spanish Church so distinctive among the churches of Western Europe, so comparatively well prepared to answer the challenges put to it later by the discovery of America and the threat of Protestantism. The appendixes originally printed at the end of the article have been omitted, as have the direct references to the documents in the text and the notes.

IN 1937, when we were preparing our book on the Dominican reform in Castile,[1] we had not yet had the opportunity to examine thoroughly the papal records. Hence we were acquainted with the popes' measures concerning the reform only through the records of the Order's generals. And since these records, insofar as they are able to enlighten us about the matter, do not begin until 1474, a considerable portion of the papal documentation prior to this date was not utilized in the previous study.

Later we have been able to consult these papal records in comparative leisure, though for another purpose, especially the Register of Petitions, which serves as a basis for the rest. The results of this search have not been particulary ample; but their quality compensates sufficiently for the time spent on the search, for they give us information of extraordinary interest which has been preserved only in these Vatican sources. To order and present their contents is a preliminary step in the history of Dominican reform in Castile, and this is what we propose to do in the present study.

Aspiration to the life of observance made itself felt in some of our Castilian friars beginning in the early decades of the fifteenth century. But they were isolated episodes, such as the action of the Blessed Álvaro, who retired with a few companions to live the life of a hermit, a very frequent occurrence at that time among the reformed Franciscans. In the case of the Blessed Álvaro the apostolate was kept alive; but in others it was reduced to a minimum, at the risk of sacrificing one of the specific aims of the Order.[2] Establishment of the first reform in the province, early in the second half of the century, eliminated this danger; and what might have become a deviation helped to strengthen observance when properly channeled.

Observance began to be established in an isolated way in a few houses. After the Escalaceli of Córdoba, which on the basis of a bull of Martin V is usually assigned the date of 1423, though in reality it occurred several years later, came that of the monastery of Burgos, initiated by Don Pablo de Santa María,[3] who greatly favored that particular monastic house. For the purpose, in 1435 he sent a petition to the Council of Basel, where it was admitted on May 5 of that year. On the fourteenth of the month a favorable decision was taken, which appears in the proceedings of the Council in these words: "Concerning the request of the lord Paul, bishop of Burgos, about the reform of the house of the Preachers in the city of Burgos, all deputations agree that it should be committed to the most reverend cardinal legate (Cesarini), who by the authority of the Holy Council may provide, and according to the ordinance of the general and the constitutions and statutes of the same order, that the same house may be reformed."[4]

Don Alfonso, Don Pablo's son and his successor in governing the church in Burgos, inherited his father's affection for this monastic house. At his request general study was instituted there, as is shown in a declaration of the chapter general of Montpellier in 1456, which reads as follows: "We declare that, at the instance of the most reverend lord, the bishop of Burgos, a *studium generale* has been set up in the house at Burgos in the province of Spain, without, however, degree or form, in order that brothers of the Spanish province and of other provinces may be sent there for study."[5]

This same prelate of Burgos, Pablo de Santa María, also took part in the foundation of a new monastery of observance. We cite what Father Luciano Serrano has to say about the matter: "The foundation of the Dominican monastery of Rojas, established in the church of Santa María de Cinco Altares, falls within the episcopate of Don Pablo. This foundation had formerly been offered to the Hieronymite friars, who occupied it for a few years; but on February 10, 1435, Doña Sancha de Rojas and her brother Lope de Rojas ceded it to Fray Martín, prior of San Pablo and nephew of Don Pablo, together with all the assets and properties the Hieronymites had owned, plus an income in wheat which the aforesaid Don Lope de Rojas enjoyed in this town and other towns of the district."[6]

A year later, in 1436, the foundation of the monastery of Murcia took place, also within observance and directly subordinated to the general of the Order. Alfonso Juan de Fajardo, president for that kingdom, had requested of his superiors that he be allowed to keep Fray Juan de Murcia with him for a time; this friar, a licentiate in theology, was to instruct and offer religious service to the faithful of that kingdom, who needed to be fortified in the Faith because they shared a frontier area with the Moors, "in order that they should strive manfully for the strengthening of this same faith,"[7] as he explains to Eugenius IV. He adds that this friar, with his preaching and his edifying life, "administered to the aforesaid children of Christ very many good things, doctrines, and examples."[8] He therefore requests that, in order to give stability to this laudable ministry, Fray Juan may be allowed to found a monastery of observance there "immediately subject to the general of the said Order at that time."[9] On May 9, 1436, the pontiff granted the petition, exempting the new monastery from the authority of the provincial of Spain.[10]

Not long after this, in 1439, the chapter general recommended to the Spanish provincial that he reform the monastery of Santa María de Nieva, since it was a sanctuary much frequented by pilgrims.[11]

A number of petitions presented to Eugenius IV in 1440 by Fray Rodrigo give us additional information not included in the chronicles concerning the reforming task of the Blessed Álvaro. "Formerly Fray Álvaro of Zamora of the Order of Preachers, master in sacred theology," says one of the petitions, "founded and built in the city of Seville a certain house with a chapel or oratory under the name of St. Dominic of Portaceli, in which he and a companion or companions often used to stay."[12] This foundation, the author of the petition continues, was created by Fray Álvaro so that observant religious could undertake to celebrate the Divine Office there; this is not done at present, for a certain brother who claims to have permission from his superiors occupies the foundation, for his own solace rather than for spiritual exercises. Therefore Fray Rodrigo de Valencia, doctor in theology and chaplain to the king of Castile, requests [that he] "who for a long time has attended sermons in the said town and wishes to continue hereafter to attend them, as the said Fray Álvaro, the founder of that house, used to do while he lived in the same city, insofar as you may of your special grace think it worthy to grant and mercifully allow the same Fray Rodrigo so that he may more peacefully serve God and can more fruitfully abstain from preachings without hindrance, so that he may be able to be in, remain at, and inhabit a house or oratory of this kind, which at present has no rents, with two friars of the same order, which he shall choose for the same purpose, and to rule and govern it, as long as he lives freely and lawfully without any contradiction or hindrance of any other person, so long as the agreement of the master general of that same order is secured for that project."[13] The pope granted the petition "with the consent of the master general of the said order."[14]

Eugenius IV himself, at the insistence of Fray Rodrigo, commissioned him jointly with the prior of the Charterhouse of

Seville to reform the monastery of San Pablo in that city, as well as the convents of Santa María la Real and Santa María del Val.[15] But since Fray Rodrigo feared that the general would not give consent to have an outsider intervene in the reform, he later requested and obtained permission to have the condition calling for his consent suppressed.[16] A few days later he presented a new request entreating that in the bulls of the previous concession, so that they could not be criticized as fraudulent, it be stated that he was not a master of theology but merely a lector or doctor.[17] But when the general learned of the negotiations which were being carried out behind his back by the friar, he requested and obtained their annulment, and further, "that they should be canceled and removed from the register of petitions."[18] This in fact was done, and therefore they appear crossed out in the register.[19]

The chronicles of the Order present Fray Rodrigo de Valencia as a disciple of the Blessed Álvaro. It seems likely that he was a true promoter of observance, but perhaps he was not particularly discreet, and thus obliged the general to stop him from attributing to himself some degrees to which he was not entitled. In the monastery of San Pablo which he was trying to reform, the name of Father Pedro de Villaviciosa appears as assigned there in 1434;[20] he was an extraordinarily gifted friar, who later as provincial was to carry out the reform of the province. Thus we can suppose that the picture presented by Fray Rodrigo concerning the situation in that community was deliberately distorted in order to gain his ends.

These isolated reforms did not satisfy those who were eager for a prompt and true renewal of the province. The new foundations of Escalaceli,[21] Rojas, and Murcia, since they concerned small monastic houses, could not noticeably influence the more important ones, which was what was most needed. If to this circumstance we add not only the lack of zeal in maintaining observance among the provincials, but in some cases the actual demoralization caused by their bad example, we will understand that the religious who were truly earnest, of whom there were many in the province, became seriously alarmed by the course matters were taking just at the time when other orders were seriously attempting a real restoration in the life of the regular clergy.

We lack precise data on the politico-social state, if we may call it that, of the province; but there are indications that a certain amount of unrest was being felt in it, with a great many discontented members and the prejudices which are likely to arise when matters are not progressing in their normal channels. The differences of opinion had to do with the reform advocated by some and rejected by others, the latter group constituting the majority.

From 1434 to 1436 at least, the provincial had been Father Lope de Galdo. His personal history did not make him a particularly appropriate person to carry out the transformation required by the low level of religious life in Spanish monasteries. He had taken his vows in the monastery of Vivero, where his name appears as a student of logic in a fragment of the proceedings of a certain provincial chapter held in 1383.[22] In 1410, already a master of theology, he appealed to the Luna Pope with the request that he be assigned to the minor penitentiaries of His Holiness.[23] He continued to be a member of the curia of Luna himself until 1415 or 1416, leaving him to go to Constance with Cardinal Carrillo. In a petition of March 28, 1419, he appears as one of the familiars of this cardinal, asserting that he has been a minor penitentiary of the deposed pontiff, "and for three years continuously exercising by papal authority the office of [minor] penitentiary until his own complete abandonment of Peñíscola."[24] A few months later, wishing to take advantage of this adhesion, he requested that he be granted the administration of benefices in the kingdom of Castile belonging to the Bethlemite church, which had been abandoned because its bishop—who at the time was Juan Marchand—"lives at present in distant parts."[25] By 1434 he had become the provincial for Castile, and in this capacity he accompanied, together with the Dominican Master Juan del Corral, the embassy sent by John II to the Council of Basel, where he probably remained until the Council was transferred to Ferrara in

1437. It appears that in 1438 he was already back in Spain. All his actions show that he felt extremely attached to the papal curia and regretted having to leave it.

Who was his successor in the office of provincial? In 1442 the head of the province was Father Juan de Zamora.[26] We do not even know how long his term of office lasted. In 1449 the name of Father Esteban Soutello appears in the position, and he continued in it until his deposition by trial in 1454. The chronicles tell us nothing about the matter, but papal documents charge him with lack of ability, which caused this serious decision to be made.

Because it is intimately connected with the foregoing, we must say something here about the episode of Fray Diego Ortiz. He was a Hieronymite monk from Guadalupe who passed over to the Dominican Order about 1429 and was admitted to the monastery in Seville. In the chapter general of 1434 his name appears with the title "pro doctore."[27] But later he was accused before the chapter general of having appropriated some funds, and his expulsion was decreed. The Order, according to a report presented by the provincial, Soutello, had obtained permission from the pope to turn the matter over to the bishops of Burgos and Leon (the latter probably Coutanza), who approved the decision made by the chapter general. But the accused later appealed to the Holy See, which commissioned the bishops of Cuenca and Orense to settle the matter on receipt of information about the case.[28] The bishop of Cuenca was Lope de Barrientos.[29] To judge from the date at which this took place, the bishop of Orense must have been Pedro de Silva,[30] also a Dominican. The pope's charge was formulated in such a way that both bishops, or only one in agreement with the other, could institute trial and decide on the matter. The person who in fact began the investigations was Barrientos, calling on the provincial, Soutello, and Fray Rodrigo de Marmolejo of the Seville monastery to appear before him and give information, according to the terms of the pope's charge. The provincial ignored the order, and in consequence Barrientos denounced him as disobedient and perhaps in addition accused him of other irregularities which had been attributed to him. Some juridical reports were also added to the denunciation, in corroboration of the charges being made against the provincial. The result of the accusations was the bull *Ex fidedignorum* of April 20, 1453, addressed to Barrientos himself, in which Nicholas V says that he has received trustworthy information concerning the extremely low state of observance in the province of Castile, blaming it on the provincial because of negligence in his governance and the bad example he is giving, "consumed as he is by such great avarice that he sells graces and liberties to the brethren of the said order for money, and extorts money from them and the convents by the most exorbitant means."[31] He therefore charges the bishop, in order to correct these evils, to visit the province either personally or through a representative and to patch up its defects, reestablishing observance there and attempting to foster studies. To accomplish this, he is given authority to remove the provincial from office, obliging him to return whatever he has unjustly taken, and to provide a successor; and he is given full power to carry out these changes.[32]

A plea granted *motu proprio* on February 24, 1454, to confirm what Barrientos had done in the course of this mission gives us details of how the matter was handled. In it the pope begins by recalling the reasons which led to issuance of the previous bull, and the recommendation made to the bishop of Cuenca concerning the affair. The pope later learned, through a written report made by the bishop and through other official testimony, that the bishop had convoked the chapter in order to carry out the apostolic mandate. The convocation had to take place in Toledo, according to the laws of the Order, and the above-mentioned prelate had attended it. In the chapter meeting, in agreement with the delegates, the reforms, ordinances, and corrections were made and the necessary sanctions applied, releasing and deposing the provincial from his office "on account of his demerits, and particularly because of his disobedience and rebellion and failure to obey apostolic letters and mandates,"[33] obliging him in addition to return what he had unjustly taken, and also sanctioning some other religious who opposed the reform of the province. Then Father Pedro de Villaviciosa was elected provincial, with the bishop confirming the election, and other measures were taken for the purpose of reestablishing peace and tranquillity. The pontiff confirmed all this in order to give stability to what had already been done and to make sure that in the future its legitimacy would not be subject to doubt, "motu proprio et ex certa scientia," decreeing that the appeals made by the previous provincial, Soutello, and other religious were frivolous and inconsistent, canceling all the litigation still pending in the matter, and imposing perpetual silence on the subject, to the end that everything done and agreed upon in the chapter meeting should be observed and kept in force and carried out.[34]

In an unhappy coincidence, symptoms of relaxation appeared at about the same time in the famous monastery of San Esteban, where regular life had always been fully maintained. Three months after Nicholas V's bull recommending reform of the province to Barrientos, this same pontiff signed a plea presented in the name of the bishop, dean, cathedral chapter, clergy, school, and city of Salamanca, in which they stated that the monastery of San Esteban, whose friars had formerly edified the faithful in that city with their upright life and preachings, "for some little time past . . . for lack of due reformation,"[35] had begun to stray from that wholesome path, with the result that the people were losing the esteem they had formerly held for the institution, to the detriment of their spiritual benefit. They requested, therefore, that the visit and reform of the monastery be assigned to Fray Martín de Santa María and Fray Pedro de Villaviciosa, professors of theology. The pope granted this request, but reduced to a single occasion the intervention of the visitors, which the petitioners had asked to be permanent "for as long as they lived."[36]

Although the reasons were exaggerated both in the first petition referring to the state of the province and in the second having to do with San Esteban, as was customary on such occasions, there is no doubt that the true situation left much to be desired. As for the state of the province, Barrientos or the person who made the request presented his proofs, later confirmed by the results of the visit. In regard to San Esteban, the interpretation presented in the name of all the active elements in Salamanca could only have been objective, and responded to the common desire to restore the life of our religious to its ancient splendor, to the benefit of the Christian population and the university. On the same date Nicholas V signed another petition presented on behalf of the king of Castile, in which the monarch requested that the Augustinians of Salamanca, who had withdrawn from academic tasks under the pretext of stricter observance, be returned to them. These were not, then, mere machinations, but unhappy realities which obliged the petitioners to attempt a remedy for them.

The persons designated to carry out the visit and reform of San Esteban are known to history. The first, Fray Martín de Santa María, was a nephew of Don Pablo de Santa María, bishop of Burgos, whom we have already mentioned. He had ruled the monastery of San Pablo in that city as its prior and had taken part in the foundation of the monastery of Rojas. In 1464 he was promoted to the office of provincial of Castile.

As for Father Pedro de Villaviciosa, also a master of theology, we know that in 1450 he is mentioned as assigned to Salamanca.[37] In 1454, after Father Soutello was removed from office, he was elected provincial.

It must also be noted that during those years Father Pedro de Deza was also residing in the monastery of Salamanca; he held the chair in three languages (Hebrew, Chaldean, and Arabic), from which he retired in 1468. In 1454 he is mentioned as prior of the monastery and also as vicar provincial; deputy, therefore, for Father Pedro de Villaviciosa, which supplies proof of the confidence placed in him by the reformer. Father Pedro de Salamanca, prior in 1447, 1452, and 1457, also was in residence there. There was no lack of persons of authentic religious spirit in the establishment, therefore. Perhaps the circumstantial motive which led to the petition for reform was the struggle between those who supported

Father Pedro de Santi Espíritus' candidacy for the priorship and the partisans of Villaviciosa in 1450. The former group, who represented the relaxed faction, was triumphant. The appeal to Rome must, therefore, have been negotiated by the opposing faction. The "for a few days past" of the bull, which echoes the "for some little time past"[38] of the petition, indicates that the victory of relaxation over observance was recent, probably during that priorship.

Thanks to the visitors' intervention, observance was easily restored at San Esteban, and the house was left firmly established in it. This was so much the case that when the representatives of the congregation of observance, who were sponsoring a second reform, tried to force incorporation of the monastery into their congregation in 1475, the monastery refused. It was supported in this action by Bishop Vivero,[39] the same who had intervened in the previous petition for reform, and by the city. Father Villaviciosa was also residing in the monastery at the time. With justification, therefore, the community opened an inquiry to prove that the regular life had always been maintained in the monastery, and that prelates and men of letters had come out of it, such as the bishops Castellanos, Gonzalo de Alba, and Barrientos, not to mention Torquemada, who also studied theology there. As was natural, they made no mention of the brief breakdown of religious discipline between 1450 and 1453, considering it a circumstance which had left no traces. To avoid a repetition of the attempt at forced incorporation, the friars of San Esteban had recourse to the pope; they made a presentation of the facts and in March, 1479, obtained from Sixtus IV the very important bull *Cum in agro*, which put a check on the imprudent zeal with which the congregation of observance sometimes tried to enlarge its powers.

This congregation originated in Valladolid under the protection of Cardinal Torquemada,[40] who took his vows in the monastery of San Pablo. For a number of years he had taken an interest in increasing the material prosperity of this house, and felt obliged to attend to its spiritual improvement as well. The reader can find some proofs of his efforts in favor of that monastery in the series of documents which we published some years ago in connection with the cardinal.[41] Now it is possible to add a few more.

In a petition of July 14, 1445, he speaks of the size and monumental impressiveness of that monastery and church, and of the devotion professed to it by the faithful of Valladolid, including the king, John II, who "for several years in his youth or boyhood was educated in the said house and brought up by some of the venerable religious of the said order in good ways and doctrines."[42] But since the monastery is partly ruined by reason of its antiquity, especially "the greater chapel of the same church, being of a remarkable breadth, for some time the greatest part of it has collapsed and remains in ruins,"[43] and the community does not have sufficient resources to carry out its restoration, he requests that indulgences be granted for three years to the faithful who aid in the restoration by their alms.[44]

In another petition of July 5, 1449, he first explains that, owing to bad administration and neglect by the superiors of the house in question, its possessions had been transferred or rented out long ago, without permission by the superiors of the Order or the Apostolic See, and that consequently all such contracts are void. He therefore requests that the pontiff revoke them and order the return to the community of its former possessions. He adds that certain religious of that same Order, seduced by the evil spirit, have disregarded obedience to their superiors and, using as an excuse certain privileges which they say other Orders possess to admit the entrance of all who wish to join them, are changing their habits, to the detriment and damage of their original vocation. In order to remove this occasion for scandal, he requests jointly with the provincial and the priors of the province that all who have taken advantage of these privileges to leave the Order against the will of their superiors be commanded under pain of censure to return to the houses they have left, and that the houses which received them be not allowed to keep them, since that would be contrary to the welfare and rights of the original Order.

The pope granted the first petition just as it appeared in the petition, and in regard to the second replied that it would have application for the future.[45]

We will pass over other petitions and bulls which bear witness to the persistence of the cardinal's generosity in favoring the monastery of Valladolid, and add only one more, of particular interest, to those already mentioned. It bears the date of September 28, 1458, and is given *motu proprio* (though, as we know, this does not exclude the intervention of the beneficiary in its issuance). Pope Pius II, wishing to favor the monastery of Valladolid, already notable in itself because of the quality of the persons residing there, and desirous that it may have means available for its greater development, especially for the benefit of the many friars who go there for purposes of study, and knowing furthermore that Cardinal Torquemada, since it is a house in which he took the habit and made his profession, and since he is a native of Valladolid, has done his best to make more beautiful and enlarge in divers ways, *motu proprio* annexes to it permanently the prestimony of Vecilla, together with that of Vega de Ruiponce in the diocese of Leon, the income from which was eighty *libras* a year, and which were at the disposition of the cardinal, who freely renounced them.[46]

After 1460 Valladolid was declared exempt from the jurisdiction of the provincial, depending on a vicar named by the general. But the situation there was not yet consolidated. In order to secure it the cardinal needed the help of the prior of San Benito, and further succeeded in having the general, Auribelli, make a visit to the province for the purpose of fostering reestablishment of regular life there.

The first vicar who governed the reformed monasteries independently of the provincial was Father Antonio de Santa María de Nieva. He already held this post in 1460, when he was also put in charge of the reformed monasteries in Portugal. The general, Auribelli, had complete confidence in him.

On their side, the Catholic Kings also gave very effective support to the reform, protecting all the monks in their legitimate rights, and did not hesitate to confront the general himself, who occasionally took unfavorable decisions through faulty information. One, for example, is related in a letter from Queen Isabella dated December 29, 1476, regarding injustices committed to the provincial Andrés de Toro, which disturbed the peace and progress of the province for several years. This letter casts light on and gives additional details of what we have recounted about the matter in our *Historia de la reforma* (pp. 37–40). . . .

Apart from Father Santa María de Nieva, the vicars of the congregation of observance outstanding for their religious zeal and their energy in carrying out the reform are the following: Father San Cebrián, Father Pascual de Ampudia, and Father Antonio de la Peña. Father San Cebrián was extraordinarily active in this work and was successful in overcoming the difficulties placed in the way of complete development of the undertaking. One of these directly affected studies. Since they were an essential element in Dominican life, it was very sensibly agreed to keep them vigorously alive, not excluding the granting of academic degrees. This distinguished the Dominican from the other reforms, which reduced studies to a minimum. But since the monastery of Salamanca was the academic center of the province, when its incorporation into the congregation failed it became necessary to make up for its absence in some way. The strong-willed vicar appealed to Sixtus IV, and the pontiff granted to him personally a broad *motu proprio* which swept away the difficulties and fully satisfied his desires. It bears the date of May 4, 1481. . . .

Some months later (August, 1481) the same pontiff bestowed extraordinary praise on San Cebrián in a brief addressed to the Catholic Kings, indicating that he would look favorably on his presentation for a vacancy in any church whatever, for he was sure that his promotion would benefit the people, honor the monarchs, and serve as an example to other prelates.

Thanks to such effective promoters, the reform continued to gain ground in the province of Castile, with the result that after forty years it was incorporated into the congregation of observance, as is fully described in the work to which I have previously referred.

The documentation in the Vatican also offers us interesting information concerning the beginnings of reform in the province of Portugal, in which one of the most active promoters of Castilian reform took part. Its presentation here is, therefore, a necessary complement to what we have been saying about the restoration of regular discipline in the central area of the Peninsula.

Relaxation in the Lusitanian province made necessary a prompt intervention by the general, in order to answer the petitions of the good religious there and to prevent the disorder from spreading. In Portugal also, there was a provincial unfaithful to his obligations; serious accusations were leveled against him, and it became necessary to appeal against him first to the pontiff and then to the general of the Order. His name was Juan Martínez. A plea of May 5, 1452, tells us that when Leonor, prioress of the Dominican nuns of Santarem, resigned and turned over her office to the provincial Juan Martínez, María Arias was elected in her place. The latter called for reparation of any defects existing in the election and for confirmation of it.[47] In a new appeal from the prioress and convent dated on July 7 of that year, it is stated that the said provincial,

> setting aside religious honesty, for several days almost and sometimes twice and three times a day, at hours and times which were not decent, associated not with the grave and older members as he ought to have done but with the younger and with less honest people, nor was he ashamed to enter the said convent, not for the sake of visitation and correction, but rather of making a scandal whenever he liked even beyond what the honesty of religion and fragility of the female sex allow, staying there to eat, to drink, and to perform acts which are the least suitable for honesty and religion, and beyond that by deputing the prioress at his whim and other officers in that convent, and by deposing those he had deputed without legal cause; whence very many scandals arose between the prioress or the sisters of the said convent, of which there are a large number in the convent, very many of whom are of the stock of great

magnates, and among the people of those parts a very strong ill-repute arose from that house.[48]

We can take it as a matter of course that in the statement, perhaps drawn up by some adversary of the provincial by collecting complaints from the nuns who had a grudge against him, the details of his conduct were exaggerated. The nuns who denounce him request that he be banned from making a visit to the convent, recommending that it be made by Juan, the bishop of Ceuta,[49] who was then residing in Lisbon. The pope decided that the prior of Santa Cruz de Coimbra should investigate the matter and appoint a visitor.[50]

The provincial in question, making use of the support given him by the Portuguese king, succeeded in having the general, Auribelli, grant him certain privileges and powers, among them the vicariate of two of the most important monastic houses in the province. To assure these concessions the Portuguese friar requested apostolic confirmation.[51] He must not have made good use of such favors, for the next provincial chapter meeting, in agreement with the general himself, applied to the pope in its turn to request revocation of those concessions and privileges.[52]

To give greater impetus to reform in that province, Auribelli himself, following the system he had been employing in Castile, set up a vicar general for the monasteries which had already been reformed or those to be reformed in the future, exempting them from the jurisdiction of the provincial. This new office fell to Father Antonio de Santa María de Nieva, of the Spanish province, who was also in charge of reformed houses in that country.[53]

The withdrawal of the monasteries of observance accentuated the tension between them and the cloistered ones. A dramatic proof of this disaffection is shown by what happened in the Dominican convent of San Salvador, located in the outskirts of Lisbon. About 1461 the provincial refused to name a reformed religious as confessor to that community, as had been done in the past. The clumsy intervention of the bishop, an impulsive man to judge from other episodes in his life,[54] complicated things still

more, and obliged Pius II to take new measures to reestablish
normality there. Witness of this is furnished by the two bulls
dated October, 1461, and January 1464. . . .

There is little reliable information about the progress of reform
in Portugal. Santa María presumably continued in the office of
vicar of the reformed monks until 1466, when, says Sousa, he was
replaced by Father Bartolomé de San Domingos. But the
testimony of this chronicler is unreliable, for in contrast to what
we have just seen from Auribelli's letters, he assumes that the
reformed group did not have autonomous rule until that same
year, 1466. In any case, the reform had not made great progress
in Portugal at that time, a fact which is earnestly lamented by the
chronicler Olmeda, whose statements are usually well founded.[55]

Only during the course of the sixteenth century, when the
king of Portugal, John III, took great interest in the matter, was
the implantation of true reform successful in that province.
Elsewhere we have referred to the progress of this difficult task.
To complete the documentation presented there, we must reproduce in this new study the text of three briefs of Paul III, two
of them addressed to Father Jerónimo de Padilla, ratifying at his
request and that of the Portuguese monarch the ample powers
granted to him by the general, Fenario, and later confirmed by
the vicar-general, Agustín Recuperati, in order to prevent their
being contested following Fenario's death. The second brief
further authorizes him to annul or reduce the privileges granted
by the Apostolic See or its nuncios to the religious and the
monasteries of that province which he may deem contrary to the
life of observance. The third brief is addressed to the general, Recuperati, authorizing him to install, with Apostolic authorization,
a provincial who will undertake establishment of Dominican reform in that kingdom. Naturally, the person appointed was Padilla.

Recourse to such energetic measures, the only ones which gave
a satisfactory result, demonstrates once again the need for employing those extraordinary means, without trusting overmuch in
the efficacy of persuasion. Because it was so highhanded the
procedure may seem improper, and still more so if we think of

the chain of hatreds and dislikes which such measures often left behind them. But there was no other, surer method; and to renounce it would have meant renouncing the establishment of reform. Its promoters, in our Order as well as in others, came to be convinced of this once the first steps were taken.

They did not always proceed with the tact which would have been desirable. Thus, we see that during the term of office of Vicar-general San Cebrián, the system gave results when reform was instituted in the monastery of La Peña de Francia. In Salamanca, however, it was a failure, not because the monastery was at fault but because of the rash manner in which the reformers undertook their task.

In their early stages these impositions must have appeared even more highhanded, and they produced a profound feeling of hostility against the reformed religious in the province of Castile, where they were first tried. This animosity seems to be reflected in an order issued by the provincial chapter of Córdoba in 1464, which would be inconceivable if this were not the case.[56]

The reaction of one faction against the other resulted in the almost total disappearance of the proceedings of the provincial chapters, not only for those years, but from the beginning of the fourteenth century, making it impossible for us to reconstruct the history of the Dominicans in Castile for a period of more than two hundred years. But the examples we have given here show us that, though there was much to be corrected among our religious there was no lack of good examples either, thanks to which total reform was achieved in Castile much sooner than in other provinces of the Peninsula, and a solid base was furnished for the flowering of the Order during the seventeenth century in all the regions influenced by the Spanish Empire.

NOTES

[1. Cf. V. Beltrán de Heredia, *Historia de la Reforma de la provincia de España, 1450–1550* (Rome, 1939).]

2. Concerning the tendency toward the eremitic life in the province, see our contribution to the Second Congress of Spirituality celebrated in

Salamanca in October, 1956. The theme of the paper is "Guiding Principles of Dominican Spirituality in the Early Decades of the Sixteenth Century." To illustrate this eremitic tendency in Castile, we cite a few cases below. First: Fray García Rojo, O.P., of the monastery of Burgos, aged forty-five years, states that "cum ipse propter nimias conversationes gentis et alias occupatus negotiis ordinis insistendo, quos ips[i] subire est necesse, nequeat cum animi quiete et sana conscientia inter claustralia monasteria stando gratum, prout promisit et teneret, Domino reddere famulatum, desideretque in aliquo solitario et extra loca populosa continue vitam suam ducere et sine quovis impedimento paupere vivendo de per eum commissis poenitentiam agere," he asks to have authorization to retire "in aliquo loco solitario," for example the hermitage of San Victor near Belorado, in the diocese of Burgos. Petition of January 19, 1427, Reg. Suppl., Vol. 217, fol. 14 verso.

Second: Fray Alfonso Espino, lector in theology of the monastery of Jérez, desiring "in aliquo ermitorio solitariam vitam ducere," asks permission to retire to the hermitage of Santa Catalina del Río. Petition of May 13, 1427, Reg. Suppl., Vol. 218, fol. 96. Correlative bull in Bull. Ord. Praed. II, 676.

Third: Juan de Espejo and Juan Donato, monks of the monastery of Vitoria, masters in theology, "in senectute constituti, ut commodius mundana relinquere et cum quiete animi solitariam ac regularem vitam ducere valeant, cupiant ex magno devotionis fervore ad quoddam eremitorium beatae Mariae de Auro Calagurritan. dioecesis se transferre, et preces altissimo sub regulari observantia famulando inibi perpetuo remanere." They request authorization to do so, even without the permission of their religious superiors. Petition of June 16, 1429, Reg. Suppl. 243, fol. 14.

[3. Bishop of Burgos, 1415–1435.]
[4. "Super requesta domini Pauli episcopi Burgensis super reformatione conventus fratrum praedicatorum civitatis Burgensis concordant omnes deputationes quod committatur reverendissimo domino cardinali legato (Cesarini), qui auctoritate sacri concilii provideat, et iuxta ordinationem generalis et constitutiones et statuta eiusdem ordinis ipse conventus reformetur." J. Haller, Concilium Basiliense, III, 391.]
[5. "Denuntiamus quod ad instantiam reverendissimi domini episcopi Burgensis, in conventu Burgensi provinciae Hispaniae positum est studium generale, sine gradu tamen et forma, ut ad ipsum conventum fratres tam provinciae Hispaniae quam aliarum provinciarum possint pro studio destinari." Acta capitulorum generalium Ord. Praedic., III, MOPH VIII (Romae, 1900), 265.]
6. L. Serrano, Los conversos don Pablo de Santa María y don Alfonso de Cartagena (Madrid, 1942), pp. 86–87.
[7. "Ut pro huiusmodi fidei firmitate viriliter certarent."]
[8. "Plurima bona, doctrinas et exempla christicolis ministravit antedictis."]
[9. "Generali dicti ordinis pro tempore existenti immediate subiectum."]
10. Reg. Lat. 343, fol. 9 verso–10; Reg. Suppl. 322, fol. 71 verso.

11. Acta capitul. gen. Ord. Praed., III, MOPH VIII, 244.

[12. "Olim frater Alvarus de Zamora ordinis praedicatorum in sacra theologia magister, apud civitatem Hispalen. quamdam domum cum capella seu oratorio sub vocabulo Sancti Dominici de Portacaeli fundavit et aedificavit, in qua ipse una cum socio seu sociis moram saepe trahebat."]

[13. "Qui per multa tempora praedicationes in dicta civitate frequentavit et frequentare imposterum desiderat, prout dictus frater Alvarus, fundator dictae domus, in eadem civitate dum viveret frequentabat, quatenus eidem fratri Roderico, ut ipse Deo quietius servire et praedicationibus hujusmodi uberius sine impedimento vacare possit, quod in domo seu oratorio hujusmodi, quae nullos habet reditus de praesenti, cum duobus ipsius ordinis fratribus quos ad hoc elegerit, stare morare et illam inhabitare atque regere et gubernare quamdiu vixerit, dum tamen ad id magistri ipsius ordinis generalis accedat consensus, libere et licite absque alicujus alterius contradictione seu impedimento valeat, concedere et indulgere misericorditer dignemini de gratia speciali."]

14. Petition of August 11, 1440, Vol. 366, fol. 169 verso–170.

15. Petition of August 20, 1440, Vol. 366, fol. 215 verso–216.

16. Petition of August 23, 1440, Vol. 366, fol. 243.

17. Petition of August 29, 1440, Vol. 366, fol. 288.

[18. "Ut de regestro supplicationum cassentur et deleantur."]

19. Petition of September 15, 1440, Vol. 367, fol. 73 verso.

20. Analecta Ord. Fratrum Praed., IV (Romae, 1899), 485.

21. It is clear that observance continued there during the years 1442–45; among other proofs, we have that of the friars' appeal to the pope requesting concession of indulgences to the faithful who visit the church on certain days to help in its construction. In the statement by the authors of the appeal we read, "Cuius fratres in observantia vivunt." Reg. Suppl. bol. 383, fol. 236 verso, and Vol. 406, fols. 84 verso and 168.

22. This fragment has been preserved in the endpapers of Ms. 3012 of the Biblioteca Real, at present in the Biblioteca Universitaria de Salamanca, Ms. 1986.

[23. "Dignetur s.v. devotum oratorem vestrum fratrem Lupum de Galdo, presbyterum expresse professum, in sacra theologia magistrum ordinis fratrum praedicatorum, conventus de Vivero, Mindonien. dioecesis, in poenitentiarum minorem e.s. (v.) et sedis apostolicae recipere gratiose et retinere, numeroque et consortio aliorum poenitentiarium minorum e.s.v. et sedis apost. praedictae liberaliter aggregare cum omnibus et singulis privilegiis, stipendiis ... minoribus poenitentiariis ... concessis. Fiat ut patitur. L. Datum Barcinone quarto kalendas iunii anno decimosexto." Reg. Suppl. 104, fol. 52 verso.]

24. Reg. Suppl. 122, fol. 239 verso–240. (Alfonso Carrillo, bishop of Osma, 1411–1424 [and of Sigüenza, 1426–1434], was made cardinal of St. Eustachius, September 22, 1408, and died March 14, 1434.)

25. "In remotis deget de praesenti." Reg. Suppl. 129, fol. 197 verso–198. [This petition was included in the appendix of documents at the end of the original study.]

26. Madrid, Arch. H. N. Clero (Valladolid), Leg. 440 and 456.

27. Analecta Ord. Fratrum Praed., IV (Romae, 1899), 485.

28. See Reg. Suppl., Vol. 459, fols. 127–29 and Vol. 468, fols. 66 verso–68.

[29. Bishop of Cuenca, 1445–1469.]

[30. Bishop of Orense, 1447–1462.]

[31. "Tanta avaritia detentus ut gratias et libertates pro pecuniis vendat fratribus dicti ordinis, ac ab eis et conventibus per vias exorbitantissimas pecuniam extorqueat."]

32. Reg. Vat. 425, fol. 210.

[33. "Ob eius demerita, et potissime propter eius inobedientiam et rebellionem ac litteris et mandatis apostolicis non paritionem . . ."]

34. Reg. Suppl. 475, fols. 2–3.

[35. "A paucis tamen temporibus . . . ob debitae reformationis defectu[m]" . . .]

36. "Quoad vixerint." Petition of July 21, 1453, in Vol. 468, fols. 13 verso–14.

37. Madrid, Arch. H. N. Clero (Salamanca), Leg. 220.

[38. "A paucis diebus citra" . . . "a paucis tamen temporibus."]

[39. Gonzalo Vivero, bishop of Salamanca, 1447–1462.]

[40. 1388–1468; he was made cardinal priest of St. Sixtus in 1439 and was subsequently cardinal priest of St. Mary across the Tiber (1446–1460) and cardinal bishop of Preneste (1460–1463) and of Sabina (1463 until his death).]

41. Archivum FF. Praed. 7 (1937), 210–45.

42. "Per plures annos in sua iuventute seu pueritia in dicta domo educatus necnon bonis moribus atque doctrinis a nonnullis venerabilibus religiosis dicti ordinis instructus fuit." In fact we know from Lope Barrientos, *Refundición de la Crónica del Halconero*, chaps. 7 and 9, that John II and his mother, Doña Catalina, resided in the monastery of San Pablo from 1412–1417. See Carriazo's edition (Madrid, 1946), pp. 21, 24. In Reg. Avin. 347, fols. 312 verso–318, this fact is also mentioned.

[43. "Capella maior ipsius ecclesiae, mirabilis amplitudinis existens, ab aliquo tempore citra in eius maxima pars corruit et ruina dedita remansit."]

44. Reg. Suppl. 407, fol. 28.

45. Reg. Suppl. 435, fols. 285–86.

46. Reg. Suppl. 512, fols. 105 verso–106. Correlative bull: Reg. Vat. 468, fol. 214.

47. Reg. Suppl. 458, fol. 298.

[48. "Deposita religionis honestate, singulis fere diebus et quandoque bis et ter in die, horis etiam et temporibus indecentibus, non gravibus et seniori-bus ut deceret, sed iunioribus et minus honestis personis associatus, nec cum proposito visitandi et corrigendi, sed potius scandalizandi, monasterium praedictum intrare quandiu sibi placet, etiam ultra quod patitur honestas religionis et fragilitas sexus mulierum, ibidem etiam manens comedendo, bibendo et alios qui honestati et religioni minime conveniunt actus exercendo, necnon pro sui libito priorissam et alias officiarias in eodem monasterio deputando et deputatas sine legitima causa deponendo, non erubescit; unde inter priorissam sive sorores dicti monasterii, quae ibidem in monasterio habentur copiosae, quarumque plurimae ex magnorum nobilium prosapia sint genitae, scandala plurima et apud populum partium illarum vehemens inde infamia sint secuta."]

[49. Juan Alfonso Ferraz, 1458(?)–1476 (or 1477).]

50. Reg. Suppl. 460, fols. 206 verso–207.

51. Reg. Vat. 499, fol. 8.

52. Petition of May 24, 1460, in Vol. 530, fol. 179.

53. See petition of July 17, 1460, in Vol. 532, fol. 250. In the correlative bull preserved in Reg. Vat. 503, fols. 189–90, the general's two letters are inserted, as indicated by the reformed monasteries when they requested confirmation of the general's decisions; and the papal concession also expresses this "cum insertione singulatum litterarum dicti magistri generalis." [The reader will find the letters reproduced in the appendix of documents which accompanied the original study.]

54. On March 5, 1463, the pope charged the bishop of Oporto, with others, to oblige in the pope's name the archbishop of Lisbon, Alfonso (the same to whom we have referred in the text), to return to the bishop of Coimbra, a diocese formerly occupied by him, the books and registers stating the privileges, possessions, and rights of this church, which he had arbitrarily taken with him and refused to hand over. See Reg. Vat. 511, fols. 319–20.

55. S. de Olmeda, *Chronica Ord. Praed.*, ed. Canal (Romae, 1936), p. 214.

56. We reproduce the text of the provincial chapter, in which the term *piis* seems to refer to the reformed faction, whose members at that time were beginning to vent their wrath on the members of the province. It reads as follows: "Sequela et communicatio fratrum cum piis est praecipua et maxima corruptio nostri sacri ordinis. Eapropter omnes ordinationes factas in praecedentibus capitulis provincialibus circa huiusmodi piis volumus in suo robore permanere, adiicientes quod quotiescumque contigerit aliquem de piis declinare ad aliquem conventum vel terminos eiusdem, priores teneantur tales carceri tradere, et inde non solvere absque licentia prioris provincialis expressa. Quorum bona dividimus in partes aequales inter conventum in quo capti fuerint et inter provinciam. Priores vero negligentes in hac captione et divisione suspendimus ab officio per mensem." Acta capituli provincialis Cordubensis anno 1464, in *Analecta sacri Ord. Fratrum Praedicatorum*, IV (Romae, 1899), 489.

FURTHER READING

A. Fliche and V. Martin, *Histoire de l'Eglise*, Vols. XIV, pt. i (Paris, 1962), especially 431–47; pt. ii (1964), 1097–99, and XV (1951).

8 The Economy of Ferdinand and Isabella's Reign

JAIME VICENS VIVES

In a further extract from Professor Vicens' *Historia Económica de España*, the author outlines the main economic themes for the years 1474–1516. He deals with a series of controversial issues, including the effects of the expulsion of the Jews in 1492, the encouragement given to stock-raising and in particular to sheep as opposed to arable farming, and the failure of Castilian industry to develop very far. He also assesses the importance of the monetary reform of the Catholic Kings and of their so-called mercantilist policy.

DEMOGRAPHIC RISE: EMIGRATION OF RELIGIOUS MINORITIES

The period of Ferdinand and Isabella seems to have produced a noticeable rise in population, probably due to the end of the civil wars both in Castile and Catalonia and the reestablishment of a normal economic situation.

There is much evidence of this state of affairs, though the figures are scanty and unreliable. Thus, Quintanilla's census (1482), the only one we can make use of for the whole period, gives the Crown of Castile a total of 1,500,000 households (6 to 7 and a half million inhabitants), a frankly exaggerated figure. To the central nucleus, composed of Castilians, we should have to add the inhabitants of the old kingdom of Granada (from 500,000 to 750,000) incorporated into the nation in 1492, and the subjects of the Aragonese Crown (probably 1 million, in round figures) and the Crown of Navarre (100,000?). In fact, the only proved increase is that of the Principality of Catalonia, which rose from 55,541 households in 1497 to 59,435 in 1516.

This bright demographic picture in Castile probably made up for losses through emigration, which were considerable. In first rank among these we must place the departure of the *conversos*, which took place as a consequence of the establishment of the Inquisition. It is impossible to give exact figures for the numbers involved in this movement. Next comes the departure of the *Jews*, which according to Baer[1] affected some 150,000 persons; and also that of the *Moriscos* of Granada after the revolt of 1502, a group which can be estimated at 300,000 individuals. To this we must add the emigration of the *discoverers of America*, which up to 1520 was a very small contingent. We can estimate, then, for the whole kingdom of Ferdinand and Isabella, a total of some 500,000 persons, a number whose real importance must be measured, as we shall see, more by the emigrants' economic quality than by their quantity. As for immigrants, they were few in number— select *colonies* of foreign businessmen and artisans, and in the Pyrenees the first evidences of the growing avalanche of *Gascon* shepherds and peasants.

Let us emphasize the question of *confessional minorities*, which were so important in Ferdinand and Isabella's religious and economic policy. At the beginning of their reign the Jews numbered some 200,000. Of these, 150,000 emigrated and the rest became converted, especially in certain regions of Catalonia and in Majorca. We must point out that the majority of expelled Jews settled in lands controlled by the infidel (Cairo, Alexandria, Aleppo, Tripoli in Syria, Salonica, and Constantinople), where they very soon formed a basic economic community, so that their departure from Castile not only deprived the country of this community, but benefited the enemies of the Faith, against whom the drastic measure of the Inquisition had been intended.

In regard to the *conversos*, we must handle all the figures with care. If we start with the approximately 130,000 Jews who had renounced the Hebrew religion at the beginning of the fifteenth century in Castile and the Crown of Aragon, it can be supposed that their number by 1480 was about double: some 250,000. These people made up the most powerful, most vital and active segment of the Castilian population in the fifteenth century. Everyone, both attackers and defenders, agrees on this point. When the Inquisition began to function all over Spain, between 1480 and 1486, the *conversos* accused of Judaic tendencies fled *en masse*. How many emigrated? We do not know. How many were burned at the stake? This too is unknown. There are figures to suit every taste. The most likely possibility is that in the period with which we are dealing some 2,000 Jewish-leaning *conversos* were burned and about 20,000 returned to the Church. The rest probably emigrated. This is the impression given by reading the documents of the time. The mercantile cities of the Catalonian and Valencian coasts, along with many cities in Aragon, Castile, and Andalusia, felt the departure of the *conversos* as something which profoundly damaged their economic vitality. This was the basis of the resistance made to the establishment of the Inquisition —not in its aspect as a defense of dogma, but to what it represented in the way of trials without legal guarantees, seizure of property, and paralyzation of mercantile life. The cases of Saragossa, Teruel, and Barcelona are proof of this.

The number of *Moriscos* came to 1 million, of whom there were 50,000 in Aragon, 160,000 in Valencia, 10,000 in Catalonia, and 15,000 in Majorca, a total of 235,000 for the Crown of Aragon; and in Castile some 700,000, distributed in the following manner: 200,000 in Castile before the conquest of Granada, and 500,000 in the kingdom of Granada. Some 300,000 of these departed, as we mentioned before, leaving a remainder of 400,000 in the Crown of Castile. We must keep in mind that in 1502 this group of people lost their position as a legal minority and became a dissident minority within the country, dissident in a different, but no less profound, sense from the Jewish-leaning *conversos*.

POPULATION DISTRIBUTION

How were the inhabitants of Spain distributed at the time of the Catholic Monarchs? The vast majority lived in the country. More than 80 per cent of the total Spanish population were peasants.

Urban workers, including Jews, *conversos*, and so on, amounted to 10 or 12 per cent before the expulsion. The urban middle class, counting citizens, merchants, and ecclesiastics, made up some 3 to 5 per cent. And finally, the nobles, taking together the aristocracy of both Castile and Aragon, represented less than 2 per cent, divided into 5,000 magnates (dukes, counts, barons, etc.), 60,000 knights, *hidalgos*, and so on, and 60,000 urban patricians, or aristocrats of the cities. These 125,000 individuals were at the summit of the social scale and controlled the country from above.

It was at this time that the countryside, especially in Castile, first began to show signs of depopulation. When we seek the origins of the unfavorable situation in the seventeenth century, with deserted lands and an army of vagrants and beggars infesting the country, we tend to put the responsibility on the Hapsburg government. In reality the phenomenon goes back to the time of Ferdinand and Isabella, as can be observed in several famous contemporary chronicles, such as Carvajal's.[2] The peasant classes, unable to make a living from the soil, began their exodus to the cities. Thus, the urban population grew at a rate higher than the general rhythm of the country. Seville and Valencia were famous for having 80,000 inhabitants; Barcelona had 35,000; Córdoba, Toledo, Granada, Valladolid, Salamanca, Murcia, Málaga, Saragossa, Majorca, and Perpignan between 15,000 and 25,000; and there was a large group of cities with 10,000 to 15,000 inhabitants.

STABILIZATION OF PROPERTY:
RISE OF THE CASTILIAN ARISTOCRACY

During the fifteenth century property and revenue from land had passed from hand to hand all over Spain, in Castile as well as in the Crown of Aragon. In the greater part of Spain, around 1476, no one could say "this is mine" and "this is yours," for the luck of a battle, the favor of a sovereign, a change of sides, were enough to cause a person's property to be confiscated and given to someone else. It was a state of general chaos. Ferdinand and Isabella reestablished peace and stabilized property. This fact is very important, for property, as Ferdinand and Isabella left it, underwent very few changes in the succeeding centuries, until the disentailment laws of the nineteenth century.

When Ferdinand and Isabella are discussed, one of the commonest statements made about them is that they put the nobility in their pockets; it is true that, from the point of view of authority, they let no one raise his head. But in the social aspect they maintained the economic advantages to the aristocracy stemming from the ownership of land. This fact is supremely important if we are to understand the future of the Castilian economy.

Let us look at what happened. In Catalonia the civil war had ended in 1472, but John II allowed the confusion to continue. In 1479, when Ferdinand the Catholic took over the government, he began to bring a little order out of chaos. In 1481 he decreed a general restitution of property, issuing, with the compliance of the Cortes, a pragmatic sanction setting forth the restitutions which were to be made. For this purpose he exacted from the Cortes a donation of 100,000 libras with which to pay his supporters for the property they unjustly occupied and were going to have to give up. The result was that with a fairly moderate sum of money, the country was able to blot out the past errors of the civil war. If we also keep in mind the publication of the Sentence of Guadalupe, in 1486, and that it very cleverly gave the peasant effective possession of his land, leaving jurisdictional control to his lord, we will understand that Ferdinand the Catholic's accomplishment was truly democratic, for it gave some 50,000 individuals access to a fair-sized property. This is why there have not been, up to the contemporary period, any attempts at agrarian revolt in Catalonia.

What happened in Castile? There the Cortes of Toledo met in 1480, and the necessity was recognized of putting the exchequer in order. Estimates were made, and it developed that enormous quantities of maravedís were owed. It was then decided to cancel the gifts and hereditary pensions enjoyed by the nobles. Thanks to the studies of Matías Usón,[3] it has been proved that the nobles, who possessed some 63 million maravedís of revenue, in fact had to give up some 30 million. However, in Castile this reduction was very superficial; the nobles lost half of the income they had violently and unjustly usurped after 1464, but the order was explicitly given to preserve the properties, grants, and pensions they had possessed before the upheavals of Henry IV's reign. That is, the destructive work performed by the Castilian aristocracy during the reign of Henry II, and completed during that of John II, was formally respected. Since these usurpations were the most important ones, it can be stated that the law of 1480 served only to ratify the absolute social and economic control of the noble class over the State and the rest of the country. The known figures could not be more conclusive: about the year 1500 the nobles owned 97 per cent of the territory of the Peninsula either directly or by jurisdiction. This is the same as saying that 1.5 per cent of the population owned almost the entire Spanish territory. This fact is of capital importance.

Of this 97 per cent, 45 per cent belonged to bishoprics, high ecclesiastics, cathedral chapters, canonries, the urban aristocracy, and the knights. The rest belonged to the grandees and formed true latifundia. We shall mention a few names. Andalusia was divided among the following landowners: the Guzmáns, dukes of Medina Sidonia; the Cerdas, dukes of Medinaceli; the Ponce de Leóns, dukes of Arcos; the family of Fernández de Córdoba in both branches, as counts of Cabra and lords of Montilla, the latter soon elevated to dukes of Sesa; the Mendozas, counts of Tendilla and Priego. The archbishopric of Toledo was sole owner of the rest. Extremadura was divided, almost half-and-half, between the family of Súarez de Figueroa and the Order of Alcántara. In Murcia the largest landowners were the Fajardos; in Salamanca the Estúñigas, dukes of Béjar, and the Álvarez de Toledo family; in La Mancha, the Orders of Santiago and Calatrava, the archbishopric of Toledo and the Marquis of Villena; in the Alcarria, the Duke of the Infantado.

The remaining 3 per cent had to be shared by some 4 or 5 million Castilians. We can easily understand that Ferdinand and Isabella's social reform amounted to nothing, for in addition the following took place: first, the monarchs confirmed and extended the right of establishing *mayorazgos* (Laws of Toro, 1504),[4] that is, the right of hereditary transmission which entailed property to the firstborn of a family; second, they approved a policy of matrimonial connections whose only result was to produce a concentration of property in the hands of those who already had it; and third, in Granada they carried out a policy favorable to the aristocracy. Granada was a new conquest, but with the exception of the western regions of the kingdom (Ronda, Málaga, Alora, Coín), which were given to peasants and workmen from lower Andalusia, the rest was turned over to the nobles in compensation for what had been taken away from them in 1480. So to those who had was given—practically the whole kingdom of Granada.

To these facts we must add another which was no less important: the sale of the lands of free farmers because of the agrarian crisis at the beginning of the sixteenth century, followed by depopulation of the countryside and the appearance of the specter of famine. This movement could only benefit those who had money with which to buy; namely, the aristocracy again.

The sum total of the events we have just described explains the enormous fortunes of the Castilian lords of the period. As Marineo Sículo says, one-third of the country's revenues belonged to the king, one-third to the nobility, and the other third to the Church,[5] which is like repeating "the aristocracy," for its second sons owned the choicest part of the ecclesiastical benefices. Sixty-one nobles enjoyed an average annual income of 20,000 ducats (1 ducat = 375 maravedís = 8 days' wages of a specialized worker). The wealth of the grandees can be estimated at 1,245,000 ducats annually; that of the Church, 6 million overall—fabulous sums, which render comment unnecessary.

THE MIDDLE AND PEASANT CLASSES IN CASTILE, ARAGON, AND CATALONIA

We have just described the result of Ferdinand and Isabella's social policy: the consolidation of the nobility's economic potential. If it is really true that they tried to weaken the aristo-cracy's political power by bringing the educated middle class into the royal councils, it is no less true that subordinate executive power was turned over to the grandees, in viceroyships as well as in high military posts. On a larger scale, it was from the ranks of the lower nobility that Ferdinand and Isabella recruited the royal governors of the cities, who formed the Castilian State into the rigid mold characteristic of an authoritarian monarchy.

As for the middle class, we cannot say that it particularly benefited. Order and authority, combined with a relative econo-mic prosperity, made up for loss of liberty in the Cortes and in municipal government. This is why the Castilian town councils recalled the times of the Catholic Monarchs with special affection. The same occurred in the Crown of Aragon. But now a particularly grave problem arises: the elimination of the dissident middle class—Jews, and Jewish-leaning *conversos*. Both groups occupied three key positions: in the first place, they were the financiers; in the second place, they held the chief public offices related to the court and the municipal governments; and last, they represented an artisan class which was lively, intelligent, and alert.

It is difficult to take up this problem from a purely economic point of view. Knowing the number of *conversos*, their vitality and influence, it is understandable that their wealth and preponderance should have aroused hatred among certain social classes in Castile. Generally "the hatred of the people" is spoken of, but the facts we possess limit the acceptance of this term to certain concrete classes which were, as a matter of fact, the aristocracy and the Church. Though we admit the animosity of part of the Castilian popula-tion for the *conversos* who refused to abandon the religious practices inherited from their ancestors, we will have to state that Ferdinand and Isabella were totally intransigent when they decided to sacrifice the country's economy to its spiritual well-being. There can be no doubt whatever on this score, for in the face of the reasonable arguments made to them by the city governments of Seville, Toledo, Barcelona, Valencia, and Saragossa, in the face of the serious dislocation which the establishment of the Inquisition and the consequent flight of the *conversos* meant for these cities, the king and queen always replied that in the first place, they were taking into account the religious benefit of the country, that they had the economic factor well in mind, and that in consequence they were sacrificing it to the spiritual policy which had been decreed.

In view of all this, it is possible to state that the elimination of religious dissent was due to an inalterable desire to maintain orthodoxy, over and above all material concerns. However, this feeling was not the only one, but was perhaps accompanied, in circles connected with the Court, by less lofty purposes. There is a historiographic tendency, lately centering around Américo Castro's work *The Structure of Spanish History* (*La realidad histórica de España*),[6] which insists that the Inquisition was created under the sole pretext of "robbing" the *conversos*. A number of texts are quoted in support of this thesis which would seem irrefutable were they not a product of the violent polemics of the period. At any rate, we cannot reduce the elimination of the Jewish-leaning *conversos* to such an uncompromising word as "robbery." On the other hand, it is possible to state that at the time the Inquisition was established the State was undergoing a profound financial crisis, and that the voices of those who counseled economic measures against the *conversos* prevailed. But even in this case the problem cannot be solved in such a simplistic manner; for although Ferdinand and Isabella could attack the *conversos* in order to take over their wealth, their elimination from national life was prejudicial to the treasury's future revenues; that is, it was an operation which quickly brought in a certain amount of money, but which resulted after a time in the stagnation of the sources of public revenue (this was what happened in a number of Castilian cities, which obtained tax exemptions by pleading the departure of the Jews and *conversos*, the only ones who really contributed to the public treasury). We need to weigh matters carefully, therefore, and admit on the one hand the spiritual necessity felt in the Castile of the time to avoid all religious dissent, and on the other the urgent need to face the undeniable necessities of the public treasury.

If we accept as approximate figures the 20,000 who returned to the Church, the 2,000 burned at the stake, and the 120,000 who fled, among whom were commanders of the military orders, canons, friars, city magistrates, people of all classes, for the *conversos* were imbedded in the very fabric of Castile, we will realize what an enormous paralyzation of the country's resources took place; not only because a vital sector of the nation fled, but because even before the introduction of the Inquisition, which was established slowly, first in Andalusia, then in Castile, and finally in the Crown of Aragon, the *conversos* were responsible for the flight of capital on a large scale. This brought about a stagnation in the capitalization of the middle class that, in combination with the preponderance of the aristocracy, was on the point of causing the monarchy's financial collapse between 1485 and 1490.

A no less serious problem was the expulsion of the Jews; the apologists for this measure thought that it was necessary in order to eliminate the element which controlled the Castilian *conversos*, while its critics felt it was only an excuse to seize the Jews' property and wipe out the debt incurred by the war in Granada. These opinions could be reconciled if we possessed impartial critical studies. The documentation is in the archives, but no one has yet had the courage to tackle this material, which is abundant but scattered.[7]

As for the peasant classes, the policy of Ferdinand and Isabella varied from region to region. In Catalonia, where a social doctrine existed in regard to the *remença* serfs (a total of 15,000 to 20,000 households, or one-fourth of the total population), Ferdinand the Catholic assured their liberty and stability by means of the Sentence of Guadalupe (1486), which eliminated the problem of serfdom and evil practices. The keystone of this measure, to which the nobles and the cities were stubbornly opposed, was to give freedom to the peasant by assuring him effective possession of the land that he tilled. In Aragon, however, where the analogous problem of the *exarchs* existed, not only was the situation of this group not improved but, conversely, it was changed in favor of the lords. As for Castile, in 1481 the right of landed serfs to abandon their lord was confirmed. If we keep in mind that this right was theoretical, since it appeared in legislation but not in the reality of the social fabric (for, as we have observed, 97 per cent of the land in Castile belonged to the civil and ecclesiastical aristocracy), the freedom of 1481 meant only the freedom to die of hunger, as was immediately shown during the great crises of 1502 and 1509 in Castile.

STAGES IN THE CONTAINMENT OF CATALONIAN ECONOMIC DECLINE

The economic decline of Catalonia had reached a new low at the end of John II's reign, so much so that Ferdinand's accession to the throne was awaited as if it were the coming of the Messiah.

It has been said over and over that Ferdinand the Catholic's policy brought about the economic ruin of Catalonia. This statement, made by the romantic school of Catalan historians, has gone over into Castilian and foreign works. But the truth is exactly the opposite: during Ferdinand and Isabella's reign there was economic recovery in Catalonia.

In 1479 and 1481 the first step was taken to arrest Catalonian economic decline. In the Cortes of 1481 two important measures were taken for this purpose; the first was general restitution of property, of which we have already spoken, and the second was the restoration, or "redreç," of trade. This consisted of a long catalogue of protectionist measures, in which a schedule of customs duties was established, the entry of certain foreign products was forbidden, measures were taken to safeguard the coral industry, and the monopoly of Catalonian fabrics in Sardinia was decreed. This atmosphere of recovery received a setback in the years immediately following, between 1481 and 1488, owing to the double phenomena of social revolution in the countryside and the establishment of the Inquisition in Barcelona. In 1486 Catalonia was really exhausted. But after 1488 Ferdinand's good will, plus the people's desire to live and the artisans' will to work, resulted in a visible rebirth of mercantile and industrial activity in the Principality.

In 1488 a number of measures were taken which were to affect the total situation: stabilization of the currency, a study of the establishment of a monopoly on Catalonian cloth in Sicily, and the fight against privateering. Piracy had been one of the causes of Catalonian economic decline, especially because of the reprisals it provoked from the affected countries. In 1491, however, all safe-conducts and privateering licenses were suspended, and in 1492 a pragmatic decree was issued freeing the galley slaves. This event contributed toward calming relations between Barcelona and Genoa, and permitted both to concentrate their efforts on eliminating the pirates who infested the Barcelona-Valencia-Balearic triangle. At the same time, an order was issued prohibiting the traffic of ships from Genoa and Nice in Catalonian ports (1491), and the export of Catalonian wool was limited so that local industry, stimulated by the monopolies in Sardinia and Sicily, could be better supplied.

The problem of the Catalonian textile industry's monopoly in Sicily was slowly solved. First an entry tax (5 per cent) was placed on French cloth (1498), and then it was totally banned not only in Sicily but also in Naples (1506). So by 1506 Catalonian cloth had preferential rights in Sardinia, Sicily, and Naples, three great consumer markets. There is no doubt that these facts influenced Catalonian mercantile recovery, revealed in the resumption of trade with Egypt. In 1495, after half a century of paralysis, the fleet of Juan Sarriera, general bailiff of Catalonia, again reached Alexandria. The Catalan consulate was at once reestablished in that city. After 1495 this profitable trade was not interrupted, though it declined in proportion to the growing success of the Portuguese in their voyages to India and the Spice Islands.

The last stage, from 1503 to 1516, was one of clear prosperity: the cities' population grew, Barcelona recovered, sea trade with the Atlantic countries was renewed, Catalonian ships traded with Flanders and England, the insurance companies did excellent business, and finally, the Crown of Aragon's great traditional market in North Africa was reopened. In 1511, after Bougie, Oran and Tripoli were taken, a pragmatic decree issued in Burgos on the eighteenth of December granted the Catalans the right to impose a duty of 50 per cent on any non-Catalan article imported into those seaports.

On the other hand, we should point out that Ferdinand's improvements in Catalonian industry and trade also affected agriculture. In this regard, the Sentence of 1486 which resolved the *remença* problem was complemented by the decree of the Cortes of Monzón in 1511, prohibiting the passage of flocks through cultivated lands. This was a measure of utmost importance for the future of Catalonian agriculture, which, compared with the radically opposite policy decided upon ten years earlier in Castile, shows that the decrees of Ferdinand and Isabella should not be considered simply as royal decisions, but as responding to social structures in existence in the two countries. What was possible in Catalonia was not possible, as we shall see, in Castile.

To sum up: except in the matter of trade with America, which we shall take up shortly, it is proved that during the reign of the Catholic King, either because of the monarch's favorable attitude or because of the country's vital recovery, Catalonia progressively regained the stature she had lost in the middle of the fifteenth century.

AGRARIAN AND GRAZING POLICY IN CASTILE: EXPANSION OF THE MESTA

The fundamental fact of Ferdinand and Isabella's economic policy in Castile is the solution, favoring livestock over agriculture, of a problem which had existed since the beginning of the thirteenth century.

No historian, no matter how great an apologist he has been for the Catholic Monarchs, has been able to defend this decision. Ballesteros Gaibrois states in a work on Queen Isabella, "The result was permanently harmful for the Spanish economy."[8]

And, trying to find some excuse, he adds, "This was one of the subjects which the great policy-makers of the time simply did not have within their mental range." This conclusion seems unfounded to us, for the problem of famine in Castile was one that Ferdinand and Isabella lived with daily, and it was intimately related to the dilemma which they found already in existence and solved in favor of livestock.

The fact that Ferdinand and Isabella favored the Mesta is obvious. This appears not only in the legislation we are about to describe, but also in the less important decrees of their government. Torres Fontes speaks in a recent article of a disagreement that developed over a grazing ground in Murcia which some good farmers had planted with trees, sowed with grain, and then fenced in to prevent the passage of flocks; he shows that the royal decision condemned this act, and tells of the solemn moment when the herdsmen destroyed the fence and chopped down the trees.[9] There is something here—a negative element, which must have been very deeply rooted—which strikes very deep in Castilian economic history and explains the anguish of the farmers. And this is not a personal, subjective impression. It is borne out in hundreds of texts. Let us choose one of these: the protest of the delegates of the city of Cáceres in the courts of Valladolid in 1501, when, referring to these attempts against agricultural property, they exclaimed, "Such things cannot be called just nor honest, since they are not for the public good but for the private advantage of a few favored men."[10]

Let us examine a number of decrees issued by Ferdinand and Isabella favorable to herding, detrimental to agriculture.

The *royal cédula of 1480* ordered evacuation of the enclosures set up by farmers on communal lands during the time of Henry IV.

The *ordinance of 1489*,[11] called *Defense of the Cañadas*, decreed the redrawing of the boundaries of these sheepwalks in order to expel from them the farmers who had settled there during the previous fifty years. This law caused considerable losses, for it greatly widened the paths along which the flocks passed, and especially banned the setting aside of land for enclosures.

The *edict of 1491* banned enclosures in the kingdom of Granada.

A law of the same year, confirmed in succeeding years, authorized shepherds to "lop"; that is, "to cut down the smaller trees for their branches during the winter or when pasture is scarce." This measure, together with the absence of any measure stipulating punishment for the burning of forests to encourage growth of grass for grazing, resulted in deforestation of the country in spite of the interest shown by Isabella the Catholic in perpetuating the forests. As Julius Klein writes, "This reign was indeed the crucial period in the history of Castilian forestry; and the desolation which was wrought in the wooded areas of the kingdom had its beginnings in the uncompromising partiality of Ferdinand and Isabella for the pastoral industry."[12]

But all these edicts pale into insignificance if we consider the famous *land lease law* of 1501. When the law in defense of the sheepwalks began to be enforced, the herdsmen tried to invade the farmers' fields and the city councils defended themselves. A fundamental solution had to be found: the law of 1501. By its provisions the Mesta could extend the lease of a field indefinitely, paying for it the sum originally agreed upon, and keeping for its own purposes any grazing ground it had occupied for a few months, without the owner's knowledge. This last decree implied a presumption of legal usufruct in favor of the herdsman, a presumption established independently of the desires of the owner of the land, who was obliged to lease it for a ridiculously low rent. Great stretches of Andalusia and Extremadura were thus linked to the Mesta and to the interests of the Mesta's ruling minority. For agriculture, the result could not have been more unfavorable.

What were the reasons for Ferdinand and Isabella's policy toward the Mesta? Its first motive is crystal clear: *monopolistic regulation of the wool trade*. Over and above any other consideration, they were ruled by the need for obtaining "great quantities of gold and other advantages from abroad" (J. Klein). And the reason for this was that the monarchy was the chief beneficiary of the Mesta. In fact, since 1466 indirectly, and 1493 directly, the Crown had controlled the great masterships of the military orders. This means that it received, through the Order of Santiago, 100 per cent of the *servicio y montazgo*[13] taxes which constituted the Crown's chief financial resources. Therefore, instead of waiting for a few years until the development of agriculture would bear fruit, the monarchs chose to follow the easy path of their predecessors and collect money on something as tangible and easily taxable as sheep. This brings us to the second motive: *the financial crisis undergone by the Crown after 1484.* Owing to the expansion of the Inquisition and the flight of capital in the hands of the *conversos*, and subsequently, in 1492, to the expulsion of the Jews, quick remedies were needed; and none was closer to hand than the wool which was exported. Hence the protection of the Mesta. Hence too, after the time of Ferdinand and Isabella, it could be said that, "The exploitation and preservation of sheepherding is the chief support of these kingdoms."

It now seems hardly necessary to add more details on the state of agriculture in Castile at the time of Ferdinand and Isabella. But does evidence of the decline of Castilian agriculture at the time derive solely from legal testimony?

No. It is a fact based on the conscientious studies carried out by Ibarra[14] and Hamilton[15] on the evolution of the grain problem in Castile. And as their findings agree, and are incontrovertible, we can state that in 1504 Ferdinand and Isabella's agrarian policy began to bear fruit in the form of a frightful crisis in the grain market, resulting in the massive importation of wheat, called "bread from oversea," after 1506.

If we study production during this period, we find an uninterrupted series of insufficient harvests from 1502 to 1508. Scarcity had been known before (1486 and 1491) and had forced the placing of a ceiling price on the *fanega* of wheat, setting it at 124 maravedís (the normal price in years of a good harvest was 50). But after 1502 this price-fixing not only failed to correct the scarcity of wheat, but its price rose out of all bounds: 600 maravedís in 1504 and 1506. Only the prompt importation of wheat avoided continuation of the ravages of famine; but the fatal result was that the fall in prices ruined the farmers who had sowed wheat under great difficulties in 1505.

The very serious threat of famine in 1506 was not the result of a series of adverse climatic circumstances, but of a deficient agrarian structure, produced by one-sided protection of livestock, absenteeism in rural areas, the expulsion of the Moriscos from Granada, latifundism, and the growth in power of the aristocratic class.

DEVELOPMENT OF INDUSTRIAL ECONOMY IN CASTILE

The traditional thesis holds that the Catholic Monarchs fomented Castilian industrial activity in every direction, and that they brought it to an extraordinary level of expansion. We must confess that we do not find evidence to confirm this statement. The industries usually mentioned in the books were either luxury items or had only a local market. The only flourishing industries worthy of the name were the iron production of the North and the fabrics of the central Castilian zone: Segovia, Soria, Ávila, and Toledo in particular. And even in the development of the cloth industry we can observe two sharply differentiated phases— the first, a stage of crisis produced by the authorization to import foreign cloth, as a counterweight to the export of raw wool; the second, a stage of relative prosperity, coinciding with the early colonization of the Antilles (1505–1520). After that the Castilian cloth industry continued to grow, exporting its products not only to America and the traditional Portuguese market, but also to North Africa.

It would also seem possible to distinguish, as Klein does, between Ferdinand's policy and Isabella's. That is, after the death of the queen (who was the chief beneficiary of the Mesta's trade), the king effectively protected Castilian industry. But these are speculations which we have no time to look into. The incontrovertible fact is that after 1505 there was growing prosperity in Castilian industry, coinciding with the initial colonization of the Antilles and a favorable change in the direction of the long-term business cycle.

There is one other product which also underwent considerable development: the manufactured silk of Granada. (But only until 1503, the year in which the revolt of the *Moriscos* in Granada caused the silk industry to fall into a decline from which it did not emerge until the time of Charles V.)

The growing number of decrees regarding manufactures, which are so constantly mentioned in the texts, cannot hide the basic lack of coherence of Ferdinand and Isabella's industrial policy. For underneath them all, one fact sapped their effectiveness: the flight of the *conversos*. They had been the basic artisan class, and thus we can observe that soon after the Inquisition was established, Ferdinand and Isabella had to issue decrees calling for the presence in Spain of foreign artisans (1484). The lack of skilled manpower came to be felt even more strongly later, when America needed cloth and other products of the Spanish market.

EXPANSION OF THE CASTILIAN WOOL TRADE

It is in this area that Ferdinand and Isabella's favorable reputation among the historians of the past is fully justified. Their success derives not only from the fact that they carried out a mercantilist policy, but that they protected and favored the country's traditional wool trade.

Once Ferdinand and Isabella were seated on the throne, the wool trade was systematically organized. Thus, for example, they sent agents abroad who traveled to the various markets to find out about their needs, prices, and competition. The chief agents were permanent, residing in Bruges, La Rochelle, London, and Florence, from which cities they sent reports to the Court. Once they had collected the necessary information, they contacted the merchants of Burgos and the officials of the Mesta in order to organize exports.

In this regard we must point out the competition between the cities of Burgos and Bilbao, which had begun to appear during the previous reign. While Burgos controlled the wool market, Bilbao had control of shipping. The classic struggle between producer and carrier took place here, because Bilbao tried to carry out the transport of the raw product at high prices, counterbalancing Burgos' desire to control its rival's fleet in order to lower freight rates.

When Bruges gave the Biscayans great economic and commercial advantages in 1493, Burgos retaliated by obtaining from the sovereigns the famous privilege of 1494 creating the Consulate. This law granted Burgos *the monopoly of foreign trade in the Cantabrian Sea*, with the right to set freight rates on the coasts of Guipúzcoa, Biscay, and Santander, after informing the markets of the interior: Segovia, Vitoria, Logroño, Valladolid, Medina del Campo, and Medina de Ríoseco. This was a partial victory for Burgos, but, because it caused reprisals from Bilbao, one which resulted in the compromise agreement of 1499; Burgos obtained the exclusive right to authorize wool shipments to Flanders, Nantes, La Rochelle, and England, and permission to organize one annual fleet, while Bilbao retained the right to iron exports and one-third of the tonnage Burgos needed for wool shipment. In spite of this agreement, relations between Bilbao and Burgos continued to be strained, owing to the influence of citizens of Burgos at Isabella's court. Finally, Bilbao obtained from Ferdinand the privilege of 1511 creating the Consulate of that city, and then Burgos had to capitulate. This led to the agreement of 1513, which resembled that of 1499. But the merchant fleets of Santander and other Cantabrian ports lost their independence, and were not to recover it until 300 years later.

Let us mention at this point the internal wool markets. In accordance with the centralizing policy of Ferdinand and Isabella, they were reduced to three at this time: Medina del Campo, which was the queen's fair: Villalón, that of the Duke of Benavente; and Medina de Ríoseco.

Commercial life was given a strong stimulus because Ferdinand and Isabella made an effort to develop the technical instruments of trade. We cannot state unequivocally whether Isabella had a feel for commercial life or not. It is very possible that she did. On the other hand, we *can* make such a statement in regard to Ferdinand the Catholic, a great promoter of public works in the Crown of Aragon and in America. To demonstrate this we need only cite the fact that, when he got the news of the discovery of the Pacific by Vasco Núñez de Balboa, Ferdinand immediately ordered the creation of a port in Panama. In Spain itself too, the port of Bilbao dates from this period, as well as the paving of some highways and the organization of two important bodies, the *Brotherhood of Teamsters*, which in 1497 brought together the owners of oxcarts furnishing transport service within the country into the so-called *Royal Association of Teamsters*; and the great *Brotherhood of the Mails*, whose spiritual center was the chapel of Marcús in Barcelona. In the network of international communcations of the period, Barcelona became the center of postal service for Italy, Germany, France, Aragon, Castile, and Portugal. In 1505 the monopoly of the Spanish postal service was granted to an Italian family named Tassis, and became the General Postal Service of Castile.

One fact should be pointed out concerning the technical organization of the merchant marine, apart from the laws on navigation which we shall discuss later. In 1498 an order was given by the terms of which the State paid a subsidy on the construction of ships of more than 600 tons. This measure has been very much argued over, for some historians accuse it of having been detrimental to merchant shipping in favor of a navy. At that time a ship of 200 tons could be sailed very satisfactorily; this was the size of the caravels which made the Atlantic crossing. Therefore, raising the tonnage limit to 600 in order to receive the subsidy meant favoring the construction of those enormous seagoing structures which were simply floating fortresses, rather than naval ships.

INSTITUTIONALIZATION OF THE CASTILIAN ECONOMY: GUILDS AND CONSULATES

The institutionalization of the Castilian economy is only one facet, in the economic sphere, of the transmission of administrative and technical information from the Crown of Aragon to Castile. Ferdinand the Catholic organized trade by setting up consulates and guilds copied from Catalonian models, just as he organized the chancellery, the administration of justice, and a number of other institutions imitating those of the Crown of Aragon.

As for the Consulates, their organization leaves no doubt that this was so. In the very document granting the Consulate of Burgos (1494), the statement is made that the merchants of the city ask for the same privileges as those enjoyed by the Consulate of the Sea in Barcelona. And when the Consulate of Bilbao was set up in 1511, it simply copied that of Burgos, which in fact meant returning to the original source, the Consulate of Barcelona.

The institutionalization of the guilds is no less obvious. Until 1475 the Castilian crown was opposed to guilds. Even in Henry IV's last Cortes "closed groups" (guild corporations) were banned once again, and the purpose of the brotherhoods was limited exclusively to pious concerns. This attitude changed radically after Ferdinand the Catholic came to the throne of Castile. Then guilds were set up with authorization from the State, which gave the cities power to grant ordinances concerning them. This was the case of Seville, Burgos, Segovia, and Valladolid after 1470, and especially after 1484.

It was also at this time that entrance examinations for trades, and the labor hierarchy of masters, journeymen, and apprentices, were introduced into Castile. The law-giving spirit which had characterized the last phase in the Catalonian guilds' evolution was also introduced. When Ferdinand dictated the Ordinances of Seville in 1511, which contained no less than 120 rules on the art of weaving cloth, he did no great favor to Castile, for its textile industry became influenced by the routine into which the Catalonian industry had fallen. At the end of the fifteenth and beginning of the sixteenth centuries, just at the moment when all Europe was starting to break loose from the guild, Ferdinand the Catholic put the corporative strait-jacket on the Castilians. If it had had more freedom of movement, perhaps the industrialization of Castile would have become a fact.

REFORM OF THE CURRENCY

Here also the Catholic Monarchs had a broad field of action for a positive policy, after the enormous dislocations brought about by the civil wars in Catalonia and Castile. They did not apply any exceptional ideas; what they did was to impose an honest and honorable administration on the minting and distribution of money.

Ferdinand and Isabella's system of monetary reform was very simple. Just as the Italian florin had been copied in the Peninsula in the fourteenth century, at the end of the fifteenth it was decided to imitate the medium of exchange which had the greatest acceptance in the international market: the *Venetian ducat*. In 1481 Ferdinand the Catholic created in Valencia the *excelente*, a coin which exactly corresponded in value to a Venetian ducat. It must be kept in mind that Valencia was the financial capital of Spain at the time, and this explains why the monetary reform stemmed from that city. The result was so propitious that in 1493 Ferdinand established a new monetary standard in Catalonia: the *principat*, equal to the Venetian ducat and to the Castilian excelente.

Reform was slower in Castile, for the war with Granada and the expulsion of the Jews did not permit the delicate operation of stabilizing the currency. Finally, on the fourteenth of June, 1497, Isabella and Ferdinand published the pragmatic decree or basic law of the Spanish monetary system that was to obtain for future centuries. The excelente of Granada was created as a *gold coin*, minted in $65\frac{1}{3}$ pieces from the mark of $22\frac{3}{4}$ carats, which had the same value—like the Valencian excelente and the Catalonian principat—as the Venetian ducat, and was often called so: *ducat*. The new *real* was introduced as a *silver coin*, minted in 66 pieces from the mark of 11 *dineros* and 4 grams (pure silver was considered to be divided into 12 dineros), as were its multiples (quadruples and octuples = the piece of 8 reales, issued especially by Charles V and equivalent to the Bohemian or Saxon "thaler") and subdivisions (half-, quarter-, and eighth-real coins). And finally, besides these gold and silver coins, a vellon coin was minted for small change, with a small quantity of silver. The coin called the *blanca* was minted of this metal, at the rate of 192 coins from the 6-gram mark. Ferdinand and Isabella, wishing to avoid inflation, had only 10 million blancas minted, an insufficient quantity that was to result in the influx of French vellon in exchange for American silver. To solve the problem, Charles V was obliged to lower the amount of silver in the blanca in 1552, and to mint 10 million more of these coins in 1558.

The coins we have just described were real ones. All of them were related among themselves by a money of account, the *maravedí*, to which they bore the following relationship: the excelente of Granada or ducat = 375 maravedís; the real = 34 maravedís; the blanca = one-half maravedí. A ducat, therefore, was worth 11 reales and 1 maravedí, or 750 blancas.

To sum up: for the first time, by about 1500, the three most important Spanish coins, the "excel.lent" of Valencia, the "principat" of Catalonia, and the excelente of Granada, or Castilian ducat, were all worth exactly the same. This was, in fact, *the only measure of economic unification* established by Ferdinand and Isabella. In regard to silver, on the other hand, since Castile kept receiving shipments from the Indies, little by little this metal began to spread from Castile into the kingdoms of the Crown of Aragon, devaluing the silver which circulated in Valencia and Catalonia; that is, the Valencian and Catalonian real. And this is why the Cortes of Valencia and Catalonia protested over and over in an attempt to avoid the influx of Castilian silver into their kingdoms, where it would produce loss in value and inflation. The Cortes of Monzón in 1511 succeeded in preventing this insofar as Valencia was concerned.

ORIGINS OF CASTILIAN MERCANTILISM: STATE MONOPOLIES

The origins of Castilian mercantilism have been studied by Hamilton. According to this author, its essential traits are as follows:

First, *imperialism*, brought about by the war with Granada and the military expansion into Italy and Africa. Second, the *prolonged drop in prices at the end of the fifteenth century*; the fall of prices favored mercantilism to the degree that it necessitated a measure of control over the money situation. Third, the *discovery of gold* in Hispaniola. Fourth, the *preponderance of the wool trade* and extractive industries, and the scarcity of manufactured goods. And fifth, the *need to develop the merchant marine in the Atlantic.*

Faced with these conditions, Ferdinand and Isabella took a number of measures to control the economy.

First, *the State undertook a monopoly of gold and silver.* This was a typically mercantilist measure, stemming from the belief that precious metals are the chief sources of well-being and universal wealth.

Second, a *system prohibiting the export of gold and silver* was established. There were already laws concerning this, but in 1480 Ferdinand and Isabella issued a famous pragmatic decree detailing the punishment, which even included the death penalty, for anyone who dared to take these metals out of Castile. This set a premium on smuggling, and consequently gold and silver went out of the country at a terrifying rate, so that in 1515 a new law on the subject had to be issued establishing an even more rigorous system of inspection.

Third, an attempt was made to maintain a *trade balance* which, if not favorable, would at least not be unfavorable. This is the sweet dream of mercantilism; so much bought, so much sold. The law was applied after 1491 in trade relations between Biscay, Navarre, and Castile, with the result that no merchant could cross a border unless he agreed to take out of the country as much merchandise as he brought in.

Fourth, *strict control of the metal coming from America* was decreed. When we speak of the Castilian monopoly in America, we are apt to forget that as far as metal was concerned, the monopoly was in the hands of the Castilian State. It was to the State's interest to control mines and ports of embarkation and disembarkation of the metal. The fewer people involved in the course of these operations, the smaller would be the leakage.

Other measures of a mercantilist type were the *navigation laws*, especially that of 1501 prohibiting the shipment of merchandise in foreign ships so long as there were Spanish ships in the ports (this measure was an imitation of the pragmatic decree issued by Alfonso V to Catalonia in 1451); and laws of *industrial protectionism*, such as the Ordinance of Seville of 1511.

FISCAL SYSTEM

Ferdinand and Isabella were certainly successful in their attempt to organize a State. In the administrative field their accomplishment was decisive, creating a number of organizations —the Councils—which centralized the work of government. Reform of the treasury was begun in 1480 by creating within the Royal Council the "Office of Chief Accountants of the Treasury Books and Royal Patrimony." This section was turned over to a hardworking Asturian, Alonso de Quintanilla. After that time royal revenues increased prodigiously, rising from some 800,000 maravedís in 1470 to the 22 million of 1504.

Although the administration functioned well and in consequence taxes were used more advantageously, there was no essential tax reform. The immunities of the nobles and clergy were maintained while the poor commoner continued to be weighed down, as always, by the *alcabalas*, *sisas*, *tercias*, tithes, and the whole series of taxes which had come down from the Middle Ages. The only uniform contribution was the Bull of the Holy Crusade, obtained by Ferdinand and Isabella for use in the war with Granada. It produced a handsome sum of money for the Crown.

ECONOMIC LINKS AMONG THE KINGDOMS OF THE SPANISH MONARCHY

In 1479, just as Ferdinand and Isabella commenced to rule, the merchants of Catalonia felt that they had entered on a period of

Hispanic "brotherhood"—according to words found in the documents. It is obvious that for the impoverished people and stagnant commerce of Catalonia, the idea of being able to count on markets such as Castile and Andalusia for their cloth, tools, coral, and spices was extremely attractive. They would also have been able to take part in the wool trade much more easily than other foreign intruders. However, these desires were frustrated, not because Castile had anything against the Catalans, but because its high financial circles were controlled by Genoese. Unfortunately, at that particular moment the Catholic Monarchs needed the Genoese more than the Catalans, and since the latter were in economic ruin, the sovereigns paid no attention to their insistent demands. The Cortes of Castile, for its part, shortsightedly refused to admit the Catalans to the fair of Medina del Campo on an equal footing, so that they continued to be regarded as foreigners. Thus the two sides of the Hispanic medieval economy, the Mediterranean and the Atlantic, lived separate lives throughout Ferdinand and Isabella's reign, establishing a fateful tradition which was not to be broken until the last third of the eighteenth century.

This fact is essential if we are to realize that Ferdinand and Isabella did not in fact aspire to the attainment of an effective unity in Spain; for the unity of a country, as we know all too well, begins with its economic infrastructure. The only link that existed among the kingdoms of the Hispanic monarchy was the monetary one. America could have been the decisive unifying force. Since in Castile the interests of the Genoese and the Mesta were so sacred that they could not permit an economic union between the Crowns of Aragon and Castile, America at least would have been an ideal field for a truly Hispanic common task.

Why, then—in practice, for there was no legal exclusion—was trade with America prohibited to the subjects of the Crown of Aragon? So many thousands of pages have been written about this problem that it would be a gigantic task even to try to sum it up. Let us point out, though, the conclusions to which the argument has led. The political version: Castilian-Catalan antagonism, and the desire of Ferdinand and Isabella to annihilate Catalonia.

The legal version: America was the exclusive patrimony of Castile. As for the first point, there is nothing that proves such an assertion, and it is totally romantic; it will prove more useful to mention, later on, the opposition of the Sevillian monopolists to any kind of outside competition, including Catalan competiton. As for the second point, the thesis of Ferdinand and Isabella's common property put forward by Professor Manzano[17] undermines this solution and affirms Ferdinand's right and the right of his vassals to make use of half of the discoveries.

The controversy raised by these two points is outside the scope of the present discussion. But we should like to point out three aspects of it which have not been adequately dealt with. First, the *mercantilist* aspect. From an economic point of view, it is obvious that the presence of non-Castilians in American trade was wholly disadvantageous to the Castilian State. Somebody had to carry on this trade, and it turned out to be the Castilians, for the Indies had been discovered by the Crown of Castile, though some Catalans and Aragonese took part in the discovery. This mercantilist position seems very justified to us, especially if we take into account the tradition created by the *Casa de Contratación de las Indias*, or House of Trade with the Indies, where this legislation was applied. Besides the mercantilist aspect, we must refer to what might be called *Catalonia's lack of interest*. This is an undeniable fact. The Catalans were not interested in America until well into the sixteenth century, when they took formal steps to engage in trade with the Indies. They were totally unconcerned during the reign of Ferdinand and Isabella. There was some question, as we have seen, of their taking part in Castilian trade, but of the Indies there is not a trace in the documents we have examined.

Last—the third aspect—this attitude of the Catalans was accompanied, on Ferdinand and Isabella's side, by a firm desire not to permit any Catalan, Aragonese, or Valencian noble or merchant to go to the Indies; they wished to avoid any application of the legalistic, pactist, and contractual spirit which had grown up in those regions during the Middle Ages. They had a hard enough time controlling the Castilians, in spite of the fact that the latter were accustomed to obeying an all-powerful monarchy. It is clear that the exclusion of the Catalans from America had something to do with the monarchs' desire *to rule the Indies without any sort of impediment.*

NOTES

[1. Y. F. Baer, *Die Vertreibung der Jüden aus Spanien,* in *Sefarad,* VI (1943), 163–88.]

[2. Lorenzo Galíndez de Carvajal, *Anales breves de los Reyes Católicos,* ed. R. F. Robles y Encinas, *CODOIN,* XVIII (Madrid, 1851), 227–422.]

[3. *Rectius* A. Matilla Tascón, author of *Declaratorias de los Reyes Católicos sobre la reducción de juros y otras mercedes* (Madrid, 1952), p. 17.]

[4. See below, p. 282. The 83 so-called Laws of Toro began to be compiled after the Cortes of Toledo in 1502 and were finally published only in 1505 (cf. R. T. Davies, *The Golden Century of Spain* (London, 1954), p. 5, n. 3).]

[5. L. Marineo Sículo, *Obra de las cosas memorables de España* (Alcalá de Henares, 1539).]

[6. A. Castro y Quesada, *La realidad histórica de España* (Mexico, 1954); *The Structure of Spanish History,* trans. E. L. King (Princeton, 1954).]

[7. Cf. now L. Suárez Fernández, *Documentos acerca de la expulsión de los Judiós* (Valladolid, 1964).]

[8. M. Ballesteros Gaibrois, *La obra de Isabel la Católica* (Segovia, 1953), p. 114.]

[9. J. Torres Fontes, *Yecla en el reinado de los Reyes Católicos* (Murcia, 1954).]

[10. J. Klein, *The Mesta* (Cambridge, Mass., 1920), pp. 316, 324.]

[11. Cf. *ibid.,* pp. 316 ff.]

[12. *Ibid.,* p. 321.]

[13. See above, p. 52.]

[14. E. Ibarra y Rodríguez, *El problema cerealista en España durante el reinado de los Reyes Católicos (1475–1516)* (Madrid, 1944).]

[15. E. J. Hamilton, *American Treasure and the Price Revolution in Spain, 1501–1650* (Cambridge, Mass., 1934); *Money, Prices and Wages in Valencia, Aragon and Navarre (1351–1500)* (Cambridge, Mass., 1936).]

[16. J. Manzano Manzano, "La adquisición de las Indias por los Reyes Católicos y su incorporación a los reinos castellanos," AHDE, XXI–XXII (1951–52), 5–170.]

FURTHER READING

Apart from the works of Klein and Hamilton mentioned in the footnotes, *Cambridge Economic History* ed. M. M. Postan and H. J. Habbakuk, III (Cambridge, 1963), 152–53.

9 The Science of Law in the Spain of the Catholic Kings

JUAN BENEYTO PÉREZ

The appearance of the *letrados* in the Royal Council in the fifteenth century is only one aspect of the importance of law (and lawyers) in this period. The author of this article discusses a number of its manifestations, from the law books in the library of Ferdinand and Isabella to the outstanding lawyers themselves, men like Alonso Díaz de Montalvo, Palacios Rubios (the author of the *Requerimiento*), and Galíndez de Carvajal. He shows that despite the efforts of the Catholic Kings in the legal sphere, it was not until the reign of Philip II that the law in Spain received its definitive codification in the shape of the *Nueva Recopilación*. Moreover, the influence of Bologna on the training of Spanish lawyers, especially after the foundation of the Spanish College by Cardinal Albornoz, was clearly maintained and prevented the emergence of a strong school of legal commentators in Spain itself.

I

First of all, a question of nomenclature: Is it possible to speak of a science of law in the last years of the fifteenth century? In what sense was the word "science" used at that time? That is, on what epistemological bases did the formulation of juridical theory rest?

The idea of science had reappeared in medieval times as a result of the revival of Aristotle's philosophy. In his commentary on the *Liber sententiarum*, Egidio Romano emphasized the significance of reason in science: "Human knowledge is primarily subject to reason."[1] Through the works of St. Thomas Aquinas in particular, science was brought face to face with exegesis, and there is no doubt that a scientific work was considered to be one which resulted from the effort of reason.[2]

But this effort of reason—which with the advent of humanism became subtlety and *elegantia*—was initially based on experience. Here too, the scientific movement of the Late Middle Ages arises out of Aristotle. In the lecture given by Palacios Rubios[3] when he inaugurated his lessons in the *Prima* chair at Salamanca, his point of departure is the Aristotelian principle: "Since as the Philosopher (i.e., Aristotle) says, 'An artist gets from nature talent, his skill from craftsmanship, readiness from practice ...'".[4] We are reuniting the scientific with the artificial, with that which is a human creation. And Palacios Rubios adds: "For through knowledge and experience every notion is acquired, and every skill is increased by practice; for Experience is the powerful mistress of life."[5]

So we have come to the point we were seeking: experience, united to reason, is the mistress of science.

And what was the Late Medieval view of juridical theory? Two possibilities were offered by life in the Law; teaching and the magistracy. The two were firmly interlocked, and reason and experience were embraced by both.

Law studies reveal the predominance of outlines and considerations arising from Roman and canonical law, as well as the lack of doctrinal preparation in those who cultivated the common law which arose out of the symbiosis of the two systems. There was also—and humanist criticism was to make a special point of this—a total lack of historical sense, necessary as this was; but perspective was broken as the sources were left further behind. With the use of the gloss, which constituted exegesis—and therefore had the least possible resemblance to science—casuistry proliferated and the accumulation of opinions flourished.

There was also, according to testimony in the Cortes of Toledo in 1480 which proves the existence of the evil, an unjustified use of academic titles, leading to contempt for them. Written into the *Ordenanzas Reales*, as passage [Lib.] 1, [tit.] 10, [cap.] 5,[6] this measure emphasizes the interest taken by the sovereigns in this science, and the obligation they recognized to honor learned men and to protect those who, by their merits and competence, had received academic investiture. The Cortes had convinced the rulers that many so-called doctors, licentiates, and bachelors were circulating in Castile, when in fact they possessed no such titles.

Palacios tells us in his "repetitio" *De donatione inter virum et uxorem* that Salamanca conferred the title of doctor only on those whose studies had occupied many nights, and then only when their work seemed to be exemplary and well seasoned. Improvisations were not acceptable, therefore, and this explains why fraudulent titles were so common. The prestige of the great university rested on the prestige of its graduates. Let us recall that the Constitutions of Salamanca of 1422 required, after thorough instruction in grammar, six years of juridical studies leading to the degree of bachelor; then the bachelors taught for five years, and once their merit was established they were admitted to the degree of licentiate after a rigorous and secret examination. Still later, after writing their theses, they attained the doctorate.[7]

The reform of Bologna in 1440 must have had some influence in Spain, for the information given by Marineo Sículo in his *De laudibus Hispaniae*, published in Salamanca in 1495, mentions fifty professors, of whom ten held chairs in canon law and eight in civil law, not counting teaching of a monographic nature. The typical Bolognese curriculum dealt with civil law through the study of the *Code*, *Old Digest*, *New Digest*, *Volumen*, and *Infortiatum*, and canon law through the *Decretum*, *Decretales*, the *Liber Sextus*, and the *Clementinae*.[8] In the reform of 1440 the chair of *Volumen* was divided into three, and there is evidence that greater depth was given to this study. Soon after, Salamanca put the two specializations on the same plane, assigning ten chairs to each.

The sovereigns took an interest in this great formative center, sometimes in defense of its freedom to appoint chair-holders, sometimes to maintain the solvency of its professors. Henry IV had taken measures to ensure that the men who taught there should be "scholarly and knowledgeable persons, such as can be heard with advantage by both students and auditors."

In the sixteenth century studies in Spanish law were instituted. Along with the six hours a day spent on the Digests and Codes, the students also had to cope with the *Partidas*, the *Fuero Real*, and the *Liber iudiciorum*.[9] The Laws of 1505, which are, as we shall see, a most important point, were also perused by the students.

II

But in teaching as well as in practice, the book—still not easily come by—was fundamental. We know that in the medieval libraries many books were chained to prevent their being stolen. Now an extremely interesting document—the will of the eminent doctor Alonso Díaz de Montalvo—gives witness of the importance of juridical books in the training of students. The noted jurist divided his books into two categories, depending on whether they concerned civil or canon law, and gave them to his two grandsons, who, he says in his last testament, "shall cast lots between them, and the one who gets the law books shall study civil law, and the one who gets the books of canons shall study canons."[10] What an ingenious way of choosing a profession, by the fall of the dice. But it also demonstrates that a student was in a position to be a good jurist if he possessed good books.

We can also form an idea of what these books were for which lots were to be cast; not only by inference, judging from the books important jurists of the time were likely to possess, but also through the sources which Díaz Montalvo himself cited or utilized in his works. In fact, we find mentioned the most famous compendia and glosses: Accursius, with his great gloss, and especially Bartolus. But the names of Baldus and Odofredus, Lapus de Castlebono and Johannes de Imola, Durandus and Johannes Andreae are also mentioned.[11] Bartholomeus Salicetus, Johannes de Platea, the "Archdeacon," and Hostiensis[12] are there too: an excellent selection of the cultivators of juridical science in the two branches his grandsons were to study.

An examination of the catalogues of libraries of the period, or of inventories made following the death of some great jurist or famous bishop, would cast no little light on this problem; but none more than an examination of the royal library. Let us see, then, what law books the Catholic Monarchs had on their shelves.

To begin with, we know that Sancho de Paredes, Queen Isabella's chamberlain, had procured two copies of the *Siete Partidas*: one was a manuscript on parchment, with decorations of gilded silver forming the initials of the two rulers, the *Y* and the *F*. The other was printed: "cast," says the inventory. There is also evidence of the presence of legal books in the Alcázar of Segovia; books of canon law, such as the *Decretales* and the commentaries of Johannes Andreae; those of civil law, such as the works of Bartolus, Baldus and Buttrigarius.[13] Collections of definitions abound; not only the famous one by Arias de Bustamante called *La Peregrina*, but several others, generally important ones, which the catalogue calls repertories or which it shows to be collections of definitions: "one which begins abbas," "another which begins ambassadors. . . ." There were also Castilian texts in Segovia: the *Fuero de Burgos* and the *Fuero de las Leyes* (that is, the *Fuero Real*), the *Ordenamientos* of Seville and Madrid (laws laid down by the monarchs themselves), and of course the *Partidas*, which occupied a well-deserved place between the tales of Boccaccio and the *Fiammetta*, which Sánchez Cantón considers the favorite reading matter of the queen herself.[14]

III

The presence of the *Ordenamientos* of Seville and Madrid among the law books in the royal library seems to me to be symbolic. Few monarchs displayed as much regard for tradition as Ferdinand and Isabella in their efforts toward modernity. They acted on that petition of 1438 in which the deputies to the Cortes had requested a summary of the laws of the kingdom in one volume. At the beginning of the so-called *Ordenamiento de Montalvo* —the first effort at compilation, as we know—it is specifically stated that "the true office of the sovereigns is to do judgment and justice . . . that justice may flourish and be done and administered justly and uprightly." Not least among the merits earned by the Cortes of Toledo of 1480 for its great work was its order to

Dr. Montalvo to compile the laws of the kingdom. Montalvo had long experience and was already an old man; he was seventy-five years old at that date, for he had been born in 1405. Over the span of his life from Arévalo, where he was born, to Huete, where he was working at the time, a very clear feeling of necessity weighed upon him: the necessity of giving an adequate framework to the legislation then in force, a framework which would serve to impart a better knowledge of Castilian law and prevent men of law from indulging in the diabolical practice of adducing opinions.

In Juan de Mena's *Dezir* the situation in Castile is expressed in the following lines:

> Now the suit has come to court;
> there are Bartolus and Cinus, the Digest,
> Johannes Andreae and Baldus and Henricus,
> who give more opinions than grapes in a basket . . .[15]

Montalvo collected and included in his *Ordenanzas* (1.4.6) a law of 1427 in which John II commanded and decreed that the parties to a suit or their lawyers, either in writing or otherwise by verbal disputation, "cannot allege an opinion, determination, decree, or authority, nor gloss of any doctor, canonist, or legist, of those who came after Bartolus or Johannes Andreae, nor of the doctors who shall exist from this time forward." The situation must have been very serious, to judge from the sanction imposed: "The lawyer or solicitor who shall do otherwise shall be deprived of his office in perpetuity, and likewise the judge who shall agree to it; and the party who alleges it shall lose his case." The Catholic Kings themselves had had to insist on the point in their pragmatic of 1499, issued in Madrid, in which adducible opinions were limited to those of the four doctors alluded to above: Bartolus and Baldus in civil law, and Johannes Andreae and Nicholas de Tudeschis as canonists.[16] The need for a thorough reform was obvious.

The compilation carried out by Montalvo was based on the Alfonsine model of the *Fuero Real, Fuero Castellano,* or *Fuero de las*

Leyes, as it was variously called. Included with it were the standards laid down in Alcalá in 1348 and the measures agreed upon in the Cortes.

A second effort in this direction was the work of the scribe Juan Ramírez, who brought together in one volume an important collection of bulls and pragmatics, beginning with the law against blasphemy issued in Valladolid in 1492. The problem here was the same: these were bulls which had been granted in favor of the royal jurisdiction, and which it was well to make known "so that they may come to the attention of all."

Moreover, Queen Isabella insisted on the necessary compilation in a measure which appeared in the codicil to her will, issued in Medina del Campo in 1504. Ferdinand, adding his word to her desire, charged Galíndez de Carvajal with this duty, and in the end it was he who gave us the *Nueva Recopilación* of the laws of the Spanish kingdoms.

IV

Thus, thanks to the efforts of the Catholic Monarchs, a laudable impetus was given to formulation of the laws of the kingdom, culminating in the Laws of Toro issued by Doña Juana in 1505. In this text it is stipulated that all lawyers, judges, and magistrates who are in charge of the administration of justice cannot hold office "unless they have made the required study of the aforesaid laws of *Ordenamientos* and Pragmatics and *Partidas* and *Fuero Real*." How far this is not only from 1427, when the date of adducible opinions was cut off with the period of the post-glossators, but even from 1499, date of the limitation to four doctors! Thus, from this point onward—the point of this compilation of laws and these standards of procedure—a national juridical sense arises. I do not think that this has been sufficiently recognized, and it is to the credit of Federico de Castro that he has emphasized the point. "After the Laws of Toro," he writes, "the new value acquired by native Spanish laws is shown in the fact that they are considered worthy, like Roman and canonical laws, of being commented upon."[17] Even if this statement is not entirely true, it does at least show a configuration which we recognize as new, for although commentaries existed before this, they become frequent only after 1505.

With these measures the Catholic Monarchs came to be justly compared to Alfonso the Wise. In his gloss of the *Siete Partidas* (and remember that it was prior to the Laws of Toro) Alonso de Montalvo reminds us of the laudable memory left by that king, a legislator par excellence. Plato and Seneca flow from Montalvo's pen and praise Alfonso's works with their writings; and then Montalvo sings the praises of Isabella and Ferdinand, most sacred sovereigns, true gift of God. Juridical literature is presented as an important nucleus of science and culture. From Montalvo to Gregorio López, we recognize the concentrated and valuable effort of a whole generation during these years of the Catholic Monarchs' reign.

The closest antecedent is Arias de Balboa, bishop of Plasencia,[18] who in the mid-fifteenth century had made a commentary on the *Fuero Real*, and whose work was used by Montalvo, as he tells us himself. This famous jurist also used the collection of definitions of González Bustamante, known for his *La Peregrina*. Montalvo says in the prologue to his gloss of the *Partidas* that he used him as a principal source: "As a kind of gloss on the *Fueros* I chiefly made use of a golden and extremely useful repertory, divided up alphabetically, known in Castilian as *La Peregrina*."[19]

Dr. Alonso Díaz de Montalvo offers us an excellent example of a figure of transition: he was born in Arévalo in 1405 and died in Huete in 1499. He had written glosses to the *Ordenamiento* of Alcalá, the *Fuero Real*, and the *Partidas*. Some of these works were printed during his last years, for example that of the *Partidas* in Seville in 1491; but others were printed after his death, like that of the *Fuero Real*, which issued from the presses of Salamanca a year after the author's death. Only after reaching full maturity in his long career in the magistracy did he undertake his crowning task. Here again, science was based on experience; a councillor and judge under the predecessors of the Catholic Monarchs, he writes at the end of his life, in old age, when, as he says, his memory is weakening and his eyes are dim (*memoria torpescit et oculi caligant*). He uses a large number of sources in his work. His satisfaction in those books he had his grandsons cast lots for was not mere vainglory! He tells us that he works on the notes he has collected from the masters and doctors in the manner of a gleaner (*post terga metentium, quasi spicas colligendo vado*). And among these ears of grain he always knows how to choose those which are in accord with orthodoxy, no doubt in the manner of that Italian glossator so highly praised by the cardinal of Ostia because he interpreted problems according to the spirit of divine law. Along with Bartolus and Baldus, with Johannes Andreae and the "Abbot,"[20] Seneca and especially St. Augustine come into the hands of this gleaner. Sincere or not (the problem of Montalvo as a *converso* has already been referred to by Fermín Caballero, but this is not the appropriate place to discuss it), Montalvo gives every evidence of being a fervent Christian. We find the morning prayer *Actiones nostras* at the end of one of his prefaces: "Actiones igitur meas, o bone Jesu, aspirando praeveni et adiuvando prosequere, ut cuncta nostra operatio a te semper incipiat et per te cepta finiatur."[21] In another place—when he is compiling and summarizing the *Ordenanzas* of Castile—he says that, in order to make up his mind to undertake the task, he invoked divine aid.

It has been said that Montalvo appears to be an entirely medieval author. It would be preferable to say that he is, as I have suggested, a man of the transition period. Methods are slow to be revised, in his case with no little effort. His working technique is the well-known one of the commentator: correlation, concordance. What fundamentally concerns him is the comparison with canon law. It is clear that this was his chief preparation, as we can see in his *Repertorium super Ab[b]atem Panormitanum*, the first of his printed works; and moreover, he tells us so: "To make a complete concordance with canon law for the most part."[22]

Palacios Rubios is another important figure. He arises as the most forceful personality of the period and occupies the central position just at the time of Montalvo's death. He became a judge in Valladolid in 1491 and in Ciudad Real in 1494, and was a man who linked his experience in the magistracy with his academic formation and his teaching career, for we soon find him holding a chair. He is the first glossator of the Laws of Toro, in a work written about 1518. His commentaries are of special value, for he explains what we might call the private history of this elaboration, with intimate details of the discussions and points of view and interests which came into play, pointing out in each case who their author was. Like Montalvo he was a man with a tremendous capacity for work, and this capacity was thoroughly exploited by the sovereigns, who charged him with such difficult questions as that of justifying the law on Indians (and, as we know, he was the author of the very famous *Requerimiento* to the Indians, which was ordered to be read by the members of Pedrarias Dávila's expedition when they found themselves in contact with the natives of America) and the incorporation of the kingdom of Navarre (on which question he had been an arbitrator in the Council). If we add that he was the author of a study on vacant benefices in the Curia, and of a treatise on the islands, we will appreciate the breadth of his learning. But he was a canonist first of all. His *Repeticiones* on marital donations, printed in Valladolid in 1501, and his *Recollecta iuris canonici*, the unpublished record of his lectures in Salamanca, show us that he was learned in decretals.

He was, therefore, like Montalvo, a jurist with a canonical formation, and also like Montalvo a man of wide experience. Nothing more clearly describes him as such than his own words when he took up teaching for the second time, after having served in the Royal Chancery: the experience obtained in practice, he admits to his students, will surely be very useful to him. . . . Thus he is not only the learned jurist who piles up quotations of laws and opinions, or the political figure who suggests innovations and draws up plans for reform, but also the man who analyzes the facts in an anatomical sense, dissecting the law through study of all the cases that he knows.

Galíndez was a contemporary of Palacios. Don Lorenzo Galíndez de Carvajal is the third example we can cite here of this combination of reason and experience. And he constitutes a further proof that the Aristotelian concepts we brought up at the beginning of this study, using the words of none other than Palacios Rubios, were not mere erudition but the evidence of true learning. Galíndez, councillor of the Catholic Monarchs, was able to dedicate less time to juridical science than the others, but he did complete some fundamental tasks: an edition of the *Partidas* and what was to become—and soon became—the long-desired *Nueva Recopilación*.

And finally, another figure who should be included here is the grammarian Nebrija. A grammarian among the authors of law? Certainly, for he was a reformer of the science of law and gave us a lexicon of civil law. This *Aenigmata iuris civilis*, which saw the golden light of Salamanca in 1506, must be included in the tendency to consider mere legists—as the phrase had it—as thoroughgoing asses (*meri legisti sunt puri asini*).

Although he does not abandon his special point of view, as he tells us in the preface of his *Lexicon*, he writes on themes connected with the jurists; but with jurists whom he attacks as having fallen away from their archetype. He calls them a contemptible crowd of men who, pretending to possess profound knowledge, advise others on questions of law, control the administration of justice, and even occupy positions of command. . . . He gives witness against them and deals with questions related to the law, he says, but in order to avoid envious attacks he will not do so as an expert jurist but as a grammarian. And furthermore, he will not exhaust the material; he will raise only "those points which the interpreters of the laws, being ignorant of them, give the appearance of knowing, recognize that they have no idea of them, or confuse in a lamentable manner."

As an effort to bring to juridical science the historical sense it lacked, and within the renewing and humanistic current which was soon to flower, thanks to the work of a number of Spaniards, the mention of Nebrija rounds out the group of jurists of Ferdinand and Isabella's time.

V

"They advise others on questions of law, control the administration of justice, and even occupy positions of command." So Nebrija tells us. To issue judgments and hand down decisions are their typical and peculiar functions; but this third function of occupying positions in the government is a novelty worthy of emphasis.

In one of the manuscripts preserved in the university library in Salamanca is the inaugural address delivered by Palacios Rubios when he returned to teaching as the holder of the *Prima* chair in canon law. The text, brought to light by Professor Bullón, discusses this third function.[23] The usefulness of juridical studies, says Palacios Rubios, who had recently left the Chancery and the Council, is extraordinary; for besides perfecting the intelligence, they lead to honors and high position; "and I myself," he says, "can give testimony of this [*de quibus ergo rectus fidusque testis existo*], for at the time when I formerly taught law at this university I was spontaneously called by Their Majesties to their Council and named judge in the Royal Chancery. . . ."

And Palacios' was not the only such example. We know of the case of Dr. Oropesa, who must have been well settled in Salamanca, for when Don Diego Ramírez de Villaescusa went there as visitor he lodged in Oropesa's house. We also know of a fellow professor of Palacios', the bachelor Francisco Malpartida, with whom he was associated in the *Colegio Viejo*, who became a councillor to the Crown and, together with Dr. Oropesa, governor of the kingdom in 1500, when the king and queen had to go to the war of the Alpujarras.[24]

The great skill of the Catholic Monarchs lies in this, that they attracted the jurist, the self-made man, the exemplary type of person who had recently risen in the world. And I believe, though I do not underestimate Isabella's part in the preferment of these men, that Ferdinand must also have had a hand it it; for not only were the jurists to whom he gave most preferment all Aragonese, but also because the regions of the Spanish Levant had begun very early to raise men of law to preeminence (aside from the point that it was the nobles who were closer to the queen during the whole bitter struggle carried on by the monarchy). And the jurist had attained prominence precisely in opposition to the nobility.

Dámaso Alonso is perfectly right when he is astonished to find no support for Joanot Martorell's *Tirant lo Blanch* as one of the highest creations both in the sphere of the novel and in universal literature. Fame has not deigned to follow Cervantes' suggestion when he called for the reprinting of this book, saying that it ought to go to the galleys—not to row, but to pass through the typesetter's hands. If the *Tirant* were as well known as it deserves to be, this typification of the jurist as opposed to the nobleman would be almost topical. For Tirant, in Chapter XLI, praises that duke who had two scaffolds made and ordered three jurists hanged head down on each, the better to do them honor. And he even claims that this was a virtuous act.

And if any doubt remained that Joanot Martorell reflects a current attitude here, Martín de Riquer has published, in the correspondence of this highly praised but forgotten author, an exchange of letters between Martorell and Monpalau in regard to the wedding of the former's sister.[25] Martorell accuses him of delay in arranging for the duel he is demanding, and says that such behavior is typical of women and jurists, "los quals en la ploma y en la llengua tenen lur defensió" (who find their defense in the tongue and the pen). "I do not want words," he says, "for they are feminine, but deeds, which are masculine." Nothing could be more expressive and revealing as a link between the author and his work. But, to add one more touch, we shall cite a text from Tomás Mieres which reveals the bourgeois origin of the Catalan jurists and demonstrates the opposition of the nobles, influenced by hatred—I translate literally—for men of the law (*infecti odio contra iurisperitos*).

It is not the moment, nor do we have the time, to go into the reasons for this. The fact suffices, and we find the fact in the *Levante*. Ferdinand takes it from the *Levante*, for he has seen that the noble class is his enemy. Thus, under the Catholic Monarchs one of the advantages arising from study of the law was the new circumstance that it led to high position.

Hurtado de Mendoza confirms this for us: the Catholic Monarchs placed the administration of justice and public affairs in the hands of learned men, people who occupied a middle ground between the great and the humble, without offending either of these two groups; their profession consisted in legal letters, discretion, secrecy, truth, plain living, and uncorrupted habits.

As for the results of this utilization of the man of law, Alonso Ortiz, in the first of his *Cinco tratados*, specified the following advantages: integrity in keeping the laws, execution of justice without regard to persons, and prompt dispatch of law suits. . . .

VI

We might ask what would have happened if this renewal of the selective system of appointments had not resulted in an excessive number of students of the law, and if the jurists had passed their time in lecture halls and libraries instead of engaging in public affairs. But the answer is given already by what happened in the *Levante*, where the fifteenth century had witnessed the entry of the man of law into the government, just as Castile began this practice under the Catholic Monarchs without detriment to the cultivation of the science, and perhaps because the proximity of Toulouse and Bologna meant that the *Levante* did not have to maintain a center such as Salamanca, for Lérida was never able to compete with that university.

The countries of the Crown of Aragon had succeeded in creating what began in Castile only after the Laws of Toro: a juridical school. It was not merely the tradition of a couple of bishops such as Bustamante and Balboa; it was a solid and vigorous movement whose visible sign was an abundant and excellent bibliography.

Using the technique of the gloss, and under the double influence of Bologna and Toulouse, Mieres, Marquilles, Vallseca, Callís, and Peguera, in Catalonia, and Pedro de Villarrasa and Bonifacio

Ferrer, in Valencia, worked on a common basis and formed the foundation for a general theory. Obscure points were revised; classical and modern knowledge was collected and corrected by experience. Marquilles, though he can be compared to Montalvo, worked more than fifty years before him; his commentary on the *Usatges* is dated 1448. Perhaps the fact that a work like the *Partidas* was received in the *Levante* as a doctrinal text, and therefore had greater flexibility, especially because of the admission of equity as *bona rahó*,[26] stimulated and encouraged the kind of theorizing which resolved problems and upheld decisions. The use of *sententia et responsa*, as is emphasized in my study *Sobre las glosas al Código de Valencia*, is very eloquent. Since the compilations of their legal texts were earlier in date than those of Castile, the legal process was improved, and textbook resources gave good evidence of the fact.[27]

It is still more strange that a country which had possessed, ever since the middle of the medieval period, the most marvelous book of law known to the history of the West, those *Partidas* which I think we are justified in describing as an encyclopedia of law and letters, did not produce a precocious juridical science. It was not until the reign of the Catholic Monarchs that this goal was achieved, and even then in a very irregular form.

One interesting problem which arises out of the consideration of the possible autonomy of the Castilian juridical school resides in the language which the fifteenth century raised to the category of a vernacular. Since Spain had had a work in Romance ever since Alfonso X, why did not a juridical literature emerge in the country's own language? Why such insistence on Latin? There was some such feeling in the *Levante* also, and there it was no doubt due to contacts with France and Italy; but while the books of *Usatges* and the Code of Valencia were translated from Latin into the vernacular tongue, in Castile Montalvo translated into Latin (*de ydeomate in Latinum translate*) the *Ordenanzas* he had compiled, which he then offered as a summary, printed in Seville in 1496.

However, there are some indications of a certain possible movement in favor of the use of Romance in juridical literature.

During Villaescusa's visit to Salamanca in 1512 the *maestrescuela* announced that "all must speak Latin *intra scolas*, lectors as well as auditors, on pain of excommunication." Some, Father Olmedo tells us,[28] refused to enter because of the Latin requirement, and the visitor complained of this; but Latin won the day and went into the university statutes. Section II of the Statutes of 1538 indicates the possibility of a tendency toward the vernacular: Item, we decree and ordain that the lectors be obliged to read in Latin, and that they shall not speak from the chair in Romance "except when referring to some law of the realm or giving an example." And this must have been imposed very much against their will, for in 1561 the order is repeated and a punishment is added: "For each lesson they shall be fined three *reales*."

There is another aspect in which it is important to look for autonomy: the doctrinal one. In general, the attention of the jurists was centered on Toulouse and Bologna. Many Spaniards, among whom we should single out Don Gil de Albornoz, had flocked to Toulouse, especially at a certain period; but large groups had been going to Bologna since earliest times—and still more went after Albornoz created his Spanish College there. I believe that it was Bologna, during the reign of the Catholic Monarchs, which served as a model. I have spoken of this when I mentioned curricula; but here it is important to emphasize the fact in the administrative aspect.

A friend of Palacios Rubios, praising—in verse, as was the custom —the excellencies of his treatise on donations, wrote: "Italicis nullius cedat . . ." [He would in no way take second place to the Italians . . .].

And in fact this must have been the highest possible compliment.

I believe, therefore, that in Bologna—and in Italy in general and in Spanish expansion into two continents—lies the key to the absence of a juridical school such as would be assumed to have been formed after Ferdinand and Isabella's initial effort.

Bologna had been the center of diffusion, but it often launched its graduates into paths which led them out of their own countries. There were many Spaniards who returned, like Rodrigo Infante, a student at San Clemente in the last year of the fifteenth century, or the notable Fortún García, also one of Albornoz' pupils, a student in 1510 who became an illustrious figure during the reign of Emperor Charles; but others stayed in Italy, like Antonio de Burgos, a student in 1484, who taught in Padua and Bologna and occupied the post of *referendarius* to the Roman pontiffs, or like Luis Gómez of Orihuela, a professor at Padua, called "the subtle" and also connected with the Holy See, and a figure of even greater fame as chief collaborator on a certain volume entitled *Elenchus*, in which an editor of Frankfurt caused to be collected the juridical knowledge of the period. Nor will we mention others who went as far away as Poland or Lithuania. The interesting thing to note is that the great seminary formed by Cardinal Albornoz' Spanish College, in the center where juridical science was cultivated, became a novitiate to prepare those men employed by the Crown of Spain to govern, with the law in their hands, advising viceroys and captains, the great domains which God had granted it.

I have already suggested in general terms, in my *España y el problema de Europa*, that when Spain stretched herself so thin she neglected to organize herself; therefore theologians and poets predominated, and jurists were lacking.[29] We were like the pelican that pulls out its feathers for its young; we paid more attention to what was entrusted to our care than we did to ourselves. And thus the instrumental aspect, so much valued by Ferdinand the Catholic, was soon abandoned in a teleological interpretation of politics.

All this goes far to explain the writings of Pedro Simón Abril on the reform of doctrines—civil law among them—as well as the observations of Juan Luis Vives and Miguel Tomás' statement concerning the ignorance of dialectics and the abandonment of the use of reason. It was already late when in 1553 Philip II put jurists and doctors on the same level as the nobles; Callís had theorized on the same point a hundred years before. By then the decision merely served to emphasize the many difficulties undergone by jurists in the effort to qualify themselves, and the lack of persons willing to engage in this profession.

Were the dreams of recompense announced by Palacios Rubios

from his classroom in Salamanca no longer sufficient? Or was it that all of Spain had rushed into action, that now there were only soldiers who fought and friars who prayed, and that men who wished to think no longer found a single ivory tower in our country?

This question must remain unanswered, for a reply to it would require the study of that moment when a generation of men of law arose, to the glory of Spain, who united experience with reason.

NOTES

[1. "Scientia humana principalius inmittitur rationi."]

2. Beneyto, *Los orígenes de la ciencia política en España* (Madrid, 1947), pp. 14–19.

[3. Juan López de Palacios Rubios, 1450–1524; professor of canon law at Salamanca; one of the more important of the *letrados* of the Catholic Kings; a member of the councils of the Mesta and of the Indies, partly responsible for the Laws of Toro.]

[4. "Quoniam ut philosophus inquit; natura potentem ars facilem, usus promptum reddit artificem ..." The *Prima* professor had to lecture in the morning for 90 minutes. His chair was proprietory and inalienable.]

[5. "Enim et experientiam omnis acquiritur notitia et omne artificium per exercitium recepit incrementum; et enim experientia efficax rerum magistra."]

[6. In 1433 and again in 1438 the Castilian Cortes had asked for a codification of the laws. The collection known as the *Ordenanzas Reales*, compiled between 1480 and 1484, was the first attempt since the time of Alfonso the Wise to answer this long-felt need. Its author was Dr. Alonso Díaz de Montalvo, a well-known and experienced jurist, specially commissioned for the job. The popularity of his work may be judged by the nine editions listed by Haebler between the first (Huete, 1484) and 1500 (cf. C. Haebler, *Bibliografía Ibérica del siglo XV* (The Hague/Leipzig, 1904), nos. 214–23). The sections are referred to by *libro*, *título*, and *ley*, in a similar way to that used for references to the *Corpus Juris Civilis* or the *Corpus Juris Canonici*. (Cf. also R. de Urena, "Los incunables jurídicos en España," BAH, 95 (1929) 1–36.)]

7. Huarte and González de la Calle, *Constituciones de la Universidad de Salamanca* (Madrid, 1927).

[8. The *Corpus Juris Civilis* of Emperor Justinian (483–565) was made up of the *Institutes*, the *Digest*, the *Code*, the *Novels*, and the *Authenticum*; the *Digest* itself comprised three parts: the *Old Digest*, the *Infortiatum*, and the *New Digest*. The *Code* consisted of twelve books of imperial constitutions, though in the medieval period only the first nine were usually included under this name. The last three books were known as the *Volumen*, or *Volumen Parvum*. The *Decretum* was a great collection of canon law, made by Gratian and published probably in 1248. The *Decretales* were another canonical collection drawn up for Pope Gregory IX in five books. The *Liber Sextus*, or Sext, was added by Boniface VIII in 1298. The *Clementinae*, or Clementines, were the work of Clement V and included the decrees of the Council of Vienne (1311).]

[9. The *Siete Partidas* of Alfonso X made up a great law code compiled between 1256 and 1265, but not promulgated until the reign of Alfonso XI (1348). The *Fuero Real* was a royal code promulgated by Alfonso X early in his reign to supplement the existing customary laws known as the *fueros*. The *Liber iudiciorum*: reference untraced.]

10. Fermín Caballero, *Elogio del doctor Alonso de Montalvo* (Madrid, 1950).

[11. With the exception of Durandus, who was French, all these authors were Italian jurists. Francis Accursius, 1182–1260, was the author of a commentary on the *Code*, the *Institutes*, and the *Digest* of Justinian, known as the Great Gloss. Bartolus, 1314–1357, was the author of a commentary on the *Corpus Juris Civilis* and numerous other treatises. Petrus Baldus, 1327–1406, wrote on the *Code* and other commentaries. Odofredus was a student of Accursius, professor at Bologna (1228), and a commentator on the *Corpus Juris Civilis*. Lapus (or Lapo) da Castiglionchio il vecchio was a canonist who lived chiefly in the fourteenth century and was a friend of Petrarch; among his works were a commentary on the *Clementinae* and another on the fifth book of the *Decretales*; he died June 27, 1381. Johannes de Imola was professor of canon law at Bologna and at Padua (1408); he died in 1436. Guillelmus Durandus, *ca.* 1230–1296, French canonist and bishop of Mende (1286–1296), wrote *Speculum Judiciale* and *Repertorium Juris Canonici*. Johannes Andreae, 1275–1348, was a famous Bolognese canonist.]

[12. Bartholomeus Salicetus (de Saliceto), professor at Bologna, 1363–1370, was the author of a commentary on the *Code* (1389); he died in 1412. Johannes de Platea: reference untraced. The "Archdeacon" was Guido de Baysio (Bajiso, Bassio), a disciple of the Bolognese civilian Guido; he wrote commentaries on the *Decrees* and the *Decretales*. Hostiensis was Henricus de Susa, cardinal bishop of Ostia, a Parisian canonist who died 1271.]

[13. Jacobus Buttrigarius, 1274–1348, was a Bolognese doctor of law who taught Bartolus.]

[14. Sánchez Cantón, *Libros, tapices y cuadros que coleccionó Isabel la Católica* (Madrid, 1950).]

[15. "Dezir que fizo Juan de Mena sobre la justicia e pleytos de la grant vanidad del mundo," ed. E. Foulché-Delbosc in *Cancionero Castellano* del siglo, xv, i, BAE (Madrid, 1912), 200. Cinus was a poet and professor of canon law at Perugia who introduced the doctrines of the French civilians into Italy. Enrique: the canonist Henricus Bohic.]

[16. Niccolo de' Tedeschi (1389–1466), Sicilian canonist, professor at Parma and Bologna; sometime abbot of Santa María di Maniace, and arch-

bishop of Palermo, hence he is often referred to as "Abbas" or as "Panormitanus"; he wrote on the *Decretales*, the *Sext*, and the *Clementinae*.]
[17. Federico de Castro, *Derecho Civil de España* (Madrid, 1940).]
[18. 1489(?)–August 28, 1506.]
[19. "Per maioritate[m] a repertorio aureo et multum utili partitatum per alphabetum [*L*]*a Peregrina* vulgariter nuncupato ut in glossis fori legum servabi."]
[20. For the "Abbot," see n. [16.] above.]
[21. "Before I act, therefore, O Good Jesus, inspire my action and by thy help ensure that my every activity always begins with thee and, once begun, by thee is brought to a conclusion."]
[22. "Cum iure canonico per maiore[m] parte[m] simpliciter concordare."]
23. Bullón, *El doctor Palacios Rubios*, App. ii.
24. P. G. Olmedo, *Diego Ramírez de Villaescusa* (Madrid, 1944), pp. 93, 48.
[25. Reference untraced. The *Levante*=Catalonia and Valencia.]
[26. Catalan term, i.e. *buena razón*.]
27. Beneyto, AHDE, 13 (1936–41).
28. Olmedo, *op. cit.*, p. 102.
29. *España y el problema*, Austral ed., p. 193.

10 Fernando del Pulgar and the *Conversos*

FRANCISCO CANTERA BURGOS

This article has been chosen to represent the problem of the *conversos*. The fifteenth century in Spain saw the expulsion of the Jews, first from Castile and then from Aragon (for the economic effects of the expulsion see the comments of Professor Vicens Vives above, p. 57). Faced with the terrible dilemma of expulsion or conversion some chose conversion. The converts, or *conversos*, included zealots who sought to outshine their old Christian brethren in enthusiasm for Christianity and many others who were more or less reluctant over the change. One of the outstanding chroniclers of the reign of the Catholic Kings, and their secretary, was Fernando del Pulgar. In a piece of very detailed and concentrated argument from the texts of letters and from the *Crónica*, Sr. Cantera, following and correcting others, shows how and why Pulgar must be added to the long list of distinguished Spaniards who were *conversos*. The story takes us back to the earliest days of the Spanish Inquisition. (The great majority of the original notes to readings in different manuscripts have here been omitted.)

WE have previously mentioned the interesting edition of the *Crónica de los Reyes Católicos*, written by those monarchs' chronicler and secretary Fernando del Pulgar, which has been published by the learned professor of the University of Seville, Dr. Carriazo.[1] One of the most important new aspects of this publication is undoubtedly the information and contributions it brings to bear on Pulgar's Jewish origin, and the remarkable unpublished letter which Carriazo has discovered, referring to the Inquisition directed against the *conversos* of Seville during Pulgar's lifetime.

The subject seems to us of sufficient importance to be treated very fully here, carefully reviewing the information we possess, especially in the light of Pulgar's own writings. Thus we shall not only ascertain more precisely the problem of the chronicler's ancestry, but will also give examples of his notable historical passages on the subject of the *conversos*.

PULGAR'S JEWISH ORIGIN AND HIS LETTER CONCERNING THE STATUTE OF GUIPÚZCOA ON PURITY OF BLOOD

According to Carriazo, the most concrete information concerning Pulgar's Jewish descent is to be found in Clemencín's *Elogio de la Reina Católica Doña Isabel* (Madrid, 1820), when he writes (p. 486):

> In the palace the secretaries Fernando Álvarez, Alfonso de Ávila, and Fernando del Pulgar served in close proximity to the queen and enjoyed her favor and confidence; all three were New Christians.

Professor Carriazo notes (*ibid.*, pp. xxi–xxii) that Clemencín, "always well informed," . . . "does not declare his sources here," and that there is "a slight doubt as to whether . . . he made use of trustworthy evidence from the fifteenth century itself, or whether he simply constructed a hypothesis." "Only this doubt," he adds, "seems to me to explain the fact that Pulgar's modern biographers maintain an embarrassing silence on this point, with the exception of Walsh, who has exploited it on a large scale."[2]

Carriazo further adds (*ibid.*, p. xv) that the manuscript letters he publishes, and the references he has gathered from other works of Pulgar's, "give considerable credence to Clemencín's statement, unfortunately not documented, that Pulgar was a New Christian; that is, a *converso* or the son of *conversos*, of Jewish descent."

Faced with these vacillations and assertions, we believe that we can point out with certainty just what "trustworthy evidence" of the fifteenth century was used by Clemencín, and can state that the source used by the eminent commentator of the *Quijote* was obviously the letter written by Pulgar himself "to the cardinal of Spain," concerning the Statute of Purity of Guipúzcoa, a letter which has not been sufficiently taken into account either by Pulgar's biographers or by Carriazo himself.

We do not believe that Clemencín can have read it very carefully, to judge from the rather vague terms in which he wrote about it; and if Pulgar had had careful biographers and editors of his writings who paid attention to an adequate commentary on them and not merely to their purely mechanical publication, it would long ago have come to their attention—as it seems to have done in small measure to Clemencín and recently more fully to Carriazo—that the chronicler uses many expressions which point to Jewish ancestry. This occurs particularly in the letter we have just mentioned concerning Guipúzcoa, a letter not properly utilized up until now. In it Pulgar could not have proclaimed more flatly his Jewish descent, that descent which Carriazo seems to think (pp. xx–xxi) muzzled and muted the writer in the personal confidences which might have been expected in his writings in view of his expansive and open character.

He begins the letter to Cardinal Don Pedro González de Mendoza by referring, with delicate humor and sharp irony, to the statute just established in Guipúzcoa regarding New Christians. With this statute Guipúzcoa had taken a roundly defensive attitude, responding to the surge of suspicion toward converted Jews which had arisen everywhere in Spain at that time. Their extremely large numbers constituted a real danger, especially after the catechizing activities of St. Vincent,[3] the persecutions of 1391, and the Dispute of Tortosa;[4] and so did their sometimes proven insincerity and bad faith; their large fortunes and influence, giving rise to envy; their determined assault on the highest government positions (tax-farming contracts on the royal revenues, etc.), which, just as they had formerly made Jews the object of hatred, now turned that hatred against the *conversos*; their infiltration into the highest social ranks of Spanish society, and into families of the most ancient Christian ancestry: all this made them particularly distrusted and hated.

Pulgar writes as follows:[5]

Most illustrious and most reverend lord: Your lordship surely knows of that new statute passed in Guipúzcoa, in which it was decreed that *we* should not go there to marry or to dwell, etc.; as if we had no other desire than to go and inhabit that fertile domain and that blooming countryside. It seems a little like the ordinance the stonecutters of Toledo made, not to teach their trade to any Jewish proselyte.

He is making fun, then, of the poverty of the soil and fields of Guipúzcoa, which he compares by antiphrasis and irony to fertile domains and blooming countryside; then he alludes, no doubt sarcastically, to the social opposition to the *conversos* which had been nourished in Toledo ever since the bloody riots of 1449.[6] It appears, therefore, that Clemencín was not strictly accurate in stating (*loc. cit.*), undoubtedly in reference to this letter, that "*at the same time*" that Isabella the Catholic was employing three New Christians as secretaries "a statute was being passed in Guipúzcoa providing that those who came from Jewish families could not marry or dwell in that province, and the stonecutters' guild in Toledo passed another not to admit them as apprentices."

Pulgar continues his barbed commentary at the expense of the Guipúzcoan region and people:

I swear to God, my lord, when I think upon it I never saw anything more laughable for one who knows the quality of the land and the condition of the people. Is it not laughable when all or most of them send their sons here to serve us, and many of them for stirrup-boys, that they do not want to be united by marriage[7] with those whose servitors they desire to be?

This argument of Pulgar's loses much of its force if we recall that Guipúzcoa, like all of Spain, would have been able to reply that it was perfectly clear that the *conversos* would not care to seek matrimonial connections among the families who had provided the Jews of former times with their stirrup-boys, but among more powerful and ancient families than these; and that this fact and that servitude were precisely one of the major causes for the separation between the races. However, the writer continues his arguments, and even puts forward some personal experiences of his own:

> I do not know for certain, my lord, how this can be reconciled; to spurn us as relatives and choose us as masters; still less do I understand how it can be suffered on the one hand to prohibit our dealing with them, and on the other to swell the houses of the merchants and scribes here in Castile with the sons of Guipúzcoa, nor that the fathers make ordinances injurious to those who instruct their sons and give them employment and wages, and who did the same to them when they were young. For I, my lord, saw more of them in the house of the Relator learning to write than in the house of the Marquis Iñigo López learning to joust. I also assure your lordship that there are more Guipúzcoans in the houses of Fernando Álvarez and Alfonso de Ávila, secretaries, than in your house or the constable's, though both of you are from their land.

We feel that these brush strokes with which Pulgar illustrates the social life of his period are of great interest: we see youths from the north filling the houses of the *converso* merchants and scribes, of whom there were doubtless many in both these lucrative occupations, and who offered to the Guipúzcoans "employment and wages." The author seems to take pleasure in pointing out the humbleness and ignorance of the inhabitants of Guipúzcoa, who are obliged to come to Castile in order to be instructed and to learn a trade, and whose country does not produce the sort of gentry who learned skills in jousting and carrying arms in noble houses, such as that of the constable of Castile, but in modest employment, etc.

In fact, such language is surprising in a letter addressed to a person who was a native, according to Pulgar himself, of the region he so severely censures, and whose social condition he thus describes; but this was one of the chronicler's *idées fixes*, for in other places in his works he takes pains to show us the low opinion he has of the inhabitants of the noble and industrious regions of

Guipúzcoa and Vizcaya: "turbulent folk and in need of firm treatment" (*Claros Varones*, p. 30, Clásicos Castellanos ed.), "folk to be mistrusted," and quick to anger (*Crónica*, I, 436).

As for the "Relator" mentioned above, he must be Fernán Díaz de Toledo, also of a *converso* family, who had been much honored by John II and who had intervened in favor of the Hebrew nation in 1449. And Pulgar has left a magnificent portrait of the marquis of Santillana, Iñigo López de Mendoza, who died in 1458, in his delightful book *Claros Varones*;[8] it is known that he was the descendant of a noble house in Álava. We also recognize the names of the secretaries of the Catholic Monarchs, Álvarez and Ávila, Pulgar's friends; all three are mentioned by Clemencín. And the constable is Don Pedro Fernández de Velasco, son of the "good count of Haro" described by the chronicler.[9]

He rounds off these remarks by giving us an interesting piece of biographical data, utilized by Carriazo (pp. xlvii–xlviii):

> By my faith, my lord, I am bringing up four of them in my house now, the while their fathers pass this ordinance to which you are a witness; and in that land are more than forty honorable and married men that I brought up and instructed, but indeed not to make those ordinances. *Omnium rerum vicis[s]itudo est.*

The end of the letter gives us a further allusion to the Jews and, as so often in his writings, bubbles with Pulgar's robust and sarcastic humor when he adds, making a rather irreverent play on the words of Scripture and referring somewhat inaccurately to Moses and his laws:

> Now these are paying [referring to the ban on marriage to persons of Old Christian extraction] for the prohibition made by Moses, that his people should not marry with Gentiles; but we cannot say of him "Moses began both to do and teach," as we say[10] of Christ our Redeemer; for the two times that he married, he took women for himself that he had proscribed for others.

And he ends with these words:

> Returning once again, my lord, to speak of this matter, it is certain, my lord, that these men have done a great offense to God when they ordered in His church what was contrary to His law, and greater offense did they do to the queen when they ordered it in her land without her license.

By this Pulgar undoubtedly wished to emphasize that the Guipúzcoan statute was in open opposition to pontifical decisions such as those of Pope Nicholas V,[11] who in 1449 had decided in favor of the *conversos* the dispute maintained against them by the Toledans in an attempt to eliminate them from public office; and he is also attempting, very cleverly, to incite Isabella of Castile, always jealous of her royal prerogatives, to take some action against the statute as a major law passed without her permission. Clemencín assures us (*loc. cit.*) that Pulgar indicates in this letter that these statutes "were displeasing to the Queen Doña Isabel." We do not know whether they were or not; but it is certain that Pulgar is attempting in his letter to influence the queen against them.[12]

Clemencín believes (*ibid.*, p. 487) that the letter was written "about the year 1482," adding that Pulgar "stated his opinions about the matter[13] in several passages of his *Claros Varones* and in his printed letters,[14] as well as in another letter to Don Diego Hurtado de Mendoza, archbishop of Seville,[15] concerning the manner in which the *conversos* of that city were treated, which has not been made public."

This letter is the one published by Dr. Carriazo, who believes (p. lii) that Clemencín must not have known it directly, for in that case he would have used it; he must, adds Carriazo, have known of it only through the Catalogue of the Manuscript Section of our National Library, in Volume II of Gallardo's *Ensayo*, where it is included.[16] But we cannot be sure of all this.

Pulgar's biographers not only were unaware of this letter and the impugnation to which it gave rise, but, out of pure mental indolence, they passed over the passages we have mentioned in the

Claros Varones and *Letras*, as well as the different parts of the *Crónica* which Clemencín did not take notice of, although Carriazo does. On noting the words of the learned Jesuit on those who "regretted that such delinquents (i.e., heretics) should not be given the death penalty," among whom "was seemingly Fernando del Pulgar, a man of sharp and graceful mind," Carriazo writes, "Thus wrote Mariana appositely of the letter which Pulgar sent to the cardinal ... although it has not survived until our time." "Well could Llorente feel this way," adds Carriazo (p. li), "since the letter which he took for lost would have provided a valuable argument for the position which he took up in the discussion."

The said professor offers it to us not without a certain emphasis: "Nothing less," he says, "than an unedited letter of Pulgar—the most important document for the history of ideas in the last decades of the fifteenth century, as for the biography of our chronicler." It obviously merits our study and commentary, which we will undertake by reproducing the text of Manuscript 1517 of the Biblioteca Nacional, folio 1º, on the understanding that the said edition contains certain errors of a particular kind, and without taking account of the very numerous variations in spelling, punctuation, etc.

In this copy, of the second half of the sixteenth century in the opinion of Carriazo (p. liii), the letter has the following title: "A letter which Hernando del Pulgar wrote to the most reverend sir, Don Diego Hurtado de Mendoça, archbishop of Seville,[15] patriarch of Alexandria, cardinal of Sancta Savina, concerning what is being done to the *conversos* of Andalusia."

Such a title seems to Carriazo (*ibid.*) " artificial, false, and late," insofar as chronology indicates that the addressee of the letter was not Don Diego Hurtado but his uncle Don Pedro González de Mendoza, the grand cardinal of Spain. Pulgar speaks of this letter "in his *Letra* XXI, printed in 1486, and certainly written at least some five years before," and "he could not give those titles to the second cardinal of Spain, who was only archbishop of Seville in 1486, patriarch of Alexandria in 1495 at the earliest, cardinal of Santa Sabina in 1500, two years before his death."[16] But more than these arguments from the titles which could have been accumulated at the time is the internal examination of the letter, which must convince us that it was directed to the archbishop of Seville, Don Pedro, and not to his nephew.

The letter begins with a brief introduction:

> Most illustrious and reverend Sir
>
> I received the letter of your lordship, and your secretary wrote to me, and some others have told me that your lordship awaits an account of what I should describe about what is going on in Andalusia.

What were these things? It would be interesting to know what is referred to in order to penetrate to the meaning of the letter. Let us examine the question a little from its beginning.

The whole fifteenth century is full of stifled warfare, at times revealing itself in loud explosions between Christian society and those converted from Judaism. The *conversos* were watched with envious eyes and grim hostility for the reasons pointed out above, and their strength acquired a certain reinforcement in the time of María de Aragon and John II of Castile, on whom Pablo de Santa María and his *converso* family exercised such a powerful influence.[17]

The figure of the great and enigmatic statesman, Don Álvaro de Luna has not yet been studied as it deserves to be, nor his policy toward the Jews, apart from that of the aforesaid family, nor the influence which could have been exercised at the time of his disgrace by the indifference with which he had witnessed the bloody calamity of the *conversos* of Toledo in 1449. Let us say in passing that, in our opinion, there is not sufficient proof that, once Don Álvaro was dead—the one defender of the Jews at the time, as is often said—their public position grew any worse; rather than reverse. What is clear is that the ferocious outbreak at Toledo was the first serious sign of that social repulsion, and that the ruling given by Pedro Sarmiento and the commune of that city against the *conversos*, removing them from public office, represents the echo of Spanish public opinion. We can hear that opinion also in the determination shown from 1452 by Espinosa de los Monteros to eject the New Christians and seize their goods; in the statute of Guipúzcoa, criticized so wittily by Pulgar, in the revulsion of Catalonia from the mixture of races, etc., etc.

The danger which Spain thought it saw in the false New Christians was denounced again and again, and the outcry which Fray Alonso de Espina raised through his *Fortalitium Fidei* in the time of Henry IV, was repeated many times until the time of Fray Alonso de Hojeda under the Catholic Kings.

In addition to this we have the riots of Toledo of 1467, the year in which the *conversos* are the cause of bloody and cruel scenes; and, between 1472 and 1474, the scandals of Valladolid, the war-fare between the New and Old Christians of Córdoba, the sacrilegious assassination of the Constable Iranzo[18] together with the robbery and murders of *conversos* which followed it, the occurrences at Andújar and other Andalusian places, and the disturbances at Segovia. Thus we come to the year 1478, in which the embers of Toledo, never quenched, revived with the intention of getting up a conspiracy against the Catholic Kings, and during which the situation was much aggravated by the discovery of a ring of false *conversos* who indulged in blasphemy and mockery of the Christian religion. In different parts of the kingdom and particularly at Seville, where it seems that the affair reached its most acute state, different individuals, both ecclesiastical and lay, raised up their voices against those sovereigns, seeking from them swift measures for defense and reprisal.

The cardinal of Spain and archbishop of Seville promulgated an apostolic constitution of instruction in Christian doctrine, at the same time as Don Ferdinand and Doña Isabella and the same prelate commissioned various secular clergy and religious to undertake apostolic preaching with the dual aim of demonstrating Catholic truth to all and giving warning that strange rites should be abandoned. But neither the gentle admonitions employed at the beginning nor the subsequent threats achieved anything, and the Kings had to inform the pope of the gravity of the affair. A bull of Sixtus IV[19] in 1478 enabled the Monarchs to set up inquisitors of the Faith in their kingdoms and to punish the heretics whom they discovered.

Nevertheless things did not move rapidly. In 1480 the Cortes legislated for the setting aside of the Jews in order especially to avoid the contamination of the *conversos*, and on September 27 in that year the Kings nominated at Medina del Campo the two first inquisitors, Fray Miguel Morillo and Fray Juan de San Martín, who began work at Seville in January, 1481.

Carriazo (p. xxxviii) thinks that Pulgar had to "utter in some form his protest against particular aspects of the way of interpreting and applying the bull of Inquisition, announcing his intention of writing about this affair," and then the cardinal would seek his view. It is possible, but from the words which Pulgar puts at the head of his letter, which we have transcribed above, one does not come to that conclusion; it was natural that, given his condition of being a *converso* and his relationship with the prelate of Seville, the latter should await with curiosity the reaction which the new occurrences sketched out above were having on his learned friend.

Let us now enter upon what Pulgar wrote; it begins like this:

> Certainly, my lord, it is some long time since I had written down in my mind, and even on poor authority, the great extent of the blind stupidity and stupid blindness of those people, for I saw well that this must bring forth the fruit which all stupidity usually yields.

In these words he tells us how great were the things which preoccupied him and which he held engraved on his heart—that of a sincere *converso*—and even on bad authority, the stupidity and blindness of the Judaizers (*aquella gente*), for he foresaw the sad consequences which they must occasion. We encounter a clear echo of them in the first version of the *Crónica* of Pulgar, edited by Carriazo, when he tells us (p. 335) that the pertinacity of those who were Judaizers "was a blindness so stupid and an ignorance so blind . . .", terms which in the later version were modified as we shall see later.

The letter goes on:

> It also seems to me, my lord, that the queen our lady does what she ought to do as a most Christian queen is obliged to do, and her duty to God requires it no less.

Thus Pulgar prudently leaves without criticism the inevitable activity of Isabella of Castile in the instructions made with regard to the incipient heresy; it being noteworthy that he seems to attribute them in a special way to the Most Christian Queen and not to Don Ferdinand, contrary to what we read in the *Crónica*. The chronicler would in due course receive the admonition, as is well known, that he should attribute sovereign acts to both. . . .

But, with that proviso, Pulgar enters frankly into criticism of the activity of the inquisition at Seville and sets up his sensible theory of public repression, which he founds on St. Augustine and St. Paul:

> But in the "How shall this be?"[20] by her ministers lies the whole point. For, as your lordship knows, one form of treatment should be used for the few who have relapsed, and another for the many: for the few, punishment is good; but forasmuch as it is good in the few, so is it dangerous and even difficult for the many. For of such, St. Augustine says that the judge must deal with them like Our Lord with each of us; for He, though He knows we fall into sin "until seventy times seven,"[21] expecting our conversion has mercy on us. This is set down in an epistle that he wrote to the emperor Marcianus[22] on the relapse of the Donatists, exhorting him to forgive them and not to flag in his efforts to convert them; and he presents as an example how many times the Children of Israel fell into sin after they left Egypt, and how many times God showered His mercy on them. And even that *argue, insta, obsecra, increpa*, that St. Paul wrote to Timothy that he should do to the multitude, should be done, he says, *in omni patiencia et do[c]trina*, for otherwise there would not be faggots enough for the burning.

The sometimes difficult paleography of the copy led Dr.

Carriazo astray, for he transcribed the Pauline passage quoted
(II Tim. 4:2: "Argue, obsecra, increpa" (i.e., "Rebuke, warn,
advise") as follows: "E aun aquel arguillista (?) obispo lo increpa
que Sant Pablo ... leña bastante" (i.e., "And even that disputatious (?) bishop criticizes the fact that St. Paul ... tinder
enough.").[23] And those last words of Pulgar's are worth noting,
for they remind us, by contrast, of those other terrible words in
Bernáldez' *Historia*.[24] "For the fire is lighted ... it will burn until
the driest part of the wood is consumed." We believe that it was a
person of similar temperament and an equally rigid criterion who
later wrote the impugnation against Pulgar. Thus we do not
think that Father Llorca is entirely accurate when, in *Sefarad*, II
(1942) 115, he attempts to *confirm* Bernáldez' opinion on the
conversos by using the witness of our chronicler, which is diametrically opposed.

Pulgar begins the second part of his *letra* by offering his opinion
on the spiritual situation in Andalusia, and especially that of the
conversos:

> I believe, my lord, that there are some there who are bad
> [Christians], and others, the largest number, are so because they
> follow those bad ones, and would also follow good ones if there
> were any. But since the Old Christians there are such bad
> Christians, the New Christians are such good Jews. I believe
> without a doubt, my lord, that there must be ten thousand
> maids in Andalusia from eighteen to twenty years of age, who
> since they were born have never left their houses, nor heard or
> known of any other doctrine than that which they saw their
> parents do behind the doors of their houses. To burn all of these
> would be a most cruel thing and very difficult to do, for they
> would flee in desperation to places where no correction would
> ever be expected of them; which would be a great danger for
> the ministers, and a grave sin.
>
> I also know for certain that there are some who flee from the
> enmity of the judges more than from fear of their own conscien-
> ces.

These interesting statements, full of prudent good sense, seem accurate along general lines. We observe the barb Pulgar directs in passing at the Old Christians, which was probably in large part justified. The number of maidens of *converso* families that he gives is also very curious, those who "since they were born have never left their houses," knowing no more of doctrine than the example of their own homes. Curious also is the warning that the extreme penalty for so many guilty persons would be very cruel, hard to accomplish, and would lead to desperation on the part of many, who would flee without hope of repentance, which would involve grave sin and could mean "great danger" for the inquisitors. And curious, lastly, is the flight of the *conversos* more out of fear of their inquisitors' enmity than for their own crimes.

What solution was to be found, then, for this difficult situation, so real and so evident? Pulgar, who does not wish to defend the guilty, but to give a truly Christian solution to the problem, writes:

> I do not say this, my lord, in favor of the evil ones, but in correction of the repentant ones; and it would seem best to me, my lord, to place in that land notable persons, together with some of their own nation, who by the example of their lives and with words of doctrine would reconcile some and correct the others little by little, as has already been done in the kingdom and even outside it. All the rest, in my opinion, is to confirm them in their obstinacy and not to reform them, to the great peril of souls, those of the correctors as well as those of the corrected.

As we see, the chronicler is arguing, following a plan already used both in and out of Castile, for the utilization of outstanding persons, intensely Catholic in their life and doctrine, chosen even from among the converted Jews, so that with their example and teaching they might attract New Christians who were either backsliders or in danger of straying from the true path of the Catholic faith. Any other procedures might be counterproductive.

The *letra* concludes with these sarcastic words:

> Diego de Merlo and Dr. Medina are good men, certainly;

but I well know that they will not make such good Christians with their fire as the bishops Don Pablo and Don Alonso[25] made with water. And not without cause; for the latter were chosen by our Redeemer Christ for the task, and these others have been chosen by the licentiate our chancellor for theirs.

This is a clear thrust at these agents of the Sevillian Inquisition, and we shall see it mentioned again in the reply to which Pulgar's letter gave rise. He is not referring here to the Dominican inquisitors whom the monarchs had named in September, 1480, as we have seen, but only to the two he mentions by name: the assistant, Merlo (one of the three who drew up the first plan for the Inquisition), and Medina, a priest of San Pedro (one of the first three inquisitors appointed along with the Dominicans mentioned, as Bernáldez tells us). Pulgar is emphasizing here the contrast between them and the bishops of Burgos, themselves converted Jews, Pablo and Alfonso de Cartagena: the latter chosen by Jesus Christ, the former by "the licentiate our chancellor"; the Sevillians aspiring to make Christians by way of the inquisitorial fire, those of Burgos through baptism by water.

Such is the very interesting letter published by Dr. Carriazo, who discusses (pp. lv–vli) its authenticity with extremely convincing arguments, dwelling particularly on the circumstances that "this letter has its closest parallel within Pulgar's work in another document unknown up until now: Chapter cxx of his *Crónica*, which is found only in the manuscript version. . . ." In our opinion, it has a still more intimate connection with Chapter xcvi, which coincides with the *letra* sometimes even word for word, as is shown by Pulgar's words which we quoted above.

We do not know what answer the cardinal of Seville gave to his friend's letter. Undoubtedly he must have informed him of the efforts toward peaceful and apostolic persuasion already employed, either on his own initiative or in agreement with the monarchs. Pulgar was to allude to these later, in his *Crónica*, especially in its last version. It is also certain that Pulgar's letter must have made a deep impression on the prelate, and encouraged him to take suitable measures.

ANONYMOUS IMPUGNATION OF PULGAR'S LETTER

It is a pity that we do not know the cardinal's reply, if, as we suppose, it actually existed. What has been preserved, however, is the immoderate, insulting, and acrimonious response addressed to Pulgar by an anonymous writer. It survives in a poor copy written by an unknown copyist, in which it directly follows a copy of Pulgar's own letter, the two forming a unit under a common title. In this lack of differentiation between the two documents— which the copyist undoubtedly thought of as forming a logical whole—Carriazo thinks he sees (p. lvi) "a sure sign, in his ignorance, of ingenuousness and good faith."

Professor Carriazo says (p. xv) that no one before himself "had seen, much less studied" this impugnation; that we doubtless owe the preservation of Pulgar's letter to it (p. liii), and that "it is an extremely valuable text for our knowledge of the earliest controversy aroused by the Catholic Monarchs' new Inquisition, a controversy contemporaneous with its establishment, mentioned by Father Mariana and which until now we could judge only by the letter of our chronicler to his unnamed friend." Carriazo also tells us that he intends to reproduce this controversy and discuss it in detail, and we await this interesting study with curiosity; but since, in order to treat properly the theme upon which we have embarked, it is essential that we present in its entirety the document which Carriazo has published only in part, and since on the other hand his fragmentary edition is flawed by a certain number of errors and misunderstandings of the manuscript —perhaps because the learned professor considered it only one of several aspects of his study—he will forgive us, we are sure, if we reproduce the entire document here ... with all the fidelity permitted by its intricate paleography, which is full of abbreviations. We shall also deal with some of the "numerous questions" which, as Carriazo points out (p. lv), are posed by Pulgar's letter and its impugnation, those questions which are of most interest for our particular point of view.

The heading of the impugnation reads as follows:

> Difinsorium juxtum prorsus doctorum inquisitorum per quemdam venerabilem virum hujus Sancti Ofitii contra dictum Fordinandum [sic] del Pulgar curat ac rremedius fuerat quam in pugnare proçesum.[26]

This interesting heading, which Carriazo did not study with care,[27] was made in the light of the preceding letter by "*dictum* Pulgar," and shows us that the document was written as an attack on it, on the side and in the defense of the doctors of the Inquisition, by a "certain venerable and virtuous member of this Holy Office."

It begins as if it were being addressed to the queen, with some allegorical phrases which are so badly preserved in the copy and so unclear in themselves that at the head of them someone (the copyist?) has had to give us the key or explanation of these allegorical terms, without which we would find it totally impossible to understand this beginning. Carriazo did not reproduce them, limiting himself to the remark (p. liii) that they are "incoherent and not easily intelligible," owing to a defect either in the original or in the copy. They read as follows:

> Speech is addressed first to the queen, of whom it is written [Psalm 44:10] "On thy right hand stood the queen in golden raiment"[28]—who is the Church; the garment—the faith; the alchemy—vain poetry; Christ—the touchstone; the King is the letter; copper—lack of faith.
>
> So that your garment of fine gold be not false and of feigned alchemy, O illustrious queen, with the touchstone we shall see whether the proofs of this king be not of copper.

It appears that by this the author wishes us to understand, addressing himself to the Church (the queen), that so that the Faith (the garment) may not be falsified and vain poetry produced (feigned alchemy), he is going to test Pulgar's letter (the king) with the touchstone which is Christ, and perhaps it will be demonstrated that his proofs or declarations are of copper; that is, pure lack of faith, or declarations contrary to the true Faith. We believe that Pulgar's anonymous enemy is attempting nothing less than this, and he continues:

> For in order to give value to a thing which in itself is without value, you slavishly undertake the task of dressing it in colors and supporting itself on the authority of others; and likewise Seneca in his tragedies and comedies brings to mind irrelevant and insidious examples which, when placed on the scale, do not weigh one carat more than those which you adduce here.

By these statements Anonymous levels against Pulgar the accusation that, just as the tragedian Seneca hides behind other authorities who, if looked at carefully, are valueless and prove nothing, he too in his letter has covered up, under the embellishments of Church authorities, arguments which in themselves have no value.

He then continues—"still without much clarity," says Carriazo, in spite of the fact that he has simply passed over the chief difficulties in the manuscript:

> And since this cunning [of mine][29] does not shrink from this task, which is a defensive rather than a harmful statement, and since in your service, my lady, I wield my stylus for the purpose of castigating the tenor rather than the subtle arguments of this phrasemaker whose intent is to defend as best he can what he would not want to see punished; and, in order to give authority to his evil words, he sends his message to the Most Reverend Cardinal, hiding his bile, together with his offended heart, under the guise of a very small quantity of the honey of rash and vain boasting.

In our opinion, the author continues here to drive his sharp dagger into Pulgar, and, to protect himself in advance, states that his missive or embassy, rather than having been written with intent to wound, is a defense, and that when he wields his pen or *stylus* in the service of so lofty a lady, he does so more to attack

Pulgar's protection of the Judaizers than the subtle argumentation of this *phrasemaker*, whose intention is to defend, if he can, that which he would not wish to see punished: namely, heresy. He further accuses him of having wished to shield himself, rashly but vainly, behind the cardinal of Spain, by sending him his harmful letter in order to clothe it with authority. This is the interpretation we believe can be assigned to the last words of Anonymous, who, having finished off the heading of his defensive document, indicated his purposes, and driven the dart into his enemy as deeply as possible, now directs the rest of the missive to him, beginning with some vicious new attacks by way of introduction before going on to deal with the letter:

> I now turn my pen to you, O man of note among your people, like the thumb on a hand, even though you may say that I am like Moses, who, though he was not called to do so, reproached the Egyptian Jew who insulted his brother, and this must be because you do not know that the Divine Spirit commands every one of the faithful, and says: *Answer a fool according to his folly, lest he be wise in his own conceit*. For leaving the blessed Moses aside, who so closely resembles you, accept willingly the great name of Jesus and do not in any wise fear the deadly poison, for rather you will deliver your life and good name from the sorrow which so much discomforts you.

In this passage, obviously, there is an attempt to insult our chronicler by a scornful reference to his "people," among whom he is described as standing out, sarcastically playing with the meaning of his name, like the thumb on a hand. However, Anonymous must have had no obligation through either his office or his person to intervene in the matter; for he states that he does so only in obedience to Holy Writ (Proverbs 26:5) and even at the risk of being criticized for interfering in an area which is none of his concern. As for his allusion to the case of Moses, he shows us that he is not very strong on Sacred History, for the leader of the Children of Israel, as we read in Exodus 2:11–12, did rather more than upbraid the Egyptian (not an Egyptian Jew) who was smiting (not insulting) a Hebrew. . . . Note also how he ends these introductory sentences with a weight of intention even more poisonous than his words.

After these two short prologues by way of dedication, Anonymous goes into an analysis of Pulgar's letter, and after stating that it had circulated widely and alluding, undoubtedly, to ancient courts like those of the medieval Inquisition,[30] tells us that since, when Pulgar referred to the punishment ordered by the Catholic Monarchs, he attacked the cause, the manner, and the ministers of inquisitorial correction, he is going to refute these points in order. He says that he is going to do this by using what he has been able to deduce from Pulgar's "confused sayings." However, Pulgar was infinitely clearer and easier to understand than his opponent both in style and in content, although on the second point, Carriazo says, there are certain distinctions to be made:

> You criticize in your narration, which we have seen so widely published—in this holy punishment that the Holy Spirit, governor of the Church, has from time immemorial ordered, and that our most Christian lords the king and queen now favor anew—the cause, and the manner, and the ministers, to judge by the meaning I can extract from your confused sayings; so I intend to go about it in that order, for lack of a better opinion.

1. As for the tribunals' method of procedure he writes, sometimes with a certain argumentative force:

> As to the manner in which justice is executed, you criticize the fact that because they are so many it is not right to punish them, using a sophistical argument; for those who you say love the quality of justice but not within their own homes, allege and say that, for the many, punishment is not proper because it gives rise to scandal, and because the erring majority ought to be brought to the Church by exhortation rather than by threats, and that severe punishment cannot be meted out to the many as effectively as to the few who have erred. What the

holy doctor Augustine says is true; but you conceal the holy intention of his saying: and it is that, when the Republic suffers harm, schism, or dissension from such a punishment, the judge, whose concern is for the common good, may set aside the execution of the penalty deserved by many; and this is done not for their sakes, but because the wheat should not be mixed with the chaff and the just suffer for the sinners; but in this case, since the harm arising from ignoring the sin and witholding the punishment is greater than the harm that would follow from administering it, from which error would ensue the breaking of the Faith, corruption of true doctrine, and destruction of virtuous life; and even though their punishment would constitute a scandal, it is the doctrine of Christ to punish, and not to open the door of pardon either to the few or to the many; for it is better to enter Paradise with one eye than to suffer in Hell with two; nor can the quality of silent or feigned justice exist in such a case, without grave sin on the part of him whose office it is to correct; and those who zealously pursue vice and make efforts to defend the *conversos* with doubtful authority deserve neither honor nor much less communion.

We see in these last words the treacherous intention of Anonymous, who takes advantage of every circumstance to plunge in the sharp dagger of his harsh criticism. He then proceeds to demolish, not without a certain sly wit, Pulgar's arguments and the interpretation he had given to the lofty authorities adduced on the side of his position:

You allege that saying of Christ's about "until seventy times seven" and Paul's "patience in all things,"[31] etc., but in this case it is as if one were to compare Magnificat to Matins; for he speaks of the fraternal correction whose aim is to save one single person, an aim which would be thwarted if to the method of punishment were added distress; but in the execution of *this* punishment we are dealing with the common good, the preservation of which lies in punishing obstinate sinners, and disregarding their distress, for that must be subordinated to the common good, which is considered divine; just as for the survival of the body it is advisable to cut off the rotten limb.

To give greater authority to the force of these arguments and to counterbalance the repeated instances of divine pardon to the chosen people, the author brings forward a number of examples of severe Biblical punishments, which prove once again how poor his knowledge of the Bible is:

And if in your opinion God was reconciled many times with His people, it is also well that you recognize how many times, and more times than those, He harshly punished evildoers without deigning to notice the few things that you speak of, whether they are many or few, as a lord of such power that He could raise up new children from the stones unto Abraham.[32] And take careful note of the example of what happened at the time of the Flood, when all the people in the world perished except eight; and in the desert, because of the sin of the Golden Calf, 23,000[33] died by the sword of the Levites and at the hands of their own fathers and brothers; and the case of Dathan and Abiram[34] and their many followers, with the censers in their hands, and the fire consumed them and the earth swallowed them up, etc.; only Joshua and Caleb[35] entered into the Promised Land of all that host that departed from Egypt, because of their doubt when Moses took up the stone from which the waters flowed, etc.; and how because of the blasphemy of Rabshakeh the angel burned in one night 185,000 men;[36] Joshua burned and destroyed Jericho, and God accepted it as a signal service; and Saul was deprived of his kingdom and his life, with all his family, because he had not done the same to the Amalekites. Of acts of vengeance such as these the books are full; where do you find those mercies?

And the anonymous author concludes, referring to these examples—taken from the Old Law, of awe and justice, and not from the New, of grace and love, as Pulgar could have responded:

In the present case the vengeance of God comes nowhere

near to those great numbers; therefore do not complain of cruelty, for surely you may trust that God, once the evil men are eradicated, will bring His mercy.

2. He then goes on to deal with the second point attacked by Pulgar: the cause of the punishment, which Pulgar had tried to palliate by citing extenuating circumstances, and continues:

You next criticize the cause of this punishment, which seems to you to be innocence that excuses the penalty of this sin; indeed, I believe that in this you go against your own knowledge, for this ignorance is ignorance of the Faith, in which salvation consists, and excuses no one—for "Their sound hath gone forth unto all the earth,"[37] etc.—and much less those who live under the name of Christians and dress like them, and hear the bells ring for divine offices, and hide themselves for evil purposes and Judaize both in public and in secret; and for this cause Paul reproached so bitterly the Prince of the Church because he dissimulated in this case when the Church was still so young; and now that she is so much older, what greater cause for punishment do you require?

Anonymous protests indignantly and demands punishment for the sharp barb which Pulgar had directed at the religious life of the Old Christians in Andalusia:

You say, greatly to the insult of all Christians in Andalusia, that they are bad, and according to the terms you use, that they lack faith; what you say is very untrue and makes you liable to judgment; for the faithful there use the sacraments of confession, etc., and through these they believe that God forgives their sins; and if some violate the walls of Holy Church by their evil lives, the edifice of the Law remains intact; but once the first stone of the whole edifice is removed, which is the Faith, then tell me, what remains? This is what those whom you call good Jews do, for they are liars in both laws.

These last words obviously reflect the popular opinion held concerning the *conversos*, among Old Christians as well as among

Jews. On the other hand, Anonymous, with his sharp critical spirit, makes clever use in his argument of the adjective "good," which Pulgar had used to describe the Jewish-leaning *conversos* as a pure stylistic device—though a trifle dangerously, since it lent itself to twisted interpretations which his enemy did not fail to exploit.

He also seizes the opportunity to apply a crude insult to the *conversos*, and concludes this portion of the argument with some rather unclear expressions which appear to allude to the bad Christians in Andalusia taken as dangerous models by the Judaizers, whose bad conduct is not thereby excused. He says:

> And if you do not know their name, read the last part of the first letter to the Corinthians, where the Apostle calls them *marranatha*,[38] which in our language means, plainly and simply, *marranos*; nor is the guilt removed by their blindly following such men; just as the blindness of sensuality does not excuse the guilt of reason, although this is very common; for the attempt to cure blindness by following the lead of the blind does not excuse the stumbling and perilous falling of whoever follows their lead.

After this the author returns to his arguments against what Pulgar had said about the method by which the Judaizers were punished, and further states that the peaceful and persuasive means proposed by Pulgar had already been tried, with complete lack of success and even with disadvantage.

> You criticize the method of punishment, and you are wrong, because it was instituted by holy councils, and has now been decided upon by the ripe counsel of our most Christian monarchs. And the very plan that you suggested was adopted, appointing a member of your nation whose name you know, and I do not know whether more harm than good was done; and the same occurred with the punishment and holy example and life of the Reverend Father Fray Alonso Espina, master in sacred theology, friar minor, who is now with God; for many

years and many days he went to their houses to seek them out, along with many of the faithful, shedding his blood, and carrying before him the holy image of Him who suffered for us upon the Cross.

In this passage he is undoubtedly alluding to the efforts of a zealous convert from Judaism—*of your nation*—to bring erring Judaizers back into the righteous path, with results as negative as those achieved by the burning zeal of the Franciscan *converso* Fray Alonso Espina.

3. Finally, Anonymous replies to the censure implied by Pulgar against the ministers of the Inquisition, and, seeing in his words imaginary allusions to the papacy, seems to lose all control once again, and criticizes and accuses Pulgar more harshly than before:

And lastly, you insult the ministers, and your irresponsible attacks spare no one, from the head of Christendom, the minister of Christ, down to those whom you name. Therefore, pardon my impatience, and, answering your evil words—and disregarding your intention, which is more to injure than to flatter—I say that both the dead and the living have the right to complain of your knavish wiles; and that neither those reverend bishops to whom Christ entrusted His flock, nor the nation of Burgos, are what you say, nor were they ever what you imply, nor were they like the nation you are trying to defend; for they, without need of correction, followed Jesus our salvation, and follow Him to this day.

Not only Merlo and Medina, therefore, were entitled to quarrel with Pulgar's perfidious intentions, worthy of the worst punishment, but even the deceased bishops Pablo de Santa María and Alfonso de Cartagena, to whom Pulgar had referred.

We are surprised to find this extemporaneous defense of the people of Burgos, as if Pulgar, when he said that those *converso* bishops made good Christians with their baptismal water, had wished to indicate that the people of that noble land were all *conversos* or Judaizers. The *nation of Burgos*, replies Anonymous angrily and unnecessarily, follows Jesus irreproachably, and is not and never has been "what you imply, nor . . . like the nation you are trying to defend"; that is, the nation of the Judaizers, for it does not seem clear that he is alluding to the Andalusian "nation." Was Anonymous from Burgos, or was he connected with one of the inquisitors of Seville, like Fray Juan de San Martín, who we know was a native of that city?

And then, in answer to Pulgar's ironic play on the words "fire" and "water," he responds with a grave and gross accusation, not wholly clear, in which he uses the words of the Savior rather unworthily:

> He came with fire to burn the cold earth in charity, not with water to cool it; unless you mean that it was *the burning water with which baptizing was done in your homes*,[39] and perhaps that is what really disturbs you; nor were those lords the bishops, of holy memory, sent for that purpose, nor those that you call ministers by the authority of the chancellor (may he be with God), who died by poison, as it is said, for the benefit of the new chancellor, so that he might take a hand in changing the minds of the king and queen.

After the insinuation of attributing to poisoning the death of the chancellor who had appointed the inquisitors Merlo and Medina, the defense concludes by offering a charitable attitude which had been so clearly missing from the previous part of his letter, and ends thus:

> I will write no more for the present in order not to disturb you further; and I desire that you take and receive this with that charity of which it is said that it is better to receive the punishment of one who loves you than the flattery of one who hates you.
> From a place of little memory: for the fish, water; for the wild beasts, a cage. May Jesus Christ Our Lord save you.

Carriazo (p. lviii) interprets the last paragraph as follows: "From Toledo, where they do not remember, or do not wish to remember, that Pulgar is from a family of Jews." "But in Toledo," he adds, "they should have been well used to this situation; and in fact, as we have seen, it was to Toledo that Pulgar went in those years when he lived away from the court." We see no need to give such an interpretation to this paragraph, which could very well mean, as it does in so many other cases: from a town which does not deserve or wish to be named, a place of no importance. . . .

PULGAR'S REPLY TO ANONYMOUS

But the controversy did not end here. Editions of Pulgar's *Letras* contain one extremely interesting letter connected with the matters we are discussing, and which, as Carriazo has so rightly said (p. lvi), his earlier biographers "have not given the attention it deserves." Carriazo has duly pointed it out, but we believe that his commentary can be amplified and should be corrected on a few points.

Let us begin by stating that we think it entirely clear ("It seems evident," says Carriazo with excessive caution) that this *letra* refers to the letter and impugnation studied above.

In the printed editions (as, for example, in Clásicos Castellanos, pp. 93–97) it is entitled: ["For a hidden friend of his"], and it must be pointed out—for Carriazo has not made this sufficiently clear— that the letter in fact contains two parts. The first reads as follows:

> Señor compadre: I have seen a letter which was delivered by night and found under my door. The letter was addressed to my lord the cardinal, and the matter of it was an attack directed against me; and because I discovered that it had come into your hands before mine, and that you were publishing its contents in that city, I decided, after reading it, to send it to his lordship, seeing that you had not done so. I entreat you, that if at any time you learn the identity of the anonymous person who wrote it, you will give him this reply that I make to him.

As we see, this letter is addressed to a *compadre*, or close friend, who had received the anonymous attack before Pulgar did, and who, instead of *sending*[40] it to the person to whom it was addressed, as was his duty, had made its contents public in "that city" (that of the *compadre*; we cannot be entirely sure whether this was the same city as that of the hidden friend). Could he have been some secretary of the cardinal's, or rather of the Holy Office, and could the letter have been sent or delivered to him by the [author of the] *Difinsorium* so that it could be passed on to the prelate? We do not know; what is clear is that Pulgar, under whose door the damaging letter had apparently been secretly placed by night, had been obliged to pass it on per. onally to the cardinal.

At the same time as he announces all this to his *compadre*, he asks him, if he should some day discover who the anonymous author is (Pulgar may well have known his identity, and uses a euphemism to give the appearance that he does not), to give him Pulgar's reply; and then he continues:[41]

> My hidden friend: I have seen the letter that you sent to my lord and cardinal, in which you insult me and inform him of the errors which it seemed to you were included in a letter I sent to his lordship concerning the heretics of Seville.

There follows a fine and beautiful lesson in Christian humility and charity, which the anonymous author had so much vaunted:

> . . . and as for my offenses, if you are speaking truth, I will make amends; and if you are not, make amends yourself. But no matter how that may be, though you did not see fit to keep Christian doctrine in regard to your insults, I am pleased to keep it by forgiving you; and, both in this world and before the presence of Him who ordered us to forgive all offenses, I forgive you, and in such measure that I retain no scruple or rancor against you; for I believe that he who seeks vengeance rather tortures himself than avenges, and becomes so greatly changed that he tortures his body and does not save his soul. And therefore Our Redeemer and True Physician also gave us doctrine helpful for the body as well as the soul, when he commanded us to pardon those who despitefully use us, just as I in this present

letter pardon you for the ill usage that you give me. But I leave
you to have it out with God, who reserved to Himself the
judgment of vengeance.

Carriazo calls these ideas, as beautiful in meaning as they are
gracefully and felicitously expressed, "embellishments which
evade the basic issue"!

Pulgar follows them with a protest and accuses the anonymous
writer of being cowardly in his anonymity and secrecy, using very
logical arguments:

> Señor Anonymous, either you speak the truth in your letter,
> or you do not: if not, why do you write it? If the truth, why
> hide yourself, if it is true that every Catholic Christian, as you
> show yoùrself to be, should not hide his doctrine, and much less
> his person? And it seems to me that you are doing just the
> contrary: you hide your person and publish your insults, which
> ought to be private reproof, as St. John Chrysostom says of
> Matthew, and not public insult, as Christ has prohibited in the
> Gospel.

And then he goes into an analysis and reply to his adversary's
arguments, saying with impeccable logic:

> You attack me for the things contained in the letter that I
> sent to my lord the cardinal, and if either it or I were worthy of
> reproof, who could better, or should better, administer it than
> the cardinal himself, to whom my letter was written, since he
> is one of the pillars of the Church of God? But there is no
> doubt that he did not rebuke me either personally or by letter,
> nor did other prelates who saw it; for they are the words of
> St. Augustine, epistle one hundred and forty-nine, concerning
> the relapse of the Donatist heretics. If you find these words
> reprehensible, then have it out with St. Augustine, who spoke
> them, and not with me, who merely quoted them.

His adversary had accused him, "to give authority to his evil
words," of having sent his letter to the cardinal, "hiding his bile,

together with his offended heart, under the guise of a very small quantity of the honey of rash and vain boasting"; and Pulgar, feeling certain of the illustrious prelate's esteem, challenges his enemy to try to destroy it; and, judiciously protecting himself with this esteem, as Carriazo observes, replies by telling how much appreciated and sought-after his learned opinions are.

> Furthermore, it seems that in the beginning of your letter you accuse me of the sin of vainglory, because I said that His Lordship was expecting my letter; and this sin, indeed, I believe you cannot correct in me; for His Lordship and other lords and learned men have written to me, and are continually writing to me and commanding me to write to them, and I must needs do what they command me to do; make them stop these commandments, and you will have punished my vainglory.

And then he writes:

> You reproach me also as a buffoon because I sometimes write jestingly; and certainly, Señor Anonymous, you say the truth; but I have seen those noble and magnificent men, the marquis of Santillana Don Iñigo López de Mendoza, and Don Diego Hurtado de Mendoza, his son, duke of Infantado, and Fernán Perez de Guzmán, lord of Batres, and other famous men write messages of sound doctrine, putting in some few jesting words which add savor to what they say. Read, if you like, the family letters of Tully[42] . . . etc. Do not believe that I use this example because I presume to compare myself with any of these; but, they being who they are and I what I am, why should you not allow me, my friend and accuser, to jest about what I know if it injures no one, if it suits me to do so and does you no wrong? But with all that, Señor Anonymous, I tell you that if you find I have ever written a line of jest where there were not also fourteen of truth, then I am willing to be called the buffoon you take me for.

The preceding paragraphs suggest some observations to us. In the first place, we cannot be sure to which passage in the *Difinsorium*

Pulgar is alluding here. Certainly, in no passage in the extant copy is he called an *albardán* or buffoon[43] because he "sometimes" writes jestingly; perhaps the copyist skipped the paragraph, or perhaps Anonymous used the expression verbally when he made the letter public. After the obscure phrase "evil words . . . hiding his bile, together with his offended heart, under the guise of a very small quantity of the honey of rash and vain boasting" (*vano blasón*), Carriazo places the word "albardán?" We do not, however, find this obvious, and in the expression "vain boasting" it seems that Pulgar is referring to the fact that he was accused of boasting of his friendship with the cardinal. Furthermore, although Carriazo writes (p. li) that the phrase about "some jesting things" is a detail which certainly agrees with Pulgar's unpublished letter, we find no passage in it alluding to jokes or jests, unless we read them into the final paragraphs, when he says that the bishops of Burgos converted many more with their baptismal water than the inquisitors were going to convert by fire.

Anonymous had twisted some of Pulgar's words, and blamed him for having accused the inquisitors of Seville and even the queen herself; and Pulgar, who failed to reply to a great many things in the letter, did not wish to pass over this serious and dangerous accusation, and hastens to reply to it:

You also say that my letter says that the inquisitors of Seville err in what they do, and that it follows from this that the queen our lady must have erred in giving them the charge. I, certainly, wrote no letter saying any such thing; and if it seems I know the letter so well, then it cannot say what I did not make it say; for neither do I say that they err in their office, nor the queen in her commission, though it would be possible that Her Majesty had erred in charging them with it, and even for them to have erred in their procedure, and that both did so without evil intent, but because of false information from others. Certainly the King Don John, of glorious memory, was a good man and prudent; but, thinking that he did well, he turned over that city of Toledo[44] to Pedro Sarmiento to keep for him; and he, perverted by evil men there, rebelled against the king and cast down his royal title, and even threw stones at his tent. The queen our lady thought well of what she was doing when she confided the fortress of Nodar to Martín de Sepúlveda; but he rebelled with the city and sold it to the king of Portugal. Therefore, señor my corrector, it is no marvel that Her Highness may have erred in the charge that she made, thinking that she was doing well, and they also in the trials, thinking that they were not ill-informed; although I never said it, nor will I now affirm any such thing.

Pulgar was perfectly right here, and Carriazo correctly says (p. lvii) that "a fabulous command of language" permits him "these marvels, saying a thing and not saying it. With such statements he avoids their consequences, and politely defends himself against the greatest danger in this affair: the queen's indignation." Let us also note how Pulgar takes advantage of the chance to criticize John II's error in the matter of Pedro Sarmiento and the injustices committed against the *conversos* of Toledo, to which Pulgar refers so many times in his writings.

The letter ends by begging Anonymous' pardon for not going fully into the question he has raised; Pulgar evades it, but at the same time challenges him to come out in the open so that he can confront him:

> As for the other things you mention having to do with Holy Writ, I do not answer because I do not know who you are: make yourself known and I will satisfy you as much as I can, and will even show you clearly how greatly you have fallen into the sin of lying, in order to stain me with the sin of heresy.

Thus ends this delightful and witty letter of Pulgar's in which he discloses to us all the grave danger contained in the intent of his enemy's missive, and the strict and firm conviction of innocence that the chronicler possessed. Everything we know about him and his literary work proves his orthodoxy; and this is further accredited by the slender text adduced by Carriazo (p. xxv) when he declares, and rightly, that Pulgar was a fervent Christian and must be exonerated from all suspicion.

DATE AND CONSEQUENCE OF THIS CONTROVERSY BETWEEN PULGAR AND HIS ENEMY

In the edition of the *Letras* I have mentioned (p. 322) Domínguez Bordona writes, obviously in error, when referring to the last of the letters we have quoted here, that it was "apparently written in 1478, date of the publication of Cardinal Mendoza's edict for establishment of the Inquisition. Cf. *Crónica*, Rivadeneira, p. 331." Carriazo, however (p. lii), believes that this letter, included in the edition of the *Letras* printed in Toledo in 1486, was "certainly written some five years earlier at least." It could not be more than five years, for we must date the whole dispute later than January, 1481, when the first inquisitors began to work in Seville; and they were appointed, as we have said, on September 27, 1480.

What were the consequences for Pulgar? In Carriazo's opinion, the new documents would explain his removal from the court, "probably because of his criticism of the first inquisitors' conduct" (pp. xv–xvi). "We know nothing with certainty," he says more cautiously elsewhere (p. xxxviii), "and only with all kinds of mental reservations do I dare to present the hypothesis that this absence was related to Pulgar's opinions on the first steps taken by the new Inquisition . . . and still more, perhaps, to his observations and reservations concerning the procedures of some inquisitors than to his own personal position as a presumed New Christian." The inclusion of the letter to the hidden friend in this edition of 1486 and the fact that the queen commissioned him to write her Chronicle prove, according to Carriazo, that "he was able to justify himself. But for the moment an embarrassing situation was created, sufficiently so to remove him temporarily from his posts and from familiarity with the sovereigns. Let us keep in mind the circumstances that his last known official act took place in Seville in October, 1477. In any case, he was away from the court in

1479. . . ." Finally, Professor Carriazo writes in another passage (p. lviii): "For, in fact, no matter how strong his position was, and no matter how successfully he had justified himself, no matter how highly placed his protectors were, and even supposing great good will on the part of the queen, it is clear that Pulgar had issued a serious criticism of an act of government, had placed himself in opposition to a strong current of opinion, and was left in a difficult and perhaps dangerous situation, at the very least an uncomfortable one. His departure from court and from familiarity with the monarchs was decreed, and Pulgar retired to private life, to the cultivation of letters and the instruction of Vizcayan pupils. But in the long run the incident was smoothed over to everyone's satisfaction; and Pulgar returned to court, summoned by the queen, and was given nothing less than the extremely delicate and responsible task of writing the history of her reign.[45] Not even a Galíndez, whose attitude toward Pulgar was one of suspicion, seems to have known anything about this whole affair. The letter to the anonymous friend remained, printed in Toledo itself, as if to demonstrate that Pulgar did not need to be ashamed of what had happened. As for the other letter, which had given rise to the whole matter, every possible effort was made to forget it. . . ."

The reader will pardon these long but necessary quotations, for they contain many unproved statements, lacking in detail and a trifle gratuitous, which the critical historian cannot accept at face value. To begin with, we do not have one word showing whether the first letter was eliminated from the edition of 1486 for this reason, and we are completely ignorant of the causes and circumstances of Pulgar's temporary removal from court. If this took place before 1479,[46] as Carriazo writes in the quoted passage, he would have to agree with us that the event could not have been a result of the controversy under discussion, which took place more than a year later.

The impression we now have of the matter, then, is that a gap really exists in our knowledge of Pulgar's life during the years 1477 to 1480—as in so many other years of his life—and that we do not know the circumstances of his departure[47] from court either; for, so long as there is no proof to the contrary, Pulgar's simply being away from court does not mean that the absence was involuntary. And we know still less about the reasons for this supposed *forced* retirement.

Now let us go on to examine *how Pulgar's position in respect to Jews and conversos, as well as his situation as a New Christian, is reflected in his other writings.*

A. As for *Claros Varones de Castilla*, where, according to Clemencín, Pulgar had shown "in a number of passages" "his opinions on the matter," we can state that after diligently examining the work we have found, along with the most fervent praise of the Catholic Monarchs, the following references to *conversos* or Jews:

1. When he deals with the cardinal of St. Sixtus, Don Juan de Torquemada,[48] he states that the cardinal was from the city of Burgos and that "his ancestors were of the lineage of the Jews converted *to our holy Catholic faith.*" Domínguez Bordona notes (p. 108) that Pulgar was ill-informed, for the cardinal was neither from Burgos nor of Jewish descent, but was the son of Álvar Fernández de Torquemada and great-grandson of Lope Alfonso de Torquemada, upon whom Alfonso XI conferred knighthood on the day of his coronation in the Castilian capital.

2. Pulgar writes very high praise of Bishop Alonso de Cartagena, of Burgos,[49] after stating (p. 125) that his father Don Pablo "was of the lineage of the Jews, and so learned a man, that he was enlightened by the grace of the Holy Spirit; and, having knowledge of the truth, was converted *to our holy Catholic faith.*"

3. He writes of Don Francisco, bishop of Coria[50] (p. 129), that "he was a native of the city of Toledo: his ancestors were of the lineage of the Jews converted to the Catholic faith"; he lavishes lengthy and high praise on him and concludes by saying that he was an example of doctrine for all who wished to live a good life, "for neither did this regard that we have for lineage enhance him, nor his bodily appearance, nor did wealth make him an eminent

man ... but the perseverance that he had in the virtuous life opened the doors for him to enter into high places. ..."

Carriazo, who has emphasized the *insistence* with which Pulgar points out the Jewish descent of various prelates whom he describes and extols in his *Claros Varones*, says (p. xxv) that "it strikes a false note, coming from a possible *converso*, to say of the count of Cifuentes that 'he was an *hidalgo* of pure blood,' when it would have been enough to say '*hidalgo*'." But undoubtedly the chronicler does not use the expression "pure blood" here as a contrast to that tainted by origins considered less pure.

B. Insofar as his *Letras* are concerned—which so far have not been carefully analyzed—we can make a few observations in addition to what we have already indicated about those we considered most important, and to point out among them some which abound in Biblical erudition of the Old Testament, together with some quotations from the New, as well as from St. Augustine and Josephus; for example, in *Letras* 1, 2, 3, 6, 7, 9, etc.

On *Letra* IV, addressed to "a knight, his friend, of Toledo," he recalls having heard Fernán Pérez de Guzmán say that Bishop Don Pablo of Burgos wrote to the old constable, who was then ill "and in Toledo: I am glad that you are in a city with such notable doctors and such excellent medicines." "I do not know if he would say it now," Pulgar adds, "for we see that the leather-bottle-makers have cast the famous physicians out of there, and so I believe that you are furnished with much better rebellious bottle-makers than with good natural physicians." Although Domínguez Bordona writes that it can be presumed that in this reference to bottle-makers Pulgar is alluding to those who conspired with the prelate Carrillo in favor of the Portuguese king, we believe that he refers here, as in other passages of his works, to the followers of the famous bottle-maker who, after the year 1449, when he mounted a rebellion, aroused the imperial city against the *conversos*: "When the bottle-maker blows, Toledo will riot."[51]

The very interesting *Letra* XIV must also refer to Toledo and its disturbances; it too is addressed to "a friend of his" in Toledo, and begins, like the one previously analyzed, with the words "Señor

Compadre." It seems to be an answer to one in which the friend had referred obliquely to events that had taken place in Toledo in connection with the well-worn theme of purity of descent, for Pulgar writes:

> I have received your letter, and so that you may see that I understand it, I shall say plainly what you say under your breath.
>
> In that noble city it is not to be endured that some whom you judge not to be of pure descent have honors and offices of government, for you believe that the defect of blood deprives them of the ability to govern. And also, it is a grave affront to see riches in men who, it is believed, do not merit them, especially those who have gained them recently. From these things . . . arises a pang of envy so great that it torments men, and impels them to take up arms irresponsibly, and deliver insults. . . .

It is regrettable that we do not have space here to explain this curious missive, dated in 1478 and included almost in its entirety in Pulgar's *Crónica*, in the long speech which the *alcaide* Gómez Manrique "made to the men of Toledo" who, incited by Carrillo's bribes and promises, had secretly conspired to kill the commander of that city and take the Portuguese monarch for their king. It contains open allusions to the chief causes which, as we have said, fed the riots against *conversos* and Jews, and to the old dispute which the citizens of Toledo maintained concerning the exclusion of New Christians from public office, the envy of their wealth, etc.

Pulgar does not fail to remark on that quarrel over lineage: "They sustain a very old dispute, certainly, and a very ancient quarrel and one not yet extinct in the world," in which they err "against the law of nature, for all of us are born from the same stuff and had a noble beginning; it is also contrary to divine law, which commands us all to be of one fold and under one shepherd; and especially is it contrary to the shining virtue of charity. . . ." He repeats this idea later, assuring that we must believe that God made men and not lineages among which to choose, and that He made all men noble at their birth; vileness of blood and humbleness of lineage are chosen with his own hands by the man who, having departed from the path of virtue, inclines toward the vices and blemishes of the erring path. . . .

This theme of lineage, which apparently was an obsession with Pulgar, reappears in the long and beautiful *Letra* XXIV to a daughter of his who is a nun, and whom he first urges to hold and believe "firmly the Catholic faith of our Savior and Redeemer Jesus Christ, and that which His holy mother Church believes and holds . . .," and then writes (p. 119): "St. Jerome in a prologue to the Romans and Jews who gloried in their lineage, rebuked them, saying . . ."

We could also cull some interesting allusions from *Letra* XXV (dated in 1473) to the bishop of Coria and dean of Toledo, in which he speaks of "this our kingdom of Toledo," of its important men and its internal strife: "What shall I say then, my lord, of the body that noble city of Toledo, stronghold of emperors, where the humble and the great live a very sad life, surely, and full of misfortune?" (p. 129).[52] And we could also add a quotation from the *converso* bishop Alonso de Cartagena (*Letra* XXXII, p. 152).

C. Glosses on the *Coplas de Mingo Revulgo*: these, printed with the *Letras* in Domínguez Bordona's edition, offer copious biblical references from the Old Testament, and sometimes Pulgar makes very felicitous commentaries on them, as for example (pp. 208 *et seq.*), on *manna*, or the comparison of the two laws, Mosaic and Christian (pp. 200–201), which recalls that of Cartagena in his *Defensorium*. . . . Moreover, many ideas and expressions whose background and inspiration are biblical are found everywhere in the *Coplas* as well as the glosses, and show obvious scriptural imagery.

On page 185 there is a reference to Christians (the sheep of Cristóbal Mexía), Jews (those of the other stammerer, Moses), and

Mohammedans (those of Meco, the clever Moor) mingled in a single garment during the troubled reign of Henry IV.

We did not find, however, any special allusion to the themes studied in this article.

D. The opposite is true in Pulgar's *Crónica*, A good many years ago, when we first read this delightful history in the B[iblioteca de] A[utores] E[spañoles] edition, Volume 70, we were amazed by the wealth of passages he offers which throw light on the Jewish question at the time of the Catholic Monarchs, and especially on the problem of the *conversos*. Now we shall utilize the notes we took at that time, expanding them by comparison with the new revision offered by Carriazo's recent edition.

First of all, we were surprised by certain curious silences of Pulgar's, which have not been noticed and are worth pointing out. Thus, in dealing with the uprising instigated in Segovia in 1473 by Don Juan Pacheco against the chamberlain Cabrera, he merely says that the former "attempted to raise the city," and that "there was a great commotion . . . among its citizens," partisans of one man or the other. He makes no mention, therefore, of the *conversos*, who had so large a part, to their sorrow, in the plans and maneuvers of the odious royal favorite.[53]

The short shrift he gives to the assassination of the constable, Iranzo, in the cathedral of Jaén in the course of that year is also startling: "He was evilly and cruelly murdered by some peasants of the district of Jaén."[54] He has nothing at all to say, then, about the violence done to the *conversos* "who were killed afterward for no cause." (See Valera, *Memorial*, chap. LXXXIV, p. 79, of the BAE edition, Vol. 70.)

Nor does he write a single line about the serious occurrences which took place during those very days in Córdoba between Old and New Christians. (See *ibid.*, chap. LXXXIII, p. 78.)

On the other hand, when he gives us a description of Queen Isabella (BAE ed., p. 257; Carriazo, 77) he does not fail to say that "this queen was she who rooted out and destroyed the heresy that existed in the kingdoms of Castile and Aragon, of *some*[55] Christians of the lineage of the Jews, who returned to Jewish practices, and she made them live like good Christians. . . ."

But let us turn to the passages in which Pulgar deals directly with the subjects we are studying here.

None is as important as Chapters XCVI and CXX of the old version (A), which it is extremely instructive to compare with Chapter LXXVII of the later version (B), not only because it is a sufficient illustration of the events reflected in Pulgar's newly discovered letter, but also because it permits us to understand his position in the matter of the Judaizers, and the agreement or conflict of his opinions on the method of dealing with them. Therefore we shall publish the text of those first two chapters according to Professor Carriazo's edition,[56] placing at the foot of the page, in Chapter XCVI, the variations introduced by B (according to the BAE edition, pp. 331 *et seq.*); but when these consist of omissions we shall place them in the text between brackets, thus: [ ] and in the case of additions, thus: ⟨ ⟩; we shall italicize what is peculiar to each version. We shall edit the text of Chapter CXX in double column with the original Chapter LXXVII, which it modifies considerably.

Chapter XCVI. Of the Heresy That Was Found in Seville.

1   Some clerics and religious persons *and others of the city of Seville* informed the king and queen that in *that city* many Christians of the lineage of the Jews *were returning* to Jewish ways and performing *rites of the Jews* secretly in their houses,
5   and they neither believed the Christian faith nor did the works that Catholic Christians ought to do. And *this weighed on their consciences*, requiring of them, that since they were Catholic rulers, they should punish that so [*foul and*] detestable error; for if *they* [*allowed it to occur and*] *left* it unpunished and it was
10   not [*quickly*] checked, *it would grow* in such a manner that our holy Catholic faith *would receive* detriment.

1–2 *and many other secular persons*   2–3 in *their kingdoms and seigniories there were* . . . who *were returning*   4 *Judaic rites*   6–7 *this case weighed on them*   9 *they should leave* it   10 *it might grow*   11 *might* receive

This being known by the king and queen, they were greatly troubled, because persons were found in their king-dom⟨s⟩ who were not in accord with the Catholic faith and

15 were heretics and apostates. On this matter the cardinal of Spain, [who was] archbishop of Seville, drew up a certain constitution ⟨*in the city of Seville*⟩ according to the sacred canons, of the way ⟨*in*⟩ which the Christian should act from the day he was born, in the sacrament of baptism as in all the

20 sacraments he ought to receive, and of *the usage that* he ought to use and believe like a faithful Christian, in all the days and time⟨s⟩ of his life, and *at the time* of his death. And he commanded it to be published in all the churches of the city and placed on signboards in each parish, as a firm constitution.

25 And he showed moreover what the priests and clergy ought to preach [*and show*] to *the* parishioners, and what the parishion-ers ought to hold, and teach to their children.

And moreover, *the king and queen* [*and the cardinal commanded*] some friars and clerics and other religious persons, that both

30 by public preaching and in private and individual speech they should inform those persons in the Faith and instruct them and lead them once more into the true belief of our *Savior* Jesus Christ [*and that they exhort them and require them to leave off doing those Jewish rites*] and that they show them how much

35 perpetual damnation of their souls and perdition of their bodies and possessions they were incurring because of *doing this*.

These religious persons to whom this charge was given, no matter how much they endeavored, first with gentle exhorta-

40 tions and then with sharp reproaches, to reclaim those who were Judaizing, it was of little avail, *for their obstinacy was so foolish a blindness and so blind an ignorance that,* although they denied and concealed their error, they secretly fell into it again *and performed and kept their Jewish rites.*

20 *the doctrine that he should be taught and*   22 *until the day*   26 *their*
28 *the king and queen gave orders to*   32 *Lord*
36–37 *performing Jewish rites*   41–42 *against the blind obstinacy in which they per-sisted; and they, though*   43–44 *blaspheming the name and doctrine of our Lord and Saviour Jesus Christ*

45   The king and queen, considering the evil and perverse
nature of that error, and wishing to amend it with great
study and diligence, sent notice of it to the supreme pontiff,
who gave his bull by which *he granted them power to place
inquisitors of the Faith in their kingdoms and to attack and punish*
50 *those of that* sin of heretical iniquity.

48–50 *he commanded that there be* inquisitors *in all the* kingdoms *and seigniories
of the king and the queen, who should make inquiry into the Faith, and punish those
guilty of the*

Chapter cxx. *Of What Was Done in Seville Against the Heretics*

We have told how the king
and queen were greatly distressed by the heresy that
existed among some Christians
of the lineage of the Jews, who
were returning to Jewish rites
and were not in accord with the
Faith.

And therefore the king entrusted to a friar of the Order
of St. Dominic, who was
superior of the monastery of
Santa Cruz of Segovia, the
general Inquisition of all the
kingdoms and seigniories of
the king and the queen.

And this prior, who was the
chief inquisitor, entrusted his
authority to two learned
friars, one a native of the
kingdom of Valencia and the
other of the city of Burgos,
and to a doctor named Juan de
Medina, so that they would be

And he gave principal charge
of this inquisition to a friar of
upright life who had great zeal
in the Faith, who was called
Fray Tomás de Torquemada,
confessor to the king and prior
of the monastery of Santa Cruz
of Segovia, of the Order of
St. Dominic.

This prior, who was the chief
inquisitor, put other inquisitors
in his place in all the other cities
and towns of the kingdom of
Castile, and Aragon, and Valencia, and Catalonia.

inquisitors in the city of Seville and in its archbishopric.

These inquisitors instituted trials and inquisitions, and through these discovered, as we have said before, that many of the Christians who came of the lineage of the Jews had returned to Jewish ways and were performing Jewish rites.

These made inquisitions on that matter of heretical iniquity in every land and district where they were assigned; and in these places they set their charters and edicts, founded upon law, so that those who had engaged in Jewish practices or who were not in accord with the Faith, within a certain time might come to confess their faults and be reconciled with Holy Mother Church. And by these charters and edicts many persons of that lineage, within the term that had been set, appeared before the inquisitors and confessed their faults and the errors that they had committed in this crime of heresy. And these were given penances according to the degree of the crime that each one had incurred. These were more than fifteen thousand persons, men as well as women.

And if some were guilty of that crime and did not come to be reconciled within the period of time that had been decreed, once there was information from witnesses of the error they had committed, then they were taken prisoner and trial was instituted against them, by means of which they were condemned as heretics and apostates and turned over to secular justice.

Of these, up to three hundred men and women were burned on different occasions, and many others were arrested.

Up to two thousand men and women among these were burned on various occasions and in some cities and towns; and others were condemned to perpetual imprisonment; and to others was given as a penance that for all the days of their lives they should go marked with great red crosses placed on their clothing, both on the breast and on the back. And they as well as their children were declared unfit for all public office of responsibility, and it was decreed that they could not carry or wear silk or gold or camlet, on pain of death.

Likewise inquisition was made whether those who had died within a certain time had Judaized; and because they found some who in life had committed this sin of heresy and apostasy, judicial trials were brought against them, and they were condemned and their bones taken out of the tombs and burned publicly, and their children barred from holding offices or benefices. A great number of these were found, whose goods and inheritances were taken and applied to the treasury of the king and the queen.

Others fled and went to the kingdom of Portugal and to the lands of the Moors and to other places in the seigniories, to protect themselves with the favor of the lords; and against these the inquisitors proceeded in their absence. And their possessions were seized, from which was paid the armada that was formed against the Turks, and also many things necessary for the war against the Moors; for the king and queen commanded that those goods should not be distributed except in things that concerned the defense of the Faith.

When they saw how this was done, many of those of that lineage, fearing those proceedings, abandoned their houses and possessions and went to the kingdom of Portugal, and to Italy, and to France, and to other kingdoms; and the inquisitors proceeded against these in their absence, and their possessions were seized; from which, and from the fines paid by those who had become reconciled, and from everything belonging to those who had gone against the Faith, the king and queen commanded that it be not distributed in anything except in the war against the Moors, or in other things which would serve to exalt the Catholic faith.

Some of the relatives of the prisoners and the condemned informed the king and queen that that inquisition and procedure was not being done in the form in which it ought to be done in justice, and that it was very harsh, for many

Some relatives of the prisoners and the condemned protested, saying that that inquisition and procedure was rigorous beyond what it ought to be.

reasons. Especially they said that the bull received from the pope concerning this matter included only the Christians converted to the Faith from the lineage of the Jews, and not any others, and hence they supposed that the person who issued it wished to taint all those of that lineage, making a special case in that bull of them and no others.

They likewise said that in the manner of conducting the trials, and of taking witnesses and information, and in the tortures that were applied, and in the execution of the sentences, and in the other circumstances, the ecclesiastical inquisitors and the secular executors had behaved cruelly and showed great hatred, not only against those on whom they passed sentence and tortured, but even against them all, and showed a desire to taint them and defame them for that horrible sin. And that, mindful of the mercy of God and that which Holy Mother Church commands in this case, those erring folk should be brought to the Faith with gentle reasoning and soft exhortations and good doctrines and exam-

and that in the manner in which the trials were conducted and in the execution of the sentences,

the ministers and executors showed that they had hatred for those people.

ples. And, following the precepts and rules of holy canons, they should be reduced and subjected to the penalties which the laws provide, and not with that cruel punishment of fire. Especially those who confessed their error and were converted to the faith of Christ our Lord; for they said it was an inhuman thing, and a cruel, to condemn to the fire anyone who invoked the name of Christ and confessed himself to be a Christian and wished to live as a Christian.

When these things were seen by the king and the queen, they ordered them to be discussed in their Council, and that whatever the law decreed should be done. And for the purpose they appointed the cardinal of Spain, who then[57] was the archbishop of Seville, and the bishops of Jaén and Palencia, and ten doctors and four masters of sacred theology who, after they had discussed the matter, gave a certain order in writing, which was to be used from that time forward, founded on the laws and the sacred canons, as to how they were to be called and reduced, and as to the confession and abjuration they

The king and the queen turned over this matter to certain prelates, men of conscience, who were to look into it and justly remedy the matter.

were to make, and the penalty which each was to incur, according to the measure in which he had erred.

In Seville and its archdiocese at that time, there were three thousand households and more where those folk lived, and they departed with their wives and children. They went by land and by sea to other, foreign places. And since the absence of those folk left a large part of that city depopulated, the queen was informed that the great commerce carried on there had diminished, and thus her rents were very greatly reduced; but she considered the diminution of her rents a thing of very little importance, and said that, all interest aside, she wished to cleanse her kingdom of that sin of heresy, for she knew it was to the service of God and herself. And the supplications and pleas that were made to her in this affair did not make her change her mind about it.

There were at that time, especially in Seville and Córdoba and in the cities and towns of Andalusia, four thousand and more households where the folk of that lineage were dwelling; and they departed from the land with their wives and children. And since the absence of those folk depopulated a large part of that region, the queen was notified that commerce was diminished; but she, giving little heed to the diminution of her rents and esteeming very highly the cleansing of her lands, said that, all interest aside, she wished to cleanse her lands of that sin of heresy, for she knew it was to the service of God and herself. And the supplications that were made to her in this affair did not make her change her mind about it.

And because it was discovered that the communication which these folk had with the Jews who lived in the cities of Córdoba and Seville and their dioceses was a partial cause of that error, the king and queen

> gave orders that no Jew, on
> pain of death, should dwell in
> that land for ever and ever; and
> they were forced to leave their
> homes and go to dwell in other
> places.

The comparison of A and B in these passages suggests deductions of great interest, which we should like to point out.

Carriazo believes (p. xxii) that Chapter cxx is "new," and "provides texts for out investigation; texts no less substantiating than those already referred to" by Clemencín, and that "it may be considered as an amplification and more extensive first version" of what the known version states in Chapter xcvi.

These assertions seem to us to be a trifle hasty and inaccurate. In the first place, this chapter, whose newness we shall consider later, does not offer more convincing proofs than, for example, the letter about the Guipuzcoan statute; moreover, in a number of places the ampler and more detailed test is represented precisely by the later version. We must go into detail, therefore, as follows:

Obviously, Chapter lxxvii is a recasting of the two others in version A, which has been made more systematic and more polished in style, avoiding repetitions, etc. The original Chapter xcvi has gone over almost whole into the new revision, but in it Pulgar presents the question of the Judaizers not as a problem in Seville alone, but everywhere in the kingdom. From this new focus and its elevation to a more general plane, major subsequent changes arise. And there is also, it should be noted, greater circumspection in ideas and expressions.

Finally, in B the pope *commands* the naming of inquisitors to uncover and punish the heresy of which he had been informed, while in A the pope *had granted powers* to establish an inquisition.

Chapter cxx underwent a still greater transformation when it was combined with Chapter xcvi, and it will be useful to point out some of the changes. First, while in A it is the king who turns over the matter to the inquisitors, in B—as if there were a desire not to involve the sovereign too directly—it is the pope who gives the main responsibility of the Inquisition to Torquemada. Moreover, B adds some words of praise for the inquisitor general, adding that he was the king's confessor.

A cited specifically the inquisitors of Seville and its archbishopric; B refers *in genera* to those of all Spain. The general character of B, as we mentioned before, brings up new variations in the number of persons condemned, the places to which the Judaizers fled, what happened to their goods and the monetary penalties imposed on condemned persons, etc.

B presents striking amplification concerning the inquisitorial procedure, penalties imposed, etc.; in this respect it is, therefore, much more precise than A. On the other hand, the notable passage referring to the complaints by relatives of the condemned is given more space in A, though perhaps not in such strong terms.[58] B omits information showing that the papal bull was directed only against the Hebrew race, and about the manner of conducting the trials, the taking of witnesses and information, and the application of torture. B merely alludes in a general way to formal irregularities either in procedure or in execution of the sentences.

Furthermore, B omitted the following paragraph in A concerning the Church's gentle standards of procedure in such cases, and the methods of attracting erring persons. Perhaps Pulgar had at last become convinced that all those peaceful and persuasive methods had given no result. In all these passages it is clear that there is a close connection between version A and the ideas and expressions contained in the newly printed letter, as we have already pointed out on [pages 306–7].

Finally, passing over other details, we can observe that B also abbreviates the passage concerning the commission named to examine possible abuses by inquisitors and lay prosecutors, and about the measures which they had laid down; it also raises to four thousand the number of condemned persons in Andalusia, compared to the three thousand in Seville and its archbishopric in A, and adds an interesting paragraph about the expulsion from Andalusia of all the Jewish families who lived there.

These are the most important points to be studied concerning these notable chapters in the *Crónica*. But there are still others on which we can focus our attention, even though briefly.

Thus, we consider Chapter xcviii (Carriazo's ed., pp. 347–48) particularly notable; we have already referred to it (p. 332) when we were discussing *Letra* xiv.

Chapter cxv concerns the events of 1480, and especially the Cortes held that year in Toledo. In this Cortes new measures necessary for the governing of the kingdom were passed,

> among which one measure was promulgated confirming the old order and constitution made by the monarchs their ancestors, that Jews and Moors should live apart in the cities and towns where they dwelt, and that they should not dwell among the Christians, and that they should wear the distinguishing badges formerly decreed. Moreover, that the Jews should not use gold and silver in their Torahs; and to carry out this segregation they ordered charters issued in their name, and sent out persons to give the order in this matter and to accomplish it within a year.[59]

In Chapter cxxxiii (pp. 25–26 in Vol. ii of Carriazo's edition) version B adds a final paragraph on the tax on the Hebrews in their kingdom which Ferdinand and Isabella decreed for the war in 1482:

> In that year they imposed a tax on the Jews and Moors of all Castile and Leon, that each should pay a gold piece of the kind called Castilian, that was worth fifteen and a half *reales* of silver.

In this, as Carriazo tells us (p. xc), "Pulgar demonstrates once again that he is interested in matters pertaining to the Jews."

Chapter clxxxii (pp. 209–11) reads, referring to 1481:

> In that year, since the inquisition begun in the kingdom against the Christians who had been of the lineage of the Jews

and who were Judaizing continued, there were some men and women in the city of Toledo who were secretly celebrating Jewish rites, and who, in great ignorance and peril to their souls, were not keeping either one law or the other; for they did not circumcise like the Jews, as the Old Testament advocates, and although they kept the Sabbath and performed some of the fasts of the Jews, they did not keep all the Sabbaths or fast during all the fasts, and if they celebrated one rite they did not celebrate the other, so that they were false both to the one law and to the other. And it happened that in some households the husband kept certain Jewish ceremonies and the wife was a good Christian, and that one son and daughter might be good Christians while another son was of the Jewish faith. And within the same household there was diversity of beliefs, and the members of the family concealed themselves one from the other.

Many of these were reconciled to the Faith and received into the Church, and penances were given to each one according to the confession that he made. Some others were condemned to perpetual imprisonment, and others were burned. And because in this case of heresy testimony was received from Moors and Jews, and servants, and wicked and vile men, and because of their testimony some were arrested and condemned to death by fire, there were in the city some Jews and poor and vile men who through enmity or malice gave false witness against some of the *conversos*, saying that they had seen them practising Jewish rites. And [once the truth was known] the queen commanded that they be brought to trial ⟨as perjurers,⟩ and eight Jews were stoned and tortured with pincers.

This is, according to Carriazo (pp. xxiii–xxiv) "the text most indicative of Pulgar's thought and position"; but we have adduced others which are no less so. And we must point out that in our opinion, though we accept the great importance of the passage, Carriazo has erred in stating that Pulgar, speaking here on his own account, "explicitly recognises the legitimacy of both laws [the

Jewish and the Christian], that he places them almost on an equal plane, and that he denounces the transgressions of both with equal fervor, especially that vacillation which involves sinning against both laws." The chronicler merely states a fact: that those false *conversos* kept neither the Jewish nor the Christian religion, and in trying to ride two horses at once, sinned against both faiths; therefore he does not make the slightest objection to the severe punishment meted out to them. The rest of what Carriazo reads into Pulgar seems gratuitous to us.

Nor do we believe he has had a more felicitous idea when he points out (p. xxv) that, when Pulgar describes "with real satisfaction" the exemplary justice meted out to the Moors, Jews, servants, and wicked and vile men who testified falsely against the *conversos*, "*the reproaches he heaps on the Jews who denounced them*" seem to reveal "the pen of a *converso*, and even that of a *converso* of Toledo." If we read the passage carefully we find no such accumulation of reproaches against the Hebrew denouncers; but it is very natural that Pulgar should have had a special interest in recording their punishment.

In the preceding pages we have collected from Pulgar's writings as much as can be gleaned today about those consuming problems of his time.

The question of the chronicler's Hebraic origin has been definitely cleared up, through analysis of his extremely interesting letter concerning the Guipuzcoan statute, which contains his most forceful and explicit statement in this regard, in contrast to the attitude of prudent and calculated reserve maintained by Pulgar later, even when it appears that unequivocal statements can be expected of him, as in his reply to the attack of the *Difinsorium*. We have succeeded in amplifying and correcting both Clemencín and Carriazo on various points.

We have also studied with a certain amount of detail and breadth the polemic unleashed by the revelation of Pulgar's opinion in respect to the activities of the inquisitors of Seville after 1481. The editing and study of the *Letras*, the anonymous *Difinsorium*, and Pulgar's reply to it have cast much light on several aspects of his life, and especially on the problem of the *conversos*, so vital at that time. In addition to improving Carriazo's edition of the former document and correcting and amplifying the fragmentary edition he made of the second, we have corrected and added more detail to Carriazo and Domínguez Bordona in important statements relating to Pulgar's biography, insofar as the date and consequences of the dispute are concerned.

The examination of Pulgar's remaining writings has led us to weigh his interesting statements and his position in the problem of *conversos* and Judaizers, permitting us to make further corrections in the scholars mentioned. Likewise, the careful analysis of passages in the *Crónica* and the comparison of its two editions suggest important deductions which correct and clarify Carriazo's recent study, casting light both on Pulgar's biography and on the history of the subject of the *conversos*.

We lack the space here to make a thorough study of this subject, and of the position itself of our chronicler in the debate being carried on in Spain at the time in regard to the problem. We cannot, therefore, go into an examination of the writings of defenders of the *conversos*, such as Juan de Lucena or the anonymous author of the note written at the end of Paulo Burgense's manuscript[60] of the *Scrutinium Scriptorum*; or their impassioned detractors, such as Bernáldez; or accounts of such high human, Christian, and historical value, as those of Pulgar's intimate and admired friend, F[ernán] Pérez de Guzmán, in his *Generaciones y Semblanzas*; or of chroniclers such as Diego de Valera[61] or the writer who continued Pulgar's history, etc. Perhaps we shall do so at a later date.

But Pulgar is particularly outstanding for both his attention to Jewish themes and, in general, his presentation of the political doctrines which guided the Spain of the Catholic Monarchs. Carriazo was correct in criticizing (p. xii) Fueter for stating that Pulgar mentioned the most important things only in passing, "mixing, for example, the Inquisition's measures against the Judaizers with matters of mere curiosity." However, we should not neglect to state that, in our opinion, Pulgar does not equal

Bernáldez in showing the most vivid interest in the subject of *conversos*, Judaizers, and Jews.

NOTES

[1. *Crónica de los Reyes Católicos por su secretario Fernando del Pulgar*, ed. J. de Mata Carriazo (2 vols; Madrid, 1943), reviewed in *Sefarad*, IV, i (1944), 209–11.]

2. W. Thomas Walsh, *Isabel de España*, trans. A. de Mestas (Burgos, 1937). Walsh mentions Pulgar twice as a *converso* or New Christian who referred to Torquemada's Jewish descent (p. 71, n. 7 and p. 344).

[3. St. Vincent Ferrer, Catalan saint, the hero of the Compromise of Caspe (1412), which settled the disputed claims to the Aragonese throne in favor of Ferdinand of Antequera.]

[4. A famous dispute between Christian and Jewish doctors held at Tortosa in 1413 at which St. Vincent Ferrer was present.]

5. In this and Pulgar's other *letras* we follow the text of the Seville edition by Estanislao Polono, April 24, 1500 (Biblioteca Nacional, 1–2493), which followed *Los Claros Varones d'España*. Cf. Jesús Domínguez Bordona's edition of the *Letras* and *Glosa a las coplas de Mingo Revulgo* in Clásicos Castellanos, Vol. 99 (Madrid, 1929); and the edition of *Claros Varones de Castilla*, *ibid.*, Vol. 49 (Madrid, 1942). This author follows the 1486 edition of all these works, utilizing in part the Zamora edition of 1543 in the mistaken belief that "it is the oldest extant in the Biblioteca Nacional." He knows the edition of 1500 only through Gallardo y Salvá, and thinks, erroneously, that the title "should be spread over four lines," etc.

6. Cf. Manuel Alonso, *Defensorium unitatis christianae*, Publicaciones de la Escuela de Estudios Hebraicos, (Madrid, 1943). In the bloody events of 1449 Pero Sarmiento, the *alcalde mayor*, seized power at Toledo; anti-Jewish measures were introduced and the Jewish quarter was sacked.

7. The phrase used by Pulgar, "ser consuegros" ("united by marriage') corresponds exactly to the Hebrew התחתן.

8. Clásicos Castellanos edition, title IV, pp. 36–47.

9. *Ibid.*, Title III, pp. 28–35.

10. Cf. Acts 1:1.

11. Cf. M. Alonso, *ibid.*, pp. 367 *et seq.* [Nicholas V, pope, 1447–1455].

12. Neither regional nor general historians refer to this statute (cf. M. Arigita, "Influencia social, religiosa y política de los judíos en el País Vasco", in *Euskal-Erria*, LXXV (1916), 110–24, and LXVI (1917), 59–67, 98–104, 155–62; and Gorosabel, *Cosas memorables de Guipúzcoa* (1889), Vol. 1, sec. V, pp. 317 *et seq.*). We consulted the learned Guipuzcoan scholar Don Fausto Arocena, who has kindly informed us by letter that the Registers of the period are missing and that there is no proof that the *Juntas* of Guipúzcoa adopted the agreement to which Pulgar refers.

Because of the opposition which it probably aroused (and Pulgar's influence as well?) it may never have received royal approval, and consequently may not have been incorporated into the code of laws drawn up later, the *Fuero de Guipúzcoa*. In this code the demand for purity of blood is based on two decrees, both approved by Charles V and his mother, Juana, on July 12, 1527, according to which no New Christian or descendant of New Christians could live or dwell or settle in the entire province; nor could anyone who was not a *hidalgo* be admitted as a resident in town or village councils. But this agreement, approved by the "Decree of Cestona" of 1527, "was very probably decreed at a much earlier date, for its practice appears to authorize the delay of royal approval. For all this, cf. the pamphlet printed by Guipúzcoa in 1773 with the title "La forma, y método uniforme, con que se deben sustanciar las causas, o pleytos de filiación, nobleza, y limpieza de sangre en esta M[uy] N[oble] y M[uy] L[eal] Provincia de Guipúzcoa." We are grateful to Sr. Arocena for this interesting information, which provides a very useful commentary on Pulgar's *letra*, and which reached us after this study was complete, through the good offices of our good friend Dr. Zaragueta.

13. He is undoubtedly referring to the subject of the *conversos*, though the sentence lends itself to misinterpretation.

14. Here he is obviously alluding to the *letra* on the Guipuzcoan statute, etc.

[15. Diego Hurtado de Mendoza was archbishop of Seville, 1486–1502.]

[16. Bartolomé José Gallardo (1776–1852) wrote *Ensayo de una biblioteca española de libros raros y curiosos*. Cantera is right to doubt whether Clemencín consulted it. If he did so, it must have been in manuscript, since it was published (with additions) only after Gallardo's death, by D. M. R. Zarco del Valle and D. J. Sancho Rayón in 4 vols. (Madrid, 1863–89).]

17. Cf. Luciano Serrano, *Los conversos D. Pablo de Santa Mariá y D. Alfonso de Cartagena*, Publicaciones de la Escuela de Estudios Hebraicos (Madrid, 1942).

[18. The constable Miguel Lucas de Iranzo, count of Quesada, was killed in Jaén cathedral in 1473.]

[19. Pope, 1471–1484.]

20. Luke 1:34. Carriazo's edition reads, "En el como de fiat istud." [In the Latin "comodo fiat istud." Carriazo's emendation is unnecessary: "comodo" = "quomodo"—"how."]

21. [Text: *seties septuagesis*]; cf. Matthew 18:22: *septuagies septies*. We have not succeeded in finding the passage in St. Augustine to which Pulgar alludes here.

[22. The reference is to Letter 159 (not 149 as Pulgar says), written to the *tribune Marcellinus!*]

[23. The text is evidently corrupt.]

[24. Andrés Bernáldez, author of *Memorias del reinado de los Reyes Católicos*, Cura de los Palacios, 1488–1513, chaplain of Diego de Deza, archbishop of Seville.]

[25. Pablo de Santa María, bishop of Cartagena, ca. 1405–1415 and of Burgos, 1415–1435. Alonso de Cartagena, bishop of Burgos, 1435–1456, son of Pablo.]

[26. "A Just Defense by every means of the doctor inquisitors, by a certain venerable man of this Holy Office against the said Ferdinand del Pulgar and it was an antidote rather than an attempt to impugn a process." Title corrupt.]

27. He reproduced only the *difinsorius justus* (sic).

[28. Text: "Astitit regina a dextris tuis in vestitu deauratu." Psalm 44:10 (Vulgate); 45:9 (Authorized Version).]

29. The manuscript is somewhat unclear here.

30. We know that it was established in a definitive form by Gregory IX about 1230 or 1232.

[31. Text: "setuagesis seçies" . . . "in omni patientia."]

32. Cf. Luke 3:8.

33. Cf. Exodus 32:28 (not 38 as in text), where the figure given is 3,000.

34. On Dathan and Abiram and their followers, cf. Numbers 16.

35. Caleb: cf. Numbers 14.

36. On Rabshakeh and the death of those "hundred fourscore and five thousand" men, cf. II Kings 19:35.

[37. "In omnem terram exiuit sonus eorum." Psalms 18:5; 19:3–4 (Authorized Version).]

38. The manuscript possibly reads "Marranacha." We shall leave for another occasion a discussion in *Sefarad* of the word *marrano* and its origin (*marrano* means "pig," "hog," and was a word of abuse for a Jew).

[39. Reference not traced.]

40. The manuscript uses this word *enviar*, "to send," rather than *entregar*, "to deliver."

41. Carriazo writes, "Then, and following the pattern of the impugnation, he changes direction and addresses himself to the author."

[42. I.e., Marcus Tullius Cicero.]

43. Cf. Bernáldez, *Historia*, chap. 32, "un jodío albardán (ed. BAE "albadán") del Rei que llamaban Alegre" (a Jewish buffoon of the king's that they called Alegre). Compare the Arabic *farhán*, "merry, jovial," from which "perhaps" is derived the Spanish *farfán*. In his study *Etimologías árabes* (published shortly before his sudden death, in Al-Andalus, IX [1944], 9–43). Don Miguel Asín [Palacios] does not include the word *albardán*.

44. Perhaps the anonymous accuser lived there.

45. Carriazo remarks (p. xv) that it is "strange and hard to believe" that the queen would confide such a task, and summon to such close contact with herself, any New Christian under such circumstances. But was it so unusual at that time?

46. On p. xviii he tells us that the letter sent at the time of Prince Don John's birth (June 30, 1478) to Dr. Talavera was "written after he had already left the court"; and on p. xxxvii that we should date his departure back to "sometime after October, 1477; but it had already occurred" by the time of the prince's birth.

47. Nor do we know when it began or ended. According to Carriazo, in 1482 he was "away from court," and during that same year he "announced to the queen that he was leaving for the court." Domínguez Bordona, on the other hand, states (Clásicos Castellanos, Vol. 49, p. xiv) that in 1481, when Pulgar was living in retirement in his home "and almost free of the pangs of envy and beginning to enjoy the benefits of contentment" (cf. *Letra* xxix), he was summoned by the Catholic Monarchs to write their *Crónica*, part of which he may already have written, "for in that same year he wrote to the queen informing her that he would go with the part he had written 'so that she could examine it'" (*Letra* xi). Note the phrase "beginning to enjoy," perhaps indicating that he had not lived in peaceful retirement for long.

[48. The uncle of the Inquisitor. Cf. p. 236, note 40.]

[49. See note 24.]

[50. Francisco, bishop of Coria, after 1449(?)–1458.]

51. Cf. M. Alonso, *ibid.*, pp. 22 *et seq.*; Amador de los Ríos, III, 118.

52. The letter contains frequent quotations from St. Augustine, St. Matthew, St. Peter, St. Paul, Boethius, St. Gregory, etc., and also from Josephus, but nothing from the Old Testament.

53. Cf. p. 247 in the BAE edition, and p. 53 in Carriazo's.

54. Cf. pp. 248 and 53, respectively, in the above editions.

55. Note the restriction.

56. We shall only alter, in certain cases, the punctuation he gives to the text.

57. As he was until 1483, the year in which he was appointed archbishop of Toledo; these words were obviously written after that date.

58. A speaks of their *informing* the monarchs of their opinions; B says that they *protested*.

59. This is the version given in B (BAE ed., p. 354); A (Carriazo's ed., pp. 423–24) says: "Therefore they decreed that all the Jews ... persons with proper authority ... and they saw to it that it was done ..."; also, A omits the passage between < >.

60. Ms. Dd. 13,086, Biblioteca Nacional.

[61. Chronicler, 1412(?)–1488(?), author of *Crónica de España*.]

FURTHER READING

J. H. Elliott, *Imperial Spain*, pp. 94–99.
H. Kamen, *The Spanish Inquisition* (London, 1965), especially chaps. 2 and 3.
A. A. Neuman, *The Jews in Spain* (2 vols; Philadelphia, 1942).
Fernando del Pulgar, *Claros Varones de Castilla*, ed. R. B. Tait (Oxford, 1971).

11 The Holy See and the Reconquest of the Kingdom of Granada (1479-1492)

JOSÉ GOÑI GAZTAMBIDE

The conquest of Granada was one of the "great deeds" of the reign of Ferdinand and Isabella. But behind the heroic exploits described by the chroniclers lay an immense diplomatic and financial effort. Sr. Goñi Gaztambide shows how the Spanish monarchs, requiring every resource, kept up a steady diplomatic pressure on the papacy in order to secure essential grants for the "crusade" and subsidies. The popes, especially Innocent VIII, felt the necessity for paying for the war against the Turks almost as much as the Catholic Kings did for that against the Moors. The Spanish Crown and the papacy are here shown as partners (as they were in the matter of episcopal appointments or the reform of the Church or the practice of the Inquisition), but they were partners who were constantly rubbing up against each other and having tiffs, even if these never led to an open break.

The series of documents printed as an appendix to the original study are here omitted, but references to them have been retained.

The humanist Lucio Marineo Sículo condemns the medieval kings and popes because, through their negligence and lack of incentive, they tolerated the Saracens for seven hundred years in one corner of Spain, not without grave offense to Christendom.[1] In 1890 the French historian Lavisse echoes the same reproach: "The popes and monarchs sent only a few isolated groups of knights across the Pyrenees, leaving to Spain the task of liberating herself."[2]

Such accusations are absolutely unfounded insofar as they refer to the Holy See. The papacy did not wash its hands of a struggle involving the future of Catholicism and the reestablishment of the Church in a country which had been Christian for a very long time. Sixtus IV and Innocent VIII,[3] when they upheld the war with Granada, were simply imitating their predecessors of the eleventh to fifteenth centuries, who constantly supported and encouraged the Reconquest, as is demonstrated by unnumerable concessions of "crusades" and tenths granted in aid of the fight against Islam. During the reign of the Catholic Monarchs the memory of the Bull of 1457 was still very much alive; it had been the first to contain a plenary indulgence applicable to the dead, which turned out to be very profitable for the royal coffers.[4] It is not strange that when Ferdinand and Isabella resolved to dislodge Islam from its last redoubt in the Peninsula, they immediately thought of appealing to the papacy for aid.

SIXTUS IV AND THE WAR WITH GRANADA; THE PACT OF CÓRDOBA

Sixtus IV (1471–1484) received the plan with the greatest enthusiasm. In the Catholic Monarchs he saw a combination of all the qualities necessary for the success of so difficult an undertaking: suitable age, nobility of spirit, talent, experience, authority, prudence, and intelligence. Therefore, at their request he issued the first Bull of the Crusade in favor of the war with Granada on November 13, 1479, in essence limited to granting plenary indulgence to all those cooperating in it.[5] But this was not enough for the Spanish monarchs. They wanted a new type of crusade offering greater inducements, one which would, in consequence, be more productive. At the outset of military operations they had great hopes of the total conquest of the Nasrid kingdom, but they clearly understood that the struggle would be long and costly.[6] How was it to be financed?

The queen's mind was constantly at work trying to think of ways to obtain money.[7] For his part, Ferdinand tried to make arrangements in Rome for imposition of a tithe on the revenues of ecclesiastical benefices. On May 2, 1481, the king of Naples complained because the pope was taking such a long time to find a solution for the problem. On the 14th of the following month he was told that the vicar of San Cebrián had arrived from Rome, bringing with him the tithes and certain suggestions by the pope.[8] These suggestions must have displeased the Spanish king, for undoubtedly the Roman Curia reserved one-third of the moneys to be collected for use in the war against the Turk. However, the Catholic Monarchs believed that for the time being it would be more useful to arrive at an understanding with the Holy See in this as in other matters pending between them.

By the terms of an agreement arrived at in Córdoba on July 3, 1482, the Spanish sovereigns and the pontifical representative Dominico Centurione agreed to launch an offensive against the infidel: the pope would attack the Turks, and the Catholic Monarchs the Moslems of Granada. To cover expenses, Sixtus IV was to impose on the ecclesiastical establishment of Castile, Aragon, and Sicily a 10 per cent tax on benefices and revenues from tithes for a year. He would also extend the "crusade" in compliance with an appeal to be drawn up by the monarchs, on condition that this did not exceed the usual form in such cases. One-third of the revenue from the "crusade" and the 10 per cent tax was to be applied to the war against the Turks, and would be delivered punctually to the person named by His Holiness. On the side of their majesties, the deputies were to be Fray Hernando de Talavera,[9] prior of the Hieronymite monastery of Nuestra Señora del Prado near Valladolid, and Pedro Martínez de Préxamo,[10] master of sacred theology, and on the pope's side a person freely chosen by him.[11]

From the military point of view the plan for the offensive seemed to favor Ferdinand and Isabella's designs, for if the Turks and Moslems were attacked simultaneously the Moors could not get reinforcements from the Turks. On the other hand, the pope was not asking for anything exceptional. In granting indulgences he often included the condition that part of the alms collected were to be sent to Rome for the struggle against the Turk.[12] However, Ferdinand and Isabella disapproved of the pope's request for one-third, and gave their consent only most unwillingly. In their opinion this requirement was an invention of persons who were laymen and lacked the fear of God, rather than the will of the pope,[13] as if they doubted His Holiness' warlike intentions or knew that Sixtus IV was not wholly scrupulous in the use of the funds destined for the fight against the infidel.[14]

True to his word, the pope imposed a tax on the ecclesiastical establishment and "sent his Apostolic nuncio to the king and queen with his Bull of the Crusade, containing generous indulgences for all who acquired it. The king and queen received this papal nuncio and the bull in the monastery of Santo Domingo el Real in Madrid with a solemn procession, in which marched the cardinal of Spain;[15] Don Alonso de Fonseca, archbishop of Santiago; Don Diego Hurtado de Mendoza, bishop of Palencia; Don Gonzalo de Heredia, bishop of Barcelona; Don Juan de Maluenda, bishop of Coria, and many other prelates."[16]

THE BULL OF THE CRUSADE OF 1482

If those venerable bishops from the most diverse dioceses of Spain paid attention to the contents of the bull, they undoubtedly observed the marked difference which existed between this concession of a crusade and the previous ones, for example that of 1479. And if their view had been able to take in the future at a glance, they would have seen that this bull, though somewhat modified, would continue almost without interruption during the coming centuries.

In fact, a rapid glance at the pontifical document suffices to show that the Bull of 1482 is not like those formerly granted to Spain, but is much richer in graces and favors. While previous bulls contain merely the indulgence for the crusade and an odd privilege or two, this one spurs on the crusade as well as the contributor in money by offering a number of advantages.

It begins with a solemn exordium in which Sixtus IV, perceiving that the resources of the Catholic Monarchs are not sufficient to recover the kingdom of Granada, but that it is necessary to seek warriors and other aid both in Spain and abroad, exhorts all men to assist Ferdinand and Isabella with their wealth and persons according to their various abilities. Those who take personal part in the expedition, pay for their own substitute, or at least give a minimum contribution of two silver *reales* can take advantage not only of the plenary indulgence customarily offered to crusaders in the Holy Land, but of other spiritual privileges, such as that of freely choosing a confessor with almost total power to absolve major crimes, omission of canonical hours, simony, censure, and to commute vows. They are also given the right to ecclesiastical burial in a place subject to interdict, and anyone who gives two additional *reales* for the care of those who fall ill in the course of the war, and for the construction of churches in conquered territory, is given a share in all the good works performed within the Church.

Chaplains and soldiers are granted special favors. Priests accompanying the armies can celebrate Mass in the camps before dawn and are exempted from the obligation of residence, fasting, and recitation of the Divine Office during the time they are occupied in the war and it may not be convenient for them to recite the Breviary. Soldiers are exempt from the law of Sunday rest and from fasting.

To increase revenues still more, the pope applies to the crusade legacies left for the ransom of captives and moneys which would have been spent on public feasts. He proclaims peace, issues a prohibition on interfering with the wars against the Moors or using the crusade's funds for any other purpose, and names as his deputies Maestro Francisco de Ortiz,[17] Pedro Martínez de Préxamo, dean of Toledo, and Fray Hernando de Talavera, prior of El Prado, giving them broad powers to pass judgment on illegally acquired profits, to absolve from simony, censure connected with simony, and irregularities, to absolve in certain degrees, to regularize marriages and legitimize offspring, and, finally, to enforce exhibition of wills.

Sixtus IV, who understood the significance of the struggle,

presented a great silver crucifix to the Catholic Monarchs as a standard, which was carried before the army throughout the entire campaign.[18] The fight against Islam took on the air of a crusade, as in the best times of the Reconquest. The Spanish Church mobilized all its propaganda resources. The pope's appeal to the religious feeling of the faithful resounded from every pulpit in Castile, Aragon, Sicily, and Sardinia, and exalted the ideal of holy war against the infidel.[19]

Its success was astonishing. Thousands of crusaders from France, Germany, England, Ireland, Poland, and especially from Switzerland flocked to fight under the silver standard of the Holy Cross.[20] The Swiss "are warlike men and fight afoot, and are determined never to turn their backs on their enemies," says Fernando del Pulgar, the Catholic Monarchs' secretary and chronicler.[21] Brackmann says that they had the best troops of their type at that period, and were Spain's teachers in military art, thus laying the foundation for the Spanish army's later fame in war.[22] But the foreign crusaders were no more than simple auxiliary troops. The chief weight of battle fell on the Andalusian and Castilian armies.

However, the bull's effectiveness was shown much more in the economic sphere than in recruitment of volunteers. Before it was issued, the Catholic Monarchs had thought of the crusade as one of the chief supports for the struggle,[23] and they were certainly not mistaken. They themselves were the first to give an example, contributing to the indulgence by donating a hundred florins.[24] Their example was imitated by the nobles and the people, and thus "great sums of money, which were spent on wages and in the other things required for the war against the Moors," as the chronicler mentioned above puts it, were obtained.[25]

Ferdinand and Isabella could feel satisfied and grateful in regard to the pope who had made possible such an abundant and reliable source of revenue. And now the moment came to turn over part of the profits to him, according to the terms of the agreement made in Córdoba. However, when the pope's nuncio and collector, Firmano di Perugia, tried to carry out the terms of the pact, he encountered systematic opposition, and his attempt to collect the sum agreed upon met with total failure.[26] Rome added an energetic claim to his protests.

INNOCENT VIII AND THE CAMPAIGN OF GRANADA; REVALIDATION OF THE "CRUSADE" IN 1485 AND THE TERCIA

The new pope, Innocent VIII (1484–1492), was in no position to give up any of the rights of the Apostolic Chamber, in spite of his personal good will.[27] He had found the papacy's resources not only exhausted but burdened with heavy debts,[28] and he also had to ward off the Turkish threat which menaced the coasts of Italy.[29] Immediately after his accession he invited the European powers, Spain among them, to join forces against the common enemy; and in a special brief he exhorted Ferdinand to the defense of Sicily, at that time united to the Spanish Crown.[30] The pope foresaw the preparation of a great fleet which would be of effective help in the defense of the Sicilian coasts.[31]

All his attention seemed to be concentrated on the Mediterranean battleground. Would Spain's forces also go there, abandoning her national war?

The Catholic Monarchs impressed upon him the importance to Christendom of continuing the task of reconquest. If it were interrupted, all the expenses and efforts so far invested would be lost, and the Spanish kingdom exposed to grave danger. Convinced by the strength of these arguments, on January 29, 1485, Innocent VIII revalidated for one year the crusade of Sixtus IV, which had been canceled at the beginning of his pontificate according to the usual rules of the pontifical chancery.[32] He also declared that in Aragon the indulgence could be earned by turning over in *dineros* the amount equivalent to six *reales*, at the rate of twenty-two *dineros* per *real*, for the latter coin did not circulate in Aragon.[33] He banned wearing of the insignia of the Cross by combatants unless they had received it at the hands of the deputies,[34] and extended the graces of the crusade to the kingdom of Navarre.[35] But however great his desire to please the monarchs, the financial straits of his treasury were such that he found it impossible to grant them the one-third corresponding to the Apostolic Chamber, which the Spanish ambassador Francisco de Rojas had so persuasively requested of him.[36]

Holding firm in this attitude, the pope charged his new deputy and collector, the Genoese merchant Cipriano Gentili, to demand and collect the third share promised to Sixtus IV. Without the intervention of the pontifical representative, the Spanish agents Fray Hernando de Talavera and Pedro Martínez de Préxamo could do nothing, on pain of nullity and invalidity. Gentili was also to take charge of the moneys in possession of Firmano di Perugia, Francesco Pinello, and other merchants, and to recover the sums of money in arrears; for this purpose the collectors were to turn over their account books to him.[37]

REACTION OF THE CATHOLIC MONARCHS; THEIR IDEAL FOR THE CRUSADE

When the king and queen learned of the pope's decision, they angrily refused to accept the revalidation of the crusade and, first to Cipriano Gentili and then to their ambassadors in Rome, made it clear that they were not inclined to accept these terms. Their reply is the document which best shows us the ideal of the crusade that inspired the Spanish sovereigns in their war with Granada. They lament the fact that the pope apparently does not believe what has been explained to him so often concerning the motive for the struggle.

We have not been moved nor are we moved to this war by any desire to enlarge out realms and seigniories, nor by greed to obtain greater revenues than those we possess, nor by any wish to pile up treasures; for should we wish to increase our sovereignty and enrich our revenues, we could do this with much less danger and travail and expenditure than we are putting forth in this. But our desire to serve God, and our zeal for His holy Catholic faith, make us put all other interests aside and forget the constant travails and dangers which continue to increase for this cause; and although we could not only keep our treasures, and further have many more from the Moors themselves, which they would give us most willingly for the sake of peace, yet we refuse the treasures offered to us and pour out our own, hoping only that the holy Catholic faith will be multiplied and that Christendom will be quit of so constant a danger as she has here at her very doors, if these infidels of the kingdom of Granada are not uprooted and cast out from Spain.

No pope had ever asked money for the granting of a crusade except Sixtus IV,

and this we believe to have been an invention of laymen who fear God little, rather than the will of the pope.

If our subjects were to learn that part of the money they are giving for the expulsion of the infidel is being put to other uses, they would refrain from taking the bull, and so the part for the pope's use would be insignificant, and the part left for us so much reduced that the emolument we would receive would be very small.

If the needs of His Holiness are as great as he says, then he has all of Christendom to which to appeal by means of a crusade, a tithe, or what he will; for, excepting Hungary, no other country has any reason to excuse itself, as we would not excuse ourselves were we not forced to it by necessity.

You must put it to His Holiness that if he refuses or delays revalidation of the crusade, he will be responsible if the war is interrupted or if the defense of Sicily is not carried out as it should be. What this would bring to pass in offense to God, scorn of the Christian religion, dishonor and a burden of conscience to the pope, we leave to his consideration. But on the other hand, if the undertaking of Granada is successful, we will place our kingdoms at the disposal of the Holy See. In case the pope obstructs or delays this concession, you will try to have an audience with His Holiness in the presence of some of the cardinals most favorable to us, and if this does not suffice, in the presence of the Sacred College; and you will declare to him that by no means will we accept the crusade on condition of giving him part of its benefits, and that he must bear the blame if the war loses its ardor.[38]

The modern writer W. T. Walsh, though he is unaware of this document, has admirably interpreted the ideal of the Spanish monarch: "Left to his own courses, he would probably have followed the example of several of his ancestors; he would have waged a valiant medieval warfare against the Moors, defeated them, made the most favorable terms he could with them, then turned to gain an advantage over France; then perhaps, at a later, more favorable time, have struck the Moors again and taken what profit he could. He was always content to take small and sure gains; like a skilled and cautious gambler, he preferred to keep part of his resources in reserve."[39]

To the weight of these arguments was added the irresistible march of events. In the spring of that same year, 1485, the king succeeded in taking over a large amount of territory within the Nasrid kingdom. After a fifteen-day siege he captured Ronda, "one of the strongest cities in Europe," liberating "more than five hundred Christians who were captive in the straitest captivity." Ferdinand decided to inform his ambassadors Antonio Geraldino and Francisco de Rojas, "so that you may let our most holy Father know, for the pleasure His Holiness will feel, that in the time of his pontificate it has pleased Our Lord to give victory to the Christians against the infidels; and also so that His Holiness may see and know on what things we spend our time and money here in Spain. And should it please His Holiness to aid us with his benediction and his word only, granting us wholly that indulgence which former popes were accustomed to grant in such cases, with the same terms under which they granted it, great things would be done in the service of God, and these my kingdoms would be relieved in order to aid and serve the Christians who in other lands are hard pressed by the infidel."[40]

According to Pulgar, "the pope and the cardinals, when they

heard this news, were greatly pleased."[41] The Catholic Monarchs' victory over the Moors was celebrated in Rome with great rejoicing.[42] Innocent VIII, compliant by nature, at last submitted. On August 26, 1485, he renounced his rights in favor of the Spanish Crown, renewing the bull unconditionally.[43] He further ordered the clergy to contribute to the war with a tenth of all their revenues, charging the cardinal of Spain with the duty of determining this and distributing the money as he thought best. The cardinal fixed the amount at 100,000 Aragonese florins.[44]

Pulgar assures us that the moneys thus obtained were to be used for the purpose assigned to them by the pope: "And out of what was collected from the crusade and the subsidy of the clergy and the fines imposed on those who had reverted to Judaism and become reconciled with the Church and other fines, and from other ordinary revenues and from every source where money might be obtained, they [the Catholic Monarchs] ordered them to be spent on things for the war."[45]

In the following year Innocent VIII gave further proof of his interest in the struggle against the infidel by replying favorably to the Spanish ambassador's petitions concerning the crusade, the tenth, and the inquisition,[46] and exhorting Ferdinand and Isabella in separate briefs to continue to wage war on the Moors so that, once the Reconquest was over, they could turn their flourishing forces against the Turks in alliance with the other Christian princes. At the same time he thanked them for the donation of 10,000 ducats obtained from the subsidy.[47]

An English nobleman, Lord Scales,[48] took part in the campaign of this year, 1486. He had come with three hundred doughty artillerymen and archers "to serve God and make war against the Moors."[49]

FURTHER EXTENSION OF THE TENTH AND "CRUSADE" IN 1487

On his side, Ferdinand was convinced that not only the glory of God but the honor of the Holy See was involved in the total expulsion of the Saracens.[50] Therefore he felt he had a right to the pope's support. Maintenance of a fleet to keep watch over the Straits, guarding of the conquered cities and castles, payment of wages, and supply of the artillery used up a great deal of money. Since the ordinary revenues of the Crown plus a new loan were insufficient, he asked for a further extension of the tenth and "crusade" through his ambassador Iñigo López de Mendoza, count of Tendilla.[51] The latter had been sent to Rome (February 8, 1486) with the double mission of settling the dispute between Innocent VIII and the king of Naples, and declaring obedience to the pope. Both before and after his embassy he fought heroically in the Reconquest, was Gonzalo de Córdoba's teacher in the arts of war, and was the first Christian military governor of Granada. The king and queen chose him for this embassy "because, besides being a valiant knight, he was well prepared in Latin letters and a discreet man of good prudence for such affairs. And they sent with him a doctor of their Council named Juan de Medina ... who was later bishop of Astorga" (1489–1493) and of Badajoz (1493–1495).[52]

After peace was concluded on August 11, 1486, between the pope and the king of Naples, he made a solemn entrance into Rome on September 13, and on the 18th of that month, in a public consistory, presented obedience to the pope in the name of the realms governed by the Catholic Monarchs. During the ceremony a speech was made by the prothonotary Antonio Geraldino, secretary and chronicler to the king, who formed part of the delegation in the capacity of third ambassador.[53] The count of Tendilla remained in Rome until August 28, 1487, when he returned to Spain.

With his dexterity and prestige he obtained great privileges and favors both for himself and for the Catholic Monarchs. He had no difficulty in procuring a further tenth on ecclesiastical revenues, set by the cardinal of Spain at 100,000 Aragonese florins.[54] The ambassador showed generosity toward the pope by presenting him with 10,000 ducats.[55] In regard to the "crusade," he encountered lively opposition from the Holy See. Innocent VIII put forward the breakdown of the Apostolic Chair's authority and the economic difficulties being experienced by the officials of the Roman Curia. If he extended it again, these officials would redouble the complaints and protests which they daily brought to His Holiness. In the end he acceded only through pressure by the Spanish cardinal Rodrigo de Borja, whose friendly pleadings forced the pope to grant the "crusade" (on February 26, 1487) for another year, counting from September 1, 1487.[56]

On September 11 of that same year, 1487, the grateful monarchs sent to the supreme pontiff of the Church a hundred Moors whom they had captured when Málaga was taken.[57] When the city surrendered on August 18, 1487, the king "sent his standard and the cross of the crusade," which Fray Juan de Belalcázar placed on the Tower of Homage, followed by the banner of Santiago and the royal flag.[58] Ferdinand "gave hearty thanks to Our Lord God and expressed his gratitude for the great victory He had bestowed on him there. And the queen and the Infanta, with their duennas and ladies and all the royal retinue, kneeling on the ground, offered to Our Lord and to the most glorious Virgin St. Mary much prayer and praise, and to the Apostle Santiago. And all the devout Christians of the royal camp did the same. And the bishops and clergy there assembled chanted the *Te Deum laudamus* and *Gloria in excelsis Deo*," says Bernáldez.[59] This same chronicler adds that "in the royal camp at Málaga were many clergy and friars of all the Orders who said masses and preached throughout the camp, to the sound as well as the ill, and gave plenary absolution to all by virtue of the Holy Crusade."[60]

The campaign which followed was crowned with such brilliant success that the king felt it necessary to inform the pope of his victories twice over. In the second of his letters he said,

These few days past, continuing this holy enterprise against the Moors of the kingdom of Granada, the enemies of our holy Catholic faith, to the praise and glory of our Redeemer Jesus Christ, I sent my army against the city of Vera, on the borders of this my kingdom of Murcia; and it pleased God that, without the slightest resistance, the city fell to me together with other towns, fortresses, and villages to the number of fifty, and in which there are twenty leagues of land and more, all won from a single owner, and among them are impregnable fortresses and some on the coasts and on ports of the sea. Your Holiness may well believe that what has been done this year in the service of Our Lord and to the increase of the Christian religion is no less worthy of esteem than what has been accomplished in any of the years past. And since it is just that Your Beatitude as immediate lieutenant and vicar of Our Lord should know of all this, I have caused this letter to be written so that you may give thanks to Him who is well pleased to act thus in His own cause, and to implore Him to grant that the work may go forward.[61]

Innocent VIII answered the first letter, congratulating him on his triumphs and urging him to dispatch quickly the undertaking he had begun. As soon as the Reconquest was over, the pope, with the help of the Catholic Monarchs, planned to pass from the defensive to the offensive and to crush the Turkish power.[62]

RENEWAL OF THE TENTH AND "CRUSADE" IN 1489:
THE POPE'S RESISTANCE; ABUSES IN SPAIN AND
SICILY

The pontiff of Rome, when he encouraged the struggle against the Moors, was working in the interest of universal Christianity. It seems, then, that he should have wanted to renew the "crusade" and tenth as soon as they expired. But in fact he always had some more or less reasonable pretext for putting off granting them. This time he took refuge behind some violations of ecclesiastical freedom and certain abuses committed by the king's officials; so firmly that neither all the pleas of the Spanish ambassadors Bernardino López de Carvajal, bishop of Astorga (1488–1489),[63] nor of Juan Ruiz de Medina, the Apostolic prothonotary, nor the mediation of the vice-chancellor Rodrigo de Borja and the datary Antoniotto Pallavicini, bishop of Orense,[64] availed to make him change his attitude.

Was it a question of opposition in principle or simply a calculated resistance? The Spanish diplomats thought it was the latter. They suspected that what the pope was trying to obtain was simply a payment larger than 10,000 ducats, owing to the increasing needs pressing upon him. It could all be satisfactorily arranged with fifteen thousand. The Spaniards themselves conceived a plan of attack. The Catholic Monarchs were to write two letters as soon as possible: a secret one for the exclusive use of the ambassadors and another to show to the pope and the cardinals. In this second letter the subject of the abuses would be brought up tactfully, with a promise to correct them if they could be proved; but the subject of the tenth and "crusade" was to be expressed very harshly, exhibiting astonishment that the pope would not give a greater favor than in previous years, when the need had increased, the revenues obtained had doubled, and the demonstration made by Their Majesties on behalf of His Holiness had also been duplicated. If the pope refused to grant the tenth and crusade for two years, the ambassadors were not to bring up the subject again; Their Majesties would remedy matters as best they could.

In the secret letter the monarchs were to state whether they would accept the "crusade" and tenth for another year for 10,000 ducats, or if they would accept the "crusade" only, on condition that it would be valid for two years. The pope, added the ambassadors, was enchanted with the count of Tendilla, who had given him 10,000 ducats in cash simply for the tenth, not counting the "crusade." They could not carry out their charge with more diligence than they were already employing, owing to the difficulties they were encountering in the Curia, difficulties which some Spaniards took care to increase by means of false letters and reports.[65]

This plan, we do not know why, failed to produce the immediate effect which its authors had hoped for. Meanwhile the needs of the war became more pressing. Since the siege of Baza "continued overlong, and the time had consumed a great sum of money which the queen had at first, from the "crusade" as well as the subsidy and from her own revenues," she had to take out a new loan, and when this was not sufficient had to pawn her jewels, pearls, and precious stones in Barcelona and Valencia.[66]

At last, on October 9, 1489, the Bull of the Crusade was extended for a year. The deputies named in it, the bishops of Ávila and Leon, Fray Hernando de Talavera and Don Alfonso de Valdivieso,[67] received authorization to preach the indulgence in all the kingdoms under the sovereignty of the Spanish Crown, even in Navarre, which still maintained its independence.[68] A few days later, on November 13, 1489, the sovereigns were warned to correct the enormous excesses of their ministers, especially in the exaction of the tenth, in the kingdoms of Castile and particularly in the island of Sicily. They should try to see that the spiritual gifts of the crusade were received uprightly and devoutly, and administered by ecclesiastical and God-fearing persons. Moderation was to be used in collecting the subsidy, so that in the future no one would have reason to complain. A storm of protest had reached Rome concerning the unjustified demands made on Spanish officials, a repetition of which was to be avoided at all costs in order to preserve the monarchs' good name and the honor of the Apostolic See.[69]

There is no doubt whatever that this reproach was justified, for the abuses were all too clear, but perhaps it made the sovereigns recall the adage of *medice, cura te ipsum* [Physician, heal thyself]. The officials of the Roman Curia were not exactly models of probity and rectitude themselves. In spite of the reprimand, relations between the supreme pontiff and the conquerors of the Moorish armies continued to be cordial. The pope was satisfied because the king and queen had subjugated almost all of the kingdom of Granada, even though the price had been very high. The conquest of Baza caused them tremendous expenditures and obliged them to contract enormous debts. Further, simply to hold on to the conquered cities was a heavy drain on the royal treasury. If the end of the war was to be brought about quickly, funds for the "crusade" would have to be increased. Therefore, at the insistence of the Spanish sovereigns, the pope reduced the quota of alms for poor regions, permitted the use of the former quota in richer districts, and authorized the use of censures against those who, after signing their names in the registry books, did not take up the bull within the specified period of time.[70]

LAST CONCESSION OF THE "CRUSADE" AND THE SURRENDER OF GRANADA

Finally, on October 1, 1491, the pope renewed the Bull of the Crusade for the last time, valid for one year.[71] On January 2,1492, the city of Granada surrendered. The count of Tendilla and many other knights entered the Alhambra and "displayed on the highest tower, first the standard of Jesus Christ, which was the Holy Cross that the king carried always with him in this holy undertaking; and he and the queen and the prince and all the host bent low before the Holy Cross and gave great thanks and praise to Our Lord; and the archbishops and clergy said the *Te Deum laudamus*; and then they displayed the banner of Santiago."[72]

The king decreed that, since all the monasteries and religious houses of Spain had offered prayers for the obtention of victory, processions should now be held and thanks given to Our Lord for so signal a favor.[73] Not only Spain; all of Europe celebrated with great rejoicing the glorious ending of the drama of reconquest, but nowhere was the victory more celebrated than in Rome. On the very day that Granada fell, Ferdinand the Catholic gave the news to the pope in the following letter:

> Most Holy Father: Your most humble and devoted son the king of Castile, of Leon, of Aragon, of Sicily, of Granada, et cetera, kisses your feet and your blessed hands and very humbly commends himself to Your Holiness. May it please Your Holiness to know that Our Lord has been pleased to give us full victory over the king and the Moors of Granada, enemies of our holy Catholic faith; for today, on the second day of

January of this year ninety and two, the city of Granada has surrendered to us, together with the Alhambra and all the troops and with all the castles and fortresses which remained for us to conquer within this kingdom, and we have it all in our power and sovereignty. I inform Your Holiness of this because of the great joy you will have of it; for Our Lord has given Your Holiness so much good fortune, after many travails, expenditures, and deaths, and outpouring of the blood of our subjects and citizens, this kingdom of Granada which for seven hundred and eighty years was occupied by the infidels, that in your day and with your aid the victory has been won which the former pontiffs, your predecessors, so much desired and aided, to the glory of God Our Lord and the exaltation of our holy Catholic faith, the glory and honor of Your Holiness and of the Holy Apostolic See.[74]

This letter reached Rome a month after the event, on the night of January 31–February 1. The pope had it entered in his archive in Spanish by the good offices of the Spaniard Luis Peñafiel;[75] and, accompanied by the College of Cardinals, went in procession from the Vatican to the Spanish national church of Santiago, where a Mass of thanksgiving was celebrated and the papal benediction given. As we know, a pageant was presented in Rome representing the conquest of the kingdom of Granada and the triumphal entry of the Spanish monarchs, while Cardinal Rodrigo de Borja gave a bullfight for the people of Rome.[76]

The queen survived the triumph of her arms only eight years. In her will she charged the crown prince and princess to continue without interruption the conquest of Africa and the struggle for the Faith against the infidel.[77] Her codicil to the will shows how scrupulous she was in the use of crusade funds: "Moreover, inasmuch as the Holy See has granted us divers times the "crusade" and jubilees and subsidies for the expenses of the conquest of the kingdom of Granada and against the Moors of Africa and against the Turks, enemies of our holy Catholic faith, so that they may be spent according to the terms of the bulls that have been granted

us, I command that if from said "crusades" and jubilees and subsidies some few *maravedís* may have been taken by our command-
ment to be spent for other things of our service, and not for the
things for which they were granted and given, the said *maravedís*
be taken and the things that have been used from them, and that
they be discharged and paid from the incomes of my kingdoms in
the year of my death, so that they may be spent in accordance with
the form of said concessions and bulls."[78]

When Diego Saavedra Fajardo speaks of the scruples of conscience of the Catholic Monarchs he says, without mentioning
the date, that "the Queen Isabella was distressed to see ninety
cuentos together which had been taken from the moneys of the
"crusade," and commanded that they be spent immediately in
those uses which the Apostolic bulls required."[79]

ECONOMIC IMPORTANCE OF THE "CRUSADE"

Although it is not possible to present exact figures of the
amounts of money collected at this time, since the account books
prior to 1509 have disappeared, there is no doubt that the economic
yield of the "crusade" was considerable from the outset. Though
we lack other more precise figures, this fact is quite clearly
demonstrated by the interest taken by the Catholic Monarchs in
obtaining uninterrupted concession of the bull from the popes,
and the efforts made by Sixtus IV and Innocent VIII to keep
one-third of its revenues for themselves. But fortunately there is
no lack of contemporary references, or references of the period
shortly following the events, which fully confirm our supposition.

We have already cited the testimony of Pulgar, who in referring
to the Bull of 1482 says that with it "a great sum of money was
obtained." We also know, through the instruction given by the
Catholic Monarchs to their ambassadors in Rome in 1485, that
Ferdinand and Isabella saw in the "crusade" "one of the chief aids
and supports to carry on" the war with Granada.

In his "Relazione di Spagna" Guicciardini, ambassador of
Florence at the court of the Catholic King in 1512–13, informed his

republic of the importance of the "crusade" in these words: "At first, when the affair was fresh, they profited from it a good deal, and say in particular that in the year the king took Málaga [1487] 800,000 ducats were collected. This sum has grown less since, for in the cities there are few who take it up; in the country many do so, almost forced to it by fear. Nevertheless, even today it usually brings in about 300,000 ducats. These popes think it a small thing to grant, but it has been so great that without such subsidies this king not only would not have taken Granada and so many other foreign realms, but he would have had difficulty in keeping Aragon and Castile."[80] Guicciardini's figures are likely to be accurate; for he, as ambassador of an Italian power, would have been able to obtain exact information from the contract holders of the "crusade" themselves, who were often Italians. On the other hand, his figures coincide with the account books of the sixteenth century, according to which the "crusade" furnished to the public treasury, between 1509 and 1571, an annual median net sum of 300,000 ducats, and therefore was one of the richest and most reliable sources of revenue in the Spanish state.

NOTES

1. Lucius Marineus Siculus, *De Rebus Hispaniae*, Liber XX (this work was published in 1530), in *Hispaniae Illustratae . . . Scriptores*, I (Frankfurt, 1603), 489.
2. E. Lavisse, *Vue générale de l'histoire de l'Europe* (Paris, 1890), p. 97.
[3. Popes, 1471–1484 and 1484–1492.]
4. Alonso de Palencia, *Crónica de los Reyes Católicos*, trans. from Latin into Spanish by D. A. Paz y Melia, I (Madrid, 1904), 239–40; Diego de Valera, *Memorial de diversas hazañas: Crónicas de los eyes de Castilla*, III (Madrid, 1878), 15 (BAE, Vol. 70); Mariana, *Historia General de España*, Book 22, chap. 18.
5. See the text of the bull in [the original] Appendix 1. At the Cortes of Toledo in April, 1480, the king and queen told the grand master of Santiago that they "had been planning to give orders for the war against the Moors, but that now they were busy with forming an armada against the Turks" (Pulgar, *Crónica de los Reyes Católicos*, part II, chap. 96).
6. Letters from Ferdinand the Catholic to the bishop of Gerona, his ambassador in Rome, and to Count Trivento, captain general of the armada of the king of Naples, dated June 10 and 12, 1482, respectively,

374   SPAIN IN THE FIFTEENTH CENTURY

published by A. de la Torre, "Los Reyes Católicos y Granada", in *Hispania*, 4 (1944), 251–57. In his letter of May 12, 1482, to the viceroy of Sardinia, the king alludes to the "infinite expenses" he has had and will continue to have (*ibid.*, p. 256).

7. Fernando del Pulgar, *Crónica de los Reyes Católicos*, part III, chap. 14 (BAE, 70, 379).

8. A. de la Torre, *Documentos sobre relaciones internacionales de los Reyes Católicos*, Vol. I: 1479–1483 (Barcelona, 1949), 145–46, 155–57.

9. On Fray Hernando de Talavera, the queen's confessor, bishop of Ávila (1485–1493[?]), and first archbishop of Granada (1493–1507), see A. Fernández de Madrid, *Vida de fray Hernando de Talavera*, ed. F. González Olmedo (Madrid, 1931); Fr. José de Sigüenza, *Historia de la Orden de San Jerónimo*, in Nueva Biblioteca de Autores Españoles, 12 (Madrid, 1912), 288 ff.; Miguel Mir, *Discurso preliminar a la edición de los opúsculos de Talavera*, ibid., Vol. 5; F. Martínez, *La España imperial, Fray Hernando de Talavera, confesor de los Reyes Católicos y primer arzobispo de Granada* (Madrid, 1942).

10. Pedro Martínez de Préxamo is the same cleric who officially accused, and refuted by the use of various works, the heretic Pedro de Osma, with whom he had studied in the College of San Bartolomé. He was a disciple of Tostado, vespers professor of theology at the University of Salamanca, canon and vicar general of Segovia, first magistral canon of Toledo, and was presented in 1486 for the deanship of the Imperial City. On January 18, 1486, he was elevated to the bishopric of Badajoz, from which he went to that of Coria on January 23, 1493, dying in 1495. Concerning him see also *Historia del colegio viejo de San Bartolomé de Salamanca*, by Francisco Ruiz de Vergara; 2d ed. corrected and enlarged by Joseph de Roxas y Contreras, marquis of Alventos, 1 (Madrid, 1766), 139–41; M. Menéndez y Pelayo, *Heterodoxos*, 1 (Madrid, 1880), 554–55; Gil González Dávila, *Teatro eclesiástico de las ciudades e iglesias catedrales de España*, 1 (Salamanca, 1618, teatro de Badajoz), 41–43; J. Solano de Figueroa, *Historia eclésiastica de la ciudad y obispado de Badajoz* (Badajoz, 1933).

11. The complete text of the agreement is in Simancas, Patronato Real, 19, 8; in the [original] Appendix 2 we reproduce the part having to do with the crusade and tithe. On Centurione's embassy, see Pulgar, *Crónica*, part II, chap. 104 (BAE, 70, 362–63); L. Serrano, *Los Reyes Católicos y la ciudad de Burgos* (Madrid, 1943), pp. 266 *et seq.* This work contains information of a local nature concerning our theme.

12. Pastor, *Historia de los papas*, IV (Barcelona, 1910), 362.

13. [See original] Appendix 5.

14. Pastor, *loc. cit.*

[15. Pedro González de Mendoza, bishop of Calahorra, 1454–1468; of Sigüenza 1468–1483; cardinal, 1473; archbishop of Toledo, 1483–1495.]

16. Pulgar, *loc. cit.*, n. 7. The bull begins with the words "Ortodoxe fidei" (August 10, 1482) and is in the Vatican Archives Reg. Vat. 621, fols. 2 verso–3 verso; there is a fragment in Raynaldus, *Annales Ecclesiastici*,

ad a[nnum] 1482, no. 41, N. Paulus, *Geschichte des Ablasses am Ausgang des Mittelalters* (Paderborn, 1923), Vol. III, thinks that its date is 1483.

17. The appointment as deputy of Maestro Francisco Ortiz, archdean of Briviesca and apostolic notary, was a reward by the pope for his loyalty to the Holy See; for in the conflict between the Catholic Kings and Sixtus IV regarding provision of the bishopric of Cuenca, Ortiz was imprisoned for having obeyed papal letters and orders. His attitude aroused the monarchs' ire, and in the agreement of Córdoba they forced him to resign the deanship of Toledo so that they could present Pedro Martínez de Préxamo for the post. (Simancas, Patronato Real, 19, 8.)

18. Andrés Bernáldez, *Crónica de los Reyes Católicos*, chap. 87 (BAE, 70, 632; also see 643).

19. See note 7. That the crusade was preached in Sardinia is shown by a dispatch concerning the crusade from the year 1484, preserved at Simancas. (Section 19, Hacienda, Expedientes, Series V, Leg. 888, not in folios.)

20. W. T. Walsh, *Isabella of Spain* (New York, 1930); Spanish ed., trans. A. de Mestas, 3d ed. (Santander, 1939), p. 309; A. Brackmann, *Das mittelalterliche Spanien in seiner europaische Bedeutung*, in Archivo Ibero-Americano 12 (1938), 16.

21. Pulgar, part III, chap. 21 (BAE, 70, 387).

22. *Loc. cit.*, n. 20.

23. [See original] Appendix 5.

24. See [original] illustration. There is preserved in Simancas (Patronato Real 27, 29) another similar papal letter of Ferdinand the Catholic's, stating that he also had received the indulgence for having contributed a hundred gold florins for the war with Granada.

25. See note 7.

26. According to a document dated at his residence in Seville on November 6, 1484, preserved in the Archive of the Cathedral of Burgos, Book 60, fol. 8 verso.

27. Immediately after his election he promised to revalidate the "crusade" and tenth and to retain none of the proceeds. A. de la Torre, *Documentos*, II (Barcelona, 1950), 145-46.

28. He complains of this many times, for example in a brief to the king and queen of Spain on December 7: "Invenimus in hac nostra ad apostolatus apicem assumptione aerarium Camerae Apostolicae non modo pecuniis exhaustum, sed debitis etiam magnis gravatum." Vatican Archive, Arm. 39, Liber Brev. 18, 74; brief to Bologna on August 2, 1486, in Hist. Jahrbuch VI; Liber 19, fols. 392, 406, and 414 in Arm. 39 of the Vatican Archive.

29. Brief of January 30, 1485, in [original] Appendix 4. Concerning Innocent VIII's efforts to combat the Turkish peril, see Pastor, V (Barcelona, 1911), 297-320.

30. Raynaldus, ad a[nnum] 1484, no. 67-68.

31. [Original] Appendix 4 and Pastor, V, 298.

32. [Original] Appendixes 3 and 4.

33. Brief of January 30, 1485, "Quoniam in bullis," in the Vatican Archive, Arm. 39, Vol. 18, fol. 107 verso.
34. Bull "Cum superioribus" of February 11, 1485, in Simancas, Patronato Real, 19, 15 original; Book of copies, no. 1, 166.
35. Bull "Nuper cupientes" of February 20, 1485, in Simancas, Patronato Real, 19, 12 original; Book of copies, no. 1, 166.
36. [Original] appendix 4. Concerning the ambassador, see A. Rodríguez Villa, "Don Francisco de Rojas, embajador de los Reyes Católicos," BAH, 28 (1896), 180–202. The rest of the study consists of supporting documents taken exclusively from the Salazar collection of the Real Academia de la Historia and the archive of the Empress Eugénie, countess of Teba. He states (p. 182) that the Catholic Kings sent him to Rome as their ambassador in 1488 and that he "returned from Rome at the end of 1491"; but in documents 4 and 5 [of the original appendix] . . . he appears to be in Rome early in 1485. Since a warrant of Ferdinand the Catholic states that he served as ambassador for three years during Innocent VIII's papacy, he must have returned to Spain early in 1488 or at the end of 1487.
37. In a special brief to "Cypriano Gentili, mercatori januensi, commissario et depositario nostro," on January 30, 1485, he writes: "Ut jura et pecunias Camere nostre Apostolice melius revidere et recuperare possis, tenore presentium tibi commit[t]imus ac mandamus, ut a dilectis Firmano de Perusio et Francisco Pinello aliisque collectoribus pecuniarum Camere nostre Apostolice ac quibuscumque mercatoribus in regnis istis Hispaniarum computa petas et recuperes, pecuniasque penes eos existentes tam cruciate et indulgentiarum et subsidii exigas et ad manus tuas reducere studeas, ut illas ad nos, sicut habes in commissis, statim mittere possis." For this purpose, he has given him authority to impose censures on the prior of Santa María de las Cuevas near Seville. (See Arm. 39, fol. 106 verso, brief "Cum nostre intentionis" dat. ut s.: that is, on January 30, 1485.) (Arm. 39, Vol. 18, fol. 107 verso.)
38. Complete text in [original] Appendix 5. The king states the same arguments in a letter of December 5, 1484, published by A. de la Torre, Documentos, II, 145–46.
39. Work cited in note 20.
40. Published by A. de la Torre, "Los Reyes Católicos y Granada," in Hispania, 4 (1944), 269–71.
41. Pulgar, part III, chap. 48 (BAE, 70, 425).
42. Pastor, V, 319, n. 1.
43. Bull "Redemptor noster" in Simancas, Patronato Real 19, 10 original; Book of copies no. 1, 168. The king of Naples had taken an interest in the matter. A. de la Torre, Documentos II, 221.
44. Loc. cit., n. 41.
45. Pulgar, part III, chap. 40 (BAE, 70, 410).
46. Brief of February 21, 1486, "Regibus Hispaniarum. Carissimi in Christo filii nostri, salutem etc. Que dilectus filius Franciscus de Rojas, orator serenitatis vestre nomine maiestatis vestre postulavit tam super negocio

cruciate et decimarum quam super rebus inquisitionis heretice pravitatis, attente omnia intelleximus ac deinde libenti animo et amanter illis providimus, dedimusque eidem oratori Bullas ac Brevia opportuna. Que maiestas vestra, Deo volente, videbit, intelligetque ex litteris oratoris abunde mentem nostram, quem carum habemus et in dies multo magis ob eius prudentiam et singularem fidem quam in servitiis vestre maiestatis ipsum continue adhibere videmus. Datum Rome, etc. die 21 Februarii 1486 anno secundo." (Vatican Archive Arm. 39, Vol. 19, fol. 204 verso. In folio 204 recto there is another brief to the Spanish monarchs recommending the ambassador, in which he repeats the same thing.)

47. *Ibid.*, fols. 182, 183 (February 8, 1486).

[48. I.e., Sir Edward Wydevill, brother of Richard Wydevill, Earl Rivers (d. 1491), with whom he is confused by Washington Irving and by Prescott (cf. *Complete Peerage*, XI, 25 n. [e]); he was brother also of Anthony Wydevill, called Lord Scales by right of his wife, Elizabeth, daughter and heiress of Thomas, Lord Scales.]

49. A. Bernáldez, *Crónica de los Reyes Católicos*, BAE, 70, 622.

50. Letter from Ferdinand the Catholic to the pope (November 14, 1486), published by A. de la Torre, "Algunos datos sobre los comienzos de la reforma de Montserrat en tiempo de los Reyes Católicos," (BAH, 107 (1935), 483–84).

51. Pulgar, part III, chap. 64 (BAE, 70, 442). Concerning the count of Tendilla's embassy, see Pulgar, III, chap. 54 (BAE, 70, 430–31), and A. González Palencia-Eugenio Mele, *Vida y obras de don Diego Hurtado de Mendoza*, I (Madrid, 1941), 3–29, especially 6, 8, and 24.

52. Pulgar, p. 431. He later occupied the bishoprics of Cartagena and Segovia and the presidency of the Royal Chancery of Valladolid. He had been a student at San Bartolomé in Salamanca, received the degree of doctor in canon law at the university there, and was *Prima* professor at Valladolid. Although the count of Tendilla returned to Spain after his embassy, Medina stayed in Rome until 1492. He died on January 30, 1507. *Historia del Colegio viejo de S. Bartolomé*, I 184–87; G. González Dávila, *Teatro eclesiástico . . . de las dos Castillas*, I (Madrid, 1645), 567–68.

53. Johannes Burkardus, *Diarium*, ed. Celani, in Rerum Italicarum scriptores, XXXII, I, 159–60; Pulgar, part III, chap. 54 (BAE, 70, 431).

54. Pulgar, part III, chap. 65, p. 442.

55. [Original] Appendix 7. See A. de la Torre, *Documentos*, II 414.

56. [Original] Appendix 6.

57. Diego de Valera, *Crónica de los Reyes Católicos*, ed. J. M. Carriazo (Madrid, 1927), p. 272.

58. *Ibid.*, p. 269.

59. *Crónica* (BAE, 70, 630).

60. *Ibid.*, p. 632.

61. Published by A. de la Torre in *Hispania*, 4 (1944), 286–87.

62. Brief of Innocent VIII to the Catholic Kings (July 14, 1488), published by Fita, "Nuevas fuentes para escribir la historia de los hebreos españoles.

Bulas y breves inéditos de Inocencio VIII y Alejandro VI," in BAH 15 (1889), 585–86.

63. This Carvajal was an ambitious man, named a cardinal by Alexander VI on September 20, 1493, ringleader in the schismatic so-called Council of Pisa (1511). Concerning him, see H. Rossbach, *Leben und die politisch-kirchliche Wirksamkeit des Bernaldino López de Carvajal* (Breslau, 1892); Pastor, v, vi, vii (index under the heading *Carvajal*); J. M. Doussinague, *Fernando el Católico y el cisma de Pisa* (Madrid, 1946).

64. Genoese, like Innocent VIII, and a brother of Jerónimo and Cipriano Gentili, whom he had accompanied to Spain as a young man, returning to Italy in 1470. Innocent VIII named him as his datary, an office which he held for five years; he was bishop of Orense and Pamplona and was named cardinal on March 9, 1489. He died September 30, 1507. A. Ciaconius, *Vitae et res gestae Pontificum Romanorum et S.R.E. Cardinalium* (Rome, 1630), pp. 1302–3, praises him highly.

65. [See original] Appendix 7.

66. Pulgar, part iii, chap. 118 (BAE, 70, 497),

67. His term of office lasted eleven years. In 1491 he was removed as president of the Chancery of Valladolid, along with four judges, for having granted an appeal to Rome, when they should have tried the cause. G. González Dávila, *Teatro eclesiástico . . . de las dos Castillas*, i (Madrid, 1645), 413. See [original] Appendix 2.

68. Bull "Ortodoxe fidei," in Vatican Register 759, 39 verso–43; Raynaldus, 1489, no. 10 (fragment).

69. [See original] Appendix 8.

70. Brief "Nuper pro exoneratione" (February 11, 1490). The quota had been reduced in the bull cited in note 68.

71. By means of the bull "Redemptor noster." Vatican Register 757, 134 verso–140; Raynaldus, 1491, no. 4 (fragment).

72. A. Bernáldez, *Crónica* (BAE, 70, 643). According to Fray José de Sigüenza, the person who placed the cross on the highest tower of the Alhambra was Fray Hernando de Talavera. *Historia de la Orden de San Jerónimo*, in Nueva Biblioteca de Autores Españoles, esp. pp. 12, 300.

73. Letter from the Catholic Kings to the chief justice of Valencia (January 2, 1492), published by A. de la Torre in *Hispania*, 4 (1944), 304. Similar letters were sent to the chief officers of the kingdom.

74. *Ibid.*, p. 305.

75. *Ibid.*, p. 305, n. 11.

76. Pastor, v, 318–19.

77. Drawn up on October 12, 1504; its text may be seen on p. 625 of the work cited on note 20.

78. *Ibid.*, p. 644. It was executed on November 23, 1504.

79. D. Saavedra Fajardo, *Razón de Estado del rey D. Fernando el Católico*, par. 12 in BAE, 25, 441. [A *cuento* was 1,000,000 *maravedís*.]

80. *Opere inedite di Francesco Guicciardini*, vi (Firenze, 1864), 296; see C. M. Alvárez Peña, "Guicciardini en la corte del Rey Católico," in *Universidad*, 26 (1949), 1–32.

FURTHER READING

J. Goñi Gaztambide, *Historia de la bula de cruzada en España* (Vitoria, 1958), includes the article printed here and develops the subject over a broader span.

12 The Significance of the Reign of Isabella the Catholic, According to Her Contemporaries

RAMÓN MENÉNDEZ PIDAL

Any collection of essays on Spanish fifteenth-century history should contain a Spanish appreciation of Queen Isabella. In this essay the late and much lamented Professor Menéndez Pidal, for many years president of the Spanish Academy and director of the monumental *Historia de España*, surveys the importance of her reign through the eyes of contemporary writers from chroniclers like Alfonso de Palencia and Fernando del Pulgar to the humanist Lucio Marineo Sículo and the grammarian Nebrija.

When a ruler, like a writer, artist, or any other creative person, brings his work into being, he can leave within it something which goes beyond the bounds of his own and his contemporaries' view of it; this occurs in the case of every lasting work. But what he set out to do, what those around him saw in his action, is always the essential factor; it is what the circumstances decreed, what opportunity demanded, and therefore it is what can best give us the measure of the creative genius and the success of the new thing that has been created.

What purposes were displayed by Queen Isabella the Catholic in her actions and her government? What assessment did the queen's contemporaries make of her? And let us begin by answering the following questions: How did historical writers regard the Spain of that time? What was their view of the destinies of the nation Isabella was to govern?

THE NEO-GOTHIC IDEAL AND DECADENCE UNDER
HENRY IV

During the last years of Henry IV's reign, and at about the time when Isabella contracted marriage with Ferdinand, Bishop Rodrigo Sánchez de Arévalo was writing, in Latin, his *Historia Hispanica*.[1] He wrote in Rome about 1469, when he was prefect of Castel Sant' Angelo, refused to recognize the great decline into which the court of Henry IV had fallen, and wrote in a highly optimistic tone. He is the last historian who speaks of "the five kingdoms" (Castile, Aragon, Navarre, Portugal, and Granada), but he sees a historical unity in this fragmentation, for all the monarchs of these kingdoms are descendants of those of Castile, and these in turn are direct descendants of the first king of the Goths. This is the reason why Rodrigo Sánchez de Arévalo himself had previously, when Henry IV began the war with Granada in the early years of his reign, enthusiastically dedicated his *Vergel de Príncipes* (1455) to him, predicting that the young king would even conquer the seas around Málaga and cross the Straits to take possession of the province of Tangier, thus completely restoring the great monarchy of his ancestors the Goths. This idea was latent in all the medieval histories and in the minds of all Spaniards. Another historian, Rodríguez de Almela, when he presented a Chronicle of Spain to the Catholic Monarchs in 1491, expounded this Gothic descent to them with the greatest enthusiasm, reminding them that when Isabella's father, John II, was buried in the Carthusian monastery of Burgos, Don Alonso de Cartagena, the bishop of Burgos, had said in his funeral sermon that the dead king was a descendant of the first king of the Goths, Alaric, "he who took Rome by force of arms," and thus for more than a thousand years there had been no change in the kings of Spain: an astounding continuity of which no other nation could boast, for in France or in England there had been at least three changes of dynasties or royal genealogies. This (somewhat fanciful) uninterrupted descent from Gothic kings in the monarchs of Leon and Castile, chief among the other kings of Spain, was an indication of their historic destiny to restore the Hispano-Tingitanian province of the Roman Empire, the province possessed by the Goths; or, which amounted to the same thing, it suggested aspiration to the unity of Spain on the one hand and the African ventures on the other.

Along with these plans for political glory which had sprung up so ambitiously at the beginning of Henry IV's reign there was, as a necessary complement, a firm belief in the country's natural resources. Fernando de la Torre, a traveler to the foreign courts of France and Italy, wrote to Henry IV in 1455 describing the power of the Castilian monarch as superior to that of the French king, and the superior wealth of the soil in Galicia, Leon and Castile, benevolently using it as an excuse for the inferiority of Spanish products compared to those manufactured in Flanders, Milan, Florence, or Naples. The reason for this superior production was the lack of fertility of those countries, which "makes them industrious and wealthy; and in Castile the fertility of the soil makes us in a certain sense proud and slothful, and not so inventive or hardworking." And, in confirmation of this point of view, we could quote a number of repetitions of the traditional praise of Spain as a fortunate land among all the countries of the West.

But although at the beginning of Henry IV's reign it was possible to dream of royal greatness and to view the prosperity of the kingdom with total optimism, the picture quickly changed when Henry's actions were those of a hapless invalid, with perverted and perverting tastes, a consummate corrupter of everything within his reach, as another chronicler, Alfonso de Palencia, tells us in lugubrious detail. It is true that this chronicler's authority is questionable, but it has been made so by the defenders of the indefensible;[2] this authority is attested by the fact that Palencia did not write his *Décadas* according to a preconceived plan, but wrote just as the events occurred, correcting his opinions at times; and it is also attested by his previously having been the official chronicler of the Impotent King and having later abandoned this sought-after post to go over to the party of those who were demanding reform in the ill-governed kingdom; reform in regard to all the religious, political, and moral bases of the nation which were daily being trampled underfoot by the king, his courtiers, the ruling classes, and the coterie of ruffianly and obscene persons who surrounded the king.

RESURGENCE

However, and surprisingly, the ruin of all the traditional forces which motivated that society was followed by a splendid resurgence of them all. When the Catholic Monarchs ascended the throne everything changed, says Alfonso de Palencia, "like the stormy sea when a fair wind suddenly springs up." However, if we look carefully at the situation, there is no such sudden change; it is only a dazzling illusion. The resurgence which took place was due to an extremely laborious process of government carried out by the Catholic Monarchs, a grandiose process precisely because it had persisted in its necessary slowness; and, moreover, this resurgence must also be understood as the effort of a large part of the nation, which had been laboring for some time (though in a disorganized way) within the disorder produced during the two preceding reigns. Structures raised in an instant and by a single stroke are but the devil's bridges; great works of God require much labor and time from men. It is frivolous to speak of the personal achievement of the Catholic Monarchs if we forget the national movement they directed.

A national reaction was imminent within the reign of Henry IV. Palencia shows us how, in the course of Henry's long reign, a multitude of forces arose which, unselfishly or selfishly, rejected the wrecking of all public and private ethical standards: the persons who organized themselves into brotherhoods, such as the one which arose in Segovia in 1466 to punish an outrage committed by the Moorish royal guard, a brotherhood that spread like a powder train through both Castiles, Vizcaya, Galicia, and Aragon, when cities and hamlets joined together to combat, crossbow in hand, the banditry practised by the great lords;[3] the nobles who conspired or took up arms again and again to demand reform in the government, often with the support of the king of Aragon;[4] and it should be noted in passing that the foreign kingdom of Aragon closely shared both popular and noble movements in the kingdom of Castile.

All the forces of reaction which clustered around the Infante Alfonso, a lad who, amid the corruption of palace life at the side of Queen Juana in Segovia which undermined all his training, kept intact a noble inclination toward whatever virtues were lacking in the court. Palencia gives us a number of anecdotes to illustrate this point. One of them tells how, when this boy Alfonso had already been proclaimed king in opposition to Henry IV, he seized power in Segovia in 1467 when he saw two of his sister Isabella's ladies-in-waiting in one of the rooms of the *alcázar* boasting about the indecency of dress, conversation, and manners which Queen Juana displayed around the modest princess; he took his sister away from the queen and carried her off to Arévalo.[5] It was then, at the age of sixteen, that Isabella came upon the stage of history, the cornerstone of public reaction against her half-brother Henry. Thus John II's own children came to lead the attacks and counter attacks which fill Spanish life in the second half of the fifteenth century; on one side Henry, son of María of Aragon, the child who inherited John II's psychic abnormalities in an exaggerated form; on the other, Alfonso and Isabella, the children of Isabella of Portugal (such an abnormal woman that she died insane); and both of them inherited from her an ethical strength still more extraordinary than their half-brother's moral looseness. It is startling to think that the Catholic Queen, daughter of a madwoman, mother of a madwoman, would never have been conceived if laws of eugenic sterilization had been in force at the time; and the modern world would have lost its royal Semiramis, a considerably greater queen than the legendary Semiramis of the ancient world.

ISABELLA AS LEADER OF THE REACTION

The many persons who were hostile to Henry IV, reformists like Palencia as well as those of uncertain and faltering loyalties like Archbishop Carrillo of Toledo,[7] would undoubtedly have brought some sort of restoration to Spain, but not with the harmony plenitude, and high level that the country reached under Isabella's leadership.

In Isabella the reaction was so extreme that it can only seem that the princess' character, as described by Pulgar, was formed by taking as a negative mold the character of her half-brother, as described by Palencia. Henry loathed any kind of occupation; Isabella was industrious, "very hard-working as to her person."[7] Henry left his tasks as ruler to his favorites and even turned over his marital functions to them; Isabella, jealous "beyond all bounds" of her husband, was also jealous of her prerogatives of government; she listened carefully to politicians, learned men, and representatives of religion, even though she might then follow her own inclinations; she never had a favorite: "Know," says Pulgar, "that the queen's only favorite is the king."[8] Henry took pleasure and profit in injustice; "even the tyranny exercised by others pleased him more than the peace of the kingdom,"[9] while Isabella was always a lover of justice and a detester of violence. Henry was indicted because he scorned the accouterments of kingship and kingly behavior; Isabella was criticized for being "ceremonious and of excessive pomp" on solemn occasions;[10] Henry took pleasure in degrading all nobility of spirit; he belittled the actions of his armies before Granada; he held up two prelates to ridicule by making them chant the benediction in unison, to the laughter of the congregation; he debased the apartments of the palace by stirring up the disagreements between his concubine, Doña Guiomar, and Queen Juana, until the queen came to blows with her; he flouted justice by expressing the opinion that the corpse of a hanged man was worthless and that it was better to free criminals from the gallows for money; Isabella, on the contrary, felt the solemn or terrible emotion of regarding every man in his most proper function: "She used to say that there were four things she enjoyed seeing: men-at-arms in the field, a bishop in his robes of office, a lady in a drawing room, and a thief on the gallows."[11] Henry undermined all the bases of national life without making any innovations; Isabella, honoring all the traditional values, transformed the nation; he was a worthless and mischievous rebel; she was a figure of meek grandeur.

REASONS FOR THE ARAGONESE MARRIAGE

Isabella was always attentive to the voice of her people, in order to direct them in best accordance with the public interests. Even Henry's historian, Enríquez del Castillo, shows us that in the first decision Isabella was to take (when she was under the disastrous control of her brother Henry), the decision concerning her own marriage, she demanded from her brother consultation with the grandees and representatives of the cities, refusing to serve the fleeting interests of the moment according to which King Henry wanted to decide.[12]

At the age of eighteen, the recognized heiress to the throne of Castile, she had as suitors the crown prince of England; Charles of Valois, the duke of Berry, possible heir to the French throne; Ferdinand, the heir of Aragon, and the great Portuguese king Alfonso V "El Africano," who five years before had taken a fancy to her as a child during some royal interviews in Guadalupe. The vacillating Henry sought a matrimonial alliance for his own momentary convenience, but the English marriage was out of the question after the Cortes of Ocaña (1469) rejected the alliance which the king had arranged without the knowledge of the kingdom's cities, and spiritedly invoked the traditional friendship with France: "being a thing more in accord with the greatness and nobility of the crown of Castile that the two greatest kings in Christendom, which are your two kings of Castile and France, should be joined together, and not any other king whatever." The French marriage was rejected in its turn by the ruling party of the kingdom, for if the duke of Berry should come to inherit the throne of France, the French would always consider the kingdoms and seigniories of Spain as "subordinate provinces."[13]

National inclinations, contrary to the desire of Henry, were in favor of a Spanish marriage. The oft-repeated observation of the historians that the Peninsular kingdoms were ruled by one family was becoming truer every day, for the Hispanic kings almost always contracted marriages with Spanish princesses; from the twelfth to the fourteenth centuries there were few alliances of a Spanish king with a foreign princess in Catalonia and Aragon, very few in Castile, and extremely few in Portugal; and even in the fifteenth century the dynastic connections among these three kingdoms grew ever closer, for all the royal marriages were being made within the three reigning families. But in Isabella's case the most widely held opinion rejected the Portuguese marriage because of the resentment left between Portugal and Castile by the battle of Aljubarrota, and because the union between the two countries would not be lasting, since "El Africano" was a widower with children. Only the Aragonese marriage promised a lasting political result. And even the common people vigorously supported it, as the chroniclers take pains to note; on the one hand, Palencia tells us that in 1469, when Henry IV threatened Isabella so rudely that he made her cry, urging the Portuguese marriage on her, the people in the streets and even the pages in the palace sang ditties in which they predicted unhappy consequences for the tender rosebud if she allowed herself to become the stepmother of the children of the Portuguese king, who were of the same age as she;[14] on the other hand, Bernáldez recalls that long before that year the young people sang a new *villancico* "with a very pretty tune,"

> Flores de Aragón
> dentro en Castilla son.[15]

"And the children took little banners and, riding on willow sticks, would say, '*Pendón de Aragón, pendón de Aragón!*'[16] And I used to say it too, and did so many times." And it was God who placed these prophecies "in the mouths of sinless babes, and in the songs of the other young folk who sang joyously," to announce the cure for all the crimes that were destroying the kingdom, and which would come to an end when the flowers and banner of Aragon came into Castile with "the holy marriage" of the princess.

Isabella sent her chaplain, Alfonso de Coca, to her suitors to look into the attributes of each, and was pleased to learn (Palencia, the chronicler of the myriad details, tells us so) that Ferdinand, in addition to his greater political power, was handsome in appearance, while the duke of Berry had rheumy eyes and skinny legs.[17] Naturally, like the consummate woman that she was, she listened to the voice of her eighteen years, but over and above this she heeded public opinion and also listened to the voice of her ancestors, for when she firmly resisted Henry IV's pressure, she not only accepted the advice of the grandees and the cities but also invoked, whether well or ill informed we do not know, the last wish expressed by her grandfather that "there should always continue to be new matrimonial connections" between the Castilian and the Aragonese royal families.[18] Thus, for Isabella the union of Aragon and Castile had been predestined long before, and in fact the recent Castilian-Aragonese marriages—such as those of the kings of Aragon, Alfonso V (1415) and John II (1446) and of Castile, John II (1418) and Henry IV (1440)—worked in her favor.

Thus the union of the two great Peninsular kingdoms was in the minds of the people long before Ferdinand and Isabella's marriage contract; the national desire to reconstruct the unity of the kingdom of the Goths showed itself in every way, even before the political fusion of the two kingdoms was accomplished.

PROPHECIES AND REALITIES

Isabella celebrated the Aragonese marriage, against King Henry's will (1469), before the expected Aragonese inheritance came about. An old writer at the time of John II, Mosén Diego de

Valera, had predicted even greater success: the total restoration of the empire of the Goths, which was, as we have seen, the great historical preoccupation of Castilian thinkers. In 1476, when Valera dedicated his *Doctrinal de Príncipes* to Ferdinand, he told him that it had been "prophesied for many centuries not only that you would be lord of these kingdoms of Castile and Aragon which belong to you in all right, but you will have the monarchy of all the Spains and will reform the imperial seat of the illustrious blood of the Goths, from whom you come, and which for so many long ages has been scattered and spilled."[19]

But such ambitious prophecies dwindled when they came into collision with reality. When the Aragonese inheritance occurred (1479), Fernando del Pulgar, the chronicler of the Catholic Monarchs, wrote that although some of the Royal Council believed that the monarchs should style themselves *King and Queen of Spain*, in the end they preferred to call themselves "King and Queen of Castile, Leon, Aragon, Sicily, Toledo, Valencia, Galicia . . . counts of Barcelona, lords of Vizcaya . . . etc.," alternating a Castilian title with an Aragonese one. And, moreover, the union of the two great kingdoms was still weak, and purely matrimonial; Ferdinand himself tried to separate them again after Isabella's death, when he married Germaine de Foix to see whether he could achieve succession and secession.

Therefore, many regretted the pompous pettiness of the Chancery-inspired formula. Diego de Valera, once more, when he dedicated his *Crónica de España abreviada* to Isabella in 1481, modifies the official title and calls her "Queen of Spain, of Sicily and Sardinia . . . etc.," a detail of considerable significance. Valera is an old-fashioned writer who writes by following the pattern of the *Crónica* of 1344; that is, within the period of the five kingdoms. But he feels, with satisfaction, that that period has come to an end; though the kingdoms of Granada, Navarre, and Portugal still exist, he apostrophizes Isabella "since Our Lord has given you, not without great deserts on your part, little less than the monarchy of all the Spains."[20]

THE FORMULA OF "THE KING AND THE QUEEN";
FERNANDO DEL PULGAR

These monarchs of Castile and Aragon, not of Spain, labored, however, not each in his own kingdom but together, to form a new Spain. But in this labor, was it the Aragonese king or the Castilian queen who led? The official chronicler, Fernando del Pulgar, writes with perfect truth that husband and wife always lived in agreement as to their government; not only did they issue all orders in the name of both, but when it was necessary for them to separate, one never gave a command that would contradict the other, "for though necessity separated their persons, love held their wills together."[21] Thus the chronicler uses the double Chancery formula in his narrative: "The king and the queen always intended to conquer Granada," "The king and the queen were in agreement in the matter of the brotherhoods," "The king and the queen commanded . . .," etc., and hundreds and hundreds of times, to the point of monotony, we do not know which of the two is acting and thinking. Isabella demanded this of her chronicler without fail, as Don Juan de Arguijo tells us, adding the joke that Pulgar avenged himself for this tiresome requirement by pretending to write in his chronicle, "The king and the queen, on such and such a day, gave birth to a daughter."

The admirable political agreement of husband and wife is certainly true, but it is also undeniable that underneath this concord in government important personal differences existed, and all those who write unhampered by the official charge which weighed so heavily on Pulgar, and who were apart from the situation in space or time, give the palm to the Aragonese king. Thus Machiavelli, Saavedra Fajardo, Gracián, and the others who take Ferdinand as the prototype of kings agree in not mentioning the Castilian queen along with him; they differ only in their basis for praising the king.

THE KING OR THE QUEEN?

Machiavelli, who finished *Il Principe* in 1513, [some] years before Ferdinand's death, declares that "he has become, in fame and glory, the foremost king in Christendom," and chooses him as the model for Chapter 21, which concerns the prince who knows how "to win reputation." Ferdinand accomplished great actions one after the other, "which have left the spirits of his subjects awed and astonished, and he has not left them leisure to attempt anything against him." And this idea is made clear in the correspondence between Machiavelli and Vettori, in both of whom we seek in vain for any shade of hostility toward the Spanish king such as we find in Prescott:[22] "What Ferdinand is attempting in his bold actions in Granada, Africa, and Naples," says Machiavelli, "is not, properly speaking, one particular deed or another, but rather to win reputation among nations, to give great expectation of himself." This seeking of expectation above all, which must not be confused with the frivolity of an Alcibiades, cutting off the dog's tail simply to give people something to talk about, is certainly not said in criticism of the king: far from it. It corresponds very well to the thought of the great Florentine statesman, absorbed as he was in studying the personal aggrandizement of the prince rather than that of the state, since the only means of founding a great state is no other than the success of a prince, as Machiavelli longs to have happen in the disorganized Italy of his time. But it is certain that Machiavelli, who was personally acquainted with Cesare Borgia and Alexander VI but not with Ferdinand, does not sufficiently stress the true inspiration of the Spanish monarch's activities. Baltasar Gracián, when he wrote *El político Don Fernando el Católico* (1640), adds something very essential to Machiavelli's description. Ferdinand owed a great deal to the impulse of his people: "He reigned," Gracián says, "during the waxing of empire, which very greatly aids the plausibility of a monarch; the greatness or smallness of a king depends very much on the state of the monarchy; for there is a great difference between reigning in its waxing phase and in its waning one." But what Gracián does not tell us is how to explain this waxing in a reign which began after the excessive waning of the kingdom produced by Henry IV. And finally, Saavedra Fajardo, when he presents the *Política y razón de Estado del Rey Católico* (1631), praises the king's accomplishments for their lasting results when he writes that the Spain of the seventeenth century owed to Ferdinand "the building of its monarchy in two worlds." Indeed, it was during the reign of this king that the grandiose political Escorial of the Spanish monarchy arose out of the heap of ruins left by Henry, not haphazardly from the sense of expectation aroused by the prince, but as an eighth wonder of the world built from an architectural plan, pursued with perfect order and persistent energy, from the clearing of its site to the construction of its cupolas.

But if we move from the opinions of outside observers to those of persons who knew both monarchs personally and breathed the atmosphere of the Spain of that time, we will observe that the greatest effort and supreme decision in drawing up the pattern for this plan, the greatest firmness in carrying it out, is due to the talent and tenacity of Isabella, who is frequently passed over in the standard history books. Isabella guided and often corrected the profound political intelligence of her husband, who is justly called the most perspicacious ruler in Europe at that time. Isabella strongly insisted on his putting the war with Granada ahead of the war with France, as an undertaking which was more lofty and more formative of national unity, and on more than one critical occasion she made him persevere in the long, ten-year war. Isabella introduced into the plan, and also put first, the discovery of America so unexpectedly posed by Columbus. She incorporated the war with Italy into the plan, using the Great Captain for the purpose and supporting him against the attacks of the envious. She conceived the plan for the war with Africa, more efficiently than it was carried out after her death. And finally, and most important of all, it was Isabella and not Ferdinand who brought the most persistent action to bear on ending the prostration left by Henry, converting it into a state on the ascendant, selective in vigor and development, the sole determinants of Gracián's *waxing of empire.*

And here we come to the difficult matter of singling out the value of the queen within the joint rule. The standard histories speak only of Ferdinand. The queen, on the other hand, receives more attention from biographers; more special books have been written about her than about the king. If we make an overall comparison of the two monarchs, we can say that the showy successes, the difficult political combinations, the keenness which persevered in attaining a difficult end by whatever means, focused on Ferdinand; for their joint motto, TANTO MONTA, implies untying as well as cutting the Gordian knot.[23] To Isabella we must attribute the firmer concern with unity, symbolized in the bundle of unbreakable arrows; to her belongs the sure and penetrating touch in discovering the necessary person and the opportune circumstance; Isabella had the constant raising of sights, the firmness of the hand that held the tiller, resisting the buffeting of personal interests, the virtues and energetic constancy, the only qualities which achieve deep and lasting effects, but which ordinary history does not customarily consider.

There is no doubt that this royal marriage has no peer. Universal history offers no other case in which a king and a queen reign together, each one of whom is equally endowed with the most outstanding gifts of government. But having said this I should like, in the centenary celebration of her birth which is now beginning [i.e., 1951, when this essay was written], to point out the very high value of the queen, insisting as I do so that I have no desire either to overvalue or to undervalue the king; I do so to mark the centenary. Here there is no childish question of "who was more valuable," but of the necessary discrimination of the qualities properly belonging to the woman in the joint government of husband and wife.

As for Isabella's great influence in the marriage, the always-revealing Alfonso de Palencia is all the more trustworthy because he is a friend of the king rather than of the queen, for he served as

Ferdinand's counselor. He tells us that when Henry IV's death occurred he and Ferdinand were away from court in Saragossa, and Isabella, in Segovia, hastened to proclaim her succession. The new queen, her exceptional twenty-three-year-old beauty heightened by a rich, jewel-encrusted dress, rode horseback under a canopy to the cathedral, surrounded by all the grandees on foot; only Gutierre de Cárdenas went mounted before her, holding up before him a naked sword grasped by the point, the symbol of sovereignty and justice. Many censured as arrogance this display by the wife of the attributes of the husband, and Ferdinand and Palencia criticized it more harshly than anyone when they were told of the matter in the course of their hasty trip to Segovia. The young husband was alarmed by the airs his wife was giving herself and asked Palencia, who was traveling with him, if he remembered having read in any history that any other queen had appropriated the masculine symbol of the sword, reserved for kings; and the chronicler, declaring that he did not recall a similar case, criticized Doña Isabella's action. The meeting between husband and wife was stormy. Ferdinand, feeling that his husbandly authority had been weakened, wished to return to his native kingdom of Aragon; there were consultations among the grandees and learned men who were partisans of the husband and of the wife concerning the attributes of each in the government; arbitrators were resorted to; they handed down a decision giving great attributes to the queen, and Don Ferdinand insisted that he was going to retire to Aragon. But Isabella's tears and the charm of her blonde beauty and her green-blue eyes, together with a few discreet concessions, triumphed—and Ferdinand resigned himself to staying, though not without boasting to his intimate advisers that his tolerance would only be temporary. But Don Juan Manuel's old wisdom had told the tale, long before Shakespeare, of how the husband brutally tamed a haughty and unmanageable woman on the wedding night, and the teller of tales had pointed out the moral: "In the very beginning the husband must show/ his bride the direction in which she must go." "If in the beginning you don't make a stand/ you'll never be able to take her in hand."

Don Ferdinand gave in at the outset, and lost his cause there in Segovia, on that January day in 1475.

Later Palencia, as he advanced further into the compilation of his *Décadas*, collected a number of instances of how people protested here and there because the King's will was subordinated to that of the queen.[24] And in his turn the traveler Nicolaus von Poppelau, who saw the monarchs in Seville in 1484, could see that the king did nothing without the consent of the queen; he did not seal his own letters until the queen had read them, and if the queen did not approve of one of them the secretary tore it up in the presence of the king himself; this traveler also observed that the king's orders, even in Aragon or Catalonia, were not held to be of much account, "but everyone trembled at the name of the queen."[25] Bernáldez confirms this: "She was the most feared and respected queen that ever there was in the world."[26] For his part, Lucio Marineo Sículo, though he had been appointed to the private service of King Ferdinand, notes in Book XXI of his *De rebus Hispaniae* that in comparison with the excellencies of the king, "in the judgment of many, the queen was of more majestic aspect, of livelier intelligence, of greater soul and more serious conduct."[27] Even Pulgar himself, in spite of his rigid undifferentiating formula "the king and the queen," corroborates the fact that Isabella was more farseeing in the affairs of both her own kingdom and that of her husband: "The king," he says, "aware of the queen's great sufficiency, gave over and entrusted to her all things, and also those things that occurred in the kingdoms of Aragon and Sicily, those which were arduous and of great importance, for she had great ability and a good natural intelligence."[28] To the testimony of these contemporaries can be added the general opinion recorded a few years later, in 1526, by the Venetian ambassador to Charles V, Andrea Navagero, who, noting the statement that "all Spain" considered Isabella to have been the strongest cause for the conquest of Granada, continues: "She was a rare and most virtuous woman, who is universally, throughout all Spain, mentioned much more than her husband, though he also was a most wise and rare person in his time."[29]

We may add that Isabella, because of the constancy of her love for her husband (for which she received a very poor return, to tell the truth) and because of her innate good taste, hid her superiority and dignified the subjection of her husband, a man who was in his turn a man of genius, and whose greatest glory, whose greatest piece of political perspicacity, was to allow himself to be affectionately guided on many occasions by a woman in whom he recognized higher ideals, greater acumen, and greater moral purity than he had himself.

A great modern historian (and much-admired friend) censures the Catholic Kings because they were concerned to weld the interests of the various kingdoms only through religious unity, and that this was insufficient. Such as assessment is unjust. We have already shown how Aragon and Castile acted in unison on some internal matters. Isabella's decisive influence on the affairs of Aragon, noted by her contemporaries, as well as Ferdinand's constant influence in Castilian matters are also proofs of this; and a special proof is the guiding participation of Castile in the historical enterprises of Aragon. Castilians were the chief actors in Sicily and Naples; the symbol of them all, the Great Captain, was placed in those enterprises by Isabella's talent for selection.

Castile was, in fact, the most valuable kingdom in Spain, and Isabella's value was equal to the task of making all the historical prerogatives of her inherited kingdom prevail within a unified Spain. Thus, the building of a new Spain was carried out through the guidance of Castile and the sincere and forceful assistance of Aragon.

What Mosén Diego de Valera prophesied in 1476, the reconstruction of the empire of the Goths, was stated by Nebrija in 1492 as an approximate reality, but now perpetually solid, indestructible, when in the much-quoted prologue to his Grammar he attributes to the "industry, labor, and diligence" of Isabella's royal majesty the fact that "the members and pieces of Spain, which were scattered everywhere, were reduced and joined in one single body and unity of kingdom, the shape and plan of which [note these words] is so ordered that many centuries, wounds, and times will be unable to break it or undo it."

THE WISDOM OF FERDINAND AND ISABELLA'S CHOICES

The complaints of lack of government addressed to Henry IV from Burgos in 1464 stated insistently that "inefficient persons were preferred, and those of little knowledge," and that offices "were sold for a price." A procedure contrary to this made possible the great deeds accomplished by the Catholic Kings, nor need we tire ourselves in searching for other causes to explain the resurgence of a nation made up of the same subjects, the same national material which had been useless before. Decadence cannot be distinguished from flowering except in the practice of this will for selection, which supports the man of a positive sign and eleminates the one of the opposite sign.

The famous magic art which transformed the life of Spain at that time was not a stroke of witchcraft performed when the Catholic Kings appeared on the scene; it was seven long years, the first years of their reign, followed by continuing later activity, which both monarchs employed to aid the triumph of men of good will, putting down the rebellion of the cities, razing the castles of the mettlesome knights, bringing to heel the many persons who had lived surfeited by what Valera calls "sweet tyranny."

The archbishop of Toledo, Carrillo, could be the prototype of the rebellious schemer. Until 1475 he battled fiercely against Henry IV, as the man most convinced of the rights and excellences of Isabella; but as soon as he saw the princess on the throne, he fought against her in favor of "La Beltraneja," threatening Isabella by saying that though he had turned her from a poor princess into a queen, he would make her relinquish the scepter and return to the distaff.[30] It was greatly to Isabella's credit that she humbled her royal dignity in order to try (fruitlessly) to placate the rebellious archbishop, and still more greatly to her credit that she did not carry her gratitude to the point of acceding to the ambitions of that brave, energetic, and powerful man, but one who was so shortsighted that he allowed himself to fall under the sway of an alchemist, Alarcón, a sort of Rasputin, a mystical, fascinating, and dissolute man.

Pulgar comments that the chief difficulty still not overcome by the Catholic Kings at the beginning was that ill-fated characteristic of the Spaniard, the one noted by Justinus[31] (in a text adduced by Sánchez de Arévalo): "The bad Spanish quality, restless in its nature, which would like if it could to freeze disturbing movements in the air, and suffer internal strife when there is none from without. Certainly, the man who described the Spaniards as slothful in war and turbulent in peace knew what he was saying. Let us give thanks to God that we have a king and a queen who hear and judge and wish for what is right, for these are things which hinder scandals and destroy them."[32]

"We have a king and a queen"; this is always Pulgar's formula. But Palencia, writing more freely, reveals to us that in the Herculean struggle against the Hydra of discord, which constantly renews its seven heads [sic], it was the queen who struck the most unerring blows: he states on one occasion that within a single year, 1477, the Andalusians complained because Ferdinand lacked a standard for rewards and punishments, and that he was known to overlook the corruption of judges, while "if anything worthy of praise was accomplished in Andalusia, it seemed to be due to the queen's initiative"; and on another, he tells us that the Vizcayans accused Ferdinand of unjust taxes and monopolies, though at the same time they did not impute to the queen any fault or lack of attention in looking after them;[33] statements which can be assessed by considering that in that year Palencia was still the king's private counselor.

Isabella had suffered ever since her childhood from this happy thirst for selective justice. On the day of her proclamation, in the ostentatious ceremony of the drawn sword, which seemed to be the mere vanity of an unwomanly woman, the young queen made clear that a straightforward, conscientious will had ascended the throne, crowned with the cross of abnegation: a will ready to consider everyone equal under justice, as the elemental basis of national cohesion. And from that time until the last day, when she drew up her will with its numerous clauses on the matter, she lived with the scrupulous preoccupation of imposing justice upon all, and first of all upon herself, combining haughty majesty in the name of the law with the most humble shedding of all personal pride, as she displayed from the beginning with her attitude toward the rebellious archbishop of Toledo.

"She was much inclined to do justice, so much so that it was said of her that she followed more the path of sternness than of compassion," says Pulgar;[34] and the quality of abnegation in her sternness is understood as a valuable factor by the chronicler himself, when he recounts at length the episode of the criminal knight of Medina (1480), who in an attempt to redeem his life "gave the king and the queen forty thousand *doblas* for the war with the Moors"; and though some members of the council urged them to accept this aid for the purposes of so holy a war, the queen had the criminal beheaded, and refused to confiscate the property of the condemned man as the law provided, "so that people should not think she had ordered that justice done being moved by greed."[35] Proofs of this moral superiority of the queen over the king are numerous. When the chronicler Bernáldez mourns Isabella's death he praises the happiness of those times. "The humble poor were weighed in justice along with the knights, and received justice";[36] and Fernández de Oviedo, recalling that he had witnessed in the *alcázar* of Madrid the public audiences held on Fridays, in which the queen administered justice at the king's side, exclaims: "That was a golden time indeed, and a time of justice; and he who had it could profit from it. I have seen that since God took that holy queen, it is more trouble to deal with the servant of a secretary than it was then with her and her Council, and costs more as well."[37] Marineo Sículo also writes of that happy age when justice was done impartially to nobles, citizens, and peasants, to the poor and to the rich. Yes; there was a golden age that was owed to the queen, to her fervid passion for justified punishment and just reward, to the delicate perspicacity of her impartial justice; it was the golden age envied far away in Italy by Baldassare Castiglione, who, shortly after Isabella's death, praised the influence exercised by the queen in that "divina maniera di governare," "which seemed as if her will alone sufficed for everyone to do his duty and not to dare, not even secretly in his own house, to do anything that might displease the queen." For me, this is the fundamental enterprise of the Catholic Kings. That divine manner of governing gave perfect health to the sick body of the nation: none of its cells rebelled against the organism of which they formed a part: there was no abscess, hypertrophy, or abnormality of any sort: an extra-ordinary vigor followed in all orders of the state's activity; it was the "waxing of empire" which Gracián was unable to understand.

The war in Africa, which entered into the Catholic King's architectural plans after the long and difficult undertakings of Granada, America, and Italy, was decided upon in April, 1504, and was to be carried out by the count of Tendilla, commander of the Alhambra, with funds which the king and queen were to supply him. But in the month of November the queen died; Isabella could do no more than to order her children and heirs in her will "not to give up the conquest of Africa." We certainly cannot accuse the king of indifference toward this war, but it must be noted that he did not readily provide money for the capture of Mazalquivir (1505) and Oran (1509) as he had done in the plan of 1504, and Cardinal Cisneros had to advance funds;[38] and Paulus Jovius tells us that when Cisneros was least in favor with Don Ferdinand, he took counsel with the Great Captain for the African enterprise, at a time when the latter in turn had retired to Loja in disgrace with the king; and on his advice chose, as captain general of the army against Oran, Count Pedro Navarro, who brought the war to a favorable conclusion. This means that the effective and executive concern for the war in Africa resided not in the king but in his vassals, who were acting "for the waxing of empire." It resided in the vassals created by Isabella, for it is well known that Cisneros, like the Great Captain, was yet another result of Isabella's wise and virtuous choice, imposed over the personal preferences and nepotistic tendencies of Ferdinand.

In that frail friar, dressed in sackcloth, in whom the jesting spirit of Don Francesillo saw only the semblance of a greyhound wrapped in a sack, and in whom the courtiers saw at most an anachronistic hermit out of the Thebaid,[39] Isabella saw not only an excellent confessor but the man worthy of occupying the primary ecclesiastical office of Spain, formerly given only to members of the upper nobility; and she made him archbishop of Toledo against all the desires of Ferdinand, who wanted that post for his illegitimate son, the archbishop of Saragossa; and even after the queen's death the king had a quarrel with Cisneros when he begged him to exchange Toledo for Saragossa, thus offending, as Jovius says, the good judgment of his dead consort. It was, therefore, Isabella alone who conferred greatness on that obscure Franciscan, an ascetic of a new type, capable of handling princely sums in great military enterprises, of founding a university, and of carrying out the first of the great modern attempts at philological criticism of the text of the Bible.

At the end of that glorious period Nebrija writes his *Decades* in Latin on the reign of Ferdinand and Isabella. In the prologue to his Grammar, which is so well known and which I have quoted before, he had praised the firm political unity achieved within the Peninsula; in another forgotten passage, in the preface to the *Décadas*, he praises the attainment of the most grandiose imperial plans. Basing his ideas on those of universal history conceived by Paulus Orosius and by St. Augustine, he believes that, just as the movement of the heavens and stars is from east to west, so also the monarchy of the world passed from the Assyrians to the Medes, from the Medes to the Persians, then to the Macedonians and then to the Romans, and later to the Germans and Gauls. "And now," concludes Nebrija, "who cannot see that, although the title of Empire is in Germany, its reality lies in the power of the Spanish monarchs who, masters of a large part of Italy and the isles of the Mediterranean Sea, carry the war to Africa and send out their fleet, following the course of the stars, to the isles of the Indies and the New World, linking the Orient to the western boundary of Spain and Africa."[40]

That was the reality. A new empire was arising in Spain, three centuries and a half after the medieval empire had been forgotten. It was no longer an intra-Peninsular empire, a mere reconstruction of the empire of the Goths, like the empire of Alfonso III, VI, and VII; it was a worldwide empire, based on the universalist ideas of philosophy of history conceived by the great Church father, the bishop of Hippo; an empire of the modern age, which left the medieval Romano-Germanic empire behind.

We can close the present overall glimpse of the opinions of their contemporaries concerning this joint reign with Nebrija's profound and enthusiastic appreciation; it was a reign which for the men of the time, like Bernáldez, Palencia, Encina, and Nebrija, had attained a fullness of triumph, sublimation, and power never before achieved by Spain; a reign which later, for such Spaniards as Gracián, Forner, Menéndez Pelayo, and Maeztu, was the splendid initiation of a period of "waxing of empire" during which Spain realized her true destiny under the monarchs of the sixteenth and seventeenth centuries; a reign which for other Spaniards, such as Cadalso, Valera, Ganivet, and Costa, meant not a waxing but the plenitude after which a waning phase began, the fatal uninterrupted decline during the Hapsburg period; a reign, finally, which for all Spaniards represents a happy golden age, remembered nostalgically as incomparable by one and all.

NOTES

[1. Cf. R. H. Trame, s.j., *Rodrigo Sánchez de Arévalo, 1404–1470* (Washington, 1958), 115–16.]

[2. For a more favorable view of one aspect of Henry's work, see the account of his economic policy given by Vicens Vives above, p. 56.]

3. Alonso de Palencia, *Crónica de Enrique IV*, trans. A. Paz y Melia, 1 (Madrid, 1904), 524 (Colección de Escritores Castellanos).

4. A. Paz y Melia, *El cronista Alonso de Palencia, su vida y sus obras* (Madrid, 1914), p. 13.

5. Palencia, *Crónica de Enrique IV*, pp. 112, 116.

[6. Bishop of Sigüenza, 1434–1446; archbishop of Toledo, 1446–1482.]

7. Fernando del Pulgar, in BAE, LXX, 257a.

8. Fernando del Pulgar, *Letras*, XII (Clásicos Castellanos, 99).

9. Palencia, *Crónica de Enrique IV*, I, 277.

10. Pulgar, in BAE, LXX, 257b.

11. Melchor de Santa Cruz, *Floresta*, II, 1.

12. Diego Enríquez del Castillo, *Crónica de Enrique IV*, chap. 136; letter from Isabella, dated in 1469 (BAE, LXX, 188a, 189a).

13. In Isabella's letter, already quoted, inserted into the *Crónica de Enrique IV* (BAE, LXX, 189a).

14. Palencia, *Crónica de Enrique IV*, pp. 207, 208.

[15. Literally, "Flowers of Aragon are within Castile." *Villancico* = a Christmas carol.]

[16. "Banner of Aragon, banner of Aragon."]

17. Palencia, *Crónica de Enrique IV*, II, 256.

18. In Isabella's often-quoted letter of 1469, in Castillo's *Crónica de Enrique IV* (in BAE, XX, 189a). The words attributed to her grandfather Henry III contain an anachronism, for Ferdinand of Antequera was not yet king of Aragon; but the will makes provision for the marriage of María of Castile with the future Alfonso V of Aragon.

19. In J. de M. Carriazo, *Memorial de diversas hazañas*, by Mosén Diego de Valera (Madrid, 1941), p. xxxvi.

20. In J. de M. Carriazo, *Memorial de Diego de Valera*, 1941, p. xxxix.

21. In BAE, LXX, 256a.

22. *History of Ferdinand and Isabella* (Boston, 1838), part II, chap. 24, n. 72.

[23. For the different interpretations of this device cf. J. H. Elliott, *Imperial Spain*, p. 73.]

24. Palencia, *Crónica de Enrique IV*, pp. 429, 455, 479–80.

25. A. Paz y Melia, *El cronista Alonso de Palencia*, p. xx, note.

26. In BAE, LXX, 722–23.

27. In *Hispaniae Illustratae . . . Scriptores*, I (Frankfurt, 1603), p. 506: ". . . tametsi multorum iudicio forma Regina pulchrior, ingenio acutior, animo splendidior, et decore gravior habebatur.'

28. In BAE, LXX, 256a.

29. *Viaggio in Spagna*, p. 58: "Fu rara e virtuosíssima donna e della quale universalmente in tutti quei paesi si dice assai piu che del Re ancoraché fusse prudentíssimo ed a sua età raro."

30. Bernáldez, in BAE, LXX, 580a. Zurita, *Anales de Aragón*, Vol. IV (Saragossa, 1668), fol. 246b,c.

[31. A second-century historian, author of *Historiae Philippicarum Libri xliv*.]

32. Fernando del Pulgar, *Letras*, XII (Clásicos Castellanos, 99, p. 62).

33. Palencia, *Crónica de Enrique IV*, IV, 436, 439; on p. 427 Palencia appears as the king's counselor.

34. In BAE, LXX, 257a.

35. *Ibid.*, 356a.

36. *Ibid.*, 723a.

SPAIN IN THE FIFTEENTH CENTURY

37. Quoted by Clemencín, in *Memorias de la Academia de la Historia*, VI, 203.
38. J. M. Doussinague, *Política internacional de Fernando el Católico* (1944), pp. 131, 186.
[39. The region round Thebae, Upper Egypt.]
40. In *Hispaniae Illustratae . . . Scriptores*, I (1603), 790.

13 The Catholic Kings According to Machiavelli and Castiglione

RAMON MENÉNDEZ PIDAL

Professor Menéndez Pidal here examines the views of two shrewd observers of the Renaissance scene on the Catholic Kings. Machiavelli, as is often stated, held up Ferdinand as his ideal and made him the prototype for Chapter 21 of *The Prince*. Much less often his views are held up for scrutiny and found unsatisfactory, as they are here. This discovery serves as a basis for a further inquiry into the real objectives of Ferdinand and Isabella and a comparison of Machiavelli's views of them with those held by Baldassare Castiglione, the author of *The Courtier*.

MACHIAVELLI AND KING FERDINAND

Machiavelli, who finished his book *Il Principe* in 1513, three years before Ferdinand's death, chose him as a model for his Chapter 21, dealing with the prince who, arising out of nothing, knows how to "win reputation" and make himself admired. "Ferdinand of Aragon," says Machiavelli, "the present king of Spain, can almost be called a new prince, for from the weak king that he was he has become, in fame and glory, the foremost king in Christendom; and if you consider his deeds you will find all of them great, and some of them extraordinary. . . . The war with Granada . . . won him reputation and power among the barons of Castile; always making use of religion . . . under this same cloak . . . he attacked Africa . . . then Italy and France; and thus he has always done and planned great things, which have at every moment held the spirits of his subjects awed and astonished; and they, noticing only the result of these things, and seeing that one follows hard upon the other, never found themselves in a state of tranquillity with time to work against him."

In that same year of 1513, in a letter to Francesco Vettori, ambassador to Pope Leo X, Machiavelli expanded and particularized this praise of Ferdinand:

> This king, beginning with small and weak fortune, has raised himself to the greatness in which we now see him. And one of the ways in which new states maintain themselves, and doubting spirits are reassured or remain in suspense and irresolution, is to give great expectation of themselves, keeping men always uneasy in considering what purposes there may be in his actions and new enterprises. This king has very clearly recognized such a necessity, and has taken good advantage of it; and from it has arisen the war with Granada, the attack on Africa, his entry into the Neapolitan kingdom, together with his various other enterprises; and all without their seeing his final purpose, for the end is not this or that victory, but to win himself reputation among his peoples, and to keep them in suspense in the multiplicity of his designs; and therefore he is a valiant initiator of beginnings, to which he later gives that end which luck places in his path, or which necessity indicates to him. And up to the present he cannot complain either of his luck or of his valor.[1]

For Machiavelli, the psychological effect (expectation, reputation) caused among the people is the primary motive in Ferdinand's exemplary political activities, while the objective result is a secondary matter, achieved later in terms of the way the situation presents itself. W. H. Prescott reads enmity toward Ferdinand into some of Machiavelli's judgements, since the latter was a friend of France;[2] but there is nothing negative in this characterization of the Catholic King as a prince primarily concerned with the expectation of the public. It is not a question of the frivolous vanity of an Alcibiades, cutting off the dog's tail to give people something to talk about, but the prestigious expectation which leads to mastery over one's subjects: *reputazione e imperio* is what

Ferdinand knows how to win, and he is one of the models used by the great Florentine political thinker to study the personal rise to greatness of a "new prince," such as Machiavelli longs for to redeem an Italy plagued by war and deeply wounded.

This assessment of Don Ferdinand has another facet in the 1513 letter we have quoted. In a previous letter Vettori had alluded to Ferdinand's reputation for being keen-witted, clever, and cunning; but, to judge from the truce just concluded with France, "perhaps," says Vettori, "I would not consider him the prudent man I always thought him to be."[3] Machiavelli answers by explaining how the king of Spain could act as a "wise man" in arranging the truce, but that in spite of this, to him Ferdinand has always seemed "more cunning and lucky than wise and prudent"; he always sees in him "cunning and good fortune rather than wisdom and prudence." And Vettori, deferring to his correspondent's enormous authority, states this same assessment a year later, in May, 1514, but this time believing that it is his own: "This Catholic King, with all the great progress he has made, I consider lucky rather than wise"; and, after examining the king's deeds one after the other since the end of the war with Granada, he concludes: "If one considers his actions well, he will judge him lucky, and find that *all things* turned out well for him; but no man of good sense will say that he began them like a prudent man."[4]

DEFECTS OF MACHIAVELLI'S ASSESSMENT

But here we see clearly that, once Machiavelli's thought is generalized in this way, its great weakness is exposed. "*Everything* turned out well for King Ferdinand!" But luck consistently helps only the man who knows how to control its whims. The prizes in the lottery do not *always* fall to the same person.

Machiavelli, who is personally acquainted with some of his other models (Cesare Borgia, Alexander VI), speaks of Ferdinand the Catholic without direct knowledge, and when he exemplifies in him the new concepts with which this author of genius was transforming the modern political sphere of ideas, he suffers in large measure from the effects of a literary prejudice. In other cases it is well known that Machiavelli regards some of the personages that he studies from a partially preconceived point of view; and I find that this is what he does in respect to Ferdinand. Machiavelli's portrait of this king is repeated by modern writers as entirely accurate, and it is rather far from being so. Ferdinand gives Machiavelli many of the elements for his conception of the politician-prince, but in his turn Machiavelli inserts a great deal of his own theory into the image of Ferdinand that he gives us.

For Machiavelli, *reputation* and *fortune* are basic ideas. The special importance he gives to reputation depends on the Renaissance evaluation of the human personality, which is exaltation of individuality; and the man whose *virtú*, that is, effort, energy, power, stands out in this way, acts in a world governed by fortune (a substitute for Providence, or, for others, *ancilla Dei*); and chance is in continual conflict with the best-laid plans of men.

Within these ideas, it is an arbitrary preconception to present Ferdinand the Catholic as a political man who, in the intricate succession of chance, enters boldly but blindly, seeking reputation, without concerning himself with the goal or with what may happen in the end, hoping to succeed with the aid of fortune, cunning or trickery.[5] This is wholly false. The Catholic King's reign is the most carefully planned reign which history can present, the one least committed to the hazards of fate. In its first years there was no thought of anything but internal reconstruction; once this was achieved, there was an argument between the king and queen as to whether the matter of France or Granada should be attended to first; the queen's opinion prevailed, and the campaigns continued without interruption for ten years, not in blind ignorance of their end, but methodically dedicated toward undermining the enemy's territory until the surrender of the capital was achieved; then the religious unification of Spain was undertaken; then the war on the infidel was prolonged with the conquests in North Africa; but this project was carried out always subordinated to the more pressing one of settling matters with France, into which Ferdinand entered with a very specific purpose, that of assuring possession of Roussillon and Naples, and both these aims were fully realized in the end. All this was done in perfect order of preference, leaving no more to chance than to shuffle the difficulties which arose in carrying out the predetermined plan, according to the nation's historical necessities.

THE HOLY WAR AGAINST THE INFIDEL

Let us repeat: the Catholic King's political program, both during his first marriage and after Isabella's death, was very far from having no other object than to provoke expectation. Ferdinand guided his actions from a very Spanish, and therefore a very traditional, point of view; he thought, and could only think, along the same lines as his ancestors the other Spanish kings, who knew that their primary occupation was to combat the infidel. This was a principle conclusively set forth by Alfonso III at the beginning of the Reconquest, about the year 880, and constantly repeated later; finally, Henry IV became the monarch whose mission was to complete by force of arms the restoration of the kingdom of the Goths over all the soil of Spain, and over the Africa of Tangier. It was an aspiration deeply rooted in time. In the Late Middle Ages the western part of North Africa lay within the sphere of influence or possible conquest of the kings of Castile, just as the kings of Aragon held the eastern part of North Africa. Therefore Ferdinand, as king of Aragon and Castile, as soon as he came to be the foremost king in Christendom, as Machiavelli called him, had to have as the chief objective of his undertakings the war against the infidel in Morocco and Tunis, and even in every other part of the Mediterranean.[6] To believe, as Machiavelli believed, that this war which had lasted for centuries in Spain was taken as a mere pretext by the Catholic King to arm himself against France is an anachronistic misrepresentation.

But there is yet more. Every medieval Spanish king expected to take personal part in the war against Islam. Thus, Ferdinand himself fought in all the campaigns of the war with Granada and, after it was over, intended to go in person to the war in Africa. He demonstrated this intention as early as 1507 and repeated it in 1510 when he planned to go to the war in Tunis; and in 1509 he proposed to go personally to war with the Turk, although his Council refused to give him permission.[7]

However, perhaps all was not always sincerity in these warlike plans. There is a curious text in Galíndez, who, when he tells how King Ferdinand, in February, 1511, was in Seville preparing his army to go to Africa and make war on the Saracens, adds that the secret reason, it was believed, was to arm himself against the French; and it was disclosed that the king of France had said, "The Saracen against whom the Catholic King, my brother, is arming is myself."[8] We can see that there was truth in these jesting words, though it was a half-truth.

THE AFRICAN WAR SUBORDINATED TO THE HOSTILITY WITH FRANCE

The "holy war," as it was called, was of course for every Spanish king a defense and propagation of the Faith, but it was also the only way to acquire territory, and was therefore the chief method of increasing their power and reputation. Ferdinand, as Gracián says, "joined Heaven and earth," and joined them very much to his own advantage. And the fact is that Cisneros, after the capture of Oran (May 17, 1509), had no difficulty in persuading Ferdinand to take intensive action in Africa. Count Pedro Navarro, appointed captain general for the war, took Bougie on January 6, 1510, and initiated what we might call the Catholic King's African year. After this beginning in 1510, Don Ferdinand felt deeply committed toward continuing the war with the Moors of the African coast and conquering some of the territory in the interior, in order to lay his hands on revenues with which to defend the coastal strongholds, for these could not be maintained for long simply with resources from Spain;[9] Algiers surrendered on April 24; Tripoli was conquered by Navarro on July 27. A month later, on August 28, the terrible and famous defeat took place on the island of Los Gerbes (Los Gelves in the Andalusian pronunciation), near Tripoli. It was due to the reckless conceit of Don García de Toledo, eldest son of the duke of Alba. A great expedition was prepared as revenge for Los Gerbes and for the conquest of Tunis and its hinterland. And so the letter of instructions which the king wrote on December 24 to the captain general, Pedro Navarro, begins with this declaration: "What happened at Los Gerbes not only has not dampened my ardor and the intention which I had and still have of taking part in this holy enterprise, but has inflamed and increased it so much that, by the grace and guidance of God Our Lord, I am entirely determined to go in person this summer [by summer here he means spring] to take part in the aforesaid enterprise; and for this purpose a sufficient fleet is being prepared for my command. ..."[10]

But Ferdinand was too much aware of realities to blind himself by thinking only of the far-off Saracens of Africa and forgetting that Saracen brother of his who was much closer. As early as May, 1510, he could see with great misgiving that Louis XII was aspiring to the "Monarchy," as the term was then; that is, the Universal Monarchy, supremacy over the other kings, for he and a number of cardinals were preparing a schism in order to depose Julius II and put a docile pope in his place, thus making it possible for Louis to take over Italy and control European politics at his pleasure. If these schismatic plans continued, Ferdinand would be obliged to use against them the preparations he was making for the war with the Moors.[11] And, in fact, the tension increased, so that in January, 1511, the royal secretary Almazán, who was privy to Ferdinand's most intimate thoughts, notified the viceroy of Naples that the fleet being prepared in Seville had "two purposes: the chief one against the Moors, and the other so that in case the king of France tries to stir up anything against His Majesty in that kingdom [Naples], the aforesaid fleet can be sent there."[12]

What Ferdinand had feared did in fact take place. During the spring in which the fleet was to embark for the conquest of Tunis, in May, 1511, the *conciliabulum* of Pisa was held by nine cardinals who were determined to depose Julius II, and Louis XII attacked the states of the Church by taking Bologna. Ferdinand declared himself on the pope's side and, without breaking off relations with the king of France, conveying to him through his ambassador sensible advice on respecting the unity of the Church,[13] disbanded the Spanish troops and English archers who had concentrated in Andalusia for the "holy war."[14] This action was intended to show the French Saracen that that fleet had not been specially formed against him; but Louis XII persisted in inciting the schism, and Ferdinand joined the pope and Venice to form the Holy League (October 4, 1511), in order to push the French out of Italy. Then, in the month of November, the Catholic King announced publicly that he was giving up the idea of going to Africa because of the need for defending the Church.[15] He was joining Heaven and earth, and always to his own advantage.

In December of that year the king of Tlemçen became Ferdinand's vassal.[16] But the Catholic King's series of African triumphs was interrupted by the hostility with France and the grave events in Italy; a definitive interruption, for it was followed by the long illness from which Ferdinand died.

He died with the ever-present idea of avenging the disaster of Los Gerbes, but this undertaking, so necessary to repair the military "reputation" he had lost there, was relegated to second place; it was to be attempted only if the viceroy of Naples saw that he could send the Neapolitan army to the Tunisian island, to keep it from being idle and ravaging the people of that kingdom.[17]

PEACE AMONG CHRISTIANS; EACH PRINCE
CONTENTED HIMSELF WITH WHAT HE HAD

This war against Islam, the customary occupation of the Spanish kings, made it necessary for Ferdinand as foremost king of Christendom to accept as a standard the desires constantly expressed by the popes: peace among the Christian princes so that they could take part freely in the war against the infidel. This double feeling of the community of Christendom and the propagation of the Faith by means of war was constantly expressed by the Catholic King, not only in public documents, which lend themselves to insincerity, but in private instructions to his ambassadors, and it was practised by him with firm conviction.

In the League of Cambrai (December, 1508), formed to strip Venice of her power, Ferdinand, like Julius II, wanted Venice to cede to each prince who participated in the League the territories which each occupied, and no more; an opinion contrary to that of the other allies, Louis XII and Maximilian, who wished to destroy the Adriatic republic. Ferdinand was enabled to recover immediately the cities of the kingdom of Naples which the Venetians held as security (Brindisi, Gallipoli, and Otranto), and did not aspire to more. The new conquests which Louis XII was trying to make in Italy, "without a single title of law," he described as "tyranny," for they sowed uneasiness among the other Christian princes, as he said in a letter to the viceroy of Naples in May, 1510.[18]

The idea of peace among the Christian nations was very sincerely held by the Catholic King, for he had adjusted the interests of his political activities to it. We shall add one more piece of evidence which is of great value because of its private nature. In February, 1516, as a direct consequence of Ferdinand's death, the first secretary of state, Pedro de Quintana, made a secret summary of the Catholic King's wishes in regard to the affairs of the state, and began with these words: "The principal end and desire held by His Majesty was general peace among Christians and war against the infidel . . . and he desired both these holy purposes like the salvation of his soul." Then he notes that the French, wishing to be masters of Italy and of the world, *practise tyranny* by attempting to occupy the states of other princes, and even the state of the Church; on the contrary, "His Majesty, desiring to open the way for general peace among Christians, twice arranged a two-year truce with France, and during the truce periods always tried to establish a true and lasting peace with the French."[19] These are the famous truces which Vettori could not understand that a wise and prudent king could make, and they prove a generous sincerity underlying Ferdinand's policies, as provident as they were astute.

THE CATHOLIC KING AS TEACHER OF CHARLES V

The striking thing is that this summary of the Catholic King's intentions was made by the secretary Quintana for the information of the prince, Charles, whom Quintana does not yet call king because his mother, Juana the Mad, was still alive; and we see with surprise that the political ideas which Charles always proclaimed later, when he was emperor, are the same as those set forth by Quintana. In his speech before the Council in Madrid in 1528, Charles calls the prince who conquers what does not belong to him a *tyrant*, and on this point he contradicts the opinion of his chancellor, Gattinara, for Gattinara believed that the empire was a just claim for the Universal Monarchy and for the conquest of any Christian land.[20] Later, in a conversation with the Venetian ambassador Contarini in Bologna, Charles roundly denied the rumor that he aspired to the Universal Monarchy; he wanted only to preserve what was his own, never to take what did not belong to him; and in this it seems that we are hearing Ferdinand the Catholic's words when he censured the ambitions of Louis XII, who aspired to that Monarchy. In his declaration before the Cortes of La Coruña in 1520, Charles also declared through the mouth of Bishop Mota that he was not going to make use of his world empire to win new kingdoms, for he had more than enough through inheritance, but that the empire did impose upon him the undertaking against the infidel, "in which he intends, with the help of God, to employ his royal person." And in fact, like a good king of the Spanish school, Charles did employ his person in his expedition to Tunis. No other sovereign in Europe could have suggested to Charles this duty to fight against the Saracen except Ferdinand in his campaigns in Granada and in his tenacious desire to embark on the expedition against Tunis.

On the other hand, the fraternal feeling of a Christian universality, the *Universitas Christiana*, was so alive and effective in the

Spanish court that a letter from Peter Martyr informs us that in 1503, while Ferdinand was fighting the French in Roussillon, Isabella, in Segovia, made constant supplications, with prayer and fasting, and wrote to her husband again and again urging him to carry on the war mercifully, sparing the blood of the enemy, because they were Christians; a recommendation which the king in fact accepted.[21] It should be recalled, along these same lines, that when Charles V received in Madrid the news of the great victory at Pavia he refused to allow this extraordinary and resounding triumph to be publicly celebrated there, because it had been obtained at the cost of Christian blood. It should also be recalled that when Francis I arrived in Madrid as a prisoner the Emperor's Council was divided into two factions: a number of Flemish [and Italians], especially Gattinara, firm in their conviction that the empire conferred the right to acquire new lands and aspire to the Universal Monarchy, wished to make territorial acquisitions at the expense of France; other councillors, among them the Spaniards Hugo de Moncada and Pescara, wished a treaty of clemency, of reconciliation with the captive king; that is, they wanted the empire of Christian peace; and Charles cast his decision with this moderate faction.

Charles V, then, shows himself to be a follower of the political ideas of his grandfather Ferdinand, and appears as the inheritor of the profound feelings of Christian universality which beat in Isabella's heart. And in his own way, Philip II must have learned from Charles, for Gracián tells of him that he said reverently before the portrait of the Catholic King, "We owe everything to this man."

THE VALUE OF MACHIAVELLI'S AND CASTIGLIONE'S
ASSESSMENTS OF THE CATHOLIC MONARCHS

Machiavelli theorized an idea of the state which was absolutely substantive and autonomous: every prince should look out only for his private interests and put them ahead of any other consideration whatever, either of ethics or of Christianity. This idea had a great deal of currency before Machiavelli's time, but especially after him, and it can well be said that only Ferdinand and Isabella were capable of completely identifying the historical interests of their kingdoms with the idea of Christian universality; and, conceiving the plan of maintaining, affirming, and expanding that universality, they succeeded in conferring on the Spanish nation its culminating moment. Their successors followed the direction they had indicated, but the idea of Catholicity broke down in Europe and hard times came upon Spain.

We have just mentioned the Catholic Queen's desperate petitions to the king at the time of the war in Roussillon. They indicate to us the enormous part owed to the queen at that time by such an opportune association of the Spanish idea of the state with the idea of the medieval Christian universality; of course, such an association is in perfect agreement with Isabella's motives and conduct, and therefore the great influence which the queen's ideas must have had on the king is very apparent; and he, after all, was one of the princes who inspired Machiavelli.

Here it would be well to add to Machiavelli's Italian assessment of Ferdinand, Castiglione's assessment, also Italian, of Isabella. Thus we shall have the testimony of two great contemporary writers of the early years of the sixteenth century, representatives of two opposite tendencies of the Renaissance, both of whom focus particularly on the Catholic Kings.

In the naturalist direction, Machiavelli thinks that the man who forgets *what is done or how one lives* ordinarily, and pays heed to *what ought to be done or how one ought to live*, is pursuing perdition, for he will be a victim of human wickedness, which is more frequent and more powerful than goodness. In opposition to this pessimistic notion is the idealist direction, based on Platonic philosophy; it does not wish, either in art or in life, to hold to *what is*, but aspires to *what ought to be*, according to abstract models of perfection, supreme exemplars which deserve to be imitated. Queen Isabella shared this conception in large measure: she united the eternal standard of Christian goodness with the Renaissance ideal of *gentillesse* as a way of living; she combined a holy horror of sin with the rejection of anything base in behavior; she often said that "the man who has good taste bears a letter of recommendation," a very great innovation in which the queen documents for the first time, in the Romance languages, the metaphorical sense of the expression "good taste." It can easily be understood that, because of this vital conjunction of moral and aesthetic principles, Castiglione should sing the praises of the Spanish queen when he presented the perfect example of a lady.

But before we describe this eulogy, let us emphasize one consideration as strongly as possible: Machiavelli and Castiglione, by exemplifying in Ferdinand and Isabella the two Renaissance theories, show us very clearly in what the singular value of this peerless royal marriage consisted. Universal history offers no other case in which two states were thus united by a king and a queen each of whom was possessed of the most outstanding gifts for government. But, moreover, each of them personified to an eminent degree two opposing tendencies of the period: one which based itself on the past, renewing it; the other, which initiated the Modern Age; and the king and queen harmonized their actions in such a way that they purified the excesses or deficiencies which were deeply rooted in both these tendencies.

CASTIGLIONE: COMPARATIVE ASSESSMENT OF THE KING AND THE QUEEN

Count Baldassare Castiglione began his delightful book *Il Cortegiano* in 1507, three years after Queen Isabella's death. At that date his knowledge of Spanish affairs came from having fought in 1503 in the second Neapolitan war against the Great Captain, but later this knowledge became much more direct when Castiglione entered the Church and after 1525 resided in Spain until his death in Toledo in 1529, acting as Apostolic nuncio in close proximity to Charles V. Since the *Cortegiano* was not published until 1528, it is to be supposed that there are additions stemming from these latter years when the author lived in the emperor's court.

The third book of the *Cortegiano* gives much space to a long eulogy of the Catholic Queen, placed in the mouth of Giuliano de' Medici, Il Magnifico; it is the most extensive among those of various women who have accomplished great deeds.

"Leaving aside all the others," says Il Magnifico, "what king, or what prince, has there been in our time, and even in many years past, that deserves to be compared to Queen Isabella of Spain?" To which Gaspar Pallavicino replies, "What king? King Ferdinand, her husband." "I do not deny it," continues Il Magnifico, "for since the queen thought him worthy to be her husband and loved him so much, it cannot be said that he did not deserve to be compared to her. But with all that, I believe indeed that the reputation he gained from her was a dowry no less than the kingdom of Castile that she brought to him in marriage."

As for this preference given to Isabella over her husband, we need only comment by recalling what her contemporaries told us about how much confidence the king had in the queen's good judgment, not only in Castilian affairs but in those of Aragon, Sicily, and Naples, and what they also told us about her having been more justice-living, more feared, and more loved by her people. For his part, Lucio Marineo Sículo, although enrolled in the personal service of King Ferdinand, tells us in Book XXI of *De rebus Hispaniae* that in comparison with the excellences of the king "in the judgment of many, the queen was of more majestic aspect, of livelier intelligence, of greater soul and more serious conduct."[22]

ISABELLA'S JUSTICE-LOVING SPIRIT

"When she began to reign," continues Giuliano Il Magnifico in *Il Cortegiano*, "she found the greater part of Castile possessed by the grandees, and, however, she recovered everything after such a justifiable manner and with such skill that the same ones who were stripped of their usurpations continued to hold her in the greatest affection and willingly gave up that which they had possessed as if it were their own." We can support this with a single event, so appropriate that Castiglione must have been thinking of it when he wrote, and it is the fact of the stormy Cortes of Toledo, in 1480, for the restitution of the royal patrimony, impoverished and undermined by Henry's excessive favors. At that time the restitution of the royal rents was accomplished with such scrupulous justice that everyone had to accept it,[23] those who most strongly supported Henry IV and his presumed daughter La Beltraneja as well as the stoutest defenders of Doña Isabella's rights to the throne; in the Cortes the following persons suffered a considerable reduction in their private rents: Don Beltrán de la Cueva, a constant supporter of Isabella's cause; Doña Beatrix de Bobadilla, the queen's intimate friend; the admiral of Castile, a relative of Don Ferdinand; the king's secretary, the chronicler Fernando del Pulgar, and a host of bishops and grandees, enthusiastic supporters of the monarchs. Pulgar admires the justice that was meted out: "And of this decision which was made, some were satisfied and many others dissatisfied, but all suffered it, each one considering how those favors had been granted with so much ease and so much dissolution of the royal patrimony."[24] A prime example of a measure prejudicial to all, and accepted by all, in consideration of the irresistible strength which the queen was always able to find within the strictest and most inflexible equity.

To this should be added the fact that it was she, not the king, who was concerned to establish, in a kingdom profoundly corrupted by Henry IV's lack of government, a justice which would be effective because unsubornable and rigid. When the chronicler Bernáldez is lamenting Isabella's death, he looks back with longing on the happiness of that good time which is past: "The humble poor were weighed in justice along with the knights, and received justice."[25] And Fernández de Oviedo retained an unforgettable memory of having witnessed, in the *alcázar* of Madrid, the public audiences held on Fridays, when the queen, seated under the royal canopy and surrounded by judges of the Royal Council, justices of the court, scribes, and mace-bearers, gave free entry to all litigants. "Indeed," exclaims Oviedo, "that was a golden time and a time of justice; and he who had it could

profit from it. I have seen that since God took that holy queen, it
is more trouble to deal with the servant of a secretary than it was
then with her and her Council, and costs more as well."[27] Lucio
Marineo Sículo also recalls that happy age in which justice was
done equally to nobles, citizens, and peasants, to the poor and the
rich. Yes; there was a golden age that was owed to the queen, to
her holy hunger and thirst for justice, to her fervid and constant
desire for justified punishment and just reward. For me, this was
the fundamental undertaking of her reign; the fact that no one
could feel himself aggrieved by the greater but undiscriminating
severity which might befall him; that justice was what restored
perfect health to the sick body of the nation; none of its cells
rebelled against the organism of which they formed a part; there
was no abscess, paralysis, hypertrophy, or abnormality of any
sort: a complete vigor followed in all orders of the state's activity.

The golden age passed with Isabella's death, but its effects
lasted for a long time, as Castiglione was to say very beautifully;
and after her, it was no longer possible to return to the prostration
of former times.

ISABELLA IN THE WAR WITH GRANADA

But let us return to *Il Cortegiano*.

Il Magnifico's speech continues: "It is well known with what
courage and wisdom Isabella always defended her kingdoms from
the most powerful foes. To her alone can be ascribed the honor of
the glorious conquest of the kingdom of Granada . . . in which she
always showed, by her counsel and by her own person, so much
effort that in our time few princes have dared, not only to imitate
her, but even to envy her."[27] It is very striking that, even when
speaking of a war in which Ferdinand had taken such an important
personal part, Andrea Navagero also repeats the general statement
that Isabella had been the strongest cause for the conquest of
Granada. Pulgar tells us the same thing, in more detail: "The
war against the Moors was begun at the queen's request, and was
continued because of her diligence, until all the kingdom of

Granada was won. And we speak the truth before God, that we knew and were acquainted with some great lords and captains of her kingdoms who, tiring, lost all their hope of being able to continue that difficult war; and because of the queen's constancy, and by her labors and the efforts that she continually made in the provisions for it, or by the other efforts which she brought to bear, with great exhaustion of spirit, this conquest, which seemed to have begun inspired by the Divine Will, was ended."[28]

ISABELLA'S TALENT FOR SELECTION

Then Castiglione, still using Il Magnifico as his spokesman, concentrates especially on the fine talent for selection which Isabella possessed: "The marvelous judgment that she had in recognizing and choosing the most efficient agents for those employments she gave to them. . . . In our time all the great men in Spain, and famous in any thing, have been formed by Queen Isabella; and Gonzalo Fernández, the Great Captain, took more pride in this than in all his famous victories and all those noble and virtuous actions which have made him so eminent and so famous both in peace and in war." Let us confirm this very accurate statement by adding that Isabella raised many others from obscurity, just as she did with the Great Captain, who rose to fame during the war with Granada: she made two rebellious vassals, the marquis of Cádiz and the duke of Medina Sidonia, into heroes of the Granadine war; and in that war, which she initiated and encouraged, there also arose García de Paredes, who later so distinguished himself in Cephalonia and at the Garigliano;[29] and we could name many more. Isabella brought Cisneros out of voluntary retirement and raised him, over Ferdinand's tenacious nepotism,[30] to the highest ecclesiastical post in Spain, seeing in him the man capable of handling princely sums in great military and cultural undertakings. Isabella, as in the case of Cisneros, established as a general rule the provision of ecclesiastical and civil posts on the basis of merit, something to which Ferdinand paid little attention, as was demonstrated after the queen's death.

"DIVINA MANIERA DI GOVERNARE"

And lastly, Castiglione stresses how profound and universal was the impression left by Isabella on everyone, and makes Il Magnifico say, answering the reservations expressed by Gaspar Pallavicino: "Unless all the people of Spain, men and women, rich and poor, have combined to tell lies in her praise, there has not been in our time in the whole world a brighter example of true goodness, greatness of spirit, wisdom, religion, honor, courtesy, liberality, and every virtue, in short, than this Queen Isabella; and though this lady's fame is very great in all places and all nations, these supreme virtues are confirmed by those who lived with her and saw her actions with their own eyes." Let us note here that at the same time that Castiglione, nuncio to the court of Charles V, published *Il Cortegiano*, Andrea Navagero, an ambassador to the emperor's court (1526), wrote an identical comment on the Catholic Queen: "She was a rare and most virtuous woman, who was universally, throughout all Spain, mentioned much more than her husband, though he also was a most wise and rare person in his time."[31]

And finally, there follows one of the most beautiful passages in *Il Cortegiano*, in which Il Magnifico eloquently sums up the essence of this extraordinary eulogy of the queen, the warmest and most graceful eulogy ever made of her: "All who knew her assure us that they found in her so divine a manner of governing that it seemed that her will alone was almost enough to make each one do his duty without any pressure; to such a degree that scarcely anyone dared, not even in his own house and secretly, to do any thing which he thought might displease her. ... She knew so well how to unite the severity of justice with the mildness of clemency and liberality that in her time there was no good man who could complain of not being sufficiently rewarded, nor any evil man of being too severely punished. And from this arose the fact that the people had the highest veneration for her, born of love and fear, which is still so deeply rooted in the minds of all that it seems as if they believed that she looks down on them from

Heaven and from thence sends them her praise or her reproval. And so, in her name and in the ways established by her, those kingdoms are still governed; so that, though her life is over, her authority yet lives: like a wheel which, having spun at high speed for a long time, still turns of itself for a good while, though no one spins it now."

A lucid figure of speech in which Castiglione gives the impression he has received, no doubt during his years of residence in Spain, when there was still a recent echo of the *Comunidades* which had demanded the laws and standards of Isabella; when those standards were being evoked anew in the measures passed by the Cortes; when the emperor, in his political ideas, still took inspiration from Isabella's lofty thoughts. Later, the happy government of this queen was remembered with longing by Spaniards who lived under the degenerate Hapsburgs; in later centuries, the figure of Isabella continued to symbolize the happiest period in the nation's life; and the wheel of that memory still continues to turn, arousing nostalgia in the soul of everyone who wishes to see a new flowering of that divine manner of governing, that just selection which produced such enviable results.

NOTES

1. *Opere di Niccolò Machiavelli*, VI (Firenze, 1783), 24–25. [The author here seems to use a slightly different version of chap. 21 of *The Prince* from that used on p. 391.]
2. *History of Ferdinand and Isabella*, II (Boston, 1838), 24, n. 72.
3. *Opere*, VI, 15–16.
4. *Opere*, VI, 31, 33.
5. *Opere*, VI, 25.
6. Ferdinand declared at the Cortes of Monzón, on August 13, 1510, that the kingdoms of Bougie and Tripoli, and even the Holy House [i.e. the Latin Kingdom] of Jerusalem, "to which he held title," belonged to Aragon. Zurita, *Anales de Aragón*, IX, chap. 14.
7. J. M. Doussinague, *Política internacional de Fernando el Católico* (1944), pp. 332, 340.
8. In BAE, LXX, 558b.
9. The king uses this as an excuse for not being able to help Emperor Maximilian in more than a limited way, in a letter dated in February, 1510, and addressed to the ambassador Jerónimo de Cabanillas. In May,

1510, the king advised Count Pedro Navarro that the African strongholds should be self-sustaining; see Doussinague, *op. cit.*, pp. 582, 615.

10. In Doussingaue, *op. cit.*, p. 641. In his chap. 226 Bernáldez, who is very reliable, also says that Don García's disastrous defeat at Los Gerbes made the king decide to go to the war in person. On December 24 Don Ferdinand notified the viceroy of Sicily that he would go personally (in Doussinague, *op. cit.*, p. 644).

11. "The French have an eye to the Monarchy." "The king of France leans toward being Monarch"; letters from the ambassadors in London and Rome in May, 1510. The second of these states that, in order to obstruct the French king's plans, "under the guise of its being for the war with the Moors, as indeed it would be were it not for the king of France, I am having the necessary arrangements made"; see Doussinague, *op. cit.*, pp. 595, 616 *et seq.*

12. Doussinague, *op. cit.*, p. 649.

13. *Ibid.*, p. 662.

14. Bernáldez, chap. 226 (in BAE, LXX, 744*a*).

15. He announced this in Seville on November 6, as reported in Bernáldez.

16. The news reached Ferdinand in January, 1512; Bernáldez, chap. 229.

17. Report of the secretary Pedro de Quintana, in February, 1516 (Doussinague *op. cit.*, pp. 677, 681.)

18. See the text in Doussinague, *op. cit.*, p. 616.

19. See in Doussinague, *op. cit.*, pp. 675, 676.

20. For the various indications of Charles V's thought as quoted here, see my article *La idea imperial de Carlos V*, 1937 (reprinted in the volume of the same title, no. 172 of the Colección Austral).

21. Petri Martyris, *Opus epistolarum*, 262 [ed. Paris, 1670, p. 151*b*. Cf. *ibid.*, ed. J. López de Toro, *Documentos Inéditos para la historia de España*, XI (Madrid, 1955), 65–67.]

22. ". . . tametsi multorum iudicio forma Regina pulchrior, ingenio acutior, animo splendidior, et decoro gravior habebatur." (In *Hispaniae Illustratae . . . Scriptores* I (Frankfurt, 1603), 506.)

[23. This passage now needs modification. The restitutions of 1480 did not apply to usurpations made before 1464, and these were very extensive. Thus too much should not be made of the resumptions of 1480. Cf. J. H. Elliott, *Imperial Spain*, p. 100.]

24. Pulgar, *Crónica de los Reyes Católicos*, II, 95; Carriazo's ed., I (1943), 421. See Clemencín, *Elogio de Isabel la Católica*, in *Memorias de la Academia de la Historia*, VI (1821), 147.

25. Bernáldez, chap. 202 (in BAE, LXX, 723*a*).

26. Oviedo, *Quinquagenas*, III, stanza II (in *Memorias de la Academia de la Historia*, VI [1821], p. 203).

27. In his translation of *Il Cortegiano*, Boscán incorrectly translates the Renaissance term *virtù* as *virtud*, virtue; I translate it as "effort," or some similar concept.

28. Pulgar, *Crónica*, II, 4; in Carriazo's edition, I, 78; I have corrected the word order, for better understanding of the passage.

[29. García de Paredes, 1466–1530, was the warrior companion of the Great Captain. Cephalonia was an Ionian island which had once belonged to the Venetians. Captured from them by the Turks, it was attacked and seized by the Spaniards in December, 1500. The Garigliano was a victory of the Great Captain over the French in two phases (October 15–31; December 27/28, 1503).]

[30. The reference is to Ferdinand's attempt to force into the archbishopric of Toledo his illegitimate son, Alfonso, archbishop of Sara gossa 1478–1520.]

[31. *Viaggio in Spagna*, p. 58: "Fu rara e virtuosíssima donna e della quale universalmente in tutti quei paesi si dice assai piu che del Re ancoraché fusse prudentíssimo ed a sua età raro."]

14 The Idea of the Discovery of America Among the Spaniards of the Sixteenth Century

MARCEL BATAILLON

No book of essays on the Spanish fifteenth century would be complete without a contribution on the discovery of America. The one chosen—the work of the most distinguished French scholar Professor Marcel Bataillon, author of definitive studies on Erasmus and Spain and on *La Celestina* of Fernando de Rojas (see p. 30)—ought by rights to be preceded by a translation of Professor Edmundo O'Gorman's book *La idea del descubrimiento de América* (Mexico, 1951), which it particularly criticizes. But that would be impossible in the available space; in any case this review-article of Bataillon has a validity of its own. It would be difficult to think of any other essay which plunges the student so effectively into the famous controversy over what in the discovery is owed to Columbus and what to Vespucci or anyone else. At the same time most of the early historians of the first half-century of Latin American history are brought into the closely packed argument, and if some of them belong to the period after 1516, the reader is not the loser by the editor's refusal to stick too closely to chronological boundaries.

Edmundo O'Gorman's latest book[1] will be read avidly by all who wish, like him, to go beyond history of a dryly objective kind, those who do not believe that the events of the past can be understood simply by recovering the factual details one after the other, but who are anxious to know what meaning a given event had for the men who lived it, and what perhaps different meaning it assumed for the men of later periods.

For some time now the author has been asking himself just

what is meant, in the history of the human spirit, by the phrase "discovering America." The little book entitled *Fundamentos de la historia de América* (México, Impr. Univ., 1942) bears on its cover a large question mark superimposed on a map of the American continent. In a later book, philosophizing about what he calls *Crisis y porvenir de la ciencia histórica* (México, Impr. Univ., 1947), O'Gorman took as his point of departure the question: "Se sabe, acaso, qué es el descubrimiento de América?" (Do we even know what the discovery of America means?). "History," said the author, referring to the history of culture, "if we consider it abstractly, cannot help appearing to be a very long series of errors: which amounts to saying that in history the notion of error, as it is understood by the physical sciences, cannot be applied unless we decide that all of history is itself an error: an absurdity on a large scale. Everything which, in history, is presented to us as an error of interpretation—for example, 'Columbus discovered America' —is not an error, it is an erring ('es un errar'); in other words, the living proof ('mostración') that the past regarded and experienced things in a different way from that in which we regard and experience them. ... It is not a question, then, of something susceptible of correction. It could be said that the historian is the man upon whom devolves the task of exculpating in the eyes of his contemporaries the mode of life of past generations. *His mission consists in giving explanations for the dead, not in quibbling with them*: a fine motto for the historian of ideas." And O'Gorman reproached all modern historical writing on the discovery for its "lack of perspectivism or historicism," understanding by these graceless abstract words "the generous attitude of the man who understands everything in order to understand something."

The new book could well serve as an illustration for Chapter 1 of its predecessor. In it O'Gorman reviews the successive interpretations of the discovery of the New World beginning with the sixteenth century (unfortunately he does not start with the fifteenth), up to the year 1942, when the works of Morison[2] and Enrique de Gandía[3] appeared, as well as Emiliano Jos's clarification.[4] An overall view very satisfying to the spirit can be extracted from all this. It could be summarized by saying that the sixteenth-century view, eminently expressed by Las Casas and prolonged into the seventeenth, saw Columbus' exploit in the providentialist perspective of a universal history which was still a theology of history; that in the eighteenth century the transcendent ends of divine rule were supplanted by the immanent ends of human progress, and the discovery of the New World because, for Humboldt, a decisive moment in the "knowledge of the Cosmos," by means of which humanity took possession of its universe; and finally, that recent historiography, in the measure in which it asserts the fortuitous character of the discovery and the disproportion between the initial act and its consequences, rather tends to accentuate the contingency of history, at the same time as it expresses a certain determinism, and disassociates itself from any doctrine of ends, either explicit or implicit.

But if this is the valuable lesson which I, for my part, extract from O'Gorman's book, I must confess to being annoyed (giving the word its full force) by the way in which he presents the "early stage" of the interpretation of the discovery. And, as I suppose that other "sixteenth-century-ites" will be equally annoyed by this, I should like to clarify what I do not find satisfactory. As we shall see, it is a way of treating the old historians which I find entirely too free and easy. But why this freedom? We must read attentively what is presented to us as the "Genesis" of the history of the discovery.

O'Gorman is well aware that, intellectually speaking, the discovery of the *New World* did not date from 1492, when Columbus landed on the islands which form the gateway to the American continent, for the discoverer believed that these lands were the gateway to Asia; it dated from the moment when recognition had been made of the fact that they were *new* lands, unsuspected by ancient and medieval geography. Did not this moment occur, then, in 1503, when the little account entitled *Mundus Novus*, by the navigator Amerigo Vespucci, appeared? That, indeed, was the revelation of the new land which came to be called America! The interminable discussion, recently revived yet again by Roberto Levillier (*América la bien llamada*, Buenos Aires, 1948), as to the authenticity, the date, and the extent of Vespucci's explorations along the shores of the continent, are unimportant. America was not ill-named if it was Vespucci who first "understood" that it was a new continent in relation to the known world. To O'Gorman this revelation seems sufficiently clear, sufficiently startling, to become fixed after the first decade of the sixteenth century, at least in the minds of savants, and to destroy Columbus' "Asiatic project" as inevitably as day replaces night.

But this is not all. The Mexican philosopher of history was struck by finding everywhere—at least after 1535—the tradition, or legend, of the unknown pilot. A navigator whose name is not known to history was assumed to have been blown by a storm to one of the Greater Antilles, to have taken an at least approximate bearing on his position, and on his return, gravely ill, to have been aided by Christopher Columbus and to have confided his secret to him before he died. In fact, the *New World* would then have been discovered by accident, and Columbus would have done no more than to definitely rediscover the route. The chroniclers who lived in America shortly after Columbus' time do not offer the tradition of the unknown pilot as a truth established by reliable witnesses. In his old age Las Casas presents it as an explanation which had some currency among the Spaniards in the islands during the first decade of the sixteenth century. What did this *vox populi* signify? O'Gorman does not dwell upon the too-simple idea that it may have been the offspring of resentment or envy, that it may in fact have been a way of depriving Columbus of the glory of having discovered a new world by failing in his daring plan of reaching Asia by way of the West. Preoccupied with his problem, which is that of intellectual comprehension of the discovery of the New World, the philosopher-historian seems to see in this *vox populi* a naïve solution of the problem, a sort of popular "Ersatz" of the learned Amerigo Vespucci's "revelation." According to him, what the legend wipes out is not Columbus' merits as a discoverer, but his error in regard to Asia. If Columbus really believed that he had reached the shores of Asia from the Atlantic, when in fact he fell so far short of them, then this insane project has no more value than a madman's dream after what he actually found there. Both for his own glory and for the sake of common sense, it was better to believe that he had rediscovered the Atlantic lands whose existence had been revealed to him by another, who had been cast upon them by the "fortunes of the sea." And that other, postulated by popular good sense, was the anonymous pilot.

Vespucci's revelation and the legend of the unknown pilot: O'Gorman believes that here he is in the presence of a double genesis of the idea of the discovery. Learned genesis, popular genesis: both are fatal to Columbus' "Asiatic project." Henceforth he can mock at the endless controversies between the Harrisses, the Vignauds, the Carbias,[5] who deny the Asiatic project, and erudite classic historiography, which denies the unknown pilot! "Let us say no longer," he proposes, "that the story of the unknown pilot is a 'falsehood' ('una falsedad'); let us say that it is the 'truth' ('la verdad') of our ancestors, and thus we will open wide the doors to historical understanding of the chief event in our American existence."

After this he has only to interpret the sixteenth-century literature dealing with the New World by following the thread of the double line he has adopted. It is here that the reader respectful of *texts* becomes dismayed. O'Gorman, who has achieved such a happy formulation of the rule of historical comprehension, "to give explanations for the dead, not to quibble with them," is thereby led to seek quarrels (and what irresponsible quarrels!) with Oviedo,[6] with Ferdinand Columbus,[7] with Las Casas;[8] to accuse one of paralogism, another of bad faith, to reproach the third for trying to be something other than what he is. Only Gómara,[9] perhaps, comes out well, because it is he who officially "consecrates" the legend of the unknown pilot by presenting it as truth pure and simple. From that point on he has the right to ignore the Vespuccian revelation. The others have their intentions and their thoughts torn to shreds by an inquisitor who prides himself on seeing more clearly than they do themselves. They are forced to "confess" their twisting of the facts in the light of O'Gorman's logic. But who is the guilty one, the old authors or O'Gorman? For a historian who takes care to read the texts looking for what they *meant to say* and not calling on them to answer *yes* or *no* to ready-made questions, is not the fact that their answers are beside the point a sign that the investigation is being badly conducted? We can almost hear the old authors protesting against the ill treatment of the accuser who puts them to the torture: "Lay on, but listen!" We wish that we could give them a chance to speak again, and make them judges in their turn of the value of O'Gorman's claims. Is it true that the "Asiatic" idea which spurred Columbus on died overnight? Was it on the threshold of the sixteenth century, and was it thanks to Vespucci, that the Spanish geographer-historians began to conceive of America as a new continent independent of Asia? Does the legend of the unknown pilot appear in their works in a context of calm explanation or of impassioned debate? Once we have prepared the ground in this way, we will be in a better position to understand that they all shared, without finding them incompatible, two concepts which O'Gorman tries to make into contradictory "theses": the discovery conceived as the fruit of knowledge and human calculations, and the discovery conceived as a providential event. Perhaps this syncretism, illogical in the eyes of an existentialist philosopher of today, is what best characterizes the comprehension of the discovery in the sixteenth century. But the discovery is infinitely greater than the problem formulated by O'Gorman. And it is indeed one of the most fascinating goals that an existentialist or phenomenological historian can set himself.

DEATH OR SURVIVAL OF THE ASIATIC IDEA?

In claiming a Vespuccian "revelation" in the early years of the sixteenth century, O'Gorman admits implicitly that this revelation casts into limbo the idea of reaching Asia by way of the West. This is to scorn too much an error which was an "erring" of medieval science. Why, then, does he make so little of the "Columbine genesis," as Emiliano Jos would express it,[10] of the idea of the discovery? It is indeed regrettable that Mr. O'Gorman has established as an early phase of his historiography a phase which was already late, and one peculiarly troubled by non-historical considerations, as we shall see. If, by sacrificing chronology to what he feels to be the logic of the interpretation of the discovery, he presents Gómara (1550) before Oviedo (1535) (though he does acknowledge many times that the latter precedes the former), this is not the most serious of the distortions to which he subjects the real process of the histography of the discovery. The most reprehensible of these, the one that falsifies everything else, is to do away with the true "early stage," that of Columbus' contemporaries, to obliterate Peter Martyr of Anghiera,[11] and Andrés Bernáldez.[12] Mendénez y Pelayo did not make so bold as this in his honestly chronological study *De los historiadores de Colón*,[13] to which O'Gorman shows so much injustice.

Once we take into account the documents and testimony prior to 1500, we cannot scornfully dismiss the explanation given to his enterprise by Columbus himself: his proclaimed intention of reaching India to the east of the Ganges by way of the Atlantic, and the illusion which he cherished that he had reached at least the outlying parts of that country. For, in the beginning, the genesis of the discovery and the genesis of his interpretation coincide. The Asiatic idea is displayed on the title page of the *Epistola Christophori Colom* "*de Insulis Indiae supra Gangem nuper inventis*," published in Rome as early as 1493. It is well known to Peter Martyr and Andrés Bernáldez, both of whom, before 1500, discuss the error of longitude it involves. The idea had a more persistent life than one might suppose; we have only to look at the cartography of the sixteenth century. It was something entirely different from the caprice of a mad genius or a mythomaniac.

It is comprehensible that a polemicist like the much-overrated Carbia should have pruned and cut at will in the documents, that he considered that historiography contemporary with Columbus was nonexistent, that he should have demanded the first and last word of truth about the discovery of America from the Oviedos and the Gómaras. Mortal enemy of the "Black Legend," he had vowed to demonstrate that Las Casas, who was responsible for that Legend, was the greatest liar of all time, that this "demented monk" had not only invented the absurd fiction of the Asiatic project, but that he had forged to support his invention the following spurious works: the *Life of the Admiral* by Columbus' son Don Fernando, the admiral's logbooks, and Toscanelli's letter.[14] It is comprehensible, I imagine, that an American advertising man of the twentieth century, if he is totally lacking in historical culture, if he knows nothing at all about the Middle Ages, might be bewildered at the thought that men could ever have considered as learned a view of the earth in which Asia extended to the point occupied by America, the existence of which was not even suspected. But, for an O'Gorman, this concept should have been a "living proof" "that the past regarded and experienced things in a different way from that in which we regard and experience them." Columbus' Asiatic project, or Toscanelli's letters which encouraged it, far from being mystifications of Las Casas or absurd ideas that made Ferdinand Columbus blush for his father after the fact, were in perfect harmony with a great tradition in medieval science. Every good bibliography of Columbus ought to include an old study dating back nearly a century, which Charles Jourdain entitled *De l'influence d'Aristote et de ses interprètes sur la découverte du Nouveau Monde.*[15] It uncovers the "learned" roots of the Asiatic project. It demonstrates that, though Columbus (or his brother Bartholomew)[16] used Pierre d'Ailly[17] as one of his chief authorities, this was by no means a fortuitous meeting of minds between two fantastic spirits. The idea that it was easy to reach the extreme east of Asia by way of the Atlantic was an old idea based on the "authority" of Aristotle and Seneca, and one which the Middle Ages had long cultivated.

It matters little that Christopher Columbus, who flattered himself that he had proved the idea, killed it. Nor does it matter that the discoverer believed in the idea to the day of his death.

The discussion began in connection with his earliest discoveries (even Bernáldez, we will recall, argued the point with him). It continued, but was based, much more than on arguments in books or Columbus' experience, on the experiences of the navigators who followed him. Much more decisive in this regard than Vespucci's voyages and his *Mundus Novus* was the first voyage around the world made by one of Magellan's caravels. The enormous error in longitude which vitiated the "Asian project" was progressively corrected within half a century. But this should not make us forget that information on the continuity or noncontinuity of the "New World" with Asia continued to be ambiguous both before and after these voyages. It was not definitely cleared up until 1726, when the Bering Strait was crossed. Throughout the sixteenth century and even later, a vast space was left on the maps in the area of the northern Pacific, which was called either "unknown land" or "unknown sea." It was through *a priori* arguments that an insular concept of the New World was chosen (by analogy with the ancient world, which antiquity had conceived of as a great island entirely bathed by "the Ocean, father of rivers"), or one which made it into an immense appendage of Asia. There is a capital text in Oviedo which has been very unluckily neglected by O'Gorman, for it is the most substantial response made by the chronicler to O'Gorman's question: How did men realize that the New World was new? (We should have to add, "To what extent did they realize it?") This is the preface to Book XVI, where the author solemnly announces that he is going to describe Terra Firma and give its latitudes. In discussing the name of *Novus orbis* first used by Peter Martyr, he explains that this world is neither newer nor older than the continent formed by Asia, Africa, and Europe. These western Indies, it is true, are not Europe or Africa or Asia. But, he adds, "if they ought to belong to one of the three, it should be Asia. This would be so if it were proved that the last land situated to the east of Asia, farther east than the kingdom of China, or any other located more to the east, were connected to the westernmost part of the Terra Firma of our Indies; that is, the far western part of

New Spain, as we call it here. But since all of that land is not yet fully discovered, we do not know whether there is sea or land at its further side, or whether it is all surrounded by the Ocean Sea on that side. I am inclined to believe this last. *My opinion, which is not solely mine, makes me suspect rather (until we have further information) that it is not part of Asia, and that it does not correspond to the Asia of the ancient cosmographers.* It is rather more likely that the Terra Firma of these Indies is *another half of the world,* as large as and perhaps larger than Asia, Africa, and Europe, and that all the land in the world is divided into two parts. . . . It is in this sense that Peter Martyr was correct when he spoke of a new world in relation to the accounts of judgments given by the Ancient ; and therefore it now appears that they were unaware of it, while we now see it (*por lo que agora paresce que ynoraron ellos e vemos nosotros*)" (Vol. III, pp. 184–85).

Vemos nosotros. . . . Here we are dealing with evidence resulting from the experience of successive navigations from 1492 to 1535. Elsewhere, right at the end of his history, in the conclusion to Book XLIX, he enumerates the chief stages: it is, first of all, Columbus' discovery which has made the others possible, "a discovery to which nothing else can be compared." Then came Balboa, who reached the Southern Sea. Then Magellan, who discovered the southern strait at $52\frac{1}{2}$ degrees of latitude south, and one of whose ships went around the world. Then came the discovery of Mexico by Cortés, and that of Peru by Pizarro and Almagro. Then the exploration of the Río Grande (Magdalena) by Cristóbal de Lugo, governor of Santa Marta, and by his lieutenant Jiménez de Quesada, conqueror of New Granada.[18]

VESPUCCI'S REVELATION

If O'Gorman had analyzed these texts, he would surely have accused Oviedo of repeatedly ignoring Amerigo Vespucci. We know, according to the Mexican philosopher-historian, that early in the sixteenth century there was a revelation which completely overturned the concept of the discovery: "Vespucio *reveló* su idea de que las regiones exploradas no pertenecían al Asia, sino que constituían un continente distinto" (Vespucci *revealed* his idea that the regions which had been explored did not belong to Asia, but constituted a separate continent). Those who, after that date, speak as though this *revelation* had not taken place, and as though they knew nothing of its author, cannot be in O'Gorman's eyes anything but Sophists, in either good or bad faith. Oviedo was a Sophist without meaning to be, when he declared quite plainly in his *Sumario* of 1525 (and was to repeat for the rest of his life) that Columbus had discovered the "Western Empire" of the Indies. It is he who is responsible for the fact that "the *Vespuccian notion* having been admitted as compatible with Columbus' exploit in a paralogical synthesis, it could come to be affirmed that Columbus had discovered America" (p. 46). He accuses Ferdinand Columbus of being a shameless Sophist, whom "the astute questioning of the public accuser" (this role fits O'Gorman to a T!) led to "pile up ambiguous and far-fetched explanations" in order to prove his thesis (p. 113). "Don Fernando . . . knew that his father had confused the new continent with Asia; he knew that Toscanelli was the authority who had had the most profound influence on the imagination of the future admiral; *he knew, in fact, that Vespucci had given the decisive indication* concerning the lands Columbus had first visited, and that in consequence Vespucci would have been justified in disputing, in the eyes of the savants, the title of 'discoverer' to which Don Fernando owed, as he himself admitted, his title of nobility and, as we all know, his fortune." If Don Fernando made no mention of Vespucci it was because, thanks to this extremely suspect procedure, he aspired to assure his father's title of "discoverer of America" in the eyes of posterity and his contemporaries; a title to which the admiral did not have the intellectual right. . . . Here we see Don Fernando Columbus as the accused, disqualified as a historian of his father's exploit! But the accusation, whether it is leveled against Don Fernando or against Oviedo, collapses as soon as it is realized that "Vespucci's revelation" is merely a historical mirage. O'Gorman, who is not always charitable toward Vignaud and his school, is their victim on this point. It is not a question, either for us or for him, of knowing which shores Vespucci *explored* first, nor whether it is just to say, with Levillier, *América la bien llamada* (we are not *historians of the discovery*); it is not even a question of knowing what in fact Vespucci comprehended and explained first. The only thing that matters to the history of ideas of the discovery is to ascertain for what accomplishment the first decades of the sixteenth century, especially in Spain, gave credit to Vespucci. It is useless to search; we find nothing. One swallow does not make a summer. The false summer of the school of St.-Dié,[19] which by 1507 had adopted the name of America for what we now call South America, had not made its warmth felt in Spain. At least, if the name proposed by Waldseemüller[20] had found some echo (and this has not yet been proved) it had not been strong enough to supplant the official name of "West Indies." Far more important than Waldseemüller for the adoption of the name "America" was to be Mercator,[21] also a non-Spaniard, and then not until after 1538. One of the first mentions of Vespucci which we find written by a Spanish pen—an emigré Spaniard's, coincidentally—is the aggressive allusion made by Michael Servetus[22] in his commentaries on Ptolemy (Lyons, 1535): "Those who try to call this continent America are completely mistaken, for Amerigo visited the same land as Columbus and considerably later than he; and he went there not with the Spaniards, but with the Portuguese, to trade there." Twenty years later Las Casas was amazed that Don Fernando had not, about the year 1538, defended his father's memory against Vespucci's usurpation; and it would have been natural for him to do so, says the Dominican, "for he possessed, I know, the record of Vespucci's voyages." It is this remark which the accuser, O'Gorman, alleges in order to denounce an "extremely suspect" silence surrounding Vespucci's name. Magnaghi[23] and Enrique de Gandía have tried to account for this silence by saying that Don Fernando refrained from attacking the letters attributed to Vespucci because he knew them to be false, and that Vespucci was his friend. The accuser closes the defenders' mouths; their explanation is worthless: "If Ferdinand Columbus knew that Vespucci's letters were false, it was an even better reason to attack them!" But the truth is less disputatious. Neither in Oviedo, who in 1535 tried to minimize Columbus' claims, nor in Don Fernando, who returned his attack and defended his family's rights as well as his father's titles, do we find the slightest allusion to Amerigo Vespucci, *for no one, at that time in Spain, dreamed of disputing Columbus' claim to be the first discoverer of the West Indies; and although there was an attempt to diminish the importance of this claim, no one dreamed of doing so to the benefit of Vespucci.*

The idea of a new part of the world, as we can easily see by reading Oviedo, gained currency little by little. But is this the result of the "hermeneutic process" so ingeniously analyzed by O'Gorman, a process which had to do solely with Columbus' first discoveries and in which Vespucci's role had been decisive? No. It was the result of forty years of navigation along shores which, as they became progressively better marked on the maps, showed more and more clearly how immense was the continent that had been discovered. It was its immensity which made it a New World. As for the rest, this *Novus Orbis* had been doubtful, ever since Columbus' first two voyages, insofar as its connection with Asia was concerned. This was disputed from the very outset, without waiting for Vespucci's *Mundus Novus.* A serious doubt still remained as late as 1530. Oviedo expressed it very well in the first part of his great *Historia* published in 1535. And it existed to a degree—let us repeat—up to Bering's time.

It is because he has closed his eyes to these pieces of evidence that Edmundo O'Gorman, forgetting the mission of the historian ("to give explanations for the dead and not to quibble with them"), charges poor Don Fernando Columbus with imaginary crimes. He accuses him of subtle maneuvering and paralogism because he spoke of the "fin oriental ignoto de la India" (unknown eastern end of India) and the "parte oriental de la India allende del Ganges" (eastern part of India farther off than the Ganges), though these formulas are the most classic expression of the imprecise Ptolemaic and medieval notion of geography which obsessed Christopher Columbus. He even makes Don Fernando say something quite different from what he did say (p. 110): he reproaches him for having falsely attributed to his father the knowledge of *an ocean between Asia and the newly discovered lands*, for he states, a propos of "India farther off than the Ganges," that "no cosmographer had ever assigned it a boundary with another land or province to the east, but only with the *Ocean* (p. 110; cf. p. 111, n. 10). But the ocean referred to here, for Christopher Columbus as well as for Ptolemy and all the ancient cosmographers to whom Don Fernando refers, is the *Atlantic*, which bathes on the one hand the far east of Asia and on the other the far west of Europe. It is the *only ocean* of the ancients. Don Fernando knew perfectly well that the *Southern Sea* (it is significant that the Pacific was not at first called an ocean) had been reached by Núñez de Balboa after his father's death. And furthermore, this discovery did not solve the problem of knowing whether the *Tierra Firme* reached by Columbus was a "separate continent" or an appendage of Asia. It was thus that Christopher Columbus fancied it to be when he imagined, on his fourth voyage, a sort of isthmus of which the shore he knew by hearsay, Ciguare, must be located in relation to that of Veragua like Fuenterrabía to Tortosa, or Pisa in relation to Venice. . . .[24] One of the historian's mortal sins is anachronism. It is not always easy to avoid. O'Gorman commits some aggressive misrepresentations because it is hard for him to dislodge from his mind the modern idea of the "American continent," incorrectly convinced that this idea must have entered men's minds, as clear as sunrise, after Vespucci's *Mundus Novus*. He does not even picture to himself the limits of medieval science, within which Ferdinand Columbus correctly placed his father's project, nor the geographical limits, already much altered but not as yet modern, within which Don Fernando moved. In a review which amply demonstrates the merits of O'Gorman's book, José Gaos[25] rightly says that "the history of ideas should not remain in the state of philological-literary history of ideas, nor of pure doxographic history." This is to recognize implicitly that the historian of ideas should first interpret the texts like a good philologist before he philosophizes about them. *Primum legere, deinde philosophari.* ... We might add that the good philologist cannot understand what he reads in the texts or correctly formulate the ideas they express if he does not know the world of notions and ideas within which the author moves. History of ideas and philology cannot get along without each other.

HISTORIOGRAPHY PLAGUED BY QUIBBLING: THE UNKNOWN PILOT

O'Gorman is certainly right in giving us the analysis of the admiral's projects, as presented by his son, as a tendentious and complex undertaking.[26] Don Fernando has but one intention, which is not exactly scientific, when he presents what O'Gorman calls the "scientific" solution of the problem of the discovery; that is, the solution which makes the discoverer a savant. This does not mean that he distorts the facts. What his analysis attempts to prove is that his father had ably planned and carried out the undertaking for which he had made a contract with the Crown: the discoverer had kept his part of the bargain, while the Crown had betrayed its part. Why this thesis, which scarcely conceals its aggressiveness? All this phase of Columbine historiography is dominated, and in certain respects vitiated, by the influence of the suit brought by the admiral's heirs against the Crown, which they called upon to respect the Capitulations of Santa Fe. Further, it was not Don Fernando who began to write the story in order to uphold the pretensions of one party to the suit, but the royal chronicler, Gonzalo Fernández de Oviedo. And he was not the last: Gómara was later to twist the story even more audaciously on behalf of the royal position.

Thus we see a process developing, between 1530 and 1550, which was perhaps "hermeneutic" in a subsidiary sense, but was chiefly polemic. To close our eyes to that other evidence is to risk not understanding very much about the manner in which the men of that time answered the question "How was the new world discovered?" Just as the discoveries were not undertaken to extend human knowledge, but to find gold and precious commodities, so their interpretation was affected by conflicts of power and interest. The chroniclers earned their wages fairly by working for the Crown. Thus Oviedo, who had stated in 1525 that Columbus had rendered the greatest possible service to his sovereigns, Oviedo who was still to offer him the same unmixed homage in the last unpublished books of his chronicle, made his little contribution to the Crown against the Columbus family in 1535.

The "fiscal" [public prosecutor] who was defending the royal interests against the admiral's heirs had not found anything very useful with which to rebut their claims. His King Charles' head was the role played on the first voyage by Martín Alonso Pinzón. He had died of syphilis shortly after the expedition's return; and this was why, it was said, he had not been able to claim his rights. But he had a family and friends. . . . The "fiscal" made the rounds of all the favorable witnesses to the "Pinzón theory" among the folk of Palos. Oviedo does not even pass over in silence this official thesis:

> As for what has been said here of Columbus' perseverance, it must be stated that certain persons deny it. They even say that he would have decided to turn back, and would not have gone on to the end, had not the Pinzón brothers made him go forward; and we say more: that it is because of them that the discovery was made, for Columbus was already drawing back and wanting to return. It is a point which better belongs to the long suit now being carried on between the admiral and the king's "fiscal," a suit where there are a great many allegations pro and con, and into which I do not propose to go. Those matters pertain to justice, and justice must settle them: let us leave them to follow their course to the end. As for me, I have expressed the opinions on both sides: let the reader choose the one his good judgment dictates.

Happily, we know through both previous and later texts what opinion Oviedo's own good judgment dictated: it was that Columbus was indeed the person responsible for the "discovery," itself the origin of a long series of discoveries in which, thanks to the determination of latitudes and longitudes, men were beginning to see more clearly. But when the time came for him to publish his *Historia General*, the official chronicler of the Indies refrained from contradicting the thesis of the "fiscal," and brought to the royal cause two arguments which, without dimming Christopher Columbus' glory behind the clouds of the "Pinzón theory," did diminish the historical importance of his initiative: the pseudo-historical legend of the Hesperides, identified with the Antilles, and the popular legend of the unknown pilot.

On the first point, let us cite the testimony of the letter in which Charles V, in 1533, thanks the chronicler for the discovery of which he had just hastily informed the king: "I have also seen what you say you have written and what you propose to send, with proofs taken from five authors: namely, that these isles belonged to the twelfth king of Spain counting from King Tubal, who became lord over certain kingdoms after Hercules, in the year 1558 before the incarnation of Our Redeemer; therefore, this year it will be 3,091 years that these lands have been under the royal scepter of Spain; and that not without great mystery, after so many years, God has restored them to those to whom they belonged. . . ."[27] We see that the emperor did not turn up his nose at this pseudo-erudite piece of nonsense. If the Antilles had been "Spanish" for more than three thousand years, he could feel easy about the legitimacy of their ownership, and especially (for this legitimacy had scarcely been contested as yet) about the excellent right with which he had deprived the admiral and his heirs of their privileges! The admiral had merely been, in fact, Heaven's instrument to return to Spain what belonged to her in any case. As for Oviedo, he was a good enough humanist not to consider these "proofs" as decisive. Not that he necessarily doubted the value of the texts in question. For every Vives[28] or Juan de Vergara,[29] who had enough critical spirit to make fun of the spurious Berossus and his fabulous series of the kings of Spain beginning with Tubal, there was a legion of credulous persons (such as Las Casas, the autodidact, who waxed indignant over

Vives' scepticism). But Oviedo was well aware that his arguments concerning his authorities were based on two unverifiable suppositions: (1) that the Hesperides had received this name from that of "Hesperus," following their annexation by that "king"; and (2) that the Hesperides were the same as the Antilles. Also, this little historico-geographical piece of fiction could never have had more than a very limited acceptance.

The unknown-pilot legend had a very different fate. And it is this which justifies the attention, however excessive, bestowed on it by O'Gorman. He is justified in finding it interesting, apart from the quantity of abstract truth it contains, and even though that quantity may be nil. It is not impossible that Oviedo invented it, though he does not take the responsibility for it. Even by denying it, he put it into circulation, thereby doing it notable service. For we seek in vain for the slightest written trace prior to his mention of it. It is significant that His Majesty's "fiscal" did not make use of it when he attempted to prove, in order to limit the recognition due to the Columbus family by the Crown, "que quando fué el Amirante a descubrir el primer viaje, *un Martín Alonso Pinzón thenía ya noticia de las Indias por cierta escritura que obo en Roma* e quería irlas a descubrir" (that when the admiral was about to announce the first voyage, *one Martín Alonso Pinzón already had news of the Indies through a certain writing that was in Rome*, and wished to go and discover them).[30] If the "fiscal" had heard any talk about this unknown pilot (whose secret could have been shared by the admiral and Martín Pinzón before the first voyage), that personage would have been a very valuable support for his thesis. Could the legend have circulated in the Antilles, as a vague rumor, without crossing the Atlantic? It is certainly very important that Las Casas, who arrived in the islands in 1503, admitted years later that such a rumor was circulating in Santo Domingo among the *pobladores* of his own nation; and Las Casas also admitted the "scientific" bases and the Asiatic project of Columbus' enterprise. I believe with O'Gorman that the reality of the fire from which this smoke arose is hardly important, and that we will never know whether there was any truth in it.

I do have difficulty in following O'Gorman when he discerns in this legend a naïve attempt at a "historical" interpretation of the discovery. Of course, any total or partial explanation of an event in the past partakes of "history." But if we ask ourselves what the "intent" of the unknown-pilot legend was, we begin to suspect that it was an opinion on Columbus' luck and skill rather than an "explanation" of a startling "novelty." We can imagine this rumor arising at the time when Las Casas landed in the islands with the Commander de Lares.[31] Discussions on the admiral's disgrace were in full spate. His partisans were indignant because the Crown had gone back on its promises, since the discoverer had tenaciously executed a wisely conceived project and had kept his word. The royalists and the indifferent shrugged their shoulders and said: "Columbus a savant? A persistent man? Of course not! A rogue. . . . Others suspected the existence of new lands in the Ocean. Who knows whether, just at the time when he was planning to go and discover the Indies, he was not in possession of the findings of someone else, a less lucky navigator whose secret he had seized?" This is the way the legend of the unknown pilot could have arisen, if it is true that it circulated very early in the Antilles. At the time when Las Casas landed in America it was already being passionately disputed. The Columbus family's suit against the Crown was just beginning. Whether the legend was born in the public square of Santo Domingo around 1502–1503 or in Oviedo's study thirty years later, its intention was doubtless the same, and equally "impure." As an explanation its value is extremely slight. It rejects less the Asiatic project than the "intentionality" itself of the discovery. It substitutes for a known discoverer, who claimed to have sought and found, an unknown discoverer who was supposed to have discovered by chance, without any plan, and whose findings were presumed to have been exploited by the other. That is all.

Its great interest lies in the varied use made of it by historians of the Indies from Oviedo to Acosta.[32] They are the ones who insert it into a "history" conceived of as human (all too human!) in its incentives, and at the same time divine in its plan. Oviedo makes no "historical" use of it; he denies it. Why does he not pass over it in silence, since no historian before him had spoken of it? Simply this: he was pleased to hand this weapon, good or bad, to His Majesty's "fiscal."

The *Life of the Admiral* by his son is explicitly a reply to Oviedo, and, less ostensibly, a reply to the "fiscal" of His Majesty. To become convinced of this we need only observe the care with which Don Fernando details the clauses in the contract requested by Columbus (Chapter XIV) and granted by the Catholic Monarchs ("They gave him everything he asked for," reads the title of Chapter XV). We can read Chapter XLIV, where he inserts side by side the actual text of the Capitulations of Santa Fe and the privileges confirmed in Barcelona after his return from the first voyage; we can observe the care he takes to pin down, in the course of this voyage, the exact role of the Pinzón brothers; we note the space (14 out of 108 chapters) given to the rebellion of Roldán (the most serious crisis of command for the admiral), the intervention of Commander Bobadilla, who returned the admiral to Spain in irons, and, at the end of this long episode (Chapter LXXXVII), the place where Columbus saw his privileges confirmed for himself and his children. So much for His Majesty's "fiscal," who is nowhere named. As for His Majesty's chronicler, Oviedo, he is specifically rebuked. We know how Don Fernando refutes the historical fiction of the Hesperides discovered twice, at an interval of three thousand years, by the kings of Spain. But what is his reaction to the legend of the unknown pilot, as he has read it in Oviedo?

Not only does he fail to take offense, but he flatters himself that he can identify the real fact of which this legend is a deformed version; a Portuguese thought he had discovered, to the west of Madeira, a land whose discovery was later unsuccessfully attempted by Genoese shipowners and Portuguese navigators. This event is mentioned in Don Fernando's ninth chapter, where it is added to a whole series of equally untrustworthy tales on which the admiral had based his hopes of finding "some isle or land of great useful-ness" before reaching the Asiatic "Indies" which were his chief objective. We know that it is this chapter which served as the basis for Vignaud's attempted "critical history," which, for no defensible reason, decreed that these purely empirical hopes had been Columbus' only incentives, the Asiatic project and its documentary bases having been invented after the fact to becloud the issue. We have already seen that the rejection of the Asiatic project as a chimera supposes a profound ignorance of medieval geography. O'Gorman's philosophical history of the idea of the discovery does not endorse this error of the "critical history" of the discovery according to Vignaud. But he seems to be influenced by it occasionally. After an attentive rereading of Don Fernando, one asks oneself how O'Gorman can find him confused and fallacious when he reconciles the Asiatic project with the hope of finding intermediate lands between Europe and Asia. Don Fernando shows his father operating on two planes. Wildly encouraged by Toscanelli's letter, the future admiral was confirmed in his theoretical conviction that it was possible to reach Cathay and the country of the Great Khan by way of the Atlantic.[33] On the other hand, the numerous tales, fabulous or not, made him agree with the opinion of the "savants and philosophers" who believed that the land surface of the earth was greater than that covered by seas; hence his conviction that "from the farthest point of Spain to the known borders of India there must be many other isles and lands, as experience has shown."[34] There is not the slightest inconsistency in all this. For Don Fernando it was a question of proving that his father had indeed found what he had promised the Catholic Monarchs. The demonstration was easier if the admiral had been looking for two things at once; the discoverer's merit would be more solidly established if his hopes had been based not only on theoretical opinions but on empirical facts like those which might have been disclosed to him by the unknown pilot.

One doubt does strike us, however, if we compare the already eclectic and complex interpretation of his father's exploit furnished by Don Fernando with the even more complex interpretation given later by Las Casas. For while the latter, though he praises

THE IDEA OF THE DISCOVERY OF AMERICA   447

Columbus' role, does not fail to emphasize the error of longitude implicit in his Asiatic project and the admiral's persistence in this error, Don Fernando, we can easily see why, piously tones it down. The only time that he brings it up he denounces it in Toscanelli,[35] forgetting or pretending to forget that his father shared it; the author of the famous letter which aroused new ardor for his project in the discoverer "committed an error in believing that the lands to be found would be Cathay and the empire of the Great Khan ... since, as experience has demonstrated, the distance between our [West] Indies and Cathay [across the Southern Sea] is much greater than that which exists between us and those countries [that is, from the West Indies by way of the Atlantic]." Don Fernando makes excuses for his father, as Jos has clearly shown. But having said this, we cannot see how his role as advocate for the family's cause makes him falsify either facts or ideas.

We are, it must be repeated, in the phase where the historiography of the discovery is disturbed by the influence of the Columbus family's suit against the Crown. But how much greater is the disturbance in the royal chroniclers than in the spokesman for the Columbuses! It reaches its peak in Gómara. The thesis he tries to demonstrate is diametrically opposed to Don Fernando's: "Columbus? An able discoverer, but lacking in genius. He and his heirs have been amply paid for the service he rendered." Gómara's procedure is extremely simple. It consists in suppressing everything which is awkward, and transforming into a categorical statement an explanation which his predecessor, Oviedo, had presented as doubtful or false, but which had the merit of reducing the discoverer's role to a minimum. Does he summarize the Capitulations of Santa Fe? Gómara omits the clauses which promised Columbus the hereditary honors of admiral, viceroy, and governor "of the isles and continents" he might discover. Although after his return the Catholic Monarchs "gave him the title and office of Admiral of the Indies, and to Bartholomew Columbus that of *Adelantado*," this is presented as a gracious and revocable concession, not as the execution of a contract long and bitterly sought, and still less as a hereditary concession. Is it, then, a question of the manner in which Columbus was led to conceive of his enterprise? Oviedo, who was personally acquainted with the discoverer's generation and who lived in the Indies almost continuously from 1514 until his death, gave the story of the unknown pilot in 1535 as a tale: ("Quieren algunos decir . . ."), a novel ("novela"), to which he personally attached no credibility ("para mí yo lo tengo por falso"). Gómara, writing in Spain about 1550, tells this story as the last word of truth on Columbus' project, and although he does point out some variants, it is in an attempt to confirm the point on which the versions agree: the existence of the pilot who died in Columbus' house. "Navegando una carabela. . . ." Gómara speaks categorically. And the reader has embarked on the caravel of the unknown pilot. . . . This does not prevent the chronicler, a bit later on, from tossing his hat into the ring of the Pinzón theory held by His Majesty's "fiscal"; Columbus, when he arrived in Palos de Moguer, received an offer of services from Martín Pinzón, "que había oído decir como navegando tras el sol por vía templada se hallarían grandes y ricas tierras" (who had heard it said that by sailing in the direction of the sun, over gentle seas, great and rich lands would be found).

Oviedo had mentioned as probable the bases of Columbus' project which were learned and stemmed from books: "Some are pleased to say that this land was first known a long time ago, and that its location, with its parallels, had been written down and noted; that the navigation and cosmography of those countries had been lost to the memory of men; and that Christopher Columbus, as a man trained and learned in this science, dared to discover these islands. *As for myself, I share in this suspicion, and cannot say that I do not believe it,* for the reason that will be stated in the next chapter" (where, of course, Oviedo substitutes his fiction of the Hesperides for the Asiatic mirages of medieval "science"). Gómara, however, contests the thesis that makes Columbus a savant, "a good Latinist and cosmographer." "No. Columbus *was not learned,* but he was extremely well informed. And, *as he had knowledge of these new lands from the dead pilot's story,* he inquired among learned men concerning what the ancients had written of other lands and worlds." The trick was played. Gómara had a fine talent for exposition. It is not the only case in which a tale given by Oviedo as "public and notorious" was improved upon rather than merely verified by Gómara, and accepted by posterity as true from A to Z.[36] In the case of Columbine historiography, the chronicler's highhanded practices have had serious consequences. Gómara's history had the widest circulation by far among general histories of the Indies, in the sixteenth century thanks to many editions and translations and in the nineteenth thanks to its inclusion in Rivadeneira's *Biblioteca de Autores Españoles* (Vol. XXII). It became one of the chief authorities, first for Vignaud and his "critical history," then for Carbia and his hypercritical attitude toward Las Casas. And finally, it marks, in the new philosophical history of *La idea del descubrimiento,* the moment in the "ancient history" of the discovery when the *vox populi* about the unknown pilot saw its explanation accepted as official doctrine.

HUMAN KNOWLEDGE AND DIVINE FOREKNOWLEDGE

Gómara's success, both old and new, as the culmination of the official historiography hostile to Columbus, was made both easier and more deplorable because the *Life of the Admiral* by his son Don Fernando, written about 1538, circulated only in manuscript until 1571; and then, published in Venice in Italian, it had little circulation in Spanish in the inaccurate translations of González Barcia (1749) and Serrano y Sanz (1892); not until 1947 did it find a place in a widely sold collection, in the excellent translation by Ramón Iglesia (México, Biblioteca Americana del Fondo de Cultura Económica). This prolonged confusion in the development of the historiography of the discovery might have been resolved under Philip II, if Las Casas' *Historia de las Indias* had been published at that time; for it, the work of a man living in the islands before Oviedo's time, draws on both Don Fernando's *Vida del Almirante* and the navigator's logbooks preserved in the Columbus family's archives; and we can agree with Menéndez y Pelayo's judgment: it is "the most exact and detailed of all the older histories, insofar as Columbus' life is concerned." But this history in its turn was condemned in 1559 to remain unpublished,[37] and was not printed until 1875–76. It is true that it was used in manuscript by Philip III's chronicler of the Indies, Antonio de Herrera, and has been, through his famous *Décadas de las Indias*, the source of everything written about Columbus up to the end of the eighteenth century.

And it is necessary to state it unequivocally, for this simple truth runs the risk of escaping the notice of the reader who enters the labyrinth of O'Gorman's analyses: in spite of the wide divergence in the two historians' focus, Don Fernando and Las Casas agree on the essential points of what Columbus planned and what he accomplished. Both take into account, to explain his enterprise, theoretical views of a bookish origin justifying the "Asiatic project" as well as empirical indications (for example, those in Don Fernando's famous Chapter IX and the hypothetical tale of the unknown pilot) on the existence of accessible lands to the west of the Azores. We must take note of Las Casas' heading for his Chapter XII: "En el cual se contienen muchos y diversos indicios y señales que por diversas personas Cristóbal Colón era informado, *que le hicieron certísimo de haber tierra en aqueste mar Océano hacia esa parte del Poniente*, y entre ellos fué haber visto en los Azores algunos palos labrados y una canoa y dos cuerpos de hombres que los traía la mar y viento de hacia Poniente" (in which are contained many and divers indications and signs by which Christopher Columbus was informed by divers persons, *which made him entirely sure that there was land in the Ocean Sea toward its western part*, and among these signs was that he had seen in the Azores carved poles and a canoe and two bodies of men brought by the sea and wind from the West). This idea of a Columbus whose expectations was based on two kinds of sources, Mr. O'Gorman should not be surprised to see, is found stated in a number of ways throughout all of what he styles the "modern history" of the discovery, nor should he tax his ingenuity to seek various names for it (Herrera's "eclectic thesis," Beaumont and

Robertson's "thesis of two possibilities," "thesis of two enterprises" of Juan Bautista Muñoz). It is the one which the "ancient history" of the discovery, thanks to the fact that Herrera used Las Casas as a source, has passed on to the "modern history" as the most complete interpretation. Las Casas has played an important role on this point.

However, we must take care not to believe that Las Casas had the monopoly on the explanation of the discovery as a design of Providence. This explanation is another constant of the "ancient history." It is certainly understandable that O'Gorman has chosen Las Casas as the spokesman for the "providential" theory, for nowhere is it expressed more insistently than in his work. But it would be a grave error to infer from such a presentation of the facts that Las Casas was the inventor of this "religious solution" of the problem of comprehension of the discovery. In fact, all the sixteenth-century Spaniards, all Columbus' contemporaries, beginning with Columbus himself, a strange mixture of businessman and prophet, thought of the discovery as the work of Providence. They could not understand it except in the light of a providentialist concept of history. I was happy to find the epithet "metahistorical" emerging from O'Gorman's pen, applied to the ultimate meaning of the great event in Las Casas, for I had adopted it myself to describe the views on the evangelization of the New World held by Fray Martín de Valencia,[38] the Motolinías,[39] and the Sahagúns.[40] But perhaps this neologism—though eye-catching—is not necessary if we say, agreeing with the best present-day historians of religion, that after Irenaeus and St. Augustine Christianity developed a "theology of history." According to this theology, history unfolds between the Creation and the Last Judgment; it obeys a supernatural course marked by single events: Original Sin, the Incarnation, the Redemption. Nothing of importance occurs unless its place in the scheme has been fixed by Providence. This theology of history was never more alive than in the two centuries which precede Bossuet's *Discours sur l'Histoire Universel*; that is, just before a breach was opened in it by the philosophy of "indefinite progress," an immanentist and purely human philosophy of history. Las Casas was a great reader of St. Augustine's *City of God* and a great providentialist. But his two bêtes noires, Oviedo and Gómara, are also providentialists; Don Fernando is no less one. Columbus' *Book of Prophecies*, from which his son discreetly borrows, implies that the discovery of the Indies had been prophesied ever since Antiquity; in Seneca's *Medea*, for example. Don Fernando does not hesitate to say that his father's name and surname are indicative of the predestination of his historic (and metahistoric) role. He is the *Christophorus*, the Christ-bearer. And also, he is *Columbus*, the dove which bears the grace of the Holy Spirit to the New World he has discovered; or Côlon (κῶλον), member of Christ, sent for the salvation of those nations; or *Colonus*, he by whom "the Indian nations were to be transformed into colonists and inhabitants of the Church Triumphant in Heaven." Well, why not? If for these Spaniards "the greatest event since the creation of the world, aside from the Incarnation and death of Him who created it, was the discovery of the Indies"? This admirable phrase was coined by Gómara. How could an event of this caliber escape the notice of Divine Providence?

To be sure, the providentialism of the historians of the discovery is not given the same emphasis in all of them. Though the "first cause" is the same for all (God), the last cause may be differently conceived. Certain of the "political" historians place themselves within the religious philosophy of history inherited from the Middle Ages, according to which, in the succession of empires, the "Roman" empire is the last, the one which is to endure until the end of time. Oviedo considers as providential the reconquest of the Hesperides, Spanish three thousand years ago, and the discovery of the continent nearby, at the moment when the reconquest of Spain was over and when the scepter of the Germanic [Holy] Roman Empire passed into the hands of the king of the "Goths" of Spain. Gómara emphasizes the providential mission of Spain in simpler terms, as a Spain pledged to fight against the infidel: "Comenzaron las conquistas de indios acabada la de moros, porque siempre guerreasen españoles contra infieles"

(The conquests of the Indians began as soon as that of the Moors had ceased, so that Spaniards could always fight against the infidels). For the political historians (who certainly considered evangelization to be one of the duties of a conquering Spain, but who were not so thoroughly persuaded of the future of an Indian Christianity), the providential discovery of the Indies happened *so that* Spain, champion of the Faith in Europe, might be given additional riches and power. For the evangelizers, for the learned Don Fernando himself (and it is one of the reasons Las Casas finds him so usable), the Indians are not the infidel against whom war must be waged; they are members to be incorporated into the mystical body of Christ. Hence the final cause of the discovery is not the puissance of Catholic Spain; it is the fulfillment of Christianity. And when we use the word *fulfillment*, we think of the eschatological perspective opened by the words of Christ: the Gospel shall be preached in all the world, and then shall the end come. This eschatological view of the discovery especially seized the imaginations of Fray Martín de Valencia, Motolinía, Sahagún, Mendieta;[41] they were all Franciscans more or less tinged with Joachimite prophetical views,[42] convinced that they were present and contributing in the great conversion whose consummation would mean the end of the world. The evangelization of the "New World" was a portent for the "end of the world."[43] All the "apostles" of the time felt this more or less strongly. Juan de Ávila,[44] who had dreamed of sailing to the Indies and who had to content himself with being an apostle in Andalusia, wrote a number of times that the discovery of the Indies, strangely accelerated by the greed of some and the evangelical impatience of others, announced the proximity of the Last Judgment.

These few indications will suffice to show how important it is, when we study the idea of the discovery in the sixteenth century, to consider it in its providentialist and metahistorical aspect rather than as a "thesis" among other theses. For all the historians of the so-called "ancient" period, it was the inescapable framework of any human undertaking. José Gaos observes the contrast which exists, in O'Gorman's book, between the chapter dedicated to Humboldt, where the historian's Weltanschauung is fully expressed, and the part dedicated to the "época antigua," where the implicit philosophy of the authors is not made at all clear. This was perhaps even more necessary because, to cite O'Gorman's penetrating comment, humanity confronted this great new event with its age-old ideas. He should have had the courage to note that this great new event was, no matter how it is looked at— witness the "Asiatic project" of Columbus, or the Joachimism of the Franciscan evangelizers—a medieval event. Or rather, we must be made to see that our perspective of history creates a number of false problems for us. To make ourselves understood by the reader who has learned history in textbooks, we think it necessary to speak to him of a medieval or a modern mentality. But take care! By attributing to these distinctions more value than he should, O'Gorman, ingenious author that he is, arrives at a statement which is involuntarily comic. When he says that Las Casas was "a modern grafted on an medieval man," well and good! This description fits more than one man of the sixteenth century. The comic element consists in saying that "he had the innocent and human weakness of *wanting to be what he was not, a rationalist in the modern sense*." This is the same as saying that Joan of Arc wanted or did not want to "go to the Hundred Years' War," or that she believed or did not believe that she was the saint of "modern patriotism." A man of reason and a man of faith: Las Casas was just that, and wanted to be that, indissolubly. But is this not also the case of the medieval Scholastics? Las Casas explains the history of Columbus as that of a providential man; that is, a man whose acts resulted from human foresights and calculations, and who, nevertheless, would have done nothing of what he did if his acts had not been foreseen by God, in whose acts all possible human knowledge is found, together with divine foreknowledge.

I cannot understand why O'Gorman does not pay more attention to the way in which his cherished legend of the unknown pilot is integrated into the history of the discovery by Las Casas and Acosta. For Las Casas, Columbus is a chosen vessel. This is seen in the magnitude of his misfortunes as well as his triumphs, in his good intentions toward the Indians as well as his grave sins of *codicia*, in his invincible ignorance as well as his knowledge. The fact that Columbus clung to his "Asiatic" illusion, which was one of the moving forces of his action, is in Las Casas' eyes a major sign that the discoverer accomplished a work infinitely greater than he, of which he was the unknowing instrument in spite of all his calculations. Let us consider Las Casas' testimony in regard to the legend of the unknown pilot. Oviedo refuses to believe it. Will Las Casas do the same, in order to exalt Columbus' role as a man of Providence? No. Once more, he refuses to share the view of Oviedo, his bête noire. When he searches his memory he seems to recall that some such rumor was circulating in Santo Domingo early in the century; and, after all, it may not have been entirely without foundation. But what did it matter whether or not an unknown pilot disclosed a precious secret to Columbus? What did it matter whether or not Columbus had this additional reason to undertake his voyage, since he already had so many others—both theoretical and empirical reasons? "It is very possible that Our Lord placed both this reason and the others into his hands, with the intention of effecting this sovereign work that He had decided to do by His own means, in the very direct and very effective will of His good pleasure. There is one thing, at least, which it seems to me we can believe without the shadow of a doubt: and it is that because of this circumstance or because of others, or certain of them or all of them together, Columbus left Spain as certain of discovering what he discovered and finding what he found as if he had had it at his disposal in a room of which he held the key." It was God who gave the key to Columbus, just as He chose him to open the door. What did it matter if the bit of the key had an extra notch, the unknown pilot? All these circumstances, or "occasions," are the occasional causes or second causes of the discovery, whose first cause was God. Las Casas had said a few pages before, speaking of the empirical indications which impelled Columbus to seek lands in the Ocean: "All these things were certainly of a nature to make him embrace this enterprise, which he was already so anxious to do; and there were some signs by which God appeared to move him as if with buffets of Fate; for Divine Providence, when it decides to do something, well knows how to prepare the times, just as it chooses persons, gives inclinations, furnishes aid, offers occasions, and similarly removes obstacles, *so that the ultimate effects which it seeks are produced by their second causes.*" If Las Casas seems to O'Gorman to be so *modern* and such a *rationalist* at the same time as he is medieval, it is because his whole career as a man of action had made him prodigiously attentive to the interplay of second causes. Perhaps this is why he imposed on himself the theological discipline of imagining the first cause at work behind the second ones, especially in events which were part of God's great design. When he tells how Fray Juan Garceto escaped death on the coast of Cumaná,[45] he is well aware of the physical cause that kept the Indians from approaching the friar as he awaited the blows from their "macanas." But he does not want to forget the role of God, to whom the missionary had commended his soul: "Esto no fué, *dejando aparte la voluntad de Dios,* sino que estaba tan cercado de espinas el fraile y los indios en cueros, que no osaron a él allegarse" (*Apart from the will of God,* this was only because the friar was so hemmed in by thorns, and the Indians being naked, that they did not dare to get close to him). A text such as this is not an isolated one in Las Casas' great *Historia.* One facet of the occurrence is natural, the other supernatural.

It is to be regretted that O'Gorman's analytical talent has not been exercised on another author he knows well, for he has edited him: Father José de Acosta. He says only a few words about him. O'Gorman could have observed in him also the contrast which seems such a singular trait in Las Casas. And he would not have treated his providentialism as a mere "pious accessory." Acosta forces the "providentialist thesis" to a para-doxical point: he accomplishes the tour de force of summing up the conquest of the New World (which he confronts, to be sure, as a "naturalist": *De natura novi orbis*) by scarcely mentioning

Columbus, and absorbing his glory in the anonymity of the un-known pilot, *ad majorem Dei gloriam*. For him the story of this pilot is an argument in the discussion of the different ways—by land or by sea intentional or fortuitous—in which America could have been peopled in the dawn of its prehistory. A fortuitous arrival by sea, he remarks, "took place in the discovery of our time, for *that sailor (whose name we do not even know, so that in so great a matter the discovery should be attributed to none other than God)* having, after a terrible and unexpected tempest, come to know the New World, gave Christopher Columbus the news of so great a thing in payment for his good hospitality." Here, stated in the same sentence, are the "providential thesis" and the "causal thesis" which O'Gorman considers to be characteristic of the crisis of Columbine historiography in the nineteenth and twentieth centuries. But this is implied in the logic of the unknown-pilot legend: it is not the most remarkable facet of Acosta's position. A few pages before this, in the course of the same discussion about the peopling of the New World, he had stated with great firmness that the New World could not have been reached intentionally in Antiquity by either European or Asiatic navigators, because *Antiquity*, either Hebrew or Greek or Roman, *had not discovered the compass*. This was to recognize implicitly that Columbus, instrument of Divine Providence, had succeeded in rediscovering the lands seen by the unknown pilot because he had the aid of this new device, thanks to the technical progress achieved during the Middle Ages, and which had already permitted men to sail as far as the Azores. Undoubtedly Acosta conceived of humanity's scientific and technical *progress* as obedient to a providential and transcendental order of things. But is it not true that such con-siderations pave the way for the immanentist philosophy of indefinite *progress*? Cannot Father Acosta, whom Humboldt hails as one of the founders of the physics of the globe, be considered perhaps as a precursor of Humboldt, the historian of the progres-sive discovery of the Cosmos by humanity? Yes, certainly, on condition we do not say that Father Acosta "is trying to be a rationalist in the modern sense." On condition we do not forget that Father Acosta moves easily within the Biblical frame of divine Revelation, that he calmly accepted the explanation of the animal and human population of the New World by the pairs who disembarked from Noah's ark, and that in this attempt he arrived at some views anticipating those of modern ethnologists, which postulate the peopling of America by land migrations passing through the region of the Bering Strait. And on condition, finally, that we do not pass over the fact that Father Acosta fixes his eyes on the eschatological perspectives opened by the accelerated discovery of the world. In his *De temporibus novissimis* he passes in review the regions still left to be discovered, to be penetrated, to be evangelized, from the heart of South America to China, only to conclude that the end of the world, which so many men of the sixteenth century had thought imminent, would not come tomorrow nor the day after tomorrow. . . .

Such speculations as these make very real the profound difference separating the early history and the modern history of the discovery. For a man of our time, accustomed to disassociating history and geography, it is not at first sight absurd to want to clear up what Columbus the navigator accomplished objectively, technically, quite apart from his ideas on what he was trying to do and what he actually did. But if we look at it more closely this attempt is illusory. We are grateful to O'Gorman for having said so in his rather too acerbic criticism of the excellent navigator-historian [Samuel Eliot] Morison. But we do complain of the fact that, obsessed by the pretended "Vespuccian revelation," he himself has curtailed his analysis of the old historians by consulting them only on the question of the spatial dependence or independence of the lands discovered in relation to the known world, more especially in relation to Asia. Is this not still the point of view of a specialist in navigation? An important point of view, certainly, even in the sixteenth century, for pilots and for the monarchs who paid the expenses of the expeditions of discovery. But it was not only a question of discovering lands better and better pinpointed on maps. It was a discovery of gold and other precious things. It was above all a discovery of men. And though, for the blind greed of the *conquistadores* seeking gold, men were only a base source of labor, for those who thought along the lines of Christian theology, for the evangelizers and the governors who listened to their counsels, for all learned folk in general, a gigantic discovery of men was an event replete with significance for a providential view of history. Geography, history, and metahistory were indissolubly linked. To use Las Casas' figure of speech, the New World, the key of which had been granted to Christopher Columbus by God, was a world teeming with men. For what mysterious design had it been so closely concealed? This gave rise to numerous problems concerning the origin of these men and the intentions of Providence with regard to them. Had they, or had they not, soon after the death of Christ, been affected by "the evangelization of St. Thomas"? Were they destined to furnish the elect of the city of God or were they irretrievably lost to the devil? Was it chiefly the gold and silver of those countries which Providence meant to go into the hands of the Spaniards? Were not the West Indies merely a halt on the way to China, a country where Christianity would at last conquer men "of great capacity," the last stage on man's journey around the world and through history? All these questions were asked insistently throughout the sixteenth century and even later. The temporal horizon which bounded all of them was that, when the discovery begun by Columbus drew to its close with the promulgation of the Gospel to all non-Christians, the world would come to an end.

The idea of the discovery of the New World in the sixteenth century meant all of this, at least to the Spaniards, for whom this discovery had been their great enterprise. If instead of employing a sublety worthy of a better use in formulating "theses" distorted in advance by the postulates of their formulator, O'Gorman had demonstrated the cosmological, geographical, historical (and metahistorical) concept implied in the different early explanations of the discovery, he would have given his work a broader and solider perspective, and would have made us understand much better the change undergone by the idea of the conquest during

Humboldt's time. He would not have played with a series of "theses" as if with a kaleidoscope, presenting the curious and irritating solutions of an attempted "aporia." He would have taken the old authors just as they are. He would have recognized the *development of the discovery* after Columbus, and even after Magellan, to explain the *development of the idea of the discovery* throughout the sixteenth century. He would certainly have gained more partisans for the philosophical history which he defends. Because O'Gorman is so talented, he is one of the most effective of the men who, nowadays, are waking strictly erudite and "factual" history out of its dogmatic sleep. We should not like to believe that he would rather shock than convert. Good scholars, whose horizons are often circumscribed, to be sure, can take pleasure in wider perspectives, can see that in those perspectives they can renew their comprehension of the old authors whom they attack at too close quarters. But it is preferable, if they are to be led into wider views, not to muddle the foreground willy-nilly, to appeal to their respect for the texts instead of damaging it. My purpose in writing these pages has been to help defend O'Gorman the philosopher of history against O'Gorman the prestidigitator of historical criticism. If honest scholars were struck, when they read the first two parts of his book, by too many arbitrary statements, by the omission of too many essential facts, they should pass over these defects; they should grasp the intent of the whole and recognize its fruitfulness. If they then go back and read the texts more carefully than O'Gorman has done, they will be grateful to him for having made them reread those texts; they will perceive that the *facts* themselves of the history of the discovery, in the fifteenth and sixteenth centuries, become more intelligible if we clarify the *ideas* of the men who successively told that history and gave it meaning.

NOTES

1. *La idea del descubrimiento de América*, Historia de esa interpretación y crítica de sus fundamentos (Ediciones del IV Centenario de la Universidad de México, centro de estudios filosóficos; México, 1951).

2. Samuel Eliot Morison, *Admiral of the Ocean Sea: A Life of Christopher Columbus* (Boston, 1942).

3. Enrique de Gandía, *Historia de Cristóbal Colón: Análisis crítico de los problemas colombinos* (Buenos Aires, 1942; 2d ed., 1951). A review of the problems and the fruit of a vast amount of reading in modern authors rather than a critical study of sources.

4. Emiliano Jos, "La génesis colombina del descubrimiento," *Revista de Historia de América*, No. 14 (Mexico, June, 1942).

[5. Henry Harrisse, an outstanding historian of Columbus, 1829–1910; author of *Notes on Columbus* (1866); *D. Fernando Colón, historiador de su padre* (1871); *Les Colombs de France et d'Italie* (1874); *Christophe Colomb, son œuvre, sa vie* (1884–85); *Colomb devant l'historie* (1892), and other works on Columbus and the discovery. Henri Vignaud, author of *Histoire critique de la grande entreprise de Christophe Colomb*, (2 vols.; Paris, 1911); *The Columbian Tradition of the Discovery of America* (Oxford, 1920). Rómulo D. Carbia, author of *Origen y patria de Cristóbal Colón* (Buenos Aires, 1918); *La patria de Colón* (Buenos Aires, 1923); *La nueva historia del descubrimiento de América*, etc.]

[6. Gonzalo Fernández de Oviedo y Valdés, 1478–1557, knew Columbus personally and took part in the Pedrarias expedition (1514); first chronicler of the Indies (1532); wrote first part of his *Historia general y natural de las Indias* in 1535; also wrote *Sumario de la natural historia de las Indias* (1525, published 1526); *Batallas y Quinquagenas, Libro de la cámara real del príncipe d. Juan, Relación de la prisión del rey de Francia*.]

[7. Fernando Colón (1488–1539), son of Christopher Columbus, was the author of *Historia del Almirante*, written *ca.* 1538. The original text is lost. It survives only in an Italian translation published at Venice in 1571. Doubt was for long cast on its authenticity. But the use made of it by Las Casas has convinced most modern critics of its validity. Ferdinand put together the famous Bibliotheca Colombina at Seville.]

[8. Fray Bartolomé de Las Casas (1474–1566), missionary and bishop of Chiapas in Mexico (1544–1550), wrote among much else, *Apologética Historia* (begun 1527); *Brevísima relación de la destruición de las Indias* (written 1542–46, published 1552); *Historia General de las Indias* (written 1552–61); the most outspoken critic of Spanish colonial practices and a warm defender of Indian rights; these he championed in a famous debate with Juan Ginés de Sepúlveda at Valladolid in 1552. His views were for a time very influential with the government of Charles V.]

[9. Francisco López de Gómara (1511[?]–1562/1572[?], author of *Historia General de las Indias* (finished 1551, published 1552), a fluent writer who had never visited America.]

[10. See above, note 4.]

[11. Peter Martyr of Anghiera (1457–1526), humanist and earliest historian of the "New World," a phrase which he himself coined. He went from Italy to Spain *ca.* 1487; was a member of the Court when Columbus was welcomed back; wrote the first history of the New World, *De Orbe Novo*, whose first "decade" appeared in 1511.]

[12. Andrés Bernáldez, curate of Los Palacios, chaplain to the archbishop of Seville. Columbus stayed in his house in 1496 and left with him the journals of the Second Voyage. Bernáldez' *Historia de los Reyes Católicos* is a standard source for the reign of Ferdinand and Isabella.]

[13. M. Menéndez y Pelayo, "De los historiadores de Colón," in *El Centenario* (Madrid, 1892), II, 433–54, III, 55–71.]

[14. Paolo Toscanelli, Florentine doctor and amateur geographer, corresponded with Columbus in 1474 on the possibility of reaching Asia by sailing to the West. He was much influenced by Ptolemy, Pierre D'Ailly, and Marco Polo.]

15. It appeared in August, 1861, in the *Journal général de l'Instruction publique*, Paris. Reprinted in Charles Jourdain, *Excursions historiques et philosophiques à travers le Moyen Âge* (Paris, Firmin-Didot, 1888).

16. See E. Jos, *op. cit.*, pp. 7, 41–43.

[17. Pierre D'Ailly, cardinal, 1350–1420, statesman of the Conciliar Movement, and geographical theorist; author of *Imago Mundi* (written *ca.* 1410) and *Compendium Cosmographiae* (written in 1413, contains a summary of Ptolemaic ideas). Colombus' own copy of the *Imago Mundi* (with his *marginalia*) survives in the Colombina at Seville.]

[18. Balboa had reached the Pacific in 1513, Magellan had sailed around Cape Horn to the Philippine Islands in 1520–21, Pizarro and Almagro had conquered Peru in 1530–35. Lugo and Quesada were *conquistadores* of Colombia. Gonzalo Jiménez de Quesada (1495[?]–1579) founded the present capital, Bogotá.]

[19. St. Dié is in Lorraine. A circle of scholars and scientists met there under the patronage of René II, duke of Lorraine.]

[20. Martin Waldseemüller, German cartographer, was the author of a world map and of *Cosmographie Introductio* (1507), in which America was given its name for the first time in a printed book.]

[21. Mercator, or Gerard Kraux (1512–1594), was a Flemish geographer and the inventor of a system of projections in which longitudes and latitudes are represented by parallel equidistant lines.]

[22. Michael Servet, or Servetus (*ca.* 1511–1553), was an Aragonese doctor and theologian, author of *De Trinitatis erroribus* (published 1531); he was burned at Geneva on the orders of Calvin.]

[23. Albert Magnaghi, author of studies on Columbus' navigation, such as "I present errori che vengono attribuiti a Colombo" and others in *Bolletino della Reale Società Geográfica Italiana*, 6th ser. (1928–33), V, 459–94, 553–82; VII, 497–515; X, 595–641, quoted in Morison, I, 256.]

24. Letter from Columbus to the Catholic Kings (from Jamaica, July 7, 1503), in Martín Fernández de Navarrete, *Colección de los viajes y descubrimientos*, 2d ed., I (Madrid, 1858), 448.

25. "O'Gorman y la idea del descubrimiento de América," *Historia Méxicana*, I, 3 (Jan.–March, 1952), 478.

26. E. Jos, *op. cit.*, pp. 13–19, has judiciously cast light on the tendentious side of Don Fernando's account. It consists merely of wanting to excuse his

father for having believed in the proximity of the Far East of Asia by the Western route.

27. Text published about 1646 by Juan Diéz de la Calle, cited by Ramón Iglesia in his preface to *La Vida del Almirante* (see *infra*, note 33).

[28. Juan Luis Vives (1492–1540), humanist and philosopher, friend of Erasmus, edited St. Augustine's *City of God*.]

[29. Juan de Vergara, Spanish Erasmian, arrested and imprisoned by the Inquisition but eventually released (1537); died February 30, 1557.]

30. See *Pleitos de Colón* (Colección de documentos inéditos relacionados a . . . Ultramar, VII (Madrid, 1892), 340; see Vol. VIII, p. 126).

[31. Nicolás de Ovando, first governor of Hispaniola (1501–1509), was a commander in the military order of Alcántara, of which Lares was a commandery.]

[32. José de Acosta (*ca.* 1539–1600), naturalist and historian, born at Medina del Campo, was one of the greater early historians of the Americas—the so-called Pliny of the New World; author of *De natura novi orbis libri duo* (Salamanca, 1589) and *Historia natural y moral de las Indias* (1590).]

33. *La Vida del Almirante don Cristóbal Colón, escrita por su hijo Don Hernando*, ed. Ramón Iglesia (Mexico, 1947), p. 50.

34. *Ibid.*, p. 51.

35. *Ibid.*, p. 50.

36. See M. Bataillon, "Cheminement d'une légende: Les 'caballeros pardos' de Las Casas," *Symposium*, XI (Syracuse, May, 1952), 1–21.

37. On this point, see the BH, LIV (1952), 216.

[38. One of the twelve Franciscan missionaries (with Motolinía) who arrived in Mexico in 1524.]

[39. Fray Toribio de Benavente, or Motolinía (d. 1565); see note 38 above. Author of *Historia de los Indios de la Nueva España*.]

[40. Fray Bernardino de Sahagún, O.M. (1500–1590), arrived in Mexico in 1529; specialized in the study of the Nahua language and ethnology; author of *Historia de las cosas de Nueva España* (written in Latin in 1569, translated in 1577 but published only in the eighteenth century).]

[41. Fray Jerónimo de Mendieta, O.F.M. (1525–1604), arrived in Mexico in 1556; author of *Historia Eclesiástica Indiana escrita a fines del siglo xvi* (Mexico, 1870).]

[42. Abbot Joachim of Flora in the thirteenth century announced the third and last age of the Church (cf. Matt. 24:14).]

43. On this aspect of the "spiritual conquest," see the résumés of my courses in the *Annuaire* of the Collège de France (1950, 1951, 1952), and an article which appeared in *L'Education Nationale*, December 11, 1952, under the title "Nouveau Monde et Fin du Monde."

[44. Author of spiritual writings (for which he was imprisoned, 1554–1559); he was venerated by the mountaineers of Andalusia.]

[45. Cf. Las Casas, "Historia de las Indias," Bk. III, chap. 159, in *Obras Escogidas*, ed. J. Pérez de Tudela Bueso, BAE, XCVI (Madrid, 1961), 562.]

Index

Fortià, Sibila de, queen of Aragon, wife of Peter IV, 222

Foscari, Francesco, doge of Venice, 223

Fouquet, Jean, painter, 216

Francis I of France, 415, 461

Franciscans, 453-4

Francisco, bishop of Coria, 330, 333, 353

Froissart, 73

Fuenterrabía (Guipúzcoa), 70, 72, 78, 80, 439

Fuero de Burgos, 280

Fuero de las Leyes or *Fuero Real*, 279-283, 294

Furtado, Juan (João), Portuguese admiral, 75

Gaddi, the, anonymous writer of, 203

Gagini, Dominico, sculptor, 204

Galdo, Lope de, O.P., provincial, 231

Galicia, 17, 21, 59, 68, 80, 82, 95, 99, 110, 140, 382-83, 389

Galíndez de Carvajal, Lorenzo, chronicler and lawyer, 251, 275-76, 282, 285-6, 329, 410

Gallipoli (Italy (Apulia)), 413

Gandía (Valencia), 212

Gandía, Enrique de, historian, 427-428, 437, 461

Ganivet, Ángel, nineteenth-century man of letters, 402

Gaos, José, 439, 453

Garceto, Fray Juan, missionary in Cumaná, 456

García, Alvar, de Santa María, *see* Santa María

García de Medina, Pedro, scribe, 158

García, Fortún, law student at Bologna, 292

García, Gallo, Professor Alfonso, 179-180, 192

Garigliano, river, 421, 425

Gassies, Arnau, 212

Gattemelata, 203

Gattinara, Mercurino Arborio, de, 44-45, 414-15

Gaucelm, Jaubert, painter, 208

Gaunt, John of, duke of Lancaster, 21, 60-62, 65, 72-73

Generalitat: of Barcelona, 34, 183, 196, 198

Catalonia, 34, 174, 176, 182

Perpignan, 196

Valencia, 177

Genoa, 19, 32, 36, 49-50, 60, 62, 66-8, 76-77, 259, 273

Gentili, Cipriano, Genoese merchant and papal collector, 361, 376-8, 378

George of Trebizond, 216

Geraldino, Antonio, Spanish envoy, secretary to Ferdinand, chronicler, 363, 365

Gerbes, Los (Los Gelves) (Tunisia), 411-12, 424

Geremia, Cristoforo da, artist, 205

Germaine of Foix, queen of Aragon, 389

Germany, 86-87, 165, 359, 401

Gerona, bishop Bernat de Pau of, *see* Pau, Bernat de

Gerona, cathedral of, 195, 199-200, 221, 224

Gerona, city of, 32-34, 182, 187-88, 190, 205

Gerona, Congress of, 195, 224

Ghiberti, 200

Giacomo, Blessed, of Ulm, 222

Gibraltar, 20, 67

"Gil Master", painter, 207

Giménez Soler, Andrés, historian, 179, 192

Giner, Tomás, painter, 213

Giuliano di Giovanni da Poggibonsi, Florentine sculptor, 200

Giuliano di Nofri, sculptor, 207

Goldschmidt, L., 190, 192

Gomar, Francí, wood-carver, 199-200

Gómara, *see* López de Gómara

Gómez de Sandoval, Diego, count of Castro and Denia, 100-1

Gómez de Santiago, Vasco, Castilian consul at Marseilles, 88

Piero Della Francesca, 213
Pimentel, family of, 99–100
Pinello, Francesco, merchant, 361, 376
Pinzón, Martín Alonso, companion of Columbus, 441–43, 445, 448
Pisa, 68, 411, 439
Pisa, Council of, 378, 411
Pisa, Isaia de, sculptor, 204, 225
Pisanello, Vittore, 25, 201–2, 205, 208, 210, 224–25
Pius II, Pope, 238, 242
Pizarro, Francisco, 435, 462
Plasencia (Cáceres), 37, 82, 101, 283
Platea, Johannes de, 279, 294
Plato, 283, 416
Plencia (Vizcaya), 75
Plymouth (Devon), 62
Poblet (Tarragona) 205; chapel of San Jorge, 196; monastery, 197, 199; palace of King Martin at, 195
Poggibonsi, Giuliano de Giovanni da, 200
Poitou, 71
Pola (Istria), Roman arch at, 204
Poland, 292, 359
Ponce de León, family of, 104, 253
Ponce de León, Pedro, 1st count of Medellín, 1st count of Arcos, 104, 138
Ponce de León, Rodrigo, marquis (later duke) of Cadiz, 104, 421
Ponce, Pedro, military commander, 104, 138
Ponsich, P., 195, 224
Ponza, battle of, 222
Poppelau, Nicolaus von, 395
Portsmouth (Hants), 62
Portugal, Cardinal of, Infante Jaime, archbishop of Lisbon, tomb of, 204
Prescott, W. H., historian, 377, 391, 406
Ptolemy, 462; Commentaries on, by Michael Servetus, 437, 439
Puigcerdá (Gerona), 208
Pulgar, Fernando del, chronicler,

secretary to Isabella, 23, 28, 30, 296–303, 305–35, 337, 339, 341, 343, 345, 347–53, 359, 363–64, 372, 374–78, 380, 385, 389–90, 395, 398–99, 403, 419–20, 424

Quijote (Quixote), Don, 103, 297
Quintana, Pedro de, secretary to Ferdinand, 413–14, 424
Quintanilla, Alfonso de, contador, 17, 248, 272
Quiñones, family of, 98–99
Quiñones, Diego Fernández de, see Fernández de Quiñones
Quiñones, Suárez de, mayordomo of Ferdinand of Antequera, 97

Rabshakeh, 317, 352
Ragusa, republic of, 203
Ramírez de Villaescusa, Diego, lodges in Dr. Oropesa's house at Salamanca, 287, 291, 295
Ramírez, Juan de, 282
Ravena, Bonomi de, painter, 202
Recuperati, Agustín, O.P., 242
Refundición del Halconero, 159, 169, 246
Reggio (Italy (Calabria)), 210
Reinosa (Santander), 98
Reixach, Joan, painter, 210–11
remença, remensa, 188, 257, 260
René d'Anjou, "king of Naples", count of Provence, 209, 216
requerimiento, 276, 285
Requesens, de Soler, family of, 35
Riaza (Segovia), 40, 152, 169
Ribera, Perafán de, adelantado, 64, 138
Richard II, of England, 62, 75
Rioja (Logroño), 97
Ripoll (Gerona), monastery of, 215
Riquer, Martín de, 288
Riudoms (Tarragona), 215
Roa (Burgos), 127
Ródenas (Teruel), altarpiece of St. John the Baptist at, 207
Rodrigo, Fray, de Marmolejo, O.P., see Marmolejo, Fray Rodrigo de

Bartolomé, 374, 377; Dominican house of San Esteban, 234–6, 239, 243; old cathedral, 208, altarpiece of high altar of, 202; province (Dominican) of, 226, university of, 27, 245, 275–78, 289, 293, 327

Salamanca, Pedro, de, O.P., 235

Salicetus, Bartholomeus, civil lawyer, 279, 294

Salonica, 249

Saltés (Huelva), 63, 75

San Antolín (Murcia), women of, 154

Sanç, Arnau, member of confraternity of Santa Marta (1439), 216

San Cebrián, Father Alonso de, O.P., papal envoy, vicar-general of Dominicans, 239, 242, 356

Sánchez Albornoz, Professor, 51

Sánchez Cantón, F. Javier, art historian, 280, 294

Sánchez, Dr. Pedro, councillor of Queen Catherine, co-regent of Castile, 132, 145–46, 150

Sánchez de Arce, García, adelantado of Galicia, 140

Sánchez de Arévalo, Rodrigo, bishop of Oviedo, Calahorra, Zamora and Palencia, 90, 110, 381, 398, 402

Sánchez de Laredo, Pedro, naval commander, 68, 77

Sánchez de Tovar, Fernán, Admiral of Castile, 62–64

Sanchís y Sivera, J., historian, 219, 221, 225

Sancho IV of Castile, 42, 46, 51–53

Sancho, Infante, son of Ferdinand I of Aragon, 124, 128; grand master of Alcántara, 123, 168

San Domingo, Bartolomé de, O.P., 242

Sandoval, Diego Gómez de, see Gómez

San Feliú de Guixols (Gerona), 187

Sanglada, Pere, sculptor, 198

Sanlúcar de Barrameda (Cadiz), 59, 64, 104

San Martín, Fray Juan de, one of the two first Inquisitors of the Spanish Inquisition, 306, 321

San Salvador de Felanitx (Baleares), altarpiece of, 200

San Sebastián, fair of, 42

Santa Cruz, monastery of, see Segovia

Santa Fe, Capitulations of 440, 445, 447

Santalínea, Bartolomeu, Valencian sculptor, 200

Santa María, Alfonso (Alonso) de, bishop of Burgos, 69, 227, 310, 320, 326, 333, 352, 381

Santa María, Álvar García de, 119, 123, 144, 155, 157–59, 168–69

Santa María, Martín de, prior of San Pablo, Burgos; nephew of bishop Pablo, 234–35

Santa María, Pablo de, bishop of Murcia (Cartagena) and Burgos, 129, 227–8, 235, 244, 304, 310, 320, 326, 331, 352

Santa María de Nieva, Antonio de, 238–39, 241–42

Santa María de Nieva, Dominican house of, 229

Santa María del Paular (Madrid), 41

Santa Marta, confraternity of, 216

Sant Celoní (Barcelona), 207

Sant Martí de Provençals, see Barcelona

Sant Mateu (Castellón de la Plana), 212

Santander, 63, 71, 87, 266

Santiago, archbishops of, 96, 99. See also Fonseca, Alfonso de

Santiago, grand master of, 22, 24, 103, 108, 123–27, 141, 147, 373; Order of, 82, 84, 103, 158, 253, 263

Santiago, Vasco Gómez de, see Gómez

Santi Espíritus, Father Pedro de, O.P., 236

Santillana, marquis of, see López de Mendoza

Santo Domingo, 357, 443–44, 455

72 73 74   12 11 10 9 8 7 6 5 4 3 2 1